Linguistics and English Literature

An Introduction

Concise and engaging, this textbook introduces stylistics, the application of linguistics to literary analysis. Assuming no prior knowledge of linguistics, H. D. Adamson discusses linguistics before addressing its application to literature, enabling students to become knowledgeable in both fields. Targeted specifically at undergraduate literature students, the book covers a wide range of topics in linguistics and literary criticism, as well as a variety of literary genres and popular culture, from poems and contemporary literature to comic book art and advertising. Providing numerous examples throughout, linguistic concepts are clearly and accessibly presented in an easy-to-digest way, accompanied by numerous examples and a Glossary of key terms. Each chapter features exercises, inviting students to apply specific linguistic knowledge to the analysis of literary texts, as well as further reading suggestions, figures and tables, and highlighted key terms. Supplementary online resources include additional exercises, further reading suggestions, useful links, discussion questions, key term flashcards, and an answer booklet for instructors.

H. D. ADAMSON is Emeritus Professor of English at the University of Arizona, where he has taught courses in applied linguistics, sociolinguistics, and stylistics. The author of five books and numerous articles in the field of Applied Linguistics, Adamson was a Mellon Fellow in the Linguistics Department at the University of Pennsylvania and has taught English in Ethiopia and Spain.

Cambridge Introductions to the English Language

Cambridge Introductions to the English Language is a series of accessible undergraduate textbooks on the key topics encountered in the study of the English Language. Tailored to suit the needs of individually taught course modules, each book is written by an author with extensive experience of teaching the topic to undergraduates. The books assume no prior subject knowledge, and present the basic facts in a clear and straightforward manner, making them ideal for beginners. They are designed to be maximally reader-friendly, with chapter summaries, glossaries, and suggestions for further reading. Extensive exercises and discussion questions are included, encouraging students to consolidate and develop their learning, and providing essential homework material. A website accompanies each book, featuring solutions to the exercises and useful additional resources. Set to become the leading introductions to the field, books in this series provide the essential knowledge and skills for those embarking on English language studies.

Books in the series

The Sound Structure of English Chris McCully

Old English Jeremy J. Smith

English Around the World Edgar W. Schneider

English Words and Sentences Eva Duran Eppler and Gabriel Ozón

Linguistics and English Literature

An Introduction

H. D. Adamson
University of Arizona

CAMBRIDGE
UNIVERSITY PRESS

University Printing House, Cambridge CB2 8BS, United Kingdom

One Liberty Plaza, 20th Floor, New York, NY 10006, USA

477 Williamstown Road, Port Melbourne, VIC 3207, Australia

314–321, 3rd Floor, Plot 3, Splendor Forum, Jasola District Centre,
New Delhi – 110025, India

79 Anson Road, #06–04/06, Singapore 079906

Cambridge University Press is part of the University of Cambridge.

It furthers the University's mission by disseminating knowledge in the pursuit of
education, learning, and research at the highest international levels of excellence.

www.cambridge.org
Information on this title: www.cambridge.org/9781107045408
DOI: 10.1017/9781107051379

© H. D. Adamson 2019

First published 2019

Printed in the United Kingdom by TJ International Ltd. Padstow Cornwall

A catalogue record for this publication is available from the British Library.

Library of Congress Cataloging-in-Publication Data
Names: Adamson, H. D., author.
Title: Linguistics and English literature : an introduction / H. D. Adamson,
  University of Arizona.
Description: Cambridge, United Kingdom ; New York, N.Y. : Cambridge University
  Press, 2018. | Series: Cambridge Introductions to the English Language |
  Includes bibliographical references and index.
Identifiers: LCCN 2018035158 | ISBN 9781107045408 (hardback) |
  ISBN 9781107623057 (paperback)
Subjects: LCSH: Language and languages–Style–Textbooks. |
  BISAC: LANGUAGE ARTS & DISCIPLINES / Linguistics / General.
Classification: LCC P301 .A325 2018 | DDC 808–dc23
  LC record available at https://lccn.loc.gov/2018035158

ISBN 978-1-107-04540-8 Hardback
ISBN 978-1-107-62305-7 Paperback

I dedicate this book to the memory of my parents, Margaret Boyle Adamson and Jack Hale Adamson.

Contents

Figures

Tables

Maps

Preface

Students of literature who would like to deepen their knowledge of the English language and also to learn how ideas from the field of linguistics can contribute to understanding literature are the audience for this book. Linguistics is a broad field that includes everything from the analysis of sound waves to theories of political power, and scholars have used insights from all of these specialties to enhance our understanding and appreciation of literature. The very old partnership between the study of language and the study of literature is nowadays called *stylistics*. I have chosen to focus on stylistic analyses that are based mainly on the central areas of linguistic scholarship, areas that are usually covered in an introductory linguistics textbook, including phonology, syntax, semantics, pragmatics, and discourse analysis. However, I have also included two more recent areas of scholarship that are particularly relevant to literature, namely metaphor and metonymy (Chapter 3), and the analysis of visual images (Chapter 9).

In order to do stylistic criticism, you must first know the relevant linguistics, and most of the chapters in the book first teach the required linguistics and then apply that knowledge to literary analysis. Therefore, the book is self-contained: you don't have to know any linguistics to use it, and you don't have to buy a supplementary linguistics text. I have not limited the linguistics discussions in the book to material that is directly relevant to analyzing literature. Rather, I have included areas of language study that are important for understanding how language works in general, and which are interesting in their own right.

Teaching Linguistics and Teaching Literature

Teaching linguistics and teaching literature are the same but different, and to explain why, I would like to take a brief detour into the field of education. Two very different approaches to teaching have been influential in American education. The *instructional approach* was nearly universal in the nineteenth century and is still widespread. The typical instructional classroom features a teacher standing at the front lecturing to students. Freire (1973) has characterized this approach with a banking metaphor, where the students' minds are like empty bank accounts in which the teacher makes deposits of knowledge. This approach is common in literature courses that cover the different historical periods, Victorian, Romantic, Modern, etc., where students might learn a bit about the lives of the authors and the cultural circumstances in which they wrote. In the instructional approach, the teacher is the center of the classroom and the source of knowledge, who states the relevant information and models the desired critical skills.

The instructional approach was challenged by the progressive education movement in the 1920s. The progressive approach was inspired by Rousseau's novel *Emile*, the story of a child who learns in a free and natural way, guided only by her own interests and curiosity. John Dewey was the father of progressive education in the United States, and his ideas have survived remarkably well. Dewey argued for student-centered teaching. He believed that students should follow an internal syllabus based on their own interests and developing abilities, and that schooling should be relevant to their everyday lives. Each of these beliefs has a corollary. The first is that instruction should begin with what the student already knows, and the second is that instruction should be interesting and fun.

The literature class seems custom-made for putting the progressive teaching philosophy into practice, and many activities have been developed for teaching literature according to Dewey's principles. I have tried to incorporate some of these activities into my linguistics and literature classes over the years. For example, I have used Hess's (2006) suggestion to help students make autobiographical or intertextual connections with a reading by asking them to infer information about a character the way we sometimes infer information about an acquaintance. This technique can be used, for example, to teach Adrienne Rich's poem "Letters in the Family" (Chapter 6), which contains a letter from a young woman named Nicole to her parents. Nicole has left an unhappy home to join the Republican cause fighting the Fascists in the Spanish Civil War. Hess suggests that students try to relate Nicole's situation to their own lives by answering questions like these:

Who is Nicole? What kind of person is she? Why do you think she has left home? What kind of relationship does Nicole have with her parents? Does anything about this relationship remind you of anything in your own life or of anything else you have read about?

Hess also suggests using role-playing to put students "into the story." As an exercise for "Letters in the Family," for example, students could be asked to write a reply to Nicole (not necessarily in verse) from her mother or father, expressing their point of view.

Another technique for relating a text to students' lives and beliefs is to select a sentence or short passage from a work of literature that presents a controversial or thought-provoking idea and ask the students to react to it, perhaps first in writing (including free-writing in class) and then orally. Here are some examples of such passages that might be used in this way to prepare the students to read the whole text.

1. Some say the world will end in fire,
   Some say in ice.
                   Robert Frost, "Fire and Ice"

(from Chapter 1)

2. (This passage describes dropouts from society during the 1960s.)
   R-r-rackety-am-m. *Am.* War, rhyme,
   Soap, meat, marriage, the Phantom Jet
   Are shit, and like that.
                   Mona Van Duyn, "What the Motorcycle Said"

(from Chapter 2)

3. It is for us the living, rather, to be dedicated here to the unfinished
   work which they who fought here have thus far so nobly advanced.
                   Abraham Lincoln, *The Gettysburg Address*

(from Chapter 3)

Beach et al. (2011) suggest another role-playing activity in which students critique a work from the perspectives of different critical schools, such as Marxist or reader-response, or as they put it, through different "lenses." Some examples of this kind of exercise are provided in Chapter 1. The critical lens adopted throughout this book is, of course, that of stylistics, but it can be interesting to ask students to interpret one of the works discussed in the text through a different lens that they may have encountered in their other literature classes. Here are some questions that Beach et al. suggest:

1. Summarize what you think it means to apply a Marxist lens to a text.
2. Underline lines that are particularly relevant to a Marxist reading.
3. Based on a Marxist reading briefly explain the meaning of the poem.
4. What larger questions about society does this text raise for you?

In doing these kinds of exercises (as well as in doing exercises through the stylistics lens), it is well to keep in mind this observation by Francine Prose (2014), "When [critical] categories get less interesting is when the category becomes the whole point – the substance and basis of how a book is read."

I have gone on at length about the progressive approach to teaching literature because although I recommend using it in moderation for teaching some of the material in this book, I have not often incorporated it into the exercises, most of which reflect an instructional approach. The main reason for this decision is that I have found that the instructional approach to teaching *linguistics* usually works best. Although it is possible to relate linguistic notions to students' lives (for example, the difference between formal and informal styles can be taught by asking students to record a friend telling a story and then counting the percentage at which the inform- ant uses a particular informal marker, such as "dropping the g"). However, this kind of learning is not very efficient, and I have found that college students can become impatient when asked to figure out well-known prin- ciples for themselves. So, it is usually more effective to teach linguistics through lecture/discussions. And, of course, it is also true that when teach- ing technical material like the phonemic alphabet or how to parse a sentence the teacher is, in fact, the expert and the students are the learners.

So, that's what I have found to be different about teaching linguistics and teaching literature. What's the same is that both the instructional and progressive approaches recognize that real learning involves hands-on doing. Courses in chemistry and biology, for example, center on the teacher, but they also require the students to spend a lot of time in the lab showing that they can apply the principles and techniques that were presented in the lecture. This is also true in teaching linguistics, where students can only master material like the phonemic alphabet by using it. Hands-on instruc- tion was also a principle of Dewey's philosophy. He wrote:

> When education fails to recognize that the primary or initial subject matter always exists as a matter of active doing, ... the subject matter of instruction ... becomes just something to be memorized and repro- duced upon demand (1916:184).

Learning to do linguistics and learning to critique literature both require a lot of practice. This is what the exercises at the end of each chapter provide, and so they should be considered as important as the expository portions of the text. Although these exercises are mostly instructional, many requiring a single right answer, they are in my opinion the only way that students can master technical linguistic material and also develop the ability to apply their knowledge to interpreting literature. However, I also encourage the use of more progressive exercises, such as those I have suggested, to increase the students' interest and enjoyment of the texts. More such activities can be found in the chapter References.

I have found that the material in this text can be covered in a 14-week undergraduate course that proceeds at all deliberate speed. If the instructor wishes to take a more leisurely pace, some of the chapters can be omitted or just touched on briefly. These less central chapters include Chapter 1, Introduction, whose material students may already be familiar with, and Chapter 5, The Rhythms of Speech and Poetry. If Chapter 5 is omitted, the students might be asked to view the PowerPoint presentation in the web materials, which summarizes the chapter. Chapter 7, Morphology, Semantics, and Pragmatics, and Chapter 9, Alternative Texts, are also less central to the book, but Chapter 9 is usually the students' favorite.

Let me end with a remark made by the great Russian linguist Roman Jakobson, who throughout his career urged a collaboration between linguistics and literary study. Jakobson said, "A linguist deaf to the poetic function of language and a literary scholar . . . unconversant with linguistic methods are equally flagrant anachronisms." I hope that this book may contribute in its own way to this collaboration.

References

Beach, R. et al. (2011). *Teaching literature to adolescents* (2nd edn) New York: Routledge.

Dewey, J. (1916). *Democracy and education*. New York: Macmillan.

Freire P. (1973). *Education for critical consciousness*. New York: Seabury.

Hess, N. (2006). The short story: Integrating language skills through the parallel life approach. In Paran, A. (ed.) *Literature in language teaching and learning*. Alexandria, VA: TESOL.

Prose, F. "Bookends." *New York Times Book Review Section*, July 6, 2014, p. 27.

Acknowledgments

I am indebted to friends and colleagues in the Department of English at the University of Arizona with whom I have spent many enjoyable hours discussing literature and linguistics. In particular I would like to thank Roger Bowen, Charlie Scruggs, and Tom Willard, who read and commented on parts of the manuscript. Former Department Heads Rudy Troike and Jun Liu provided a collegial and productive environment for both linguists and literary scholars. I owe a special debt of gratitude to Linda Waugh, whose critique of many of the chapters was insightful and supportive. I would also like to thank Dr. David Adamson, poet and editor extraordinaire, who offered valuable advice and encouragement at a time when I needed it badly. Thanks to *New York Times* best-selling author (and my son-in-law) Adam Rex for help with graphics and understanding comics, and to my research assistant Lauren Harvey for many helpful comments. Special thanks as well to Helen Barton, my Cambridge University Press editor, for cheerfully bearing with me throughout this long project.

My greatest debt is to my family, Alice, Katie, Josh, Jack, Marie, Adam, and Henry, who continue to provide love, companionship, humor, and intelligence.

CHAPTER 1

Introduction

In this Chapter ...

Stylistics is the school of literary criticism that is represented in this book, and this chapter discusses how it is related to other approaches to literary analysis. Nine schools of criticism are mentioned, and they are classified according to whether they put greater emphasis on the literary text itself or on the culture in which the text is read by the modern reader. Sample analyses of poems are given for three of the schools, including New Criticism, structuralism, and reader-response theory. The discussion shows that often literary analysis starts with a description of linguistics forms within a text and then makes an interpretation about how these forms affect the reader. Finally, two analytical tools of stylistic analysis that will be used throughout the book are considered: cohesion and foregrounding.

1.1 Literary Criticism

Which discipline has more theoretical approaches, linguistics or literature? Linguistics has at least: minimalism, lexical-functional grammar, categorial grammar, cognitive linguistics, connectionism, discourse analysis, conversation analysis, interaction analysis, and quantitative sociolinguistics. According to several popular introductions to literary criticism,[1] literature has at least: Russian Formalism, New Criticism, structuralism, stylistics, reader-response theory, Marxism, feminism, African-American criticism, and new historicism. So, it looks like a tie (though of course I cheated by choosing just nine approaches from each group – I could have listed many more). Stylistics is the approach taken in this book, but before we get to it, let us take a brief, and necessarily over-simplified, look at some of the ways that the study of literature has been practiced over the last century in order to get an idea of what literary critics do and to see how stylistics fits into this tradition. We will begin with the nineteenth-century background to some twentieth century approaches.

By the end of the nineteenth century religion was losing its power. Darwin had thrown the biblical story of Creation into doubt, and the new science of geology suggested that the earth was millions of years old, not the 6000 years confidently asserted by Bishop Usher, who had used biblical genealogy to calculate that the earth was created on October 15, 4004 BCE, in the afternoon. As the British poet and social critic Mathew Arnold wrote in "Dover Beach,"

> The Sea of Faith
> Was once, too, at the full, and round earth's shore
> Lay like the folds of a bright girdle furled.
> But now I only hear
> Its melancholy, long, withdrawing roar, . . .

The withdrawal of religion could cause a social crisis because Victorian England saw the value of religion not only as instilling moral values and uplifting the spirit, but also as pacifying the masses and preserving the social order. If religion retreated to irrelevance, what could accomplish these necessary social functions? Arnold believed that part of the answer was public education and, in particular, the study of literature, which could instill in the philistine working and middle classes "a greatness and a noble spirit" (quoted in Eagleton, 1983:24). So, one goal of teaching literature in Britain in the nineteenth century was to instill morality and good citizenship. In America, literature was also taught for these reasons. As Showalter (2003:22) notes, Yale's William Lyon Phelps considered that "teaching was

Table 1.1 *Classification of schools of literary criticism*

<--->

Text-oriented		Culture-oriented
Russian Formalism	structuralism	Marxism
New Criticism	stylistics	feminism
	reader-response[*]	African-American criticism
		new historicism

* Reader-response criticism looks at both the text and the culture in which the text is read, but, unlike the other schools, it is mainly interested in how a reader processes and reacts to a text.

preaching,"[2] and the McGuffey Readers, which were used in the public schools and included excerpts from Hawthorne, Dickens, and Shakespeare, also aimed to instill good citizenship and patriotism.

One way of looking at the nine modern schools of literary criticism mentioned at the start of this chapter is whether they emphasize the analysis of literary texts or the cultural backgrounds of their readers. Of course, all of the theories paid at least some attention to the text, so the difference between these two emphases is not clear-cut, but rather lies along a continuum, as shown in Table 1.1.[3]

1.1.1 Culture-oriented Criticism

Because we are mainly concerned with the more text-oriented schools, we can take only the briefest look at the schools that have a primary interest in the reader's culture. Let us start with one of the more recent, **new historicism**. The term implies that there is an old historicism, and indeed there is, though it is usually called "historical criticism." This was the major approach to literary studies at the beginning of the twentieth century, and it is very much alive today. Historical critics study "the canon", the great literature of the past, explaining the works of authors like Chaucer, Shakespeare, and Milton within the context of their times, and often relating them to the lives of their authors. For example, in order to understand *Paradise Lost* a historical critic might teach something about the life of John Milton, such as the fact that he was involved in the Puritan Revolution, and might even discuss why the Puritans rebelled against the Crown and how Puritan theology is reflected in Milton's great poem. One goal of historical criticism is thus an ambitious one: to use literature as a window for looking into another time and another culture.

New historicism shares these goals, but while the primary aim of historical criticism is to understand literature, new historicism pays equal attention to understanding history. To this end, new historicism borrows not only from the discipline of history, but also from economics, geography, sociology, and other social sciences to study earlier societies. A common technique is to analyze a non-literary document, such as a political tract, and a literary document from the same period, with the goal of better understanding both the politics and the literature. In short, new historicism uses literary works as texts that can shed light on past cultures.

The other culture-based theories on the list are like historical criticism in that they aim to understand a society through its literature, but they are mainly concerned with understanding present-day society. This is not to say that these schools study only modern texts. On the contrary, they are interested in all earlier periods, but rather than focusing on the culture surrounding the text and its author, like historical criticism, they focus on the culture surrounding modern readers, in order to discover how the text is interpreted in and relevant to today's society. Of course, each of the schools has a particular point of view, as their names indicate, and one goal of these schools is to point out how readers from different cultural backgrounds and identity groups can view the same text differently. In contrast, the next two schools that we will discuss have little interest in the culture of the reader, but emphasize the literary text itself.

1.1.2 Text-oriented Criticism

Does one have to teach cultural theory in order to teach literature? Showalter (2003) recounts the case of a candidate for a job in a literature department who thought so. She said that her ideal course would be,

> "Theory and – and, um – theory and *non*theory."
> "Nontheory, what's that?"
> "Well, nontheory, like, *you* know, poems, stories, plays" (p. 103).

The poems, stories, and plays are the main focus of the approaches in the left-hand column of Table 1.1.

1.1.2.1 Russian Formalism

The school at the top of the list, **Russian Formalism**, was founded by one of the great linguists, Roman Jakobson, who, it was said, could speak half a dozen languages, all of them in Russian. The Russian Formalist school began around the turn of the twentieth century in Petrograd (St. Petersburg), but it was shut down when it lost favor with the Stalinist regime. Jakobson then moved to Prague, where he continued his work, collaborating with Czech colleagues in what came to be called the Prague School of linguistics. Throughout his life, Jakobson considered the study of literature to be an integral part of linguistics.

The Russian Formalists looked at the language of literature and found it to be different from the language of everyday speech.[4] They pointed out that poetry in particular often uses syntactic patterns and diction that make it stand out and call attention to itself. The effect of this literary style is to foreground or recast familiar events and topics in an unfamiliar light, and thus heighten our awareness and understanding of them. Victor Shklovsky (1917/2004:20) expressed this idea in general terms: "Art exists that one may recover the sensation of life; it exists to make one feel things, to make the stone *stony*." The cultural context from which a work of literature came, and indeed its very content, were of less interest to the Russian Formalists than its structure. The Russian Formalists and the Prague School studied language in all of its forms, and their scholarship shaped the beginning of the social science method of *structuralism*, the tradition from which Chomskian generative grammar, which we will look at in Chapter 4, is a direct descendent. We will take a look at the structuralists' approach to literature after discussing a critical school that is often considered a first cousin to Russian Formalism, New Criticism.

1.1.2.2 New Criticism

New Criticism grew up in Britain and the United States in the 1930s and 1940s. It broke with the tradition of historical criticism by focusing on the literary work itself, without attention to the biography of the author or the social circumstances in which the work was written. The twentieth century witnessed the rise of science within the universities, and both the Russian Formalists and the New Critics tried to bring quasi-scientific methods to the study of literature. However, New Criticism focused not only on the poetic devices in a work, but also on the content. In fact, a central principle of New Criticism was that the structure and content of a good poem (and by extension of all good literature) worked together to create the poem's true meaning. "Beauty is truth – truth beauty," wrote Keats, and the New Critics looked for poetic or imaginative truth in literature as scientists looked for literal truth in nature. New Critics believed that the aesthetic experience provided by literature allowed access to a truth higher than literal truth, as it provided insights into human nature and universal human experience that evoked recognition, understanding, and even catharsis in the educated reader. The New Criticism emphasized the practice of close reading, where a passage is looked at in great detail and features such as images, sounds, and symbols are analyzed and related to each other.

A useful exercise for practicing New Criticism is to paraphrase a poem and then ask how the poem does its job of conveying truth more effectively than the paraphrase. For example, consider the following poem.

The Lake Isle of Innisfree

I will arise and go now, and go to Innisfree,
And a small cabin build there, of clay and wattles made;
Nine bean-rows will I have there, a hive for the honey-bee,
And live alone in the bee-loud glade.

And I shall have some peace there, for peace comes dropping slow,
Dropping from the veils of the morning to where the cricket sings;
There midnight's all a glimmer, and noon a purple glow,
And evening full of the linnet's wings.

I will arise and go now, for always night and day
I hear lake water lapping with low sounds by the shore;
While I stand on the roadway, or on the pavements grey,
I hear it in the deep heart's core.

William Butler Yeats

Yeats's poem not only expresses the desire to escape to a tranquil and soul-restoring retreat, it partially creates this experience. The rhythm is unhurried and a bit irregular, like a walk in a garden; the vowel sounds for the most part are soothing and low, and the repeated *l* sounds in line four allow us to hear the humming of the bees in the glade. These are some of the reasons that the poem has been enormously popular since its publication in 1888.

Now consider this paraphrase.

I will get up now and go to Innisfree and build a small cabin of clay and wattles. I will have nine bean rows and a bee hive and live there alone.

I shall have some peace there, for peace comes slowly from morning until night. There, midnight is full of stars; the light of noon is not harsh; and in the evening you can see the linnets flying.

I will get up and go now for I always hear the sound of the waves in the lake reaching the shore, while I stand on the road or on the grey pavements. I hear the lake sounds deep in my heart.

The poem is obviously more effective than the paraphrase at conveying the idea that the heart yearns for the peace that only nature can provide. The New Critic, then, would ask what poetic devices the speaker uses to accomplish this task. One device is the use of sound imagery, where a word or individual sound suggests a natural sound that is not actually heard. An example is **onomatopoeia**, where a word resembles the sound it denotes, like *whispering*, *clang* and *sizzle*. An example from the poem is the word *lapping*. Notice that the paraphrase merely tells us that the speaker hears the sound of the waves against the shore whereas in the poem the word *lapping* lets us hear this sound. Similarly, the word *cricket* lets us hear the sound that the cricket makes.

A second device of sound imagery is the **phonetic intensive** defined by Arp (1997) as, "words whose sound…, by an obscure process, to some degree suggest [their] meaning" (p. 390). Unlike onomatopoeic words, the meanings of phonetic intensives need not refer to sounds. For example, the sound *sl* suggests the feeling of slipperiness, as in "slick," "slime," and "sludge." Phonetic intensives in Yeats's poem include the words *glimmer* and *glow*, in which the *gl* sound suggests light, specifically the light that the speaker sees from the stars at midnight and from the sun at noon. Other examples of *gl* sound imagery include the words *glisten*, *glitter*, and *gleam*.

Let us now take a look at the vowel sounds in the poem. As we will discuss in Chapter 2, some English vowels are actually diphthongs, which include the sound of *y* after the pure vowel as in *mate* (MEYT), *fate* (FEYT), and *create* (KRIYEYT). The *y* sound adds a harsh quality to the pure vowel, and choir directors will tell their singers to get through the *y* quickly, or not to pronounce it at all, so that, for example, the line

You're the mate that fate had me created for …

sounds more like

You're the MEHT that FEHT had me KRIHETID for …

Vowels other than diphthongs are softer and more soothing, especially the rounded vowels produced at the back of the mouth, such as UW (as in *mood*) and OW (as in *low*). "The Lake Isle of Innisfree" contains a good number of OW sounds in strategic places in the poem. For example, the second stanza, where the tranquility and calm of the island is most clearly evoked, contains two OW end rhymes (*slow* and *glow*), and these are reinforced by the additional rounded vowels in *morning* and *noon*. In the last stanza the harsh mood of the city contrasts with the mood of the lake, and *y* sounds are prominent. For example, in the next-to-last line, the city is characterized by the words *roadway*, *pavement* and *grey*, which, besides suggesting something dreary, all contain the EY sound, with the last EY emphasized because the adjective *grey* is unexpectedly placed after rather than before the noun it modifies. In the last line of the poem, however, we return to the lake and to the softer sound of OW, this time heard not just by the ear but by the heart.

Like vowels, consonants can strike us as more or less harsh. The softer consonants, like *l* and *r*, are produced with the mouth more open than it is for the harsher consonants, like *t* and *s* (thus *l* and *r* are more like vowels). In the poem, softer consonants appear frequently in the lines that describe the isle. For example, the quietness of the lake is suggested by the repeated *l* and *r* sounds in this line:

I hear lake water lapping with low sounds by the shore.

This use of repeated consonant sounds is, of course, **alliteration**. We will examine this and the other poetic devices just discussed in more detail in Chapter 2.

While the New Critics would engage in the kind of close examination of sound imagery that I have just attempted, they would probably refrain from emphasizing the circumstances in which the poem was written, such as the fact that Yeats's father gave him a copy of Thoreau's book *Walden,* and that the young Yeats had expressed a desire to live as Thoreau had, alone in a small cabin by a lake, because these autobiographical facts are not part of the poem itself.

1.1.2.3 Structuralism

The next critical school on the list is **structuralism**, which was based on the linguistic theories of Ferdinand de Saussure, the French-speaking Swiss linguist whose book *Course in General Linguistics* is a founding document of modern linguistic science. Saussure pointed out that in language sounds usually have an arbitrary relation to what they signify (except for onomatopoeia, which is rare). For example, the sounds in the word *red* (*r*, EH, and *d*) refer to the vivid color because English speakers agree on this relationship, not because anything in the sounds themselves suggests that hue (the Amharic word for "red" is KAHIY and the Malaysian word is MEERAH). In other words, languages match sounds to concepts in an arbitrary way that is determined by the people who speak the language. Saussure also emphasized that language is a self-contained system, "òu tout se tient," where everything holds together. This idea can be seen in the system of phonemes or basic sounds in a language, which we will study in Chapter 2. The phoneme IY (the vowel in *eat*) is not defined by any inherent quality in the sound itself, but rather by its place in phonemic space, that is, its relationship to the other vowels. If the tongue dips too low in the mouth during its production, IY becomes EY, and the word *eat* becomes *ate*. In a similar way, the structuralists said, the meaning of a word depends on its contrast to the meanings of other words. For example, "cup" occupies a place in semantic space somewhere between "mug" and "bowl," and a particular vessel without a handle and with a wide base might be called either a cup or a bowl depending on what it is used for.

Structuralists also held that the system of semantic contrasts in a language affects speakers' concepts and how they think about the world. In English, a woman with medium-brown hair is called a "brunette" and is associated with the cultural stereotypes of that concept (less glamorous and maybe a bit smarter than a blonde). In Peninsular Spanish, however, that same woman is *una rubia* (roughly, a blonde), and is associated with the cultural connotations of that concept (a bit exotic and northern-European-looking). So, to understand even seemingly objective notions like cups and hair color, we need to look at the linguistic and cultural systems in which they are embedded.

The structuralists analyzed the details of literary texts, but with an eye to relating the texts to the cultural systems and traditions in which they occurred, and that is why Table 1.1 places structuralism in the middle of the textual/cultural continuum. Structuralists might observe, for example, that the metrical pattern of "The Lake Isle of Innisfree" is very flexible. The basic meter is iambic, where a stressed syllable follows an unstressed syllable, dah DUH/ duh DUH/ duh DUH, but this pattern is often violated in the poem. For example, the second half of line two is perfectly iambic, but the first half of the line contains only one iambic foot, as can be seen in this transcription:

And a | small CAB | in BUILD there | of CLAY | and WAT | tles MADE |

A structuralist might make note of this pattern in the poem and then go on to compare it to the general patterns of lyric poetry of the period, noting that this degree of metrical flexibility was not typical of the poetry of England at the time, and that Yeats was trying to establish a new genre of Irish poetry.

The structuralists also analyzed literary texts to uncover patterns of organization and contrast that might reflect similar patterns within the society in which the poem is embedded. I will attempt to do this with Robert Frost's poem, "Fire and Ice."

Fire and Ice
Some say the world will end in fire,
Some say in ice.
From what I've tasted of desire
I hold with those who favor fire.
But if I had to perish twice,
I think I know enough of hate
To say that for destruction ice
Is also great
And would suffice.

The first two lines of the poem provide a neat binary division, which can be illustrated using a **tree diagram:**

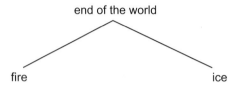

The third line makes the point that the speaker does not just mean fire (and by implication ice) literally, but also metaphorically. So, now the poem has two levels of meaning: literal and metaphorical. This can be added to the tree diagram as follows.

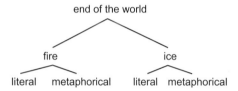

The third and fourth lines elaborate on destruction by fire. In the third line, the speaker says that he has personally experienced desire, and in the fourth line he says that he favors the fire theory. The diagram of the poem can therefore be expanded to include this information, as follows.

The fifth (and middle) line of the poem serves as a transition between the two theories of destruction. The last four lines discuss the possibility of the world ending by ice. Line 6 provides the expected metaphorical interpretation of ice, namely hate. So far, the logic of the poem has been symmetrical, as seen in the tree diagram, and if this is to continue, we should expect two propositions about the possibility of destruction by hate: the first should mention the speaker's experience with hate, and the second should mention its destructive potential. These expectations are met. Line 6 tells us that the speaker knows hate, and lines 7, 8, and 9 tell us that its destructive potential is great enough to end the world. Thus, the logical argument of the poem is neatly symmetrical, and can be diagrammed as follows.

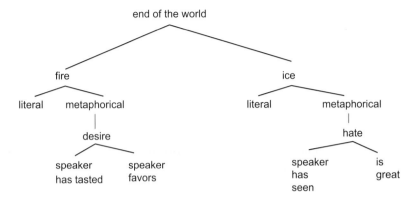

Before discussing the implications of this symmetrical structure, let us see how it interacts with the tone of the poem.

The tone of the first two lines is impersonal, even academic. We imagine that the word "some" refers to experts discussing the destruction of the earth by a natural or man-made disaster, perhaps a new ice age or a war (biblically informed readers will also recall Saint Peter's prophecy [2 Peter 3, 10] that on judgment day God will destroy the world by fire). With the third line, the tone of the poem moves toward the more personal, as the speaker mentions his own experience with desire. The fifth line of the poem serves as a transition between the two theories of destruction, and its ironic tone moves the speaker to an even closer relationship with the reader.

Although the rhetorical structure of the poem is symmetrical, the number of lines devoted to each topic in the poem is not. Only lines 3 and 4 are devoted to the discussion of desire, while twice as many, lines 6, 7, 8, and 9, are devoted to the discussion of hate. This asymmetry accentuates the change in the tone of the poem from impersonal to personal. As the tone becomes less formal, the lines become less concise and the diction becomes more familiar. In regard to destruction by fire, the speaker *holds* with those who take this view. But in regard to destruction by ice, he knows enough to *say* that it would suffice. The last two lines of the poem are ironic to the point of black humor, and the effect is to place the speaker in a familiar relationship with the reader.

The change from an academic to a personal voice over the course of the poem suggests a change in the focus of the poem, as well. Consider again the last line of the poem, "and would suffice." The subject of the verb "suffice" is "ice," but this verb requires a complement of some kind. You can't just say, "Ice would suffice," it must suffice to do something. The understood something is, of course, to cause the end the world. So, the grammar of the last line refers us back to the proposition of the first two lines, "Some say the world will end in fire,/ Some say in ice" but with an enhanced understanding of the figurative possibilities of these lines. The word "world" suggests one such possibility because it is ambiguous, referring not only to the planet earth, but also to the personal world of family and community, and in that smaller world desire and hate are especially destructive. The entire poem, then, can be read literally to refer to the destruction of the planet by fire or ice and also metaphorically to refer to the destruction of the personal world by desire or hate.

As noted earlier in this section, structuralists looked for contrasts within linguistic systems and believed that meaning was often created by these contrasts. In English phonology, IY is a basic sound (a phoneme, see Chapter 2) because it contrasts with other vowels, like EY, and in the semantic system the meaning of *brunette* is understood in part because it contrasts with *blonde*. Structuralists believed that contrastive semantic terms could be especially revealing about the structure of a culture. Such terms include: male/female, raw/cooked, and life/art. So, structuralists looked for basic semantic dyads in a work of art in order to move beyond the text and get a glimpse of larger social meanings which the text may reflect.

From this point of view "Fire and Ice" is a structuralist's dream. The title and the first line set up the basic dyad of the poem: fire and ice. The second line establishes a second dyad in which to understand these terms: literally versus metaphorically. The metaphorical meanings of fire and ice are then explored using a binary rhetorical pattern, as the tree diagram of the poem shows, where fire symbolizes desire and ice symbolizes hate. Finally, as mentioned earlier, an even more fundamental contrast is suggested in the ambiguity of the word *world*. Understood literally, *world* refers to the planet earth, but understood metaphorically *world* refers to a personal, social world. Frost suggests that the fate of both of these worlds is involved in our ability to deal with the basic emotions of desire and hate. [For further discussion of "Fire and Ice" see the online materials.]

1.1.2.4 Reader-response

So far, our discussion has characterized critical schools as emphasizing either the text or the culture in which the text is read, but we have not mentioned individual readers' responses to literary texts. That is the focus of the reader-response school. Tyson (2006) divides reader-response criticism into five separate types, which vary along a continuum according to whether they focus on an individual reader's response or assume a fairly uniform response by a community of readers.

Subjective reader-response theory, as in the work of Bleich (1978), emphasizes the feelings, associations and memories that occur in a particular reader during the reading process. Bleich's focus on the individual can be seen in his method of studying readers' responses. Because Bleich is mainly interested in how to teach literature, his method of study resembles a reading lesson. Bleich asks a group of readers to read a text and then write a response statement, describing how the text made them feel, think, or associate. These response statements often connect the characters and incidents in the text to the people and experiences in the readers' lives. Bleich then asks the readers to discuss their statements in a group, with the aim of engaging them in the text, both personally and collectively.

In an interesting variation of this method, Bleich asked readers to write a traditional "objective" essay about a literary work and then to write a subjective response paper as described above. He found that the two pieces of writing were not so different, which suggests that the traditional "objective" interpretations of texts are highly influenced, consciously or unconsciously, by readers' personal histories and experiences.

Subjective reader-response theory has been criticized as an anything-goes approach to interpretation, but this is not so because of the emphasis that Bleich puts on the group discussion of individual responses, where shared interpretations emerge and highly individual interpretations stand out as unusual. In fact, the group discussion constitutes a kind of construction of the meaning of the text, which starts with individual impressions but moves on to areas of general agreement.

Transactional reader-response criticism focuses on both individual and community responses to texts. This school was established by Rosenblatt in the 1930s, and it laid out the basic premises of reader-response theory. These included the idea that the reading process is a transaction between a text and a reader, in which the text guides the reader to an understanding of its meaning and also triggers in the reader's mind many individual feelings, associations, and emotions. Rosenblatt (1978) identified two different modes of reading a text, the *efferent* mode and the *aesthetic* mode. In the efferent mode, the reader focuses on just the information contained in the text, that is, on its literal meaning. In the aesthetic mode, the reader focuses on the feelings and memories that the text triggers and thus establishes a personal relationship with the text. There is a continual interplay between the literal meaning of a text and the personal associations that a reader makes while reading in aesthetic mode, with the text acting as a kind of blueprint to bring the reader back to a literal understanding when aesthetic associations run too far afield. Iser (1978) made a similar distinction between the *determinate* and *indeterminate* meanings of a text. The determinate meaning refers to the facts of the text, while the indeterminate meaning refers to gaps in the text where the meaning is not clear, so that readers are invited to fill in their own understandings and interpretations. These often turn out to be wrong and the reader is brought up short by the blueprint and must correct any misinterpretations. In Chapter 8 we will see that this give-and-take process is similar to what modern reading scholars call *bottom-up* and *top-down* processing. According to Iser (1978), the process of how readers form expectations of what a portion of a text will mean and how these expectations are brought up short and modified by the blueprint of the text creates a tension that makes reading enjoyable and exciting.

Fry (2009) provides an example of how the transactional process of reading works in his explication of the children's book *Tony the Tow Truck*. Here is how the text begins:

> I am Tony the Tow Truck. I live in a little yellow garage. I help cars that are stuck. I tow them to my garage. I like my job. One day I am stuck. Who will help Tony the Tow Truck?

Fry explains that at this point in the story a tension exists between the blueprint and our expectations of what is going to happen. Because this is a children's book, we expect that Tony will eventually get unstuck, but we do not know how that will be accomplished. Furthermore, because this story sounds like a folktale, we expect that there will be three possibilities for saving Tony, and that the first two will not succeed. But, we do not know how these expectations are going to play out, so we are in a state of suspense.

The text continues:

> "I cannot help you," says Neato the Car. "I don't want to get dirty"... "I cannot help you," says Speedy the Car. "I am too busy"... I am very sad. Then a little car pulls up. It is my friend Bumpy. Bumpy gives me a push. He pushes and pushes and – I'm on my way. "Thank you, Bumpy," I call back. "You're welcome," says Bumpy.

Fry says that at this point in the text, even with the problem resolved, there is still a bit of suspense because the reader expects that the story will have a moral but doesn't know what the moral will be. It could be "Don't be too busy to help others" or "Be a good Samaritan." These anticipations turn out to be wrong when we read this line near the end of the story: "Now that's what I call a friend." So, the moral is that you should help your friends, and the story is about the reciprocity of friendship.

Notice that Fry's example of how Iser would analyze a text puts a great deal of emphasis on the text itself and thus qualifies as a text-oriented theory. But, it also assumes that most readers will have the same expectations at particular points in the story. In fact, Fry's analysis assumes a reader who knows about the genres of children's stories and folktales. In other words, Fry's analysis only works for a reader who comes from a specific reading community. For this reason, reader-response criticism also qualifies as a culture-oriented theory.

Affective reader-response criticism focuses mainly on the similar responses of a community of readers rather than on the differing responses of individual readers. This school of criticism is associated with the scholar Stanley Fish, who wrote an influential book chapter in 1980 titled "Is There a Text in this Class?" One of Fish's students had asked that question to a professor, who replied, "Yes, it's the *Norton Anthology of Literature*," to which the student said, "No, no. I mean in this class do we believe in the poems and things or is it just us?" (In other words, do we emphasize texts or readers?)

Fish uses this anecdote to illustrate that the basic assumptions and background knowledge of the audience determine the interpretation of a text. In this case the text was the oral question: "Is there a text in this class?" and the assumption of the professor was that the student was asking whether there was a textbook. However, the student was instead assuming that the professor knew that she had taken Fish's class and also knew that Fish believed that the reader and not the text was of primary interest. Fish (1980) explains that readers who share background knowledge and ways of understanding constitute an interpretive community (as Fry does in his explication of how "the reader" processes *Tony the Tow Truck*), and that members of a particular interpretative community will understand a text in a similar way. Of course, different interpretative communities will have different understandings of a text. A major difference in such communities occurs across time, so that, for example, Milton's audience who believed in a literal heaven and hell understood *Paradise Lost* very differently than many modern readers, who may understand these concepts metaphorically.

The notion that ways of understanding are relative to interpretive communities goes beyond literature and is, in fact, the basis of scientific understanding. Scientific "truths," such as the belief that the earth revolves around the sun, are relative to a particular community at a particular time in history. As Kuhn (1970) pointed out, medieval European scholars held the belief that the sun revolved around the earth (The philosophical question of how we understand reality is addressed in the web materials for Chapter 8).

1.1.3 The Critic's Task

Our too-brief tour of schools of literary criticism reveals that there is considerable disagreement over how to go about analyzing literature, though there are also some areas of agreement. We have seen that the text-based schools of criticism mainly engage in fine-grained textual analysis but that some kind of close reading of a text is important to the culture-based schools, as well. In order to interpret a text, you must first describe it, so description is necessary in all criticism, and that description must involve at least some attention to a text's basic linguistic structure. For example, any discussion of "The Lake Isle of Innisfree" would probably involve some mention of onomatopoeia and alliteration.

Short (1996) provides a stylistics perspective on the text versus culture debate. He says that criticism has both core concerns and peripheral interests. The core includes interpreting a text, that is, explaining what it means, while the periphery includes matters that are external to the work itself, such as the life of the author. Short also assigns the examination of the sociocultural background of the writer and the reader to the periphery of literary criticism, but this claim is probably too strong. A new historical critic might reply that understanding those possibly very different backgrounds is important for understanding much earlier literature. For example, the critic might observe that the meanings and associations of words change over time and that understanding these changes can be important for understanding a text. When Hamlet, in his madness pose, says to Polonius, "For if the sun breed maggots in a dead dog, being a good kissing carrion … "(Act 2, Scene 2), modern readers will probably think he is just rambling like a madman, but Elizabethan readers might have detected a reference to King Claudius, who murdered Hamlet's father and married his mother. In Elizabethan culture kings were sometimes symbolized by the sun, and so Hamlet may be speaking in metaphor, suggesting that Claudius has corrupted the court, which is now like maggot-infested carrion. Critics from the reader-response, Marxist, feminist, and African-American schools would of course also say that the reader's background is crucial for interpreting a text, as will be explored further in Chapter 8. But, all critics would agree that some description of a text is a necessary step in its interpretation, and we will see throughout the book that linguistic tools can be helpful in making this description.

In our discussion of the text-based schools we saw that analyzing a text often involves two steps. First, the critic describes some feature of the text, usually a linguistic feature, and then the critic makes a claim about how that feature adds to the meaning of the text or affects the reader. Barry (1995) calls the gap between description and interpretation the "hermeneutic (interpretive) gap." In order to get over the gap, the critic must take what I will call the "interpretive leap." But, as we will see, it can sometimes be a leap off a cliff. Let us consider a couple of examples of interpretation.

Traugott and Pratt (1980) first describe and then interpret these lines from T. S. Eliot's poem "Rhapsody on a Windy Night."

> Half-past one,
> The street-lamp sputtered,
> The street-lamp muttered,
> The street-lamp said, "Regard that woman
> Who hesitates toward you in the light of the door ... "

In step 1, description, Traugott and Pratt point out (as a Russian Formalist might) that the street lamp's language is different from ordinary speech in several ways (they don't bother to mention the fact that street lamps don't talk). One difference is that the street lamp's speech at least partly rhymes. Another difference is that the lamp repeats itself. For example, line 3 repeats line 2 except that it substitutes "muttered" for "sputtered." No one could disagree with these observations. Then, Traugott and Pratt (1980) make an interpretive leap, claiming, "the repetition imitates the sputtering of the lamp" (p. 31). That point seems well-taken, and probably no one would disagree with it, either.

However, sometimes interpretive leaps can be questioned. Consider Vendler's (2009) analysis of Robert Frost's poem "Stopping by Woods on a Snowy Evening" (I will quote only the first and last stanzas of this well-known poem).

Stopping by Woods on a Snowy Evening
Whose woods these are I think I know.
His house is in the village, though;
He will not see me stopping here
To watch his woods fill up with snow.
...
The woods are lovely, dark, and deep
But I have promises to keep,
And miles to go before I sleep,
And miles to go before I sleep.

Vendler comments,

> Why does Frost, do you think, give a *subject*-position not only to himself but also to the owner of the woods...? And why does he also give it to inanimate things (the woods that fill up with snow...?).

This part of Vendler's comments constitutes the description. She then goes on to make an interpretive leap.

> The short answer is that everything in a poem that has subject-position is "alive" and can "do things"; the owner of the woods is alive enough

to see (but won't) the trespasser; . . . the woods are alive enough to be lovely, dark and deep. . . ." The whole world of the poem, in short, is animate and animated. This is far more interesting, at least in Frost's view of nature, than to make the speaker the only live person in the scene.

The claim that everything in a poem that has subject position is "alive" and can "do things" is questionable. It is true that sentence subjects are usually animate creatures that act, but this is not necessarily so. Take the sentence, "My bathtub often fills up with water." Here, the subject is "my bathtub," but that doesn't imply that it is alive or that it acts on the water. Or, to take a fairer example, namely a sentence from a poem, consider this line from "Mr. Flood's Party" by Edwin Arlington Robinson:

The road was his with not a native near.

The subject of the sentence is "the road," but it does not seem to be alive or to act. It is simply identified as belonging only to Mr. Flood, that is, to be empty. The woods in Frost's poem are, of course, alive, but the fact that they are the subject of the verb *fill up* does not imply that they act on the snow. It is also true that when something is perceived as "lovely" there must be an animate perceiver, but that does not mean that the subject of "lovely" is alive. Few would disagree with this sentence, "The Hope Diamond is lovely," but that does not imply that the diamond is a living thing. These comments may be quibbles because I agree with Vendler that the woods have an animated quality, but I am not convinced by her explanation of why this is so.

In our discussion of stylistics in the rest of the book, we will observe the two-step act of analysis many times. The first step is a description, usually based on linguistics, of some aspect of a text. If the linguistics are right, there should be no disagreement about this description, and for that reason this part of the discussion might be called rigorous or even scientific. The second step is the interpretive leap, and it is here that subjective intuitions come into play. Nevertheless, although taking the interpretive leap is risky, it is certainly the most exciting and rewarding part of a literary discussion.

1.2 Stylistics

"Stylistics," says Simpson (2004:3), "first of all, normally refers to the practice of using linguistics for the study of literature." As we have seen, stylistics shares the basic goals of all critical schools, namely understanding and interpreting a work of literature. But, because it uses linguistic tools, stylistics particularly focuses on the description of a text, as opposed to, say, comparing one character to another, or commenting on how a minority group is portrayed. Of course, all schools of criticism are free to look at all aspects of a text. In regard to the difference in focus between stylistics and other schools, Short (1996:6) observes: "The difference is ... one of degree rather than kind." To get an idea of what stylisticians do, let us look at two important tools of stylistic analysis: cohesion and foregrounding.

1.2.1 Cohesion

Cohesion refers to the elements that bind a text together, including the text's grammatical structure. Ordinary prose is full of such elements. For example, consider this story in the *Arizona Daily Star* newspaper (the bold face, underlining, and italics are explained below).

> *Locomotive No. 1673* was put into operation by the Southern Pacific Railroad in 1900 and logged 1 million miles hauling freight in Southern Arizona. In 1954, toward the end of *its* working life, *it* was used in the movie "Oklahoma!" which was filmed in Southern Arizona. It steamed into town for the last time in 1955 to mark the 75th anniversary of the arrival of the railroad in Tucson.
>
> [Locomotive 1673, a relic of transportation history, has graced city since '55, by Tom Beal. *Arizona Daily Star* April 25, 2014, p. C1]

The boldfaced words in the text illustrate the cohesion created by the use of personal pronouns. The pronouns *its* and *it* refer back to the **noun** *locomotive No. 1673*, creating connections within the text and serving to bind it together grammatically, just as the repeated meaning of these forms serves to bind the text together semantically. The capitalized words illustrate the cohesion created by the agreement of verbs with their subjects. The first *WAS* agrees with the singular noun phrase *Locomotive 1673*. If the subject had been plural, the verb *were* would be required. This fact shows that the form of an element that occurs earlier in a text can determine the form of an element that occurs later, thus creating an internal connection. The other two uses of *was* serve the same function. The underlined words in the text illustrate how relative pronouns create cohesion. Here, *which* refers back to the noun phrase *the movie "Oklahoma!"*. If the antecedent (earlier) noun phrase had been a person, the relative pronoun *who* would be used, so again the form of an element in the text is determined by an element that occurred earlier.

All texts contain cohesive devices involving grammar, but literature has some other devices that are not found in ordinary prose. For example, consider this stanza from a poem by Calvin Trillin written when France did not join the "coalition of the willing" in the invasion of Iraq.

On the Backlash Against the Perfidious French
They're relegated to the side.
This role – which they cannot abide,
Which torments Frenchmen day and night –
Can make them do things out of spite.
But could it be the French are right?

The most noticeable cohesive device in the stanza is that each line begins with a capital letter, which serves to connect the lines visually and to present the stanza as a cohesive whole. Another prominent cohesive device is that the lines rhyme, with the repeated end rhymes of *side*, *abide* and *night*, *spite* and *right*. As with the grammatical devices just discussed, an end rhyme entails that a structure in the text depends upon a previous structure, thus forming a connection within the text. In addition, the meter throughout the entire stanza is completely regular iambic tetrameter (a weak stress followed by a strong stress occurs four times in each line). Repeated without any variation, this pattern produces a sing-song effect, which would be considered a flaw in serious poetry but which enhances the humor of this satirical piece. The two sentences in the poem also, of course, contain some garden-variety grammatical cohesive devices, including the agreement of subjects with verbs and pronouns with antecedents. For example, notice that *they* in both lines 1 and 2 refers back to the noun *French* in the title, serving to connect the title to the verse.

As this discussion shows, the poem is a lot more cohesive than the newspaper blurb, and, as Jakobson famously pointed out, most literature is more cohesive than other kinds of writing. Throughout the book we will be looking at many of the cohesive devices that give literature its distinctive character.

1.2.2 Foregrounding

Writers and speakers often wish to foreground or call attention to certain elements in a text. Speakers can do this by giving a particular syllable more stress than it would normally receive, and this can be represented in writing in several ways, including italics (Don't you *dare*!) and capital letters (Her eyes opened – THUUOOCK – like umbrellas!). A speaker can also foreground an element of speech by giving it less stress, as when whispering. This device is not so easy to represent graphically, though sometimes a smaller font is used. These devices work by making the foregrounded element different from what we would expect to find. English also has grammatical devices for calling attention to particular elements in a sentence, such as the cleft sentence construction shown in example 1. The normal or expected way of putting things is shown in example 2.

1.   It was twenty years ago today that Sergeant Pepper taught the band how to play.

2.   Sergeant Pepper taught the band how to play twenty years ago today.

In the Beatles' lyric in example 1 the time of the event is stated early in the sentence in order to emphasize that today is its anniversary.

Another grammatical device for foregrounding elements of a sentence is reversing the order of nouns and adjectives. In modern English, the adjective normally goes before the noun, but in poetry it can follow the noun, and thus become more noticeable. We have already seen an example in Yeats's line:

While I stand on the roadway, or on the **pavements grey,**

Here is another example from Thomas Gray's "Elegy Written in a Country Churchyard":

Full many a gem of purest **ray serene,**
The dark unfathomed caves of ocean bear:

Adjectives and verbs can also trade places in poetry, as in these lines from Keats's "Ode on a Grecian Urn":

And, little town, thy streets for evermore
Will **silent be;**

The examples of foregrounding discussed so far are cases of *external deviation*, where the emphasized elements of a text differ from ordinary English usage. Another way that authors can foreground an element is to make it different from the surrounding text, a device called *internal deviation*. Yeats uses this technique in "The Lake Isle of Innisfree" to emphasize his desire to escape to the island, which is most strongly expressed in the final line of the poem. The last lines of the first two stanzas are in fairly regular iambic tetrameter, which sets up an expected pattern, but, as already mentioned, the last line of the final stanza ends in three stressed syllables, thus violating the pattern:

I hear it in the déep héart's córe.

Authors can also foreground elements of a text by repeating them, a kind of foregrounding called *parallelism*. One kind of parallelism is restating the same idea in different words, a technique called *chiasmus*, which is often used in the Bible, as in this verse:

> So God created man in his own image,
> in the image of God created he him; (Genesis 3, 10).

Repetition is also found in poetry and song in the form of the *refrain*, where lines or entire stanzas are repeated. For example, in the poem "Jabberwocky", included in the exercises to Chapter 2, the first stanza is repeated at the end of the poem, creating a kind of closure and a return to a natural state of affairs after the slaying of the Jabberwock. In our discussion of the musical devices in poetry in Chapter 2 we will encounter many more examples of parallelism, including rhyme, assonance, and alliteration.

As mentioned earlier, the Russian Formalists believed that literature had the capacity to "defamiliarize" ordinary experience by describing it in unaccustomed ways, thus prompting us to reconsider our prejudices and stereotypes. "Life is coated with the glass armour of the familiar," said Shklovsky (1972:68), who believed that defamiliarization can shatter this armour uncovering the unexpected, original, and strange. Cook (1994) makes the point that new forms at all levels of language from phonetic to semantic are appropriate for presenting new ideas, and as we explore the different levels of language in this book we will see how authors can break with traditional patterns, thus foregrounding the ideas that they wish to stress.

1.2.3 So, What Is Stylistics?

In the discussion of cohesion and foregrounding we saw how a literary effect was achieved by taking a close look at the linguistic structure of a text. For example, the humor of "On the Backlash Against the Perfidious French" is enhanced by its regular meter, and in "The Lake Isle of Innisfree" the greyness of life in the city is enhanced by foregrounding the word *grey*. Thus, stylistics offers a kind of psychological explanation of the experience of reading or listening to literature.

More than the other critical schools we have mentioned, stylistic critics emphasize the linguistic description of a text because it can be objective. But the claim that stylistics is more objective or scientific than other schools of criticism has been a continuing controversy. For example, Fowler (1986:3), a stylistician, claimed that linguistics-based criticism was the "objective description of texts" while other schools of criticism used "random descriptive jargon." On the other hand, critics of stylistics, for example Fish (1986), have pointed out that no matter how scientific the description of a text, a stylistic analyst must still make the interpretive leap, and this inevitably involves subjective judgments. Nevertheless, the disciplined description of a text that stylistics provides not only starts us out on a sound footing, but also offers insights into the many and seemingly magical ways that good writers can engage, delight, and inspire us through the use of language.

Notes

1 The textbooks I have consulted include: Barry (1995), Bressler (2007), Roberts and Jacobs (2007), and Tyson (2006).
2 The moralizing use of literature continues. Showalter (2003) cites the case of a professor who, in his own words, "had a theoretical agenda that directed what I said about the readings we did. . . . The students . . . would be required to write essays about race or gender, essays about poems on working-class experience, whether or not they shared these concerns" (p. 29). In reaction to this practice, the conservative Arizona State Legislature has passed a law requiring professors to warn students on the course syllabus if any controversial topics will be covered.
3 Abrams (1953) provides an analysis of literary schools according to their emphasis on one of four features: text, author, audience, and universe (which includes the cultural context in which a work was produced and the culture in which it is understood by modern readers). Of course, Table 1.1 greatly oversimplifies this picture, but I will say along with Cook (1994:129) that I seek "to maintain an awareness of the dangers of this rigid categorization, while also using it as a guide to this enormous and complex area."
4 Some critics have denied that there is such a thing as literary language. This controversy will be discussed further in Chapter 4.

Summary

The discussion in this chapter showed how the critical school of stylistics is related to some other modern schools of literary criticism. We noted that these schools can be placed along a continuum from those that focus mainly on the literary text to those that focus on the culture in which the text is read. Stylistics shares both of these concerns, but belongs mainly with the text-oriented schools. These schools use linguistic tools, such as phonetic and grammatical analysis, to describe a text, and then take the "interpretive leap" to explain how particular linguistic features affect the reader. While the linguistic description of a text can be objective and even scientific, the interpretive leap always involves subjective judgments, and is therefore uncertain and even risky, but interpretation is the most enjoyable part of literary study. Two features of a text that stylistic critics often note are cohesion and foregrounding. Cohesion refers to the elements that form internal links within a text and thus bind it together into a cohesive whole, such as the agreement of pronouns with their antecedents, or end rhyme, where the final sounds of certain lines in a poem depend on the final sounds of previous lines. Foregrounding occurs when particular elements within a text deviate from expected patterns. External deviation can involve violating rules of English usage, as when adjectives are placed after the nouns they modify (as in "purest ray serene") or before rather than after verbs (as in "will silent be"). Internal deviation involves setting up a pattern within the text itself and then violating the pattern, as when "The Lake Isle of Innisfree" unexpectedly ends in three stressed syllables.

Exercises

1.   We have seen how stylistic criticism typically consists of two parts: (1) making a linguistic description of a text and then (2) taking the interpretive leap to suggest how the text affects the reader. Consider the excerpt below and its description by a noted stylistic critic. In the excerpt Sheila is introducing her husband, whose name is Nigel, to her lover, whose name is Edwin.

> "Oh," said Sheila, "of course you two haven't met. Strange, isn't it really, Nigeledwin Edwinnigel." Anthony Burgess, *The Doctor is Sick*, p. 63

DESCRIPTION:
The two men's names are run together (from Short, 1996:53).

Now see if you can provide an interpretation of what effect running the names together has on the reader.

2.   Consider the excerpt below from William Blake's poem "The Tyger" and the linguistic analysis provided by Short.

> In what distant deeps or skies
> Burnt the fire of thine eyes?
> On what wings dare he aspire?
> What the hand, dare seize the fire?

And what shoulder, & what art,
Could twist the sinews of thy heart?
And when thy heart began to beat,
What dread hand? & what dread feet?

What the hammer? what the chain?
In what furnace was thy brain?
What the anvil? what dread grasp,
Dare its deadly terrors clasp?

DESCRIPTION:

The major deviant grammatical feature in the stanzas ... is that of deletion of grammatical elements ... . Line 4 can be normalized to something like "What is the hand which would dare to seize the fire?" ... Short (1996:73)

We might normalize line 8 to something like "What dread hand and what dread feet would dare to confront the living tiger?", though there are a lot of other possibilities.

a. Normalize line 9.
b. Provide an interpretation of what effect deleting the expected elements in the poem has on the reader.

---

3.   Consider the following poem by Shakespeare.

Come Unto These Yellow Sands
Come unto these yellow sands,
And then take hands.
Curtsied when you have and kissed,
   The wild winds whist,°   being hushed
Foot it featly° here and there,   nimbly
And, sweet sprites, the burden°bear,   refrain
        Hark, hark!
             Bow-wow.
        The watch-dogs bark!
             Bow-wow,
Hark, hark! I hear
The strain of strutting chanticleer
Cry, "Cock-a-doodle-doo!"

a. Find examples in the poem of cohesion, onomatopoeia, sound imagery other than onomatopoeia, and alliteration.
b. Which lines are foregrounded by deviating from the established meter? What is the effect of this foregrounding?

Key Terms

stylistics
new historicism
Russian Formalism
New Criticism
onomatopoeia
phonetic intensive
alliteration
structuralism
tree diagram
cohesion
noun phrase
foregrounding
   deviation
   parallelism

Suggestions for Further Reading

Students who are new to literary theory might continue this chapter's discussion with Barry (2009), which is an accessible and insightful introduction and even includes a chapter on stylistics. Bressler (2007) reviews the different critical schools in more detail than Barry, and offers relevant web sites and sample student essays. When the excesses of literary theory get you down, turn to Crews (2003), a hilarious and dead-on satire featuring essays from different critical schools that "interrogate" *Winnie the Pooh*. Guerin (2005) is a (serious) collection of essays from different critical perspectives, all of which discuss the same works of literature, including *Frankenstein*. Eagleton (1983) is challenging for the beginner, but Eagleton's Marxist approach to literary theory is engaging and has been enormously influential. Abrams (2014) is an indispensable guide to literary jargon, and Fry's (2009) free, online course is an enjoyable way to delve deeper into literary theory.

Answers to Exercises 1 and 2

1.   Short (1996:53) suggests (among other things) that Sheila's running together the names of her husband and her lover suggests that Sheila is speaking very fast and as a result "we can infer that she is either trying to appear unconcerned or is trying to get the confrontation over as soon as possible."

2.   Short (1996:73) says that deleting the grammatical elements produces an effect "of compression and the feeling of hidden power." He notes that in

the last part of the excerpt, "A much more dramatic form of syntactic deletion has taken place so that on four occasions sentences are reduced to 'what' plus an associated noun phrase .... The resultant uncertainty on the part of the reader is likely to increase the sense of fear and awe of the Tyger."

CHAPTER 2

The Sounds of English

In this Chapter ...

We first discuss how the American English vowels and consonants are formed in the mouth and how they can be transcribed in a phonetic alphabet. We then discuss phonemes, the basic sound units of a particular language, and contrast them with their different realizations called *allophones*. This detailed knowledge of the English sound system is then applied to analyzing poetry. It is shown how a phonemic description of a poem can heighten our understanding of the musical devices that poets use, including rhyme, assonance, consonance, alliteration, and onomatopoeia, and can also help us notice sound patterns that are not obvious. This increased understanding of English sounds allows us better to appreciate the poet's craft.

2.1 **Speech Production**

When we talk, sound waves issue from our mouths in a great jangle of vibrating air molecules. The study of how our speech organs cause the air to

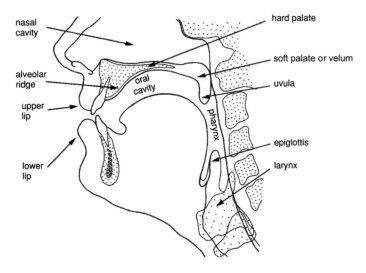

Figure 2.1 The vocal tract.
(from Fasold, R. & Connor-Linton J. (eds.). *An introduction to language and linguistics* (p. 16). Cambridge University Press

vibrate in different ways, and thus produce different sounds, is called *articulatory phonetics*. Phoneticians have found that speech sounds can be characterized along three dimensions: **voicing** (whether the vocal cords are vibrating), **place of articulation** (the place where the mouth is most narrowly constricted), and **manner of articulation** (usually, how open the mouth is as a whole).

Voicing is produced in the larynx (see Figure 2.1), which is part of the trachea, or windpipe, through which air travels to and from the lungs. The larynx contains the *vocal cords*, which can be brought together to cut off the flow of air from the lungs. When the vocal cords are almost touching and air from the lungs passes through them, they vibrate, causing the surrounding air molecules to vibrate. Our ears detect this vibration as sound. The process of expelling air from the lungs up through the vocal tract is a lot like blowing air through a trombone, where the player's lips are like the vocal cords and the tube and bell of the trombone are like the throat and the mouth.

If you have ever played the trombone, you know that you can take off the mouthpiece and blow through it, thus producing a "raspberry" sound that is very different from the sound produced when the mouthpiece is attached to the instrument. This is because the tube and bell of the instrument modulate the sound in a pleasing way. Similarly, the throat and mouth modulate the sound produced by the vibrating vocal cords, and the speaker can control this sound by changing the positions of the lips and tongue just

29

as a trombone player can modulate the sound by moving the slide. These changes produce the different vowels and consonants.

It is possible to produce a very soft noise in a trombone by just blowing through it without vibrating the lips. Similarly, it is possible to produce a soft noise in the vocal tract by keeping the vocal cords far apart so that they do not vibrate. Sounds produced without vocal cord vibration are called *voiceless* sounds (all whispering is voiceless), and sounds produced with the vocal cords vibrating are called *voiced* sounds. In English all of the vowels are voiced (though some languages have voiceless vowels). English consonants, however, can be either voiced or voiceless. Consider, for example, the sounds [z] and [s] (speech sounds are enclosed in brackets, as explained below). These sounds are produced in exactly the same way except that for [z] the vocal cords are vibrating and for [s] they are not. Thus, [z] is voiced and [s] is voiceless. You can test this claim for yourself by putting your fingers on your larynx (Adam's apple) and producing a [z] that changes into an [s]: zzzzzsssss. You will feel your vocal cords vibrating during the [z] and then stop vibrating when you change to the [s]. Another way to experience the difference between a voiced and voiceless sound is to put your fingers in your ears and repeat the zzzzzssssss sequence. You will feel the vibration in your head during the [z], but it will stop during the [s].

2.1.1 The Phonetic Alphabet

Before discussing the other dimensions along which speech sounds can differ, let us note that these sounds are written in a phonetic alphabet in which the symbols are enclosed in brackets. Many of the symbols of the phonetic alphabet that we will use are the same as the letters of the English alphabet, but there are some differences. The reason that it is necessary to use a phonetic alphabet when discussing speech sounds is that English spelling is so irregular. For one thing, the letters for vowels often represent more than one sound. For example, the letter *a* in the word *Kate* and the letter *a* in the word *cat* represent two different sounds, requiring that spelling teachers distinguish between "long a" and "short a." For another thing, English spelling sometimes uses two letters to represent one sound, as in the first sound of *phone*, the first sound of *thing*, and the middle consonant sound of *nation*. For these reasons linguists have constructed phonetic alphabets in which each symbol represents one and only one sound. Table 2.1, which shows the American English consonants, together with Table 2.3, which shows the American English vowels, is such a phonetic alphabet.[1] As mentioned, phonetic symbols are written in brackets, so that the word *cat*, for example, is transcribed [kæt].

Table 2.1 *English consonants. vl = voiceless; vd = voiced*

	bilabial	labiodental	dental	alveolar	palatal	velar	glottal
stops							
vl	p			t		k	
vd	b			d		g	
fricatives							
vl		f	θ	s	š		h
vd		v	ð	z	ž		
affricates							
vl					č		
vd					ǰ		
nasals							
vd	m			n		ŋ	
liquids							
vd				l, r			
glides							
vd	w				y		

Table 2.2 *Examples of consonants in English words*

	bilabial	labiodental	dental	aveolar	palatal	velar	glottal
stops							
vl	**p**in			**t**in		**k**eg	
vd	**b**in			**d**in		**g**et	
fricatives							
vl		**f**an	**th**in	**S**ue	mi**ss**ion		**h**i
vd		**v**an	**the**	**z**oo	mea**s**ure		
affricates							
vl					**ch**ip		
vd					**j**udge		
nasals							
vd	**m**ine			**n**ine		wi**ng**	
liquids							
vd				**l**ug, **r**ug			
glides							
vd	**w**ay				**y**es		

2.1.2 Consonants

Let us first consider how the consonants are formed in the mouth. As already mentioned, speech sounds can be described by specifying three dimensions of how they are produced: voicing, place, and manner. We have already discussed voicing, so let us now turn to the place of articulation. While reading the descriptions below, the reader should consult Table 2.1.

2.1.2.1 Place of Articulation

Bilabials are formed by closing off the vocal tract at the lips. The initial sounds of *pit* [pit], *bit* [bit], and *mitt* [mit] are bilabials. Notice that when saying *pit* and *bit* the vocal tract is completely closed at the start of [p] and [b] so that no air escapes during the first part of these sounds. When saying the word *mitt*, air does escape during the entire production of the initial bilabial sound [m], but it escapes through the nose. Therefore, [m] belongs to the class of sounds called *nasals*, in which air goes out through the nose rather than through the mouth. Nasals also include [n] and [ŋ], as described below. We can also classify the initial sound of *way* [wey] as bilabial even though the lips are not completely together.

Labiodentals are formed by bringing the lower lip into contact with the upper teeth. English has only two labiodentals, which are heard in the initial sounds of *fit* [fit] and *vat* [væt]. These sounds differ from each other only in voicing (by now you should be able to figure out which sound is voiced and which is voiceless).

Interdentals are formed by placing the tongue between the upper and lower teeth while air passes over the tongue. English has only two inter-dentals, the initial sounds of *thistle* [θisl] and *this* [ðis], which also differ from each other only in voicing.

Alveolars are formed by raising the tip of the tongue to the alveolar ridge (see Figure 2.1). English has seven alveolar sounds. The first sounds in *tip* [tip] and *dip* [dip] are made when the tongue completely closes off the vocal tract at the alveolar ridge. These sounds differ only in voicing. The first sounds in *sit* [sit] and *zit* [zit], which also differ only in voicing, are made when the tongue is very close to the alveolar ridge but does not completely cut off the flow of air. The first sounds in *night* [nayt], *light* [layt], and *right*, [rayt] are also alveolars, all of them voiced.

Palatals are formed by raising the blade of the tongue to the hard palate at the top of the mouth so that the flow of air is almost completely blocked off. English has five palatals, the first four of which can be grouped into two pairs. The first pair consists of the first sound in *shoe* [šuw] and the middle sound in *pleasure* [pležr] (these sounds also differ only in voicing). The second pair consists of the first sound in *chip* [čip] and the first sound in *jib* [jib], which also differ only in voicing. The fifth palatal is the first sound in *you* [yuw].

Velars are formed by raising the body of the tongue up to the velum, or soft palate. When the tongue touches the velum shutting off the flow of air from the mouth, the first sounds of *kit* [kit] and *get* [get] are produced, which differ only in voicing; when the tongue is in this position and air is allowed to escape through the nose, the last sound of *lung* [lən] is produced.

Glottal sounds are formed without the use of the tongue, teeth, or lips. The first sound in *he* [hiy] is a voiceless glottal consonant. As with other voiceless sounds, the vocal cords are apart and the air flowing past them is unobstructed.

The information regarding place of articulation that was just discussed is summarized in Table 2.1. This table also summarizes the information to be discussed below, namely the manner of articulation, which is the third dimension along which consonant sounds can be characterized.

2.1.2.2 *Manner of Articulation*

The manner of articulation of consonants roughly corresponds with the degree of opening of the vocal tract. There are three degrees of opening: 0 (closed), 1 (slightly open), and 2 (more open).

Stops are produced by closing the mouth at some point to degree 0 and then opening it to produce a vowel (as in the word *pa*) or a vowel-like consonant (as in the word *plot*). As Table 2.1 shows, stops can be voiced or voiceless. When the vocal tract is closed off at the lips and then opened, a bilabial stop, [p] or [b], is produced. When the vocal tract is closed off by the tip of the tongue touching the alveolar ridge, an alveolar stop, [t] or [d], is produced. The vocal tract can also be closed off at the back of the mouth by raising the body of the tongue against the velum, producing [k] or [g].

Fricatives are produced at degree 1 of opening, where the airflow is almost completely blocked off so that the air passing through the vocal tract produces friction. Like stops, fricatives differ according to the place at which the vocal tract is most constricted: [f] and [v] are labiodental fricatives; [θ] and [ð] are interdental fricatives; [s] and [z] are alveolar fricatives; [š] and [ž] are palatal fricatives; and [h] is a glottal fricative where the air is constricted in the larynx by almost closing the vocal cords.

Affricates begin at degree 0 of opening and then move to degree 1, producing a combination stop and fricative. English has only two affricates, [č] and [ǰ], which are produced with constriction at the palate.

The remaining consonants are produced at degree 2 of opening, which is too wide to cause friction when the air passes through the vocal tract. All of these sounds are voiced.

Nasals are produced by closing off the mouth at some point and lowering the velum so that air flows out through the nasal passage, as already mentioned. The three English nasal sounds are the bilabial nasal [m], the alveolar nasal [n], and the velar nasal [ŋ].

Liquids include [r] and [l]. English [r] is usually produced by curling the tongue so that the tip is pointed toward the top of the mouth. [l] is produced by touching the tip of the tongue to the alveolar ridge but narrowing the blade of the tongue so that the air can pass around the sides.

Glides include [y] and [w], both of which involve some movement of the articulators while the sound is being produced. For [y] the body of the tongue moves toward the front of the mouth, and for [w] the lips become rounded.

Using the three dimensions just discussed, namely voicing, place of articulation, and manner of articulation, it is possible to characterize all the English consonants. For example, [t] is a voiceless, alveolar stop; [ž] is a voiced, palatal fricative; and [m] is a bilabial nasal (it is not necessary to mention that [m] is voiced because in English all nasals are voiced).

2.1.3 Vowels

English vowels are produced with the vocal tract opened wider than for the consonants but still somewhat narrowed by the tongue at a particular place. They can be characterized by specifying the values of three parameters: the degree of opening (in other words, the general height of the tongue), the place where the vocal tract is most narrow (in other words, where some part of the tongue is closest to the top of the mouth), and whether the muscles of the tongue or lips are tensed or relaxed. All English vowels are voiced. In regard to the first parameter, Figure 2.1 shows the tongue in a neutral position, neither high nor low in the mouth nor bunched up toward the front or the back of the mouth. The neutral position is used for producing the most common English vowel, the first sound in *allow*, which is transcribed [ə], the symbol called *schwa*. It is possible to move the tongue higher or lower in the mouth than the position shown in Figure 2.1. The higher position produces the high vowels, [iy], [i], [uw], and [u] (see Table 2.4 for corresponding English words); the middle position produces the mid vowels [ey], [e], [ə], [ow] and [o]; and the low tongue position produces the low vowels [æ] and [a]. The relationship of these vowels is shown in Table 2.3.

The second parameter along which vowels can be characterized is the place in the mouth where the airflow is narrowed by raising the tip or the blade of the tongue: namely, the front, center, or back. This relationship is also shown in Table 2.3. Bunching up the tongue in the back of the mouth produces a back vowel [uw], [u], [ow], or [o]. Raising the tip of the tongue in the front of the mouth produces a front vowel [iy], [i], [ey], [e], or [æ]. Leaving the tongue in a relatively flat position produces the central vowels [ə] and [a]. Notice that there are five front vowels but only four back

Table 2.3 *English vowels*

	front	central	back
high			
tense	iy		uw
lax	i		u
mid			
tense	ey		ow
lax	e	ə	o
low			
lax	æ	a	

Diphthongs: ay, aw, oy

Table 2.4 *Examples of English vowels*

	front	central	back
high			
tense	P**e**te		L**u**ke
lax	p**i**t		l**oo**k
mid			
tense	pl**a**te		b**oa**t
lax	p**e**t	p**u**tt	b**ou**ght
low			
lax	b**a**t	p**o**t	

Dipthongs: ay as in *pie*; aw as in *cow*; oy as in *boy*

vowels. This is because the mouth can open wider in the front than in the back, allowing the tongue to assume more distinctive positions.

The third parameter for distinguishing vowels is whether or not the muscles of the tongue or the lips are flexed during production. Flexing the tongue muscles produces the tense front vowels [iy] and [ey] and flexing the lip muscles (in other words rounding the lips) produces the tense back vowels [uw] and [ow]. All other vowels are lax vowels. Using the three parameters it is possible to characterize all of the English vowels: [iy] is a high, front, tense vowel; [ow] is a mid, back tense vowel; [a] is a low central vowel (it is not necessary to mention tenseness because there are no low central tense vowels), etc.

Diphthongs are produced by pronouncing a vowel followed by a glide. English is often said to have three diphthongs: [ay], [oy], and [aw]. However, [ey] and [ow] also consist of a vowel followed by a glide, so they, too, are technically diphthongs. Notice that our symbols for [iy] and [uw] suggest that these sounds are also diphthongs; however, the symbols are misleading because in most American dialects these sounds do not, in fact, contain a glide.

2.2 **Phonetics and Phonemics**

Some differences don't make a difference, and in this section we will see how slightly different pronunciations of a sound still count as the same sound. So far, we have been describing speech sounds rather loosely, but it is possible to supply a lot more detail in the description. For example, the sound [p] was described as a voiceless, bilabial stop, but we could also mention the fact that [p] can be accompanied by a puff of air called *aspiration*. You can demonstrate this fact for yourself by holding a piece of paper in front of your lips and saying the word *pin*. You will notice that the puff of air that escapes after your lips part blows down a corner of the paper. So, a better phonetic description of the initial sound in *pin* would include the information that it is aspirated, and this can be done using the symbol [ʰ], which stands for aspiration, so that *pin* should be transcribed [pʰin]. Now hold up the piece of paper and say the word *spin*. The paper doesn't move. This is because in English when a voiceless bilabial stop begins a syllable it is aspirated, but when a voiceless bilabial stop is preceded by a consonant (and the only possible consonant in this position is [s]), it is unaspirated, so *spin* should be transcribed [spin].

It is sometimes necessary to write a detailed phonetic description, where you specify which variety of *p* you are talking about. Is it [pʰ] or [p]? However, for most linguistic purposes it doesn't matter which variety of a particular sound occurs in speech because all the varieties are instances of the same basic sound. An analogy is to compare [pʰ] and [p] to two models of the same make of car. For example, Chevrolet (as of this writing) makes both Malibus and Impalas, but we can imagine a Chevrolet dealer asking, "How many units do we have on the lot?" For inventory purposes it might not matter whether the unit was a Malibu or an Impala, as long as it was a Chevrolet. Similarly, for most purposes it doesn't matter whether the sound in question is a [pʰ] or a [p] because they are both instances of the same abstract category, and this category is called **phoneme**. Phonemes are descriptive units at a higher level of abstraction than the sounds we actually produce, and they are written in slanted brackets like this: /p/. Thus, using a bit of quasi-mathematical notation we can write the phonological rule: /p/ → [pʰ], [p]. This rule says that the phoneme /p/ can occur as a [pʰ] or a [p]. To continue the car analogy, we might write: /Chevrolet/ → [Malibu], [Impala]. In other words, the brand called Chevrolet includes both Malibus and Impalas. Similarly, the phoneme /p/ includes both [pʰ] and [p].

The sounds that make up the possible realizations of a phoneme are called **allophones**. Notice that no one has ever pronounced /p/ or any other phoneme because the phoneme, like the Chevrolet brand, is an abstract mental concept. You have to drive a Malibu or an Impala or a Corvette or some other realization (allocar?) of the Chevrolet brand, and, similarly, you have to pronounce a [pʰ] or a [p] or some other realization (allophone) of the phoneme /p/.

Let us consider another example of a phoneme and its allophones. As we have seen, the nasal sounds are created by blocking the passage of air at some point in the mouth and lowering the velum so that air passes through the nose. In English, vowels produced in isolation are not nasalized, so the velum is raised, closing off the nasal passage so that air passes only through the mouth. However, when a vowel is followed by a nasal consonant, the velum is lowered during vowel production in anticipation of the nasal sound, thus allowing some air to go out through the nose and producing a nasalized vowel. This nasalization is indicated by placing a tilde over the vowel as in [pẽn] (*pen*) and [hõwm] (*home*). As these transcriptions suggest, the phoneme /e/ has the allophones [e] and [ẽ], and the phoneme /ow/ has the allophones [ow] and [õw] (similarly, all of the other vowels have nasalized and non-nasalized variants).

Here are all of the allophones, along with the phonemes they belong to, that we have discussed so far. Of course, because all of the phonemes in a language have allophones, a complete chart would be much bigger.

Phoneme		Has these allophones
/t/	→	[t], [tʰ]
/p/	→	[p], [pʰ]
/k/	→	[k], [kʰ]
/e/	→	[e], [ẽ]
/o/	→	[o], [õ]

In this book we will usually use a phonemic transcription when discussing poetry. For example, in discussing rhyme, we will note that in the poem "What the Motorcyle Said" these lines rhyme even though they end in words that are spelled differently:

Hate hardhats, wear one on my **head**,
That's what the mototcycle **said**.

The rhyme can be made more obvious by transcribing the words *head* and *said* in phonemic script, namely /hed/ and /sed/, which shows that the words have exactly the same final vowel and consonant. However, some discussions of sound require using a more detailed, or phonetic, transcription to make a point. For example, if you are not from the South, you might be puzzled by the name of the motel chain *Days Inn*. Is it an inn for days? But, if you are from the South, you understand that the name is a play on words because *Days Inn* can be pronounced exactly like "day's end." So, a Days Inn is where you go at the day's end, get it? This pun doesn't work in the North because the two phrases are pronounced differently: *Days Inn* is pronounced [dayz in], just like in the South, but *day's end* is pronounced [dayz end]. The reason for this difference in pronunciation is that in the South the phoneme /e/ has the allophones [e] and [i], where [i] is always used before nasal sounds. Thus, the words *hymn* and *hem* are homonyms, as are *pin* and *pen* and *tinder* and *tender*. We can express this regularity of Southern speech with the following rule:

/e/ → [i] before nasal sounds
      [e] before non-nasal sounds

We need one more phonological rule to show how *day's end* can wind up being pronounced [deyz in], and it is this: final cononsants can be dropped from a word when they follow another consonant (actually, this rule applies in both the North and the South, but it is more common in the South). Thus, *old* can be pronounced *ol'* ([owl]) and and *last* can be pronounced *las'* ([læs]). The rule for dropping final consonants can also be represented in formal notation, and it looks like this:

C → (Ø) / C__##

In other words, you can optionally delete a consonant when it comes after another consonant at the end of a word. As this discussion has shown, describing dialectal differences in a language often requires the use of a phonetic rather than a phonemic script.

In analyzing the sound system of a language it can be difficult to tell whether two different sounds are allophones of the same phoneme or different phonemes. The traditional test is to ask whether the difference in sounds makes a difference in the meaning of words. For example, in English the difference between [s] and [z] is that [s] is voiceless and [z] is voiced. To see if this difference changes the meaning of a word, we can look to see if there are any *minimal pairs*, that is, words which differ only in the presence or absence of the sound feature in question, in this case the voicedness of the alveolar fricative. In fact, there are some minimal pairs, including *Sue, zoo; sap, zap*; and *peace, peas*. So, the difference in voicing between [s] and [z] makes a difference in meaning, and therefore the sounds in question are different phonemes, namely /s/ and /z/. Now consider whether the aspiration of voiceless bilabial stops (the difference between [pʰ] and [p]) makes a difference in meaning. Are there any minimal pairs involving this feature; that is, are there any words whose pronunciation differs only in whether [p] is aspirated? The answer is no. In syllable-initial position voiceless bilabial stops are always aspirated and after [s] (the only sound a voiceless bilabial stop can follow) they are always unaspirated. So, it is impossible for [p] and [pʰ] to contrast (they are said to be in *complementary distribution*). But, even if by mistake the word *spin* was pronounced [spʰin], it would not produce a different word, just a funny-sounding *spin*. So, there are no minimal pairs involving [p] and [pʰ], and therefore they are both allophones of the phoneme /p/.

As this discussion has shown, the symbols in Tables 2.1 and 2.3, which I have been calling "phonetic symbols," are mostly inadequate. Phonetic transcription requires more detail and therefore more phonetic symbols than are provided in these tables. However, the symbols in Tables 2.1 and 2.3 can serve very well as *phonemic* symbols, comprising a phonemic alphabet that represents the basic sounds of American English, without showing the details. This book has followed the example of other texts by teaching a simplified phonetic alphabet before mentioning the differences between allophones and phonemes, a procedure that makes sense when introducing this complicated subject. However, from this point on we will mostly use phonemic symbols enclosed in slashes. They are exactly the same as the simplified phonetic symbols in Tables 2.1 and 2.3 and are accurate enough for our purposes.

Now that we are familiar with the basic sounds of English, we can apply this knowledge to the study of literature.

Exercises 1–10 at the end of the chapter cover the material presented so far.

2.3 Sounds in Literature

Jeffries and McIntire (2010: 36) note, "Any analysis of the sounds that make up [poetry] will be partly conjecture (for example about the accent in which it could be read). But, ... there are many things that readers will know about the sounds of a poem without having to hear the poet – or any other performer – ... read it aloud." Perhaps the most noticeable such feature in many poems is *rhyme*, which can often be indicated just by the spelling even though speakers of different dialects might pronounce the rhymes differently. Strictly speaking, rhyme is the repetition of a stressed vowel and all of the following sounds.[2] If only one syllable is repeated, we have a **masculine rhyme**, as in *said/red* and *love/of*, and if more than one syllable is repeated, we have a **feminine rhyme**, as in *fertile/turtle* and *neither/either*. The term **slant rhyme** (also known as *partial rhyme*) refers to a rhyme in which the stressed vowels, and sometimes even the consonants, are slightly different, as in *black/slick* and *full/far*. When rhyming words occur at the end of a line they make an *end rhyme*. *Internal rhyme* occurs within a line, as in this example from "On the Backlash Against the Perfidious French," which was refered to in Chapter 1.

> And sure, they come on rather strong
> If you pronounce a **diphthong wrong**.
> And even if you're **quite contrite**,
> They often fail to be polite...

Alliteration is another common phonological device, which as we saw in Chapter 1, is the repetition of initial or medial consonants, as in Caesar's famous phrase, "Veni, vidi, vici" (/weniy, wiydiy, wiykiy/) – I came, I saw, I conquered). Notice that the English translation also has alliteration, with /k/ occurring three times. But Caesar's phrase is more memorable perhaps because the repeated /w/ phone begins each of the words. Consonants can also be repeated at the ends of words, and this is called **consonance**. The name "Trent Lott" (the deposed US Senate Majority Leader) is an example of consonance, which Calvin Trillin has fun with in these lines from his poem, "Republican Anger at Trent Lott."

> Republicans feel anger, unconcealed,
> Because **Trent Lott** revealed what he revealed.

Repeating a vowel sound produces **assonance**. In the movie *Educating Rita*, Rita defined assonance as, "When they don't get the rhyme right." Here is an example from Poe's poem "The Raven."

> Surely, said I, surely **that is** something from my window **lattice**
>   /ðæt iz/   /lætis/

Notice that **that is** and **lattice** almost make a feminine rhyme but that it's not quite right. The stressed vowel /æ/ is repeated but all of the following sounds are not, so we merely have an example of assonance. Usually, however, assonance involves a repeated vowel without any repeated following consonants (and thus near rhymes), as in these lines of E. E. Cummings (only one example of assonance per line is marked; there are more).

> or if your wish be to close me, i and
> my life will shut very beautifully, suddenly,
> as when the heart of this flower imagines
> the snow carefully everywhere descending;

Like rhyme, assonance adds cohesion to poetry.

Transcribing words phonemically can be helpful when analyzing phonological devices in literature because it makes obvious patterns that are difficult to notice otherwise. Consider, for example, this poem by W. H. Auden. The tabulations of assonance and consonance are explained below.

That Night When Joy Began		Patterns of assonance	Patterns of consonance
That night when joy began	/biygæn/	a	a
Our narrowest veins to flush,	/fləš/	b	b
We waited for the flash	/flæš/	a	b
Of morning's leveled gun.	/gən/	b	a
But morning let us pass,	/pæs/	a*	a
And day by day relief	/riliyf/	b	b
Outgrows his nervous laugh,	/læf/	a	b
Grown credulous of peace,	/piys/	b	a
As mile by mile is seen	/siyn/	a	a
No trespasser's reproach,	/rəprowč/	b	b
And love's best glasses reach	/riyč/	a	b
No fields but are his own.	/own/	b	a

* a and b stand for the same sound only within each stanza, not across stanzas.

Obviously, there is a lot of assonance and consonance in this poem, especially in the end slant rhymes, and above I have marked the pattern of vowel and consonant repetition. First, consider the pattern of consonance. Line 1 ends with /n/; line 2 ends with /š/; line 3 also ends with /š/; and line 4 ends with /n/. This pattern can be represented as: abba (where a = /n/ and b = /š/). Notice that an abba pattern also occurs in the two remaining stanzas. Now consider the pattern of assonance. In line 1 the vowel in the final word is /æ/; in line 2 the vowel in the final word is /ə/. In line 3 the final /æ/ is repeated, and in line 4 the final /ə/ is repeated. This pattern can be represented as abab, and again this pattern occurs in the last two stanzas. Thus, each of the stanzas, taken separately, has the same pattern of assonance and consonance. As this exercise shows, the sound patterns of the poem are extremely complex, and examining them carefully allows us better to appreciate Auden's craft.

Having made a linguistic description that, I trust, everyone would agree with, it is time to take the interpretive leap. How does this complex sound pattern add to the meaning of the poem? What is the meaning of the poem, anyway? Two themes seem to be present in the poem. The first is that of two lovers, introduced in the first stanza by the reference to a night of joy, and thereafter by the repeated reference to "us". The second theme is that of war, with the images of a leveled gun, a pass (perhaps from the front lines to a rear area), and glasses (binoculars) surveying a field, looking for trespassers. But are the lovers at war with each other, or is the world at war with the lovers? I think both interpretations are possible, and that the poem could even suggest them both.

Let us consider the interpretation of lover against lover. The first stanza suggests that after a night of love-making, they expect some trouble – the flash of a leveled gun, which might represent regret or a cutting remark. Perhaps, in the past they have found that on the morning after, relationships look very different and that they should expect a fight. But, morning let them pass – there was no trouble. Stanza two suggests that as they stay together, they remain cautious, laughing nervously, but that there is room for hope. In stanza three the lovers have almost reached a state of peace, though they are still wary of possible trouble. But no trespasser (guilt? regret?) reproaches them, and their love appears to be unthreatened. This relationship, then, is a difficult one, full of tension and worry, but it appears to be succeeding. The sound scheme, too, is full of tension – we expect perfect rhymes in a poem as carefully laid out in stanzas and as strictly metered as this one, but we don't quite get them. The assonance and consonance are just out of step. Each has its own strict pattern, but the patterns don't match up to make perfect rhymes. Nevertheless, the two rhyme schemes, abba for consonance and abab for assonance, coexist very well throughout the poem. I suggest that the lovers, too, are slightly out of step, and that this mismatch is what led to their initial worries. Nevertheless, with time they find that they can each go their own way, marching to the beat of a different drummer, and yet staying together, and in fact creating a unique kind of harmony. Well, maybe that's reaching a bit. What can be said with more certainty is that the sound patterns create a kind of dissonance, suggesting wariness and reflecting the uncertainty and cautiousness of the lovers. I think that the same basic analysis could apply to the interpretation that the lovers are ok with each other but out of step with the rest of the world.

2.4 Onomatopoeia and Phonetic Intensives

Poets use still other kinds of sound effects, and in Chapter 1 we looked at two of them: onomatopoeia and phonetic intensives. Let us take a closer look at these devices, and also introduce the topic of meter, by examining the poem "What the Motorcycle Said" by Mona Van Duyn. This poem offers a motorcycle ride through the American cultural and political landscape of the 1960s.

What the Motorcycle Said
Br-r-ram-m-m, rackety-am-m, OM, *Am:*
All – r-r-room, r-r-ram, ala-bas-ter –
Am, the world's my oyster.

I hate plastic, wear it black and slick,
Hate hardhats, wear one on my head,
That's what the mototcycle said.

Passed phonies in Fords, knocked down billboards, landed
On the other side of The Gap, and Whee,
Bypassed history.

When I was born (The Past), baby knew best.
They shook when I bawled, took Freud's path,
Threw away their wrath.

R-r-rackety-am-m. *Am*. War, rhyme,
Soap, meat, marriage, the Phantom Jet
Are shit, and like that.

Hate pompousness, punishment, patience, am into Love,
Hate middle-class moneymakers, live on Dad,
That's what the motorcycle said.

Br-r-am-m-m. It's Nowsville, man. Passed Oldies, Uglies,
Straighties, Honkies. I'll never be
Mean, tired or unsexy.

Passed cigarette suckers, souses, mother-fuckers,
Losers, went back to Nature and found
How to get VD, stoned.

Passed a cow, too fast to hear her moo, "*I* rolled
our leaves of grass into one ball
I am the grassy All."

Br-r-ram-m-m, rackety-am-m, OM, *Am:*
All – gr-r-rin, oooohgah, gl-l-utton –
Am, the world's my smilebutton.

Now, about 50 years after the poem was written, the cultural references and vocabulary require as many footnotes as a poem by Shakespeare. Here they are, listed by stanza.

1. OM (/owm/)   a mantra (i.e. silently repeated word or sound) used in transcendental meditation. The Beatles were into meditation for a while.
2. plastic   "artificial, phony"
   hardhats hats worn by construction workers who demonstrated in favor of the Vietnam war to counter anti-war demonstrators.
3. The Gap   the generation gap. Later the name of a chain of clothing stores that catered to young people.

4. Freud's path   raising children using psychological methods rather than physical punishment. This path was advocated by Dr. Benjamin Spock, a pediatrician, who advocated giving children more freedom and responsibility, and less punishment. He was an early opponent of the Vietnam War.
5. Phantom jet   the main US fighter aircraft in the Vietnam War.
7. honkies   a derogatory term for white people.
8. Went back to nature   during the 1960s some hippies left the cities and formed rural communes. They often didn't turn out too well.
9. leaves of grass   a reference to Whitman's famous poem. "Grass" also means marijuana.
10. Smilebutton   a yellow button with a moronic smiling face, which became popular in the late 1960s. ☺

With glossary in hand, we can now explicate the poem. The voice of the talking motorcycle is loud, fast, and dumb, as we might expect. In the first stanza, as the motorcycle warms up and starts out, it is filled with ambition and hope – "the world's my oyster." The counterculture movement of the sixties started out that way, too. But, like the counterculture, the motorcycle soon hits some rough road. It tells us that it hates plastic and hardhats, but wears them anyway (here, and throughout the poem, the motorcycle seems to be speaking for its rider). This contradiction introduces a theme of the poem: the motorcycle is clear on what it hates, but not on what it stands for, and the result is hypocrisy. Beginning in stanza 5 the motorcycle speeds through a list of counterculture slogans. It hates the Vietnam War, rhyme, soap, eating meat, and marriage. The theme of hypocrisy is reinforced here by the fact that the poem rhymes. This theme comes up again in stanza 6 where the motorcycle says that it hates middle-class moneymakers, but lives on Dad. The ride ends in the last stanza, where the motorcycle sputters to an anticlimactic stop. This stanza begins like the first stanza but finishes very differently. The world is no longer an oyster, but a smilebutton, suggesting that the motorcycle now buys into the mindless, commercial culture – it has sold out.

The sound effects in the poem are great. The motorcycle seems to be bilingual, sometimes talking in pure motorcyclese (br-r-r-am-m-m, rackety-am-m), sometimes in motorcycle-accented English (all – r-r-room, r-r-ram, ala-bas-ter – *Am*), and sometimes in ordinary English. These sound effects are examples of *onomatopoeia*, where, as we saw in Chapter 1, a word sounds like the thing it means. Of course, "br-r-r-am-m-m" and "rackety-am-m" aren't words, and Short (1996) calls such suggestive non-words *nonliteral onomatopoeia*. Literal onomatopoeia, the more common variety, involves a real word that names a sound and also resembles that sound, such as "buzz," "hiss," and "rattle." Onomatopoeia can also be used in a broader sense to refer to words or passages that seem to suggest what they describe, as in Shakespeare's line, "the wild winds whist," in which we can hear the whistling of the wind. An example of onomatopoeia in this broader sense from "What the Motorcycle Said" is in line 16, "Hate pompousness, punishment, patience, am into Love," where the motorcycle seems to be sputtering as it names the things it hates, but runs more smoothly when it gets to Love.

Onomatopoeia is said to be *iconic*, with the sound of the word or phrase imitating what it describes, but for the most part the connections between sound and sense in a language are not iconic but arbitrary. As noted in Chapter 1, however, we sometimes have the feeling that certain sounds suggest certain qualities without imitating them. "Glimmer" somehow seems appropriate to the meaning of a flickering light, and there are similar words that evoke this connection, including "gleam," "glisten," and "glitter." Yet these are not examples of onomatopoeia because they are not iconic; nothing in their pronunciation mimics flickering or light. This kind of sound symbolism is called *phonetic intensive*, as noted in Chapter 1. Unlike onomatopoeic words, phonetic intensives do not necessarily refer to sound. For example, in *flutter*, *flash*, *flip*, and *fling*, the /fl/ sound suggests a quick movement, and in *inch*, *slim*, *bit*, and *sliver*, the /i/ sound suggests small size.

This short discussion of English sounds shows that some concepts that are basic to linguistics are also basic to poetry. With these concepts in mind, you should be able to take a poem apart and see how it works phonemically, as requested in exercises 11–15.

Notes

1 This claim will be modified in the subsequent discussion, where it is noted that many of the symbols in Tables 2.1 and 2.3 are not detailed enough for a phonetic alphabet, but that they work very well as symbols for a *phonemic* alphabet, as explained later in the chapter. For now, consider Tables 2.1 and 2.3 to be a kind of learners' phonetic alphabet.

2 There is no general agreement about the exact meanings of "rhyme," "alliteration," "consonance," and the other terms discussed in this chapter. Some authorities define alliteration as any kind of consonant repetition; others say that it is the repetition of initial consonants. In this chapter I have tried to use the most widely accepted and consistent terms.

Summary

This chapter introduced the area of linguistics called phonetics, the study of speech sounds. We first learned how sounds are produced in the mouth and how they can be described using the dimensions of voicing, place of articulation, and manner of articulation. We then saw how speech sounds can be transcribed in a phonetic alphabet and learned the difference between a phonetic and a phonemic transcription and between a phoneme and an allophone. Turning to the sounds of literature, we discussed a number of poetic devices including rhyme, assonance, consonance, alliteration, onomatopoeia, and phonetic intensives.

Exercises

1.   Write the phonemic symbol for the first sound in the following words.

   a. university
   b. phoneme
   c. though
   d. Zsa Zsa
   e. under
   f. civil
   g. cord
   h. thought
   i. psychology
   j. judge

2.   Write the phonemic symbol for the last sound in the following words.

   a. rough
   b. plays
   c. walks
   d. mouth
   e. toy
   f. allow
   g. jumped
   h. search
   i. wrong
   j. peace

3. Write the following words in phonemic script as you would pronounce them.

   a. George
   b. swing
   c. fiction
   d. dude
   e. chain
   f. yellow
   g. thick
   h. happy
   i. soon
   j. garage

4. The following lines in phonemic transcription are from Calvin Trillin's poem "Obama Rising." Write them in English spelling.

   əlektrifayd iz hwət ðey wer, ðey sey –
   ðə deməkræts in bastən an ðə dey
   ə mæn wiθ eləkwəns æt hiz kəmænd
   hæd held ðə hol kənvenšən in hiz hænd

5. Write the phonemic symbol that corresponds to each of the following descriptions. Then write an English word that begins with this sound.

   a. high front tense vowel
   b. voiced velar stop
   c. mid central vowel
   d. voiceless alveolar stop
   e. glottal fricative
   f. palatal glide
   g. alveolar nasal
   h. voiceless palatal affricate
   i. voiceless interdental fricative
   j. voiced bilabial stop

6. a. Why are the following phonetic transcriptions incorrect?

      pick [pik], blown [blown], stick [stʰik]

   b. What are the correct phonetic transcriptions?
   c. What are the correct phonemic transcriptions?

7.   Transcribe the following quotes from Dorothy Parker using phonemic symbols and separating each word. It is not necessary to use slashes.

    a. "A little bad taste is like a nice dash of paprika."
    b. "Take care of the luxuries and the necessities will take care of themselves."
    c. "Brevity is the soul of lingerie."
    d. "This is not a novel to be tossed aside lightly. It should be thrown with great force."
    e. "I don't care what is written about me so long as it isn't true."

8.   Transcribe in phonemic script the following excerpt from D. H. Lawrence's short story "The Rocking-Horse Winner." What examples of alliteration and assonance can you find? Which three phrases contain the phoneme /k/? What effect does this alliteration create? (The first phrase is "and she could not love them."

    There was a woman who was beautiful, who started with all the advantages, yet she had no luck. She married for love, and the love turned to dust. She had bonny children, yet she felt they had been thrust upon her, and she could not love them. They looked at her coldly, as if they were finding fault with her. And hurriedly she felt she must cover up some fault in herself.

9.   Suppose that someone denied that /n/ and /ŋ/ are different phonemes in English, but rather claimed that they are allophones of the same phoneme. What evidence could you give to prove them wrong?

10.   The following data are from Sindhi, a language spoken in India. Examine the data with respect to the distribution of the phones [p], [pʰ] and [b] and answer the questions that follow.

    1.   [pənu]   leaf
    2.   [vəǰu]   opportunity
    3.   [šeki]   suspicious
    4.   [gədo]   dull
    5.   [dəru]   door
    6.   [pʰənu]   cobra hood
    7.   [təru]   bottom
    8.   [kʰəto]   sour
    9.   [bəǰu]   run
    10.   [bənu]   forest
    11.   [bətšu]   be safe
    12.   [ǰəǰu]   judge

    a. Can you find any minimal pairs or triplets for these three phones? What are they?

b. Are the three phones allophones of the same phoneme or are they different phonemes?

c. Is the relationship of these phones the same as it is in English?

11. Find one or more examples of assonance within each line of these stanzas.

Not a feather then he fluttered – till I scarcely more than muttered,
Other friends have flown before – On the morrow he will leave me,
As my hopes have flown before. Then the bird said nevermore.

Edgar Allan Poe

Thus in the winter stands the lonely tree,
Nor knows what birds have vanished one by one,
Yet knows its boughs more silent than before:
I cannot say what loves have come and gone.

Edna St. Vincent Millay

12. **The Oven Bird**
There is a singer everyone has heard,
Loud, a mid-summer and a mid-wood bird,
Who makes the solid tree trunks sound again.
He says that leaves are old and that for flowers
Mid-summer is to spring as one to ten.
He says the early petal-fall is past
When pear and cherry bloom went down in showers
On sunny days a moment overcast;
And comes that other fall we name the fall.
He says the highway dust is over all.
The bird would cease and be as other birds
But that he knows in singing not to sing.
The question that he frames in all but words
Is what to make of a diminished thing.

Robert Frost

a. Transcribe the final word in each line in phonemic script.

b. From the poem, give examples of the following terms and explain why you chose them: internal rhyme, masculine rhyme, slant rhyme, alliteration, assonance.

13. Read the following poem aloud.

Jabberwocky
'Twas brillig, and the slithy toves
Did gyre and gimble in the wabe:

All mimsy were the borogoves,
    And the mome raths outgrabe.

"Beware the Jabberwock, my son!
    The jaws that bite, the claws that catch!
Beware the Jubjub bird, and shun
    The frumious Bandersnatch!"

He took his vorpal sword in hand:
    Long time the manxome foe he sought –
So rested he by the Tumtum tree,
    And stood awhile in thought.

And, as in uffish thought he stood,
    The Jabberwock, with eyes of flame,
Came whiffling through the tulgey wood,
    And burbled as it came!

One, two! One, two! And through and through
    The vorpal blade went snicker-snack!
He left it dead, and with its head
    He went galumphing back.

"And hast thou slain the Jabberwock?
    Come to my arms, my beamish boy!
O frabjous day! Callooh! Callay!"
    He chortled in his joy.

'Twas brillig, and the slithy toves
    Did gyre and gimble in the wabe:
All mimsy were the borogoves,
    And the mome raths outgrabe.

Lewis Carroll

a. What are some of the patterns of sound repetition in the poem?
b. What other cohesive devices are found in the poem?
c. The word "chortled" was introduced to the English language in this poem. Webster defines "chortled" as: "to make or utter with a chuckling or snorting sound." Why do you suppose this word was quickly accepted into the language?
d. What does "uffish" mean? Is it an example of a phonetic intensive or of literal onomatopoeia?

14. The following is the first stanza of the well-known poem by Matthew Arnold referred to in Chapter 1.

> **Dover Beach**
> The sea is calm tonight.
> The tide is full, the moon lies fair
> Upon the straits; on the French coast the light
> Gleams and is gone; the cliffs of England stand,
> Glimmering and vast, out in the tranquil bay.
> Come to the window, sweet is the night-air!
> Only from the long line of spray
> Where the sea meets the moon-blanched land,
> Listen! You hear the grating roar
> Of pebbles which the waves draw back, and fling,
> At their return, up the high strand,
> Begin, and cease, and then again begin,
> With tremulous cadence slow, and bring
> The eternal note of sadness in.

a. Transcribe the last word in each line in the phonemic alphabet and then answer these questions. What is the rhyme scheme of the poem? Which line does not contain an end rhyme? What other features in this line make it stand out? What change does this line signal in how the speaker perceives the scene he is describing?

b. Suppose Arnold had written:

> The cliffs of England look
> Glimmering and vast, out in the tranquil bay.

Why does "stand" sound better here than "look"? What /st/ words besides "stand" have to do with strength?

c. The mood of the poem seems to change in line 7. What is the change? How does the word "only" help to accomplish this change?

d. Find some examples of phonetic intensives other than those referred to above. How do they work?

e. In what lines does the meter of the poem reflect the description of the waves? How does Arnold make this work?

15. Watch the video on how to read poetry found at https://www.youtube.com/watch?v=Cca7SRzsbBw. How do the presenter's tips for reading poetry aloud relate to the advice for scanning poetry in this chapter? You might also want to check out some of the other videos on poetry reading.

Key Terms

voicing
place of articulation
manner of articulation
phoneme
allophone
masculine rhyme
feminine rhyme
slant rhyme
consonance
assonance

Suggestions for Further Reading

Good chapters on phonetics and phonology can be found in the following introductory linguistics textbooks. Fasold & Conner-Linton (2006) features chapters written by specialists in each of the different topics covered, all of which are excellent. After ten editions, Fromkin, Rodman & Hyams (2014) is still the best introduction to basic linguistics. Yule (2010) is the easiest of the introductory linguistics books, and provides more of an overview of phonology than the more detailed treatments in the two volumes previously mentioned. Students who want to get deeper into phonetics and phonology, and who want to learn from the master, should have a look at Ladefoged (2006). The book includes a CD featuring samples of many different languages and language varieties, including Ladefoged's own voice modeling Received Pronunciation.

CHAPTER 3

Metaphor and Metonymy

"Are you a man or a mouse?"
"Throw me a piece of cheese and you'll find out."

Groucho Marx

In this Chapter …

Practically everything we say is a metaphor. Sometimes the metaphor is obvious as in "I'm as high as a kite," but more often the metaphor goes unnoticed as in "Let's move on to the next topic." In this chapter we will contrast such unnoticed metaphors with the creative metaphors found in literature, and we will see that both types are based on deeper understandings of how we think about the world called *conceptual metaphors*. Our discussion will take us into an area of psychology called cognitive linguistics, and we will see how metaphorical language is related to mental concepts. We will also look at metonymy ("Today the *White House* announced …"), a figure of speech that is as important as metaphor in both literature and cognitive science. Knowing how metaphor and metonymy work can help us understand the connection between language and thought.

3.1 Traditional Approaches to Metaphor

Metaphors and similes compare two things, asking us to view one in terms of the other. "All the world's a stage" is a metaphor that asks us to see how people in real life are like actors on a stage. "Oh, my love's like a red, red rose" is a simile that asks us to see the similarities between a rose and a woman. The difference between a metaphor and a simile is that a simile makes the comparison overt, with a phrase such as *is like* or *resembles*, while a metaphor simply equates the two things being compared. However, this linguistic difference is not important and from now on we will use the cover term "metaphor" to refer to both figures of speech. Of course, a woman isn't much like a rose and the world isn't much like a stage, but there are some similarities, and these are what the metaphor brings to our attention. A woman and a rose are both beautiful, and in real life sometimes people are just acting. Metaphors provide a mapping across two concepts, one of which contains features that are mapped onto corresponding features of the other concept. In Shakespeare's comparison of the world and a stage, the stage is called the **source concept** from which features are taken, and the world is called the **target concept**, onto which features are mapped.[1] We know that people play roles on a stage, and that feature is mapped onto the way that people act in the world to allow us to better understand how the world works. Usually, the source concept of a metaphor is more concrete and better understood than the target concept, and mapping features from the source provides a richer understanding of the target.

The metaphor "Lisa is free as a bird" compares a bird (the source concept) to Lisa (the target concept). But, notice that not all of the features of a bird are mapped onto Lisa. We don't think of her as having feathers or eating worms, only as being unconfined. The reason that only some features map from the source onto the target is that there is some preexisting similarity between the two concepts. In this case, both birds and human beings can be free, and the ability to fly is a very obvious form of freedom.

So, it helps us to understand Lisa's freedom by likening it to the ability to fly. Having feathers, on the other hand, is a feature associated only with birds, so it does not map onto the concept of Lisa.

The following poem contains an extended metaphor that compares life to a dog.

The Hound
Life the hound
Equivocal
Comes at a bound
Either to rend me
Or to befriend me.
I cannot tell
The hound's intent
Till he has sprung
At my bare hand
With teeth or tongue.
Meanwhile I stand
And wait the event.
Robert Francis

In the poem the hound is the source concept and life is the target concept, and the poem invites us to better understand life by noticing the features that it shares with a hound. The mapping of features from the source concept on to comparable features of the target concept is shown below.

In this comparison, the poem names both the source concept (hound) and

Features of the hound (source)		Features of life (target)
comes at a bound	→	events occur suddenly
can rend a person by biting	→	can damage a person in many ways
can befriend a person by licking	→	can bring desirable things in many ways
we cannot tell hound's intent till he has sprung	→	we cannot know events in life until they occur
we must wait for the hound to spring	→	we must wait for life to unfold

the target concept (life) and mentions the features of the source that transfer. However, the reader must infer which unstated features of life correspond to the stated features of the hound. In other words, the reader must mentally fill in the right side of the chart above.

The lines below require more inference on the part of the reader than "The Hound" because they do not mention either the source concepts (there are two) or the target concept, just the features of the source concepts.

> It sifts from leaden sieves,
> It powders all the wood.
>
> Emily Dickinson, "It Sifts From Leaden Sieves"

The target concept is, of course, snow, and the two metaphors are *sifts* and *powders* (actually, there is a third metaphor, *leaden sieves*, which compares clouds to a sieve, but we will focus only on the snow metaphors). *Sifts* compares falling snow to flour, so flour is the source, snow is the target and the characteristic of falling lightly is the feature that is mapped. Similarly, *powders* compares snow to powder, so powder is the source, snow is the target, and the qualities of white color and softness are the features that are mapped. Again, notice that neither of the sources nor the target are specifically mentioned, so readers must figure these out using their background knowledge of the similarities of the concepts involved.

Of course, metaphors occur in prose as well as in poetry. Cormac McCarthy uses many metaphors in this passage from *All the Pretty Horses*, which describes two cowboys riding alone at night. Some of the metaphors in the passage are printed in bold.

> They rode out on the high prairie where they slowed the horses to a walk and **the stars swarmed around them** out of the blackness. They heard somewhere in that tenantless night a bell that tolled and ceased where no bell was and they rode out on **the round dais of the earth** which alone was dark and no light to it and which carried their figures and bore them up into the swarming stars so that they rode not under but among them. . . .

The first metaphor compares the stars to bees. Construing the stars in the night sky as bees maps the features of animacy and movement and allows us to see the stars as alive. The second metaphor compares the prairie where the cowboys are riding to a dais. A dais is an area for display, like a stage, so we imagine the cowboys as large and important figures against the landscape. Also, a dais is raised up, so we can more easily picture them riding in the sky among the stars. However, other less obvious mappings can also be made. For example, some but not all readers may think of a dais as a place for royalty and therefore see the cowboys as different from ordinary men. This metaphor illustrates the point that it can be difficult to list all of the features of a source concept that are mapped onto a target concept because some readers will see similarities in the two concepts that other readers do not.

3.2 **Cognitive Approaches to Metaphor**

So far, the discussion has been compatible with how literary scholars have traditionally analyzed metaphor, but more recently scholars from the school of cognitive linguistics have looked at metaphor from a new point of view, which we will explore in this section.

3.2.1 Cognitive Linguistics

Cognitive linguistics is a branch of the larger discipline of cognitive psychology, whose goal is to understand the way the mind works, and at least some of the claims about metaphor that we will discuss in this section have been supported by psycholinguistic experiments. Cognitive scientists have pointed out that metaphors are not just found in literature. On the contrary, every speaker and writer uses metaphors in practically every sentence, though these metaphors are less creative and interesting than the metaphors in poems and stories. Here are some metaphors that have appeared in headlines in the *Daily Wildcat*, the student newspaper at the University of Arizona.

1. *No end in sight* for heat wave
2. Webmail *down* yesterday due to hardware issues
3. Bonuses may *put [Head Football Coach Mike] Stoops past $1M*

On first reading these headlines, we are not aware that metaphors are involved; the headlines seem to be just ordinary English. But, on closer inspection, the metaphors become apparent. We can't see a heat wave, so to say that no end of the heat wave is in sight cannot be literally true. But, figuratively the headline construes the heat wave as something that we can see and that stretches endlessly into the distance, like a road or a mountain range. Similarly, *webmail* is an abstract noun, not a concrete noun referring to an object that can be upright or flat. So, the metaphor construes webmail as a physical object, like a tree or a human being, which can be up (and thus in good condition) or down (and thus in bad condition). The metaphor in (3) suggests that salary figures are arranged like milestones along a path that earners travel. Coach Stoops has traveled pretty far, passing the $1 million milestone (despite not having a winning season). Lakoff and Johnson (1980) propose that metaphors like those in (1)–(3) are based on widespread metaphorical concepts in English that underlie not only the way we talk but also the way we think. These are called **conceptual metaphors**.

The metaphorical expression in (3) that views accomplishments as milestones along a road is based on an implicit understanding of the nature of life, namely the conceptual metaphor LIFE IS A JOURNEY (conceptual metaphors are written in capital letters). This conceptual metaphor allows us to make sense of expressions like, "Be sure to *stop* and smell the roses," "He's *headed for* disaster," and "It feels like I'm just *running in place*," which assume that living is like physically moving along a path. Poets have exploited this implicit understanding of life in lines like these, where Robert Frost describes choices made along life's journey:

Two roads diverged in a yellow wood,
And sorry I could not travel both
And be one traveler, long I stood
And looked down one as far as I could
To where it bent in the undergrowth

Then took the other, . . .

The underlying conceptual metaphor LIFE IS A JOURNEY is often found in biographical descriptions of people's careers. Here are some from an article on judicial careers (Barker, 2008).

"Everything I've done has helped me to *get to where I'm at* " (p. 133).

"After *passing the bar* [Judge Paul Tang] landed a job as a Deputy County Attorney" (p. 123).

"[Judge Leslie Miller] is credited with founding the Drug Court, allowing those who have *lost their way . . . to get back on track* " (p. 133).

At this point we should clarify some of the terms we have been using. In Section 1, we used the term "metaphor" in the traditional way to mean a word, phrase, or sentence that invites us to map features from one concept onto another ("All the world's a stage"). But in this section and from now on we will call such a word, phrase, or sentence a **metaphorical expression**, or just an "expression" (some scholars use the term "linguistic metaphor"). We will continue to use the term *conceptual metaphor* to refer to a mapping between two abstract concepts on which a specific metaphorical expression is based. So, "All the world's a stage" is a metaphorical expression that is based on the conceptual metaphor LIFE IS A PLAY. From now on we will not use the bare term "metaphor" unless the context makes clear whether we are talking about a metaphorical expression (actual words) or a conceptual metaphor (abstract ideas). Here are some more examples of conceptual metaphors and the metaphorical expressions that they allow us to understand.

THEORIES ARE BUILDINGS
Is that the *foundation* of your theory?
Economic models *constructed* on the evidence of past experience are of little use.
Scanlon's article *demolished* their theory.
You need to *cap off* your argument with some conclusions.

ARGUMENT IS WAR
Your claims are *indefensible*.
He *destroyed* all my *positions*.
I *outmaneuvered* them.
Marsha *won* the debate.

LIFE IS A PLAY
Quit trying to *upstage* me.
Don't make a *scene*.
He's always hogging the *spotlight*.
What's your *part* in all of this?

PEOPLE ARE PLANTS
That school is a *nourishing* environment, where children can *grow* and *blossom*.
Johnson has the IQ of a *carrot*.
She crossed the room and *planted* herself in front of the door.
After his accident he was basically a *vegetable*.

DEATH IS A DEPARTURE
She's *gone*.
He's passed *away*.
They are among the dearly *departed*.
Because I could not stop for Death –
He kindly stopped for me –
The carriage held but just Ourselves –
And immortality.
Emily Dickinson

DIFFICULT-TO-HANDLE THINGS ARE DOGS
The cable company has been *hounding/dogging* me.
"Let's see if we can unload these *puppies*" (referring perhaps to some tires).
Life the hound/ Equivocal/ Comes at a bound

Before examining metaphorical expressions and conceptual metaphors in more detail, let us take a look at a special kind of metaphor that is important in poetry called the **image metaphor**.

3.2.2 Image Metaphors

Image metaphors are like conceptual metaphors in that they underlie and motivate metaphorical expressions. But, unlike conceptual metaphors they do not map features of one concept like PLAY onto another concept like

Table 3.1 *Concepts in two semantic fields arranged according to degree of specificity*

Semantic field		
Animals	Furniture	Degree of abstractness/specificity
ANIMAL	FURNITURE	abstract
DOG	CHAIR	↓
DACHSHUND	ROCKER	specific

LIFE. Instead, image metaphors map features of one mental image onto features of another mental image. They thus allow a writer to make a scene vivid and real by accessing images stored in our minds, as when McCarthy invites us to picture stars as swarming bees. Another example of an image metaphor involves the metaphorical expression "He made the Q sign," which according to Scott Turow, in *The Laws of Our Fathers*, means that someone is dead. Here our mental image of the round part of the letter Q maps onto our image of the dead man's mouth, and the squiggle maps onto his protruding tongue.

Image metaphors are only possible when both the source and the target images are specific, like Q and *mouth* or *veil* and *snow*. To see how mental images can be more or less specific consider first the concepts listed in Table 3.1, which are taken from the semantic fields of animals and furniture:

Table 3.1 shows that within the semantic field of animals, the concept of a dacshound is more specific than the concept of a dog, which is more specific than the concept of an animal, and that there is a similar hierarchy within the semantic field of furniture. Notice that we can form rich mental images only of the most specific concepts, *dachshund* and *rocker*. Moving up to the more abstract concepts of dog and chair, we can still form mental images, but they are different. At this level of abstraction the mind pictures prototypical examples of the concepts, so we see a dog that is taller than a dachshund and a chair that does not rock, and in both cases the images are not as rich as those of the more specific concepts, containing fewer details. Moving up to the more abstract concepts of animal and furniture, we find that it is impossible to form a mental image of either because these concepts include too many different possibilities for our minds to abstract a general pattern or prototype.

Another example of an image metaphor is Tennyson's line "He clasps the crag with crooked hands" from the poem "The Eagle." In this metaphor features from the image of a hand are mapped onto the image of an eagle's claw. Notice that like conceptual metaphors, image metaphors map only some features of the source onto corresponding features of the target. For example, in the expression "crooked hands" the human hand corresponds to the eagle's claw, and the fingernails correspond to the sharp ends of the talons, but we do not picture the eagle's claw with knuckles.

Some image metaphors have fewer corresponding features than in the examples given so far. In the poem "Daffodils" Wordsworth tells us that he "saw a crowd, a host of golden daffodils ... fluttering and dancing in the sun ... tossing their heads in sprightly dance." Here the image of a dancing human figure is imposed on the image of a fluttering daffodil. The main correspondence is the movement of the two kinds of objects. We also picture both dancers and flowers standing erect, with the dancers' heads corresponding to the flowers' blossoms, but we do not picture the flowers with two legs or feet. Other image metaphors can have even fewer corresponding features. For example, in the metaphorical expressions "submarine sandwich" and "big box store" only the overall shapes of the source images (submarine and box) are mapped. Thus, we do not map the submarine's conning tower and periscope onto the sandwich.

We should also note that just because we can form mental images of the source and target concepts invoked by a metaphorical expression, we are not forced to do so. That is, we are not forced to equate the two concepts using an image metaphor, but rather can equate them using a conceptual metaphor. For example, in "Mirror," Sylvia Plath explores the perceptual processes and personality of a mirror in these lines:

I am silver and exact. I have no preconceptions.
Whatever I see I swallow immediately
Just as it is, unmisted by love or dislike.
I am not cruel, only truthful ...

Here, although the mirror is like a person that speaks, thinks, and sees, we do not map parts of the human body onto the mirror. It is still a silver object hanging on the wall. Rather, we map more abstract human features, such as vision and speech, onto the mirror by means of the conceptual metaphor MIRRORS ARE PEOPLE. Sometimes a metaphorical expression can evoke both an image metaphor and a conceptual metaphor. For example, in Tennyson's line "He clasps the crag with crooked hands," we map the mental picture of a hand onto an eagle's claw, but the line evokes more than an image. The pronoun "he" personifies the eagle and endows it with human purpose via the conceptual metaphor ANIMALS ARE PEOPLE. Another example of both an image mapping and a conceptual mapping is the metaphorical expression "John is a pig." Here the size and general shape of a pig can be mapped onto John via an image metaphor, but the expression can also evoke the conceptual metaphor PEOPLE ARE PIGS, where we transfer some abstract, not visual, pig features onto John, such as selfishness and greed, as shown in metaphorical expressions like:

> "He always hogs the cupcakes."
> "He really pigged out."

Notice that although image metaphors can be memorable, they do not serve to structure our understanding of the world the way conceptual metaphors do. For example, the conceptual metaphor LIFE IS A JOURNEY is not only highly productive, motivating many metaphorical expressions but, as we will see in the next section, it also helps us to understand the nature of life. Generally, image metaphors are more limited than conceptual metaphors, serving only to make a one-time comparison, and so they are sometimes called *one-shot metaphors.*

In summary, both image metaphors and conceptual metaphors can be characterized by the statement "A is B"; that is, both kinds of metaphor map a source onto a target. In the case of image metaphors both the source and the target are mental images, while in the case of conceptual metaphors both the source and the target are understood in terms of transferred semantic aspects, like *free, truthful, selfish,* and *occurs suddenly.*

3.2.3 Metaphorical Expressions

Let us now take a closer look at some metaphorical expressions, both creative and commonplace. First, we should note that not all language is metaphorical; language can also be literal. Compare, for example, these two sets of lines from Shakespeare's Sonnet 18 (quoted in Ungerer & Schmid, 2006:114).

> Sometimes too hot the eye of heaven shines,
> . . .
> So long as men can breathe or eyes can see
> So long lives this, and this gives life to thee.

The use of "eye" in the first line is metaphorical: it compares the sun to an eye. In the couplet, however, "eyes" refers to the organ of sight, so this usage is literal. Metaphorical expressions are so pervasive in speech and writing that it can be hard to find examples of literal usage, but a good place to look is in personal narratives, as in this true story of life in the business world from Scott Adams's book *The Dilbert Principle.*

> I created a graph a couple of years ago showing a problem with a
> circuit we had designed, and were using in most of our products . . .
> I told [the VP of Engineering] that there was a problem, and I showed

him the graph. He took the graph, looked at it, and said "Wow!...
How did you make this graph?" (p. 304).

So far so good; all of the language appears to be literal usage. But, after
noting that the VP couldn't be less interested in the problem with the circuit,
only in how to make the graph, the writer gets into some metaphorical
expressions:

> Over the next two weeks I *spent* most of my time creating graphs for
> our VP of Engineering to use in his Corporate Management Committee
> meetings, where he was finally able to *upstage* all the marketing *bozos*
> (other VPs) with their Mac graphics that their secretaries had *spent* a
> week working on (p. 304).

The verb *spend* is used metaphorically here because one cannot literally
spend time the way one spends money. This usage is based on the conceptual metaphor TIME IS MONEY, which also underlies expressions like
"I lost a lot of time," and "I'm saving up my vacation days." *Upstage*, as we
have seen, derives from the conceptual metaphor LIFE IS A PLAY, and the
metaphorical expression *bozos* compares the marketing VPs to Bozo
the Clown.

The passage from *Dilbert* illustrates the point that everyday language
contains both literal and metaphorical usage. It also shows that some
metaphorical expressions are easier to recognize than others. It takes a
practiced eye to spot the phrase "spent most of my time" as a metaphorical
expression, but "bozos" practically jumps right off the page at you. Metaphorical expressions can be placed along a continuum from creative to
conventional. As we have seen, creative metaphorical expressions are often
found in poetry, as in "All the world's a stage," and "Life the hound
equivocal." Conventional metaphorical expressions, from the hard-to-rec-
ognize end of the continuum, include "webmail down," and "no end in
sight." Expressions from the middle of the continuum are familiar, but are
still recognizable as metaphors, as in "We'll cross that bridge when we come
to it," "She devoured the book," and "jumps right off the page."

Because conventional metaphorical expressions have lost their metaphorical associations and are just the way we normally say things, they have
been called *dead metaphors*. In discussing literature we are usually more
interested in metaphors that have not completely lost their poetic quality
and Pinker (2008) offers two tests for distinguishing unconventional (i.e.
creative or poetic metaphorical expressions) from conventional metaphorical expressions, or in other words, distinguishing the living from the dead.

1. In creative metaphorical expressions the emotional coloring of the
   source blends into the target. So, in the conventional metaphorical

expression "The boxer punched his opponent's lights out," we don't have the sense that a light is being physically extinguished, but in "Out, out, brief candle," where Hamlet compares life to a candle's flame, we do get the sense that life is as easy to extinguish as a candle. This claim is simply to say that if we get no sense of the figurative associations, a metaphorical expression is conventional.

2. Creative metaphorical expressions induce a sense of incongruity in the comparison, and we can test for this by seeing if it is possible to explicitly deny this incongruity. For example, to test whether "Juliet is the sun" is creative or conventional, we can say, "Of course, people aren't heavenly bodies, but if they were you could say that Juliet is the sun." Or to take another example, it makes sense to say, "Of course, people aren't articles of clothing, but if they were you could say that Marsha cast him off like an old glove." Both of these sentences are understandable. However, this test fails for the conventional expression "She's gone," which is based on the conceptual metaphor DEATH IS A DEPARTURE. It doesn't make sense to say, "Of course, death isn't really a departure, but if it was you could say she's gone." This sentence is a non-sequitur because "gone" is just how we say "died," and no incongruity is involved.

Good writing often contains metaphorical expressions from all parts of the continuum between creative and conventional, as in these lines from Flannery O'Connor's "A Good Man Is Hard To Find."

> The grandmother offered to hold the baby and the children's mother passed him over the front seat to her.... She *rolled* her eyes and *screwed up* her mouth.... Occasionally, he *gave* her a ... smile.

The first sentence in this passage is literal, with no metaphorical expressions (although we might argue about *passed*). The second and third sentences, however, contain expressions that fall along different points of the conventionality continuum. The phrase "gave her a smile" is metaphorical because a smile is not something that can be physically transferred from one person to another, yet the phrase is so conventional that we have no sense of an actual transfer. The phrases "rolled her eyes" and "screwed up her mouth" are less conventional, and they convey a clear metaphorical sense. Applying Pinker's test we could say, "Of course a face can't physically be twisted like a screw, but if it could, you could say she screwed up her face."

So far, we have mostly discussed metaphorical expressions that are based on widely-used conceptual metaphors, such as LIFE IS A JOURNEY. But, there are many cases where a conceptual metaphor underlies very few metaphorical expressions. One example is A MOUNTAIN IS A PERSON, which is almost exclusively used in expressions involving the *foot* of a mountain. Nevertheless, with the exception of image metaphors, all metaphorical expressions are based on some conceptual metaphor even though the conceptual metaphor may not be very productive.

We should emphasize that not all creative metaphors have the same poetic quality. The musicality, rhythm, and appropriateness of the metaphorical expression are also involved, as can be seen by trying to paraphrase a very poetic creative metaphor. For example, Dylan Thomas's line "the heron priested shore" sounds a lot better than "a shore with herons standing like priests." The second version contains a creative metaphor, but it lacks the poetic quality of the original.

3.2.4 Conceptual Metaphors

Let us now consider conceptual metaphors in more detail. As we have discussed, conceptual metaphors involve a mapping of semantic features from a source concept onto a target concept, a process that can be characterized by the statement "A is B." In other words, concept A is thought of in terms of concept B, as when an argument is thought of as a war, or life is thought of as a hound. Conceptual metaphors usually map features from a more specific and better-understood concept onto a more abstract concept, allowing us to think of intangible areas of experience in terms of more concrete, better-understood areas. Some examples of specific to abstract mappings that we have already encountered include:

THEORIES ARE BUILDINGS
(abstract)   (specific)

SOCIAL ORGANIZATIONS ARE PLANTS
(abstract)   (specific)

DIFFICULT-TO-HANDLE THINGS ARE DOGS
(abstract)   (specific)

But, conceptual metaphors do more than just allow us to talk about abstract ideas in concrete terms; they can also form the basis of how we understand the abstract ideas. For example, we have seen that writers frequently employ the LIFE IS A JOURNEY conceptual metaphor when discussing careers because we unconsciously think about careers as traveling along a path towards a goal.

Another example of how conceptual metaphors structure our understanding can be seen in a passage from the novel *That Hideous Strength*, where C. S. Lewis draws upon the conceptual metaphor ARGUMENT IS WAR to describe the speech of two professors who are engaged in some spectacular word play. (Both of the professors are high, but not on anything earthly. Rather, they are under the influence of the god Mercury, patron of orators and poets.)

> Mother Dimble always remembered Denniston and her husband as they had stood, one on each side of the fireplace, in a gay intellectual *duel*, each capping the other, each rising above the other, up and up, like birds or aeroplanes *in combat*. . . . For never in her life had she heard such talk – such eloquence, such melody. . ., such *skyrockets* of metaphor and allusion.

Although the professors' debate is playful, Lewis describes it in terms of a duel and combat. This is because the conceptual metaphor ARGUMENT IS WAR is so deeply ingrained in our culture that it is simply how we think about argument. Without this understanding, the description of the professors' speech in terms of "birds or aeroplanes in combat" would not make sense to us.

A third example can be found in these lyrics from "September Song."

> Oh, it's a long, long while
> From May to December,
> But the days grow short
> When you reach September.
> > Maxwell Anderson

Literally this is true: a day in September is shorter than a day in May. Yet, few listeners would think that the song is about the diurnal cycle because of our knowledge of the conceptual metaphor A LIFETIME IS A YEAR, so we understand that "September Song" is really about a lifetime that is approaching its end. This same metaphorical understanding of life was often used by Shakespeare, as in these lines from Sonnet 73:

> That time of year thou mayst in me behold
> When yellow leaves, or none, or few do hang
> Upon those boughs which shake against the cold,

In some cases our metaphorical understanding of a concept is so complete that it is difficult even to talk about the concept in literal terms, and we are forced to use conventional metaphorical expressions. One example is the concept of time, which we often talk about in terms of space by means of the conceptual metaphor TIME IS SPACE. For example, the phrase "I'll return before eight o'clock" is metaphorical because it conceptualizes both the event of returning and the time of eight o'clock as objects placed along a path, with *returning* physically placed in front of *eight o'clock*. The literal equivalent of the sentence is "I'll return earlier than eight o'clock." Let us try to translate some other conventional metaphorical expressions used to talk about time into literal language. The first two aren't too hard.

conventional metaphorical expression	literal equivalent
They'll pick you up *after* 5:00.	They'll pick you up later than 5:00.
We'll start at the *top* of the hour.	We'll start at the beginning of the hour.

But, these expressions are harder to state literally:

I slept until *mid*-morning.	I slept until approximately ten o' clock. (?)
I'll see you this *after*noon.	I'll see you during the time period from noon to approximately six o'clock. (?)

3.2.5 Ontological Metaphors and Personification

As we have seen, conceptual metaphors help us better understand abstract concepts by thinking of them as concrete entities. Human beings are good at dealing with *things* that we can see, handle, and control, as suggested by the fact that we can only form mental pictures of concepts up to a middle level of abstraction. **Ontological metaphors** are a kind of conceptual metaphor that allows us to view abstract notions, like experiences, emotions, and events as objects or things (Ontology is the study of how we understand reality). Take, for example, the common experience of learning in a formal setting. We can think of this experience as a thing via the ontological metaphor LEARNING IS A THING, which allows us to say that someone *has* (i.e. *possesses*) an education or to ask *how much* education someone has, as we might ask how much money they have. A good place to look for ontological metaphors is on the op-ed page of the *New York Times*, and here are some examples from the September 8, 2013 edition.

> The cost of **a** university **education** has risen faster than inflation for decades.
> **Education** deserves particular attention because **its** effects are so long-lasting ...
> How we pay for **education** shows in the end how much we value **it**.

Here the experience of learning is construed as a *thing* designated by the noun "education," with the associated grammatical reflexes, including the article *a* and pronominalization with *it*. Another article from the same edition of the *Times* discusses the experience of suffering, which can be better understood via the metaphor SUFFERING IS A THING. Metaphorical expressions in the article include:

> To survive is to make sense of **the suffering** ...
> **Suffering** was **a fact** of life ...
> **Suffering brings** clarity, illumination.

67

Notice that in the last metaphorical expression suffering is construed as a person who can bring things.

As the last example shows, a particularly effective way for us to understand abstract concepts is to view them not just as physical entities, but as people, with motivations, abilities, strengths, and weaknesses, and this kind of ontological metaphor is called **personification**. Another example of personification from the article is the sentence: "Suffering breaks him open and moves him to change his ways," which implies that the experience of suffering not only can act but has particular motives for acting as it does. Here are some other examples of metaphorical expressions that are instances of personification:

> *His theory explained* to me the behavior of chickens raised in factories.
> *Life has cheated* me.
> *His religion tells him* that he cannot drink fine French wines.
> *Inflation has attacked* our economy.
> *This fact argues* against the standard theories.
>
> (from Lakoff & Johnson, 1980:33)

Personification is not, of course, limited to abstract concepts like education and suffering; it also helps us better understand concepts that are more concrete, like snow. Dickinson personifies snow in these metaphorical expressions from "It Sifts From Leaden Sieves":

> **It reaches** to the fence,
> **It wraps** it rail by rail
> Till **it is lost** in fleeces;
> **It deals** celestial veil

In sum, personification allows us to understand both abstract and concrete concepts in terms of human motivations, characteristics, and activities.

3.2.6 Schemas, Cognitive Models, and Scripts

In Section 3.1 we took a traditional approach to analyzing metaphorical expressions, an approach that emphasized their creativity and originality. This originality results in part from the fact that these expressions are based on novel conceptual metaphors. For example, Emily Dickinson's line "It [snow] ruffles wrists of posts" is based on the conceptual metaphor FENCE POSTS ARE ARMS, which if not original is certainly unusual. But, in this section of the chapter we have seen that cognitive linguistics blurs the line between poetic and everyday language because both kinds of language contain metaphorical expressions based on the same conceptual metaphors. For example, the conventional expression "The mortgage company has been hounding me" and the creative metaphorical expression "Life the hound/ Equivocal/ Comes at a bound" are both based on the conceptual metaphor DIFFICULT-TO-HANDLE THINGS ARE DOGS. Similarly, "He's passed away," and "Because I could not stop for Death/He kindly stopped for me" are both based on the conceptual metaphor DEATH IS A DEPARTURE. As Lakoff (1993) says: "poetic [i.e. creative] metaphor is, for the most part, an extension of our everyday, conventional system of metaphorical thought" (p. 205). However, writers can work with common conceptual metaphors in several ways to fashion more creative metaphorical expressions, thus recasting familiar associations in an unfamiliar light and heightening our awareness and understanding of them. We will examine two of these techniques shortly, but first we must discuss the nature of mental concepts in more detail.

From the 1920s through the 1960s the dominant school of psychology in the United States was behaviorism. Behaviorists studied the, well, behavior of animals and human beings, attempting to understand the relationship between what an organism does and the environment in which the organism is placed. There were countless studies of how rats can learn to run mazes and even some studies of how human beings can learn number sequences aided by electric shocks when they got them wrong. Behaviorism attempted to achieve scientific rigor by studying only observable events rather than speculating on what might be going on in the brain while learning activities took place. In fact, some radical behaviorists denied that complex mental activity took place at all, but claimed that behavior was an automatic reaction to stimuli in the environment, like a knee jerk.

Behaviorism has been replaced by the school of cognitive psychology, which attempts to study the internal workings of the mind by observing how it processes data. In fact, the working hypothesis in cognitive psychology is that the mind is a data processer, with the brain corresponding to a computer's hardware (the term "wetware" has been used), and the mind corresponding to the software. So, language use, for example, can be studied by looking at the input to which a speaker's brain is exposed (the surrounding language) and the output that the speaker produces, and figuring out what software, in the form of mental grammar rules, the speaker must be using and how these rules were abstracted from the input.

For example, in Chapter 2 we encountered the phonological rule that in Southern speech the phoneme /e/ has the allophonic variants [e] and [i], which can be written as:

/e/ → [i] before nasal sounds
    [e] before non-nasal sounds

Because speakers of Southern American varieties always (unconsciously) follow this pattern, the information contained in the rule must somehow be represented in their minds, and there has been a great deal of discussion about how to think about such mental representations. What is clear is that there *are* mental representations, not only of how to speak, but also of how to deal with the world around us. Such representations are called schemas, and psychologists have suggested many different types, including cognitive models and scripts, which we will now discuss.

A cognitive model is a network of information that shows how different concepts are related to each other. Consider, for example, the concept of a bird. While birds differ in many ways, they all share some features such as "has feathers," and "lays eggs," and typically they are small in size, can sing or call, and can fly.[2] But, many people know a lot more about birds than the basic information needed for understanding what a bird is. They know, for example, that birds are hunted by cats and that they are believed to be descended from dinosaurs. Such background knowledge is contained in a cognitive model that shows how individual concepts like *bird*, *cat*, and *dinosaur* are related. Sometimes it is impossible to understand a concept independently of the cognitive model in which it is embedded. For example, the concept *weekend* can only by understood in the context of a cognitive model of a work week, which contains the information that a week has seven days, that people normally work only on five of them, and that Saturday and Sunday are considered the end of the week even though calendars list Sunday as the first day of the week. Before 1922, when Henry Ford reduced the work week in his factory from six days to five, this cognitive model did not exist.

Another example of a cognitive model that we need to access in order to understand a particular concept involves the word *bachelor*. At first, it seems easy to decide whether or not a person is a bachelor. This concept has three main features: male, above a certain age, and unmarried. But, there are examples of unmarried men whom we would not call bachelors, for example Roman Catholic priests. This is because we understand the concept *bachelor* in the context of a cognitive model that contains concepts like *marriageable age*, *dating*, and *hanging out*, and that assumes a monogamous society. Priests are not expected to marry, so this case does not fit into the cognitive model in which *bachelor* is understood. Similarly, in a society with arranged marriages and little contact between men and women prior to marriage, one would not describe an unmarried man as a bachelor because the appropriate cognitive model does not apply to that society. As this example shows, many cognitive models are particular to certain cultures, and these are sometimes called *cultural models*. Cognitive models, then, show how certain concepts are related to each other, and they form the context in which these concepts are understood.

A **script** is a particular kind of cognitive model, and a famous example is the script for what to do in an American restaurant. The restaurant script, as the term metaphorically suggests, is like a little play with roles, props, and a setting. The roles consist of individual concepts including *waiter, customer, cook,* and *cashier,* and notice that without the script of what happens in a restaurant, the concept of *waiter* cannot be understood. The props include the concepts *table, menu, food, bill,* and *money* or *credit card*. The restaurant script says that first the customer is seated at a table; then the waiter brings the menu; then the customer chooses the food and signals the waiter, perhaps by making eye contact; then the customer gives the order to the waiter; then the waiter brings the food, etc. Note that this cognitive model, like the one involving *bachelor,* is culture-specific. In a working-class restaurant in Barcelona there is a different restaurant script, where you signal the waiter by whistling loudly. The restaurant script in both cultures does not specify an inflexible routine. It states, for example, that if the menu is already on the table, the waiter doesn't bring it.

Because scripts were developed by computer scientists to help computers understand language, they are often represented by means of a flow chart, like the one in Figure 3.1. You follow a flow chart by starting at the top and choosing possible branches that take you to the bottom. The various routes from top to bottom represent the various possibilities of what can happen in the situation represented by the flow chart. Figure 3.1 is a script for what to do when facing a large, unknown dog, such as a hound. In discussing the poem "Life The Hound Equivocal" we listed some of the properties of such an encounter that the poem maps onto the concept *life*. These were:

The hound comes at a bound.
The hound can rend a person by biting.
The hound can befriend a person by licking.
We cannot tell the hound's intent till he has sprung.
We cannot anticipate whether the hound will spring.

These properties are part of our cognitive model of how to deal with a strange dog that is coming toward us. Should we put out our hand? Say "nice doggie?" Run? In order to decide, we consult what might be called the Greeting A Strange Dog script. For simplicity the script in Figure 3.1 contains only two roles, the human being and the dog. A more accurate script might also include other people and even other dogs. The script begins at the top of the chart when the dog comes toward you. The dog may or may not bark. You can try to avoid the dog by turning away or, as in the poem, you can turn toward the dog and extend your hand hoping for the best. If you turn away, the dog may either stop or may spring at you, and springing will result in some pawing. If you make the other choice and

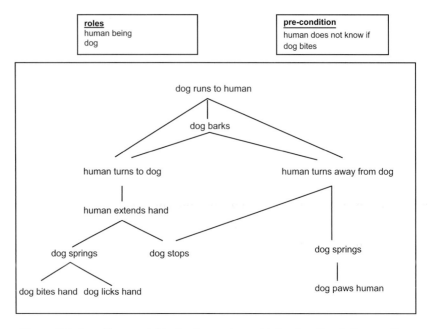

Figure 3.1 Cognitive model in the form of a script for Greeting A Strange Dog

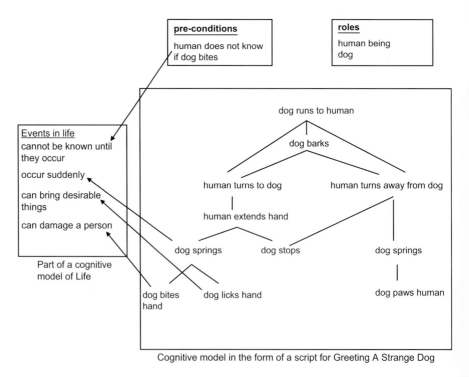

Cognitive model in the form of a script for Greeting A Strange Dog

Figure 3.2 How the poem "Life the Hound Equivocal" maps properties of the cognitive model Greeting A Strange Dog onto part of the cognitive model of Life

extend your hand, again the dog may either stop or spring. If the dog springs, it may lick your hand or bite it. In Section 3.2.7 we will discuss this cognitive model further, showing how Francis's poem maps its various properties onto the cognitive model of *life*.

To review, a cognitive model is a mental representation of the knowledge we use to understand some area of experience, like going to a restaurant, or dealing with an unmarried man or a strange dog. Cognitive models contain concepts and show the relationships between those concepts. In the rest of the discussion we will not always want to differentiate between concepts and cognitive models, so we will use a more general term that includes both concepts and cognitive models, namely, **conceptual domain** or just *domain*.

Let us now return to the question of how writers can fashion creative metaphorical expressions that are based on conventional conceptual metaphors.

3.2.7 Creative Reworking of Common Conceptual Metaphors

The traditional approach to analyzing metaphorical expressions emphasizes their creativity and originality, which often results from creating original conceptual metaphors, as in Shakespeare's line "Sleep that knits up the raveled sleave of care" (*Macbeth* Act 2, Scene 2). This expression is based on the novel conceptual metaphor SLEEP IS A TAILOR. The cognitive linguistics approach to metaphor, on the other hand, emphasizes that creative and conventional metaphorical expressions are similar because they are often based on the same conceptual metaphors, as already mentioned. Both approaches are valid. It is true that both creative and conventional metaphorical expressions can be based on the same conceptual metaphors. Nevertheless, writers can find ways to rework these conceptual metaphors so that we see familiar situations in a new light. Lakoff and Turner (1989) call two of these ways **extension** and **elaboration**.

3.2.7.1 Extension

Extension involves mapping an aspect of the source domain that is not commonly mapped onto the target domain, thus taking the conceptual metaphor in a new direction. An example from Hamlet's soliloquy is based on the conceptual metaphor DEATH IS SLEEP, as in the expressions "Rest In Peace," "Slumber Room" (a room in a mortuary where bodies are laid out), and "He's taking a dirt nap." According to Lakoff and Turner (1989) the conceptual metaphor DEATH IS SLEEP usually maps only the following features of the concept *sleep* onto the concept *death*: "inactivity, inability to perceive, horizontal position, and so on" (p. 67). But, the concept *sleep* also contains the features that people can toss and turn in their sleep, that they can snore, and that they can dream. In his soliloquy, Hamlet extends the metaphor DEATH IS SLEEP by mapping the feature of dreaming onto the concept of death.

> To sleep, perchance to Dream! Aye, there's the rub;
> For in that sleep of death, what dreams may come?

Because an unexpected feature is mapped from sleep to death, Hamlet's metaphorical expression is an extension of the underlying conceptual metaphor.

For a second example, consider this stanza of Robert Frost's poem "The Road Not Taken."

> Two roads diverged in a yellow wood,
> And sorry I could not travel both
> And be one traveler, long I stood
> And looked down one as far as I could
> To where it bent in the undergrowth
> And then took the other;

As already observed, this poem is based on the conceptual metaphor LIFE IS A JOURNEY. Here are some common mappings for this conceptual metaphor based on the main features of the concept *journey*.

Features of journey	Features of life	Example
start	birth	"She's off to a good start in life."
path	course in life	"He's stayed on the straight and narrow."
obstacles in road	problems	"Their relationship hit a rough patch of road."
end	death	"He met an untimely end."

But, as Kovecses (2010) notes, Frost extends this familiar conceptual metaphor by mapping a less common feature of a journey onto life, namely that a road may fork so that you have to choose one path or the other (contra Yogi Berra's metaphorical advice, "When you come to a fork in the road, take it").

Similarly, in the poem "Uphill" Christina Georgina Rossetti extends the LIFE IS A JOURNEY conceptual metaphor by mapping the minor feature that the path can go uphill, as in these lines:

> "Does the road wind up-hill all the way?"
> "Yes, to the very end."

For a third example of extension, consider the conceptual metaphor COMPLEX IDEAS ARE BUILDINGS, which underlies expressions like:

> "With the *foundation* you've got, you can *construct* a strong theory.
> "We've got the *framework* for a *solid* argument."
> "If you don't *support* your hypothesis with *solid* facts, the whole thing will *collapse*." ...

This conceptual metaphor is common in academic writing, as in the following passage, which discusses the legal theory of what is allowed in cross-examining a witness.

> The talk between attorney and witness in examination is, of course, *designed* to be heard ... by a jury. ... The *structural feature* that talk in cross-examination is *designed* [for] nonspeaking overhearers can be seen to have certain consequences for the sequential *patterns* and activities in talk (Drew, 1992:475)

Kovecses (2010:137) says that the conceptual metaphor COMPLEX IDEAS ARE BUILDINGS usually maps only the structural features of a building, such as the design, foundation, construction, and framework, and notice that in the passage above the author mentions "design," "structural feature," and "patterns." But, buildings also have features that are not usually mapped by the conceptual metaphor, such as windows, corridors, and ornamentation, and these features can also be mapped. For example, a writer might speak of a theory as "opaque," or with "winding corridors," or even having "gargoyles," and we are able understand such extensions because they are based on the conceptual metaphor in play.

Extension, then, can involve mapping an aspect from a source concept to a target concept that is not commonly mapped. But, extension can also involve mapping features that are not part of the source concept proper but only part of the background cognitive model in which the source concept is embedded. To see how this works, let us look again at the poem "Life The Hound Equivocal." As already noted, the poem is based on the script Greeting a Strange Dog, which is part of the larger cognitive model in which the concept *dog* is embedded. The poem maps features from the Greeting script onto similar aspects of the cognitive model for *life*. A rough approximation of this mapping was shown in Section 3.1, but now that we have a more explicit representation of the script Greeting A Strange Dog we can show the mapping in more detail, as in Figure 3.2.

Figure 3.2 matches the cognitive model represented in Figure 3.1 with part of the cognitive model for Life. (A complete cognitive model for Life would, of course, include much more information, but here only the information relevant to the mappings in the poem is included.) Notice that here the partial cognitive model for Life is not presented in the form of a script, but rather simply lists some things that we know about events in life.

3.2.7.2 Elaboration

Elaboration means expanding on and supplying details about an aspect of a source domain that *is* commonly mapped onto a target domain. Consider, for example, the conceptual metaphor ABSTRACT SYSTEMS ARE PLANTS, which underlies expressions like: "This research will *prepare the ground* for future development," "Neurological theories of behavior have *grown* out of control," and "Qualitative research methods are *rooted* in oral traditions." These kinds of metaphorical expressions are so common that their metaphorical quality goes unnoticed. However, the art historian Robert Hughes (1992) elaborates on features of the source concept *plant* when he writes,

> [Barcelona's] democratic roots are *old* and *run very deep*. Its medieval charter of citizen's rights … *grew* from a *nucleus* which antedated the Magna Carta by more than a hundred years (p. 5).

In supplying some unexpected details about the mapping of the concept of plants onto the concept of democratic traditions, Hughes allows us to see the underlying conceptual metaphor at work.

Another example of elaboration can be seen in these lines from Emily Dickinson's poem "Because I Could Not Stop For Death":

> Because I could not stop for Death
> He kindly stopped for me,
> The carriage held but just ourselves
> And immortality.

As already noted, Dickinson's poem is based on the conceptual metaphor DEATH IS A DEPARTURE. Our concept of a departure contains the feature of a means of departure, and Dickinson elaborates on this feature by picturing the departure in a horse-drawn carriage, accompanied by a kindly gentleman, Death himself. By elaborating on the means of departure Dickinson lets us see death (at least at this point in the poem) as an unthreatening, everyday kind of occurrence.

A similar example of elaboration is provided by Lakoff and Turner (1989: 67) who note that the Roman poet Horace (Carmen Saeculare, book 2) refers to death as the "eternal exile of the raft," thus elaborating on both the nature and the means of death's departure. The metaphor suggests that death is a place of exile to which we journey on a raft. Elaboration, then, means expanding on some aspect of a common mapping between cognitive domains.

3.3 Metonymy

Metonymy differs from metaphor in interesting ways. While a metaphorical expression maps aspects of one conceptual domain onto another, a **metonymical expression** (or *metonym*) uses one aspect of a conceptual domain to *stand for* another aspect within the *same* domain. In other words, a speaker can mention one aspect to bring to the listener's mind a closely related aspect. Here are some examples:

(4a)   *Barcelona* beat Real Madrid.
>   Barcelona the city stands for the football team located there.

(5a)   We don't want another *Vietnam*.
>   Vietnam the country stands for the Vietnam War.

(6a)   *Clinton* is running negative ads.
>   Clinton the candidate stands for the TV station workers who broadcast political ads.

(7a)   "The time you won your town the race
>   We *chaired* you through the marketplace;"
>>   A. E. Houseman, "To an Athlete Dying Young".
>   *Chair*, the object, stands for the whole action of carrying someone
>   in a chair.

Just as metaphorical expressions are based on conceptual metaphors, metonymical expressions like (4a)–(7a) are based on **conceptual metonymies**. Here are the conceptual metonymies that underlie (4a)–(7a) along with some other metonymical expressions that they motivate (like conceptual metaphors, conceptual metonymies are written in capital letters).

(4b)   THE PLACE STANDS FOR THE INSTITUTION
>   Signs of a booming economy give *Wall Street* jitters.
>   *India* plots cautious path to growth.

(5b)   THE PLACE STANDS FOR THE EVENT
>   There will never be another *Woodstock*.
>   After *Dallas* presidents do not ride in open vehicles.

(6b)   THE CONTROLLER STANDS FOR THE CONTROLLED
>   *The President* issued a clarification through his Press Secretary.
>   *Attorney General Sessions* will crack down on crime.

(7b)   THE OBJECT USED FOR AN ACTION STANDS FOR THE ACTION
>   They *cycled* through the countryside.
>   I'll *pencil* you in for next Thursday.

77

Metonymy can be better understood by contrasting it with metaphor. A metaphorical expression asks us to construe a target domain as a source domain, as in Dickinson's line "It deals celestial veil," which asks us to picture snow as a thin, finely- crafted garment. So, metaphor is an "in terms of" relation. A metonymic expression asks us to bring to mind some aspect of a conceptual domain by mentioning an associated aspect, as in the metonymic expression "Let's toss around the old pigskin," where "pigskin" asks us to think of a football. So, metonymy is a "stands for" relation.

3.3.1 Synecdoche

Synecdoche (/sənekdəkiy/) is a particular kind of metonymy that is often found in literature. There are two kinds of synecdoche. In the most common kind a specific part of some entity stands for the entity as a whole. This kind of synecdoche is based on the conceptual metonymy THE PART STANDS FOR THE WHOLE, as seen in these **metonymical expressions**:

"Tickle the ivories," where "ivories" stands for a piano.
"All hands on deck," where "hands" stands for sailors.

A literary example of this type can be found in Shakespeare's poem "Winter":

"And Dick the shepherd blows [on] his *nail.*

Here, "nail" stands for all ten of Dick's fingernails, and for both of his hands as well.

The second kind of synecdoche is based on the conceptual metonymy THE WHOLE STANDS FOR THE PART, as seen in these expressions:

"The University has enacted a hiring freeze," where "University" refers to the administrators of the university.

"Professional Football will have to deal with the issue of head injuries," where "Professional Football" refers to the owners and coaches of football teams.

A variation on this type of metonymy is when an abstract mental category stands for a more specific category included within it, as in Mary Shelley's line, "You exist, O divine Creature! exclaimed he," where *creature* stands for *woman.*" A second example comes from sports reporting, where this sentence described the University of Arizona Wildcat's football running back Kadeem Carey: "Three Arizona State defensive players got their hands on Carey, but the *Wildcat* crossed the goal line standing up," where *Wildcat* stands for just one of the many Wildcats who play for the University of Arizona.

3.3.2 Metonymy and Cognitive Models

To get a better idea of how metonymy works let us consider two more examples of synecdoche:

Have you read the new *Le Carré*? (meaning have you read the new book by Le Carré).

I'll wait for *the paperback* (meaning I'll wait for the paperback edition of the book).

These metonymic expressions depend on the conceptual metonymies AUTHOR STANDS FOR BOOK and FORM STANDS FOR BOOK, respectively. In these expressions concepts within the cognitive model of publishing stand for another closely related concept in the same cognitive model. A simplified version of the cognitive model of publishing is shown in Figure 3.3. The arrows in the figure show the relationships singled out by the two conceptual metonymies above. Each conceptual metonymy allows us to refer to the new book by Le Carré by mentioning a different but related concept within the cognitive model in which it is understood, namely the author or the form of the book. Like metaphorical expressions, metonymical expressions have a target, and in the expression "I'll wait for the paperback" the book by Le Carré is the target. However, the concept that brings the target to mind is not called the source (as in metaphorical reference) but rather the vehicle. Thus, in "I'll wait for the paperback" *paperback* is the vehicle. Similarly, in the conceptual metonymy on which the expression is based, namely FORM FOR BOOK, FORM is the vehicle and BOOK is the target.

Notice that only the concepts within the cognitive model of publishing that are closely related to the concept *book* can be used to refer to it metonymically. For example, we cannot say, "I bought the new Fish" even though the critic Stanley Fish may have reviewed the new book by Le Carré.

The cognitive model represented in Figure 3.3 is specific to the conceptual domain of publishing, but there are similar cognitive models for producing things other than books. For example, a bakery has many aspects that are analogous to a publishing house, such as the following:

publishing house   =   bakery
book   =   baked goods
genre of book   =   type of baked goods
date of publication   =   date of production

Like the cognitive model for publishing, the cognitive model for baking can be utilized for constructing metonymic expressions. Here are some examples along with the conceptual metonymies that underlie them.

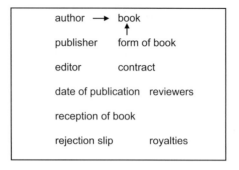

Figure 3.3 Cognitive model for publishing, showing some concepts that are contained within the model

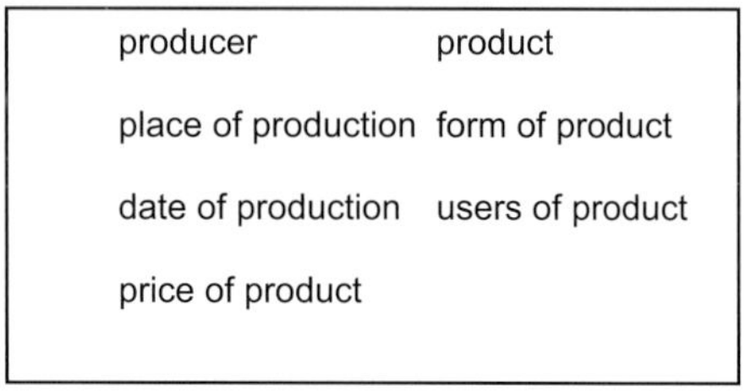

```
producer            product

place of production  form of product

date of production   users of product

price of product
```

Figure 3.4 Generalized cognitive model for PRODUCTION

"We need to buy more *sourdough*."   FORM FOR PRODUCT
"How much is the *day-old*?"   DATE OF PRODUCTION
                                        FOR PRODUCT
"*Breugers'* are the best bagels in   PRODUCER FOR
town."   PRODUCT

Clearly, there are similarities between the cognitive model for publishing and the cognitive model for commercial baking, and these can be abstracted from the two specific models to form a more general cognitive model that works for any kind of production. This more general model is shown in Figure 3.4.

Let us see how the generalized PRODUCTION cognitive model, and some conceptual metonymies based on it, would motivate metonymic expressions in the field of automobile production.

Producer for Product
I'm thinking of buying an antique *Chevy*.

Date of Production for Product
I'd like to find a *1955*.

Form of Product for Product
But, I don't want a *two-door*.

Place of Production for Producer
Detroit doesn't make them like that anymore.

3.3.3 Metonymy in Literature

As we have seen, the primary purpose of metaphor is to heighten our under-standing of a target concept, and the primary purpose of metonymy is to bring to mind a particular target concept within a conceptual domain. However, a metonymic expression can also increase our understanding of a target concept through the use of an appropriate vehicle. For example, the metonymic expres-sion "We need more *sopranos* in the choir" (where "sopranos" stands for the women who sing that part) is more informative than "We need more *voices* in the choir." Similarly, the vehicles in the following metonymic expressions involving work highlight the nature of the work in question, and, to a degree, stereotype the people involved as merely providers of that work.

> We need more *number crunchers* in the payroll department.
> Obama reduced the number of *boots on the ground* in Afghanistan.
> "For now all *hands*/ Are told to the plow."
> Robert Bridges, "November"

Robert Browning uses carefully chosen vehicles in the poem "My Last Duchess," which is a monologue spoken by the Duke of Ferrara to the representative of a nobleman whose daughter the Duke wishes to marry. The word "Duchess" in the title of the poem is a metonym where the rank stands for the person who holds the rank. The Duke could have referred to his "last lady," or "late wife," but the choice of "Duchess" implies the importance of titles to him, and this implication is confirmed later in the poem, when the Duke complains that

> She thanked men – good! but thanked
> Somehow – I know not how – as if she ranked
> My gift of a nine-hundred-years-old name
> With anybody's gift. . . .

Earlier in the poem the Duke also uses the word "hands" metonymically in the way discussed above, construing an artist as a mere workman:

> That's my last Duchess painted on the wall,
> Looking as if she were alive. I call
> That piece a wonder, now; Fra Pandolf's *hands*
> Worked busily a day, and there she stands.

John Donne's poem "Break Of Day" also uses metonymy to highlight aspects of its theme. Here is the entire poem with the metonyms that we will discuss in bold.

Break Of Day

> 'Tis true, 'tis day; what though it be?
> Oh, wilt thou therefore rise from me?

Why should we rise because 'twas **light**?
Did we lie down because 'twas night?
Love which in spite of darkness brought us hither
Should, in despite of **light**, keep us together.

Light hath no **tongue**, but is all **eye**;
If it could speak as well as spy,
This were the worst that it could say:
That, being well, I fain would stay,
And that I loved my **heart** and honor so,
That I would not from him that had them go.

Must business thee from hence remove?
Oh, that's the worst disease of love;
The **poor**, the **foul**, the **false**, love can
Admit, but not the busied man.
He which hath business and makes love, doth do
Such wrong as when a married man doth woo.

This poem is an aubade, or description of lovers parting at dawn. The voice is that of a woman who asks her lover to stay with her even though he wants to leave in order to avoid scandal and to meet his business obligations. In the first stanza the speaker indirectly requests her lover to stay by asking four rhetorical questions, the last of which (line 4) is "Did we lie down because 'twas night?" The answer, of course, is no – they lay down because of love, and the speaker asks her lover to stay for the same reason. In the second stanza, the speaker addresses the problem of a possible scandal if someone sees the lover leave, but she declares that the worst anyone could say of her is that she cares less about scandal than about love. In the last stanza the speaker addresses the question of her lover's business obligations, saying that they should not be allowed to compete with her affections, and comparing the obligations to a rival lover.

Metonymy is used throughout the poem. The first, third, and fourth lines contain the parallel structures "'tis day," "'twas light," and "'twas night." The first and third of these expressions are literal, but the second is a metonym where a feature of daytime, namely "light," stands for the whole concept. The vehicle "light" emphasizes the point that people might *see* the lover leave, which could result in a loss of honor. The first line of the second stanza addresses the problem of being seen. Here "light" metonymically refers to the sun, "tongue" refers to the ability to speak, and "eye" refers to the ability to see. In other words, the sun can only see, not gossip, but if it could gossip this is how the speaker would reply:

I loved my *heart* and honor so
That I would not from him that had them go.

"Heart," of course, is a conventional metonym for the feeling of love. Thus, the speaker says that her love is honorable, and implies that it is therefore honorable for her to be with her lover. In the final stanza, the speaker compares the man who leaves his lover to attend to business to an adulterer. In the third line of the stanza she metonymically refers to three kinds of bad lovers, using the adjectives "poor," "foul," and "false" to refer to lovers who possess those qualities. Mentioning only these vehicles, rather than the more usual full noun phrases "poor lover," "foul lover," and "false lover" foregrounds these distasteful qualities. In the fourth line the speaker uses literal language to say that the "busied man" is an even worse kind of lover, whom love cannot even admit. In sum, the poem shows how metonymy can be as effective as metaphor in poetically conveying aspects of human experience.

Notes

1 In traditional literary discussions of metaphor the source concept is called the *vehicle*; the target concept is called the *tenor*; and the mapping is called the *ground*.
2 For a discussion of the prototypical nature of concepts, see the web materials for this chapter.

Summary

A metaphorical expression allows us to understand conceptual domain A by making an analogy with conceptual domain B. The expression maps certain features from B (the source domain) onto corresponding features in A (the target domain). Most metaphorical expressions are based on ways of thinking about the world called conceptual metaphors. For example, "Marsha won the debate" is based on the conceptual metaphor ARGUMENT IS WAR. Other metaphorical expressions, like "It ruffles wrists of posts," are based on an analogy between two mental images.

A cognitive model is a network of concepts that shows how the concepts are related to each other. For example, the cognitive model for restaurant relates the concepts of waiter and customer. Metaphorical expressions can map aspects of the cognitive model in which concept B is embedded onto cognitive model A. For example, "All the world's a stage" maps aspects of the cognitive model of a play onto the cognitive model of the world. Many creative metaphorical expressions are based on novel conceptual metaphors, but most are based on the same conceptual metaphors that underlie the familiar metaphorical expressions of everyday language.

Writers can construct creative metaphorical expressions based on commonly used conceptual metaphors by means of extension and elaboration.

A metonymical expression uses one aspect of a conceptual domain to stand for another aspect of the same domain. For example, "The Dean's Office issued a denial" uses the place where the Dean works to stand for the Dean according to the conceptual metonymy A PLACE STANDS FOR THE PEOPLE IN THAT PLACE.

Exercises

1. Which of these two lines is metaphorical and which is literal? What conceptual metaphor underlies the metaphorical expression?

    a. It's a long, long while from May to November.
    b. It's a long, long way from May to November.

2. Which of the lettered clauses below are literal and which contain metaphorical expressions?

    (a) I love Pamela. (b) She is what I have been waiting for all my life. (c) I first met Pamela in the nineties (d) when she worked at the agency (e) that had just laid me off. (f) I am now a Senior Grant Writer, (g) and people tell me (h) that I am not a team player.

    Adapted from "From the Diaries of Pussy-cake" by
Gary Shteyngart

3. Consider these three quotes from an article by the late journalist Helen Thomas. Which quote contains only literal language? Identify the metaphorical expressions in the other two quotes and suggest a conceptual metaphor that underlies each one.

    a. "[Bush] has governed ... by nourishing fear in the American people ..."
    b. "No revisionist historians down the road can diminish the importance of these acts."
    c. "In waterboarding, a prisoner is strapped to a board with his face covered and water is poured over his face and nostrils."

"Bush Legacy Already Established" (downloaded from the website Seat-tlePi, June 6, 2018, https://www.seattlepi.com/local/opinion/article/Bush-legacy-already-established-1265415.php)

4. Name some metaphorical expressions that are based on these conceptual metaphors.

    a. PROGRESS IS MOTION FORWARD
    b. POLITICS IS BUSINESS
    c. ANGER IS A HOT FLUID IN A CONTAINER
    d. FEAR IS COLD
    e. ACCEPTING IS SWALLOWING

5. The following quotations all contain creative metaphors. First, identify the source domains, target domains, and mapped aspects. Then, suggest a conceptual metaphor that the metaphorical expression is based on, and list some other metaphorical expressions based on it.

    Example:
    Life is like a box of chocolates. You never know what you're going to get. *Forrest Gump*

    Source domain: box of chocolates
    Target domain: life
    Mapped aspects: life has unknowable choices, but all of them are good. This is based on the conceptual metaphor LIFE IS FOOD, which underlies expressions like, "How sweet it is," and "I want to taste all of life."

    a. And ice, mast high, came floating by/ *As green as emerald.*

    Samuel Taylor Coleridge,
    "The Rime of the Ancient Mariner"

    b. Rainbow is your sister
    She loves you.

    Leslie Marmon Silko's short story "Lullaby."

    c. Life's but ... a poor player
    That struts and frets his hour upon the stage
    And then is heard no more.

    William Shakespeare, *Macbeth*

6. In regard to the metaphorical expression below:

    a. Is the metaphor an image metaphor or a conceptual metaphor?
    b. What are the two conceptual domains?

c. Which is the source domain and which is the target domain?
d. What features are mapped?

> "The sky is barred like the sand when the tide trickles out."
>
> from "Wellfleet Sabbath" by Marge Percy

---

7. Consider these lines from Keats's "Ode To Autumn."

> Who hath not seen thee [i.e. Autumn] oft amid thy store?
> Sometimes whoever seeks abroad may find
> Thee sitting careless on a granary floor,
> Thy hair soft-lifted by the winnowing wind;

Are the lines referring to Autumn based on an image metaphor, a conceptual metaphor, or both?

---

8. Try to elaborate on some of the following conventional metaphorical expressions, as in the example.

> Conceptual metaphor: FIRE IS A HUNGRY ANIMAL.
> Conventional metaphorical expression:
>   The flames *licked at* the doorway to the house.
> Elaborated metaphor:
>   Having already *devoured* the stairs, the *hungry* flames *licked at* the doorway to the house.

a. Conceptual metaphor: IDEAS ARE FOOD
   Conventional metaphorical expression:

   The article contained a lot of half-baked ideas.

   Elaborated metaphor:
b. Conceptual metaphor: MOOD IS DARKNESS
   Conventional metaphorical expression:

   A *shadow* fell across her face.

   Elaborated metaphor:
c. Conceptual metaphor: PEOPLE ARE ANIMALS
   Conventional metaphorical expression:

   We're not political *sheep*.

   Elaborated metaphor:
d. Conceptual metaphor: PEOPLE ARE ANIMALS
   Conventional metaphorical expression:

Marsha finished writing her book with *dogged* determination.

Elaborated metaphor:

e. Conceptual metaphor: PEOPLE ARE ANIMALS
   Conventional metaphorical expression:

   The journalist *ferreted* out the information that the company would have preferred to keep secret.

   Elaborated metaphor:

---

9. Create a conventional (often unnoticed) metaphorical expression based on the following conceptual metaphors. Then write a metaphorical expression that extends the conventional metaphor, as in the example.

   Conceptual metaphor: LOVE IS A JOURNEY
   Conventional metaphorical expression: John and Marsha are *going together*.
   Extended metaphor: But, their relationship stumbled over the fact that Marsha's divorce was not final.

   a. Conceptual metaphor: A LIFETIME IS A YEAR
      Conventional metaphorical expression:
      Extended metaphor:
   b. Conceptual metaphor: SOCIAL ORGANIZATIONS ARE PLANTS
      Conventional metaphorical expression:
      Extended metaphor:
   c. Conceptual metaphor: ARGUMENT IS WAR
      Conventional metaphorical expression:
      Extended metaphor:

---

10. In this chapter, we adopted the convention of italicizing the words in a metaphorical expression that depended on a particular conceptual metaphor, as in the following sentence, which is based on the conceptual metaphor THEORIES ARE BUILDINGS:

    With the *foundation* you've *laid*, you can *construct* a good theory.

    Underline the words in the following sentences that depend on the conceptual metaphor COMPLEX SYSTEMS ARE PLANTS. The first such word in each sentence is italicized.

    a. The organization was *rooted* in the old church, and the roots ran very deep, drawing sustenance from over 2000 years of religious tradition.

b. They had to *prune* the workforce, not only trimming positions in the sales force but also lopping off entire departments at the Dallas headquarters.

c. W.'s businesses *blossomed*, and perhaps the brightest and most colorful flower to spring from the Texas soil was the professional football team.

d. Street gangs there are now *flourishing*, spreading their branches and tendrils even into elementary schools.

e. After the hostile takeover, the new owners *descended* on the company like locusts, devouring every asset and leaving only a hollowed-out shell.

---

11.   Analyze the following metaphorical mappings by asking and answering three traditional questions about metaphor.

(1) What are the two conceptual domains of the conceptual metaphor?
(2) Which is the source domain and which is the target domain?
(3) Which features are mapped?

a.   "Are you a *man* or a *mouse*?"
"Throw me a piece of cheese and you'll find out." Groucho Marx

b.   George Washington was the *father* of his country.

c.   Jane has *invested* a lot of time in the Reading Seeds Project.

d.   Sunlight falls
Through cloud *curtains* ...

from "Earth and Rain, Clouds and Sun"
by Simon Ortiz

e.   Perhaps in this neglected spot is laid
Some heart once pregnant with celestial fire;
Hands that the rod of empire might have swayed,
Or *waked* to ecstacy the living lyre.

Thomas Gray, "Elegy Written in a Country
Churchyard"

---

12.   What is the central conceptual metaphor in the following poem? Which features are mapped by metaphorical expressions from the source to the target domain? Are there any metaphorical expressions in the poem that do not depend on the main conceptual metaphor?

The Wayfarer
The wayfarer
Perceiving the pathway to truth
Was struck with astonishment.

It was thickly grown with weeds.
"Ha," he said,
"I see that none has passed here
In a long time."
Later he saw that each weed
Was a singular knife.
"Well," he mumbled at last,
Doubtless there are other roads."
Stephen Crane

---

13.   Explain the instances of metonymy in these quotations:

a.   "The *pen* is mightier than the *sword*."

b.   "Friends, Romans, countrymen, lend me your *ears*."
William Shakespeare, Julius Caesar (Act 3, Scene 2)

c.   "Instead of preaching forty year,
My neighbor Parson Thirdly said,
I wish I'd stuck to *pipes and beer*."
Thomas Hardy, "Channel Firing"

d.   "And *malt* does more than Milton can
To justify God's ways to *man*."
A. E. Houseman, "Terence this is Stupid Stuff"

e.   *Titanic* (Movie title)

---

14.   In the poem "Winter" Shakespeare characterized winter life in a sixteenth-century country house. How does metonymy work in these lines?

When icicles hang by the wall
And Dick the shepherd blows his nail,
And Tom bears logs into the hall,
And milk comes frozen in the pail,
And blood is nipt and ways be foul,
Then nightly sings the staring owl

To-whoo!

Key Terms
source concept
target concept
metaphorical expression
creative metaphorical expression

conventional metaphorical expression
image metaphor
conceptual metaphor
ontological metaphor
personification
schema
cognitive model
script
properties
conceptual domain
extension
elaboration
metonymy
metonymical expression
conceptual metonymy
synecdoche
vehicle

Suggestions for Further Reading

Lakoff & Johnson (1980) provides a brief and readable introduction to the field of metaphor within cognitive science, while Lakoff & Turner (1989) provides a more detailed look, with special attention to metaphors in literature. Kovecses (2010) is a thorough explanation of current thinking in regard to metaphor and metonymy. It is written well, but can be rough going for someone new to the field. Lakoff (1989) is a comprehensive but now dated introduction to Lakoffian cognitive linguistics, which relates the field to philosophy, color semantics, and other subjects. If you want to get deeper into the fascinating philosophical implications of cognitive linguistics, you should check out *Philosophy in the flesh: The embodied mind and its challenge to Western thought* by George Lakoff and Mark Turner (Basic Books, 1999). The subtitle says it all. An introduction to cognitive science that goes well beyond the topic of metaphor is provided by Ungerer & Schmid (2006). The book is appropriate for advanced undergraduate and graduate students.

CHAPTER 4

Syntax

"All grammars leak"

Edward Sapir

In this Chapter ...

Syntax is the study of how words can be strung together to form grammatical sentences, and it is a core area of linguistic science as well as the main concern of traditional grammar. We will look at some of the major syntactic structures of English including phrases, clauses, and sentences. The main approach to syntax adopted here is the one introduced by Noam Chomsky (who regularly appears on lists of the most important thinkers in history) called "generative grammar." This approach is a more systematic and scientific way of describing syntactic patterns than traditional approaches to grammar. Having looked at a number of syntactic structures and how they are related to each other, we will consider how authors can vary their style by varying the syntactic structures they use. We will also consider the controversial question of whether there is a specific literary style.

4.1 Introduction

Linguists use the word *grammar* to refer to a scientific description of all parts of a language including its sound system, its vocabulary, and its ways of stringing words together into possible sentences. Linguists call this latter system **syntax**. Students of literature might want to learn about syntax for several reasons. First, in order to understand how authors can manipulate language to achieve particular effects, we have to know in what ways language can be manipulated. Speakers and writers cannot put words together any way they want. Admiral Farragut wouldn't have been quoted, or even understood, if he had said, "The torpedoes damn!" instead of "Damn the torpedoes!" Although language users must follow (unconscious) syntactic rules in order to produce proper sentences, these rules allow plenty of ways for an author to express an idea. Often, one of the possibilities is memorable while the others are forgettable. For example, Robert Frost employed an unusual word order in the first line of his poem "Mending Wall." He could have expressed his idea using the usual word order as follows, "There is something that doesn't love a wall," but instead he chose to emphasize the mysterious "something" by putting it at the first of the sentence: "Something there is that doesn't love a wall." Of course, writers can also choose to violate the rules of syntax, as E. E. Cummings does in the line "anyone lived in a little how town." But, knowing in what way rules have been violated can help us understand the effect of such lines.

The second reason for studying syntax in connection with literature is that it allows us better to understand the other linguistic systems within the language. In Chapter 5 we will see how knowledge of syntax is useful for understanding poetic rhythm and meter, and in Chapter 6 we will see how syntax relates to the study of different dialects and voices. A third reason for studying syntax is more subtle. It is that the student of literature can get an idea of how language works by looking at how sentences can be formed and rearranged into their various possibilities. Syntax is the skeleton of a language, and those who wish to understand how the living organism moves and breathes can profit from studying how its bones are put together even though the bones can sometimes seem a bit dry.

4.2 Generative Grammar

The study of syntax changed drastically in 1957 when Noam Chomsky published the book *Syntactic Structures*. Chomsky was a linguistics professor at the Massachusetts Institute of Technology, and he brought to the study of syntax some concepts from the field of mathematics. One of these concepts is associated with the term **generate**. In everyday English "generate" means to produce something; for example, a turbine generates electricity. But in mathematics, "generate" means to specify or define something. For example, the set of even integers (the integers are the whole numbers plus their negative counterparts) can be defined – generated – by this equation:

$$2 \times A = B$$

where A is any integer and B is an even integer.

Any integer that can fit into the B slot in the equation must be even. Let us test the number 6. Plugging 6 into the B slot, we get 2 x A = 6. We can now ask whether there is an integer that can fit into the A slot. Yes! The number 3 will work, producing 2 x 3 = 6. So, the equation defines 6 as even. Now let's test whether the number 7 is even. Plugging 7 into the B slot, we get 2 x A = 7. Is there an integer that can be plugged in for A? No. The number 3.5 would work, but decimal numbers (and fractions) aren't integers. Therefore, 7 is not defined as an even integer. Because there is an infinite number of integers, we can't possibly test them all, but if we had an infinite amount of time, we could use the equation to test whether every integer was even or not. In this way, the equation specifies or "generates" all of the even integers.

4.2.1 Phrase Structure Rules

Chomsky's goal was to write a set of equation-like rules that would generate all and only the grammatical sentences of English. In order to figure out what the correct rules would be, he did some traditional linguistic analysis. This procedure involves dividing sentences into their component parts according to grammatical intuitions, and then using some substitution procedures. For example, consider sentence (1).

93

(1)   The dog chased a cat.

Our intuitions tell us that the first part of the sentence is *the dog* (your high school grammar teacher called this part the *subject*), and the second part of the sentence is *chased a cat* (this was called the *predicate*). These intuitions can be supported by the procedure of asking whether there is a single word that can be substituted for each of the parts. If so, the grammar treats these two parts as individual units. Notice that the pronoun *it* can substitute for the phrase *the dog*, as in the sentence: "It chased a cat." Notice also that the proverb *did* can substitute for the phrase *chased a cat*. If someone didn't hear all of sentence (1), they might ask, "What chased a cat?" and the answer would be "The dog did." So, sentence (1) can be divided into at least two syntactic units, each of which can be given a name.

Generative grammar uses some traditional terms for naming grammatical units, and also introduces some new ones. The terms for all of the syntactic units in sentence (1) are shown in the diagram below, with the traditional terms in regular type and the new terms in bold. The abbreviations for all of the terms are shown in parentheses.

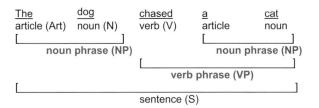

Like our intuitions, the diagram divides the sentence into two main parts, which we have called a *Noun Phrase* and a *Verb Phrase*. This fact can be represented in quasi-mathematical notation as follows: S → NP VP, which is called a **phrase structure rule** (the arrow can be read as "can be rewritten as" or "goes to"). Let us continue to examine sentence (1) to see if we can write any more phrase structure rules (from now on we will mostly use the abbreviations for syntactic units). The NP *The dog* appears to consist of two parts: the Art *the* and the N *dog*, where the Art comes before the N. So, we can write the phrase structure rule NP → Art N, which says that an NP consists of an Art followed by an N. Turning to the VP, we see that the first element is *chased*, which is a V, and that the second element is *a cat*, which is a structure we have seen before, namely an NP. So, we can write the phrase structure rule VP → V NP. Let us now review the phrase structure rules we have created so far.

(2)   S → NP VP

(3)   VP → V NP

(4)   NP → Art N

Another way to represent the information in rules (2)–(4) is to write them in the form of tree diagrams. For example, rule (2) is equivalent to the following tree (grammar trees grow upside down, with the branches spreading downward).

If we expand the tree to include graphic representations of rules (3) and (4), we get the following syntactic structure.

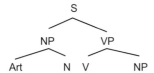

Notice that the rightmost branch of this tree contains an NP, which can be expanded by using rule (4) again. So, applying rule (4) to this lower NP, we get the phrase structure tree shown in (5).

(5)

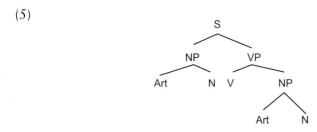

This phrase structure tree represents in graphic form the syntactic organization of the sentence *The dog chased a cat* that we arrived at using our intuitions and some grammatical substitution tests. The tree claims that the sentence has two main parts, NP and VP, each of which has its particular subparts. We have, therefore, *generated* the syntactic structure of sentence (1). Plugging the words of sentence (1) into the appropriate syntactic categories in (5) produces the final version of the tree, as shown in (6).

(6)

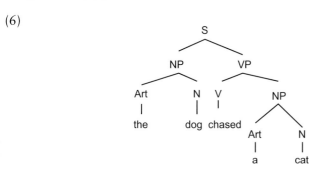

4.2.2 The Lexicon

We might now ask how the grammar knows what words can be inserted under the categories Art, N, and V. The answer is that the grammar has a dictionary, or **lexicon**, which, like Webster's, identifies the grammatical category of all the words it contains. So, the grammar knows that *a* and *the* are articles and can be inserted under any article node (changing *a* to *an* before a vowel sound is handled in the phonological component of the grammar). Of course, this means that our small grammar can generate sentences other than (1), such as "A dog chased a cat," "A dog chased the cat," and so on. Notice that all of the sentences we have generated so far are grammatical English sentences, but things get more complicated when we consider what words can be inserted under nodes other than Art. For example, the lexicon will list the word *misapprehension* as a noun, which means that it can be inserted under either or both of the N nodes in our tree, producing nonsensical sentences like * "The misapprehension chased the cat" (an asterisk indicates that a string of words is ungrammatical). A slightly more complicated grammar would generate a nonsensical sentence that Chomsky made famous: * "Colorless green ideas sleep furiously." In order to prevent this kind of semantic confusion, Chomsky introduced what he called *selectional restrictions*, which limit the kinds of nouns that verbs can take as their subjects or objects. For example, under Chomsky's proposal the lexical entry for the verb *chase* would include the information that only an animate noun can serve as the subject of this verb. This restriction would rule out * "The misapprehension chased the cat" because *misapprehension* is an abstract, not an animate, noun. Some verbs have very narrow selectional restrictions, such as the mathematical term "parameterize." You can parameterize an equation (don't ask) but that's about the only object that this verb can be used with. So, the selectional restrictions would allow only some kind of equation to serve as the direct object of the verb *parameterize*. Fortunately, we do not need to bother with selectional restrictions in our grammar because our goal is not to define which strings of words are grammatical, but rather to analyze the structure of sentences in works of literature that we already know to be grammatical. This means that our grammar will not actually generate sentences but only abstract syntactic structures (trees) like (5), which we will use to understand the structure of sentences that already exist and therefore already contain appropriate words.

4.2.3 Parts of a Sentence

Before continuing our discussion of phrase structure rules, let us take a moment to consider the similarities and differences between generative grammar and traditional grammar. Both kinds of grammar divide sentences up into grammatical categories like noun, verb, and article. In traditional grammar these are called the **parts of speech**. Both kinds of grammar also divide up sentences according to how the different parts of speech function within the sentence. For example, the first NP in "The dog chased a cat" is the *subject* of the sentence, and the second NP is the *direct object* of the sentence. Units like subject and direct object can be called the **parts of a sentence** in either kind of grammar. Generative grammar and traditional grammar use the same terms for the parts of a sentence, but they define these terms differently. Traditional grammar uses common-sense, semantic definitions. The subject is what the sentence is about, and the direct object (in many cases) is the thing that receives the action of the verb. Generative grammar, on the other hand, uses formal definitions for the parts of a sentence, which refer to sentence trees. The sentence subject is the NP that is *directly dominated by* (that is, directly under) the S. For our generative grammar, the direct object can be defined as the NP that is directly dominated by the VP. According to these definitions, in the sentence "The dog chased a cat" *the dog* is defined as the subject, and *a cat* is defined as the direct object, as you can see by inspecting tree (6).

4.2.4 Expanding the Verb Phrase

Before we can use our small generative grammar to analyze sentences in works of literature, we will need to expand it considerably. Let us begin with a closer look at the VP. Sentence (1) could be expanded to include more information in the VP, as in (7).

(7)   The dog chased a cat up a tree.

The added words *up a tree* form a prepositional phrase (PrepP), which consists of the preposition (Prep) *up* followed by an NP. This can be represented by the following phrase structure rule:

(8)   PrepP → Prep NP

We can further expand our model sentence by adding an adverb (Adv) that tells when the event occurred: *The dog chased a cat up a tree yesterday*. The rule for generating adverbs looks like this:

(9)   AdvP → Adv

Rule (9) says that an adverbial phrase consists only of an adverb (we will add more elements to the phrase later on). Of course, we will also have to change phrase structure rule (3), the rule for VPs, to allow us to add PrepPs and AdvPs to the VP. Here is the expanded rule, which replaces rule (3):

(10)   VP → V (NP) (PrepP) (AdvP)

The parentheses around (NP), (PrepP), and (AdvP) indicate that these elements are optional. As we saw in sentence (1), a VP does not have to contain a PrepP or an AdvP, and in fact does not have to contain an NP, as seen in intransitive sentences like: "The dog slept" and "The frog croaked." However, a VP does have to contain a V, and therefore there are no parentheses around the V. As we continue to build the grammar, we will find that almost all syntactic phrases contain a necessary constituent, called the *head*, and one or more optional constituents. Thus, V is the head of the VP; N is the head of the NP; Adv is the head of the AdvP; and Prep is the head of PrepP.

So far, we have used only one verb tense in our example sentences, namely the simple past tense. But, English contains other verb tenses (for a complete discussion see the online materials for this chapter), and most of them involve adding more verbal elements to the VP, as in these examples.

(11)   The dog **has chased** a cat up a tree.

(12)   The dog **will chase** a cat up a tree tomorrow.

(13)   The dog **may have been chasing** a cat yesterday.

In (11)–(13) one or more *auxiliary verbs* (Aux) occurs in front of V. When this is the case, the form of V can change depending on which Aux has been added. Thus, our examples contain the forms *chased*, *chase*, and *chasing*. For clarity, when an Aux appears in a sentence, we may want to refer to the V as the *main verb* in order to distinguish it from the Aux.

To generate sentences with Aux verbs we must, of course, change rule (10) in order to include the element Aux in the VP. The new rule looks like this:

(14)   VP → (Aux) V (NP) (PrepP) (AdvP)

Rule (14) says that a VP must contain a V and can optionally contain Aux, NP, PrepP, and AdvP. We can now generate phrase structure trees for sentences like (11)–(13). The tree for (13), for example, looks like this:

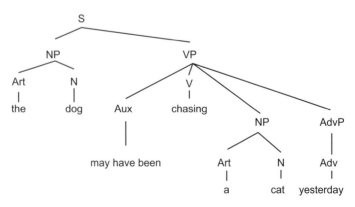

Notice that we have fudged a bit by allowing more than one verb to appear under the Aux node. A better way of analyzing sentences with more than one Aux verb is provided in the online materials.

4.2.5 Expanding the Noun Phrase

So far, we have written phrase structure rules for four of the five most important kinds of phrases in English: NP, VP, PrepP, and AdvP. The other important phrase is the adjective phrase (AdjP), which is shown in the italicized parts of the following sentence: The *brown* dog chased the *black* cat. Like the AdvP, the AdjP can consist of just an adjective. Here is a phrase structure rule for generating adjectives.

(15)   AdjP → Adj

In our example sentence the adjectives *brown* and *black* appear inside their respective NPs between the Art and N, so rule (4), our rule for NPs, must be changed as follows:

$$NP → Art(AdjP)N$$

Another component of the NP that needs to be expanded involves the Art. There are many words that pattern like articles in that they can only appear as the first word in an NP, as shown in the table below (the quantifiers don't quite fit this requirement).

Category	Examples	Sentence
articles	*a, an, the*	A cat is on the mat.
demonstrative pronouns	*this, that these, those*	Those black cats are on the mat.
possessive pronouns	*my, your, his her, our, their*	My naughty cat is on the mat.
numbers	*one, two, three*	One fat cat is on the mat.
quantifiers	*much, many*	Many cats are on the mat.

All of the italicized words in the table above are called *determiners* (Det), and all Dets except for quantifiers pattern like Arts. Therefore, fudging a little in regard to quantifiers, we can change our rule for NPs to include all determiners, as shown in rule (16).

(16) $NP → \left\{ \begin{array}{l} (Det)(AdjP)N \\ Pro \end{array} \right\}$

Rule (16) sneaks in two important facts about NPs. The first of these is that Dets, like adjectives, can be optional in NPs, as shown in these examples:

99

Cats are on the mat.
‾‾
NP

Blood is thicker than water.
‾‾‾‾
NP

The second fact about NPs that rule (16) incorporates is that they can consist of only a pronoun (Pro), such as *I*, *you*, *we*, etc. This is shown by the bracket notation, which indicates that an NP can consist of the elements on the top line within the brackets *or* the element on the bottom line within the brackets. So, the rule says that an NP must have a noun and can optionally have a determiner and an adjective phrase, **or** an NP can have just a pronoun.

We now have six phrase structure rules that will generate a lot of English phrases, but two of the phrase structure rules need to be modified a bit, and this modification illustrates an important feature about human languages that Chomsky emphasized in *Syntactic Structures*. Notice that NPs can have more than one adjective. You can say, "The **fuzzy, brown** dog chased a **playful, black** cat." But rules (15) and (16) will generate only one adjective per NP. This can be fixed by modifying rule (15) as follows:

(17)   AdjP → (AdjP) Adj

Rule (17) says that an AdjP must contain an Adj but can also contain another AdjP. It does this by using a device called *recursion*, namely allowing a rule to have the same symbol before and after the arrow. Rule (17) will generate the following phrase structure tree (to which I have plugged in a couple of adjectives).

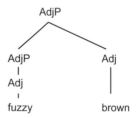

The way in which two Adj nodes are generated in the AdjP is to apply rule (17) twice. The first application expands AdjP to contain another AdjP and an Adj. The second application expands the AdjP on the left to contain just an Adj. But, of course we wouldn't have to stop there. We could repeat the process of adding AdjPs, each with its own AdjP and Adj, many times, producing long strings of adjectives like: "the fuzzy, playful, eager, young, brown." In fact, theoretically this process could go on forever. Tree structure (18) shows how a complex AdjP is embedded within an NP.

(18)

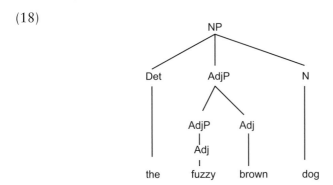

Before leaving the discussion of adjectives, let us note that an AdjP can also occur in a VP without an NP, as in sentences like: "George is hungry," which would be diagrammed as follows:

(19)

```
              S
          ╱      ╲
       NP          VP
       |         ┌─────╲
       N         V      AdjP
       |         |       |
       |         |      Adj
       |         |       |
     George     is     hungry
```

In order to generate structures like (19) we must modify phrase structure rule (14) to allow VPs to include AdjPs, and for this we will again use the bracket notation. The modified rule for VP looks like this:

(20)

$$\text{VP} \quad \rightarrow \quad \text{(Aux)} \ \text{V} \left\{ \begin{array}{l} \text{(NP) (PrepP) (AdvP)} \\ \text{AdjP} \end{array} \right\}$$

Before summing up the phrase structure rules we have written so far, we must revisit rule (9), the rule for adverbs. Like adjectives, adverbs can be repeated (in theory an infinite number of times), as in the sentence,

"That interview ended really quickly."
                      Adv Adv

So, our new adverb rule must allow for recursion. It looks like this:

AdvP → (AdvP) Adv

The following chart sums up the phrase structure rules we have developed so far.

SENTENCE	S → NP VP	A sentence consists of a noun phrase followed by a verb phrase.
NOUN PHRASE	NP → $\left\{ \begin{array}{l} \text{(Det)(AdjP)N} \\ \text{Pro} \end{array} \right\}$	A noun phrase must contain a noun, which can be preceded by a determiner, an adjective phrase, or both, **or** a noun phrase can contain only a personal pronoun.
VERB PHRASE	VP → (Aux) V $\left\{ \begin{array}{l} \text{(NP) (PrepP)(AdvP)} \\ \text{AdjP} \end{array} \right\}$	A verb phrase must contain a verb, which can be followed by a noun phrase, a prepositional phrase, and an adverbial phrase but need not, **or**, the verb can be followed by just an adjective phrase. The verb may be preceded by one or more auxiliary verbs.
PREPOSITIONAL PHRASE	PrepP → Prep NP	A prepositional phrase must contain a preposition followed by a noun phrase.
ADVERBIAL PHRASE	AdvP → (AdvP) Adv	An adverbial phrase must contain an adverb and may contain an adverbial phrase.
ADJECTIVE PHRASE	AdjP → (AdjP) Adj	An adjective phrase must contain an adjective and may contain an adjective phrase.

Exercises 1–5 cover the material presented in the last section.

4.2.6 Transformational Rules

So far, our grammar generates structures in which the grammatical categories always appear in the following order (except for sentences with AdjPs in the VP):

NP   (Aux) V   (NP) (PrepP)   (AdvP)

This order can be seen in the sentence:

Marsha	saw	that brown dog	in the yard	yesterday.
NP	V	NP	PrepP	AdvP

But in the introduction to this chapter, we noted that authors have many choices regarding the order of grammatical categories within a sentence. For example, this line from Poe's "The Raven" begins rather than ends with an AdvP,

Presently, my soul grew stronger; ...

and the following line from the same poem begins with a PrepP:

On the morrow he will leave me, ...

How shall we modify our grammar to allow for different possible word orders? One way would be to write another phrase structure rule that optionally placed an AdvP or a PrepP at the beginning of the S, such as this one:

$$S \rightarrow \quad (\left\{ \begin{matrix} AdvP \\ PrepP \end{matrix} \right\}) \quad NP \quad VP$$

But our list of phrase structure rules is already rather long. Also, whether the AdvP or PrepP comes at the beginning or the end of a sentence does not seem to make much of a difference in the meanings. "Presently, my soul grew stronger," and "My soul grew stronger presently" have the same truth value; that is, they both describe exactly the same state of affairs, and the same is true of sentences with a PrepP in first or last position. So, in order to cut down on the number of phrase structure rules and also to capture the fact that placing an AdvP or a PrepP at the beginning or the end of a sentence does not change the sentence's basic meaning, we will use a different kind of rule, which moves an AdvP or PrepP from the end of an S to the beginning. This kind of rule is called a **transformational rule** or just a *transformation*.

A transformational rule takes as input a string of grammatical categories produced by phrase structure rules and moves one or more of the categories to a different position. The transformational rule for fronting AdvPs, called the *adverb fronting* transformation, looks like this:

(21)   NP V AdvP → AdvP NP V

(The arrow in a transformational rule can be read "goes to" or "is changed as follows.") Rule (21) takes as input the string of grammatical categories on the left side of the arrow and changes it by moving the AdvP to the front of the string. This transformation will change the following sentences in the ways indicated:

My soul grew stronger presently → Presently, my soul grew stronger
Alice assessed the damage quickly → Quickly, Alice assessed the damage
My roommate has bathed recently → Recently, my roommate has bathed

It is important to note that in our grammar all transformations are optional; that is, for us transformations make only stylistic changes in already grammatical structures, as in the last three examples.[1]

Let us consider how the adverb fronting transformation can be shown graphically. The tree for the sentence, "My roommate has bathed recently" looks like this:

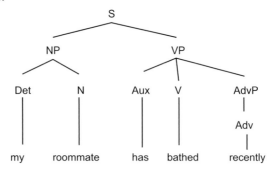

In order to see whether the adverb fronting transformation can apply to the sentence, we must check the phrase structure tree to see if all of the required input elements (that is, the elements on the left side of the arrow in rule (21)) are there. Yes, they are! We can match up the input elements required by the transformation with their counterparts on the tree as follows:

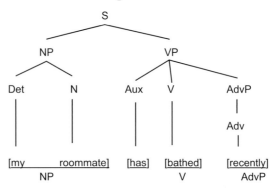

Applying the adverb fronting transformation to the categories shown at the bottom of the tree diagram above changes their order from NP V AdvP to AdvP NP V.

In other words, the AdvP has been moved to the front of the string of words. This entire operation, which is called a **derivation,** can be shown graphically like this:

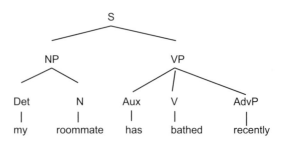

Notice that the phrase structure tree contains an element that is not mentioned in the transformational rule, namely Aux, and, of course, the tree could contain other elements not mentioned in the rule, such as a PrepP. Nevertheless, the transformation can still apply as long as the elements specified on the left side of the arrow in the transformational rule are present in the phrase structure tree to which it will be applied. There are many other transformations that change word order. For example, the NP fronting transformation changes (22) into (23).

(22)   Mac loves pizza.

(23)   Pizza, Mac loves.

This transformation is shown in (24).

(24)   NP fronting: NP_1 V NP_2 → NP_2 NP_1 V

Rule (24) says that when an NP is followed by a V and then by a second NP, the second NP can be moved to the front of the string. Let us look at this entire derivation in more detail. In the discussion of the Adv fronting transformation, we employed a shorthand way of showing the derivation, but there is a more complete way, namely, by drawing a new tree to show the changed tree structure. To illustrate, the tree for "Mac loves pizza" is shown in (25), and the effect of the NP fronting transformation is shown in the tree in (26).

(25)

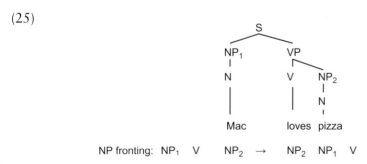

NP fronting: NP_1 V NP_2 → NP_2 NP_1 V

(26)

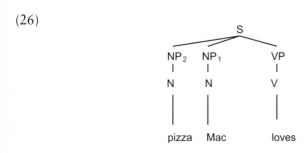

As already noted, in our grammar, transformations do not change the basic meaning of a sentence, but they can change the emphasis. Thus,

105

sentence (23) emphasizes pizza more than sentence (22). In the rest of this chapter we will encounter transformations that not only move elements around in a string of words but also delete elements and add new elements.

So far we have been looking only at sentences in the active voice. But all of the sentences we have examined can also occur in the passive voice. The passive voice is generated by applying the passive transformation to an active voice sentence. Here are some examples of active sentences and their equivalents after the passive transformation has been applied.

(27)   James Bond ate the message. → The message was eaten by James Bond.

(28)   The Governor is suing the Senate President. → The Senate President is being sued by the Governor.

(29)   Marsha has hidden the plans. → The plans have been hidden by Marsha.

What is the difference between the active and the passive versions of these sentences? The most noticeable difference is the word order. In (27) the first NP, *James Bond*, has been moved to the end of the sentence and placed in a PrepP after the word *by*. In addition, the second NP, *the message*, has been moved to the front of the sentence to serve as the subject. To state this more technically, the subject of the active sentence has become the object in a PrepP in the passive sentence, and the direct object of the active sentence has become the subject of the passive sentence. We will look at a graphic representation of this movement after discussing the other change accomplished by the passive transformation, which involves the verb.

In (27) the active sentence is in the simple past tense. Because changing a sentence from active to passive does not change its tense, the passive sentence is also in the simple past tense. But, the passive sentence in (27) has two verbal elements that the active version lacks: a form of the verb *be* (namely, *was*) and a past participle (namely, *eaten*). So, it appears that the passive transformation has added the word *be* and changed the main verb to its past participle form. Let's check out this hypothesis in the other example sentences. The active version of (28) (which is in the present progressive tense) already contains a form of *be* (namely *is*). According to our hypothesis, the passive version of the sentence should add another *be* and also change the verb *sue* to its past participle form. This is indeed the case. The passive version contains two forms of *be*, *is* and *being*, and *suing* has been changed to *sued*. How about sentence (29)? The active version of the sentence is in the present perfect tense, which already contains the past participle *hidden*. So, the passive version should add a form of *be* and change one of the other verbal elements to a past participle. This is also the case. The passive transformation first added *be* and then changed it to its past participle form *been*.

Of course, we will need to write a transformational rule that will convert active sentences to passive. As mentioned, this rule will have to do four things:

(a) move the direct object of the active sentence to subject position,
(b) move the subject of the active sentence into a prepositional phrase,
(c) add a form of the verb *be*, and
(d) mark one of the verbal elements as a past participle.

These steps can be seen in the following derivation of a sentence in the simple present tense.

Active sentence:	John loves Marsha.
Steps	Word string
(a) →	Marsha John loves
(b) →	*Marsha loves by John
(c) →	*Marsha is loves by John
(d) →	Marsha is loved by John

A formal rule for the passive transformation is provided in the online materials for this chapter, but English speakers should be able to use the guidelines above together with their intuitions to convert active sentences into passives.

Style manuals often advise writers to avoid the passive voice because the active voice sounds more direct and forceful. For example, the first of the sentences below is preferred to the second.

I will always remember my first visit to Boston.
My first visit to Boston will always be remembered by me.

Or, to take another example, compare the active and passive versions of the first sentence of James Stephan's poem "What Thomas An Buile Said in a Pub."

I saw God. Do you doubt it?
God was seen by me. Do you doubt it?

It is obvious which version is the real verse. Why, then, would anyone want to use the passive voice? One reason has to do with the notion of old versus new information. In general, old or given information is presented before new information. The sentence below would be natural if we had been talking about John; that is, if John is the old information.

John loves Marsha.

Here the predicate of the sentence provides new information about John. But, what if we had been talking about Marsha? In this case it would be natural to use a passive sentence, which presents the given information before the new:

Marsha is loved by John.

(In Chapter 9 we will see that the principle of presenting old before new information applies to pictures as well as to sentences.) Notice that the *by* phrase in a passive sentence is sometimes not important and can be left out.

> The mixture should be heated to 200 degrees F by the experimenter.
> The mixture should be heated to 200 degrees F.

The second sentence sounds better because we really don't care who should heat the mixture. The deletion of the PrepP is, of course, accomplished by a transformation.

The final transformation we will discuss is called the yes-no question transformation. Yes-no questions are questions that can be answered either yes or no. Like the passive transformation, the yes-no question transformation is somewhat complicated, so we will not provide a formal rule, but rather discuss what the rule does. When applied to sentences whose main verb is a form of *be*, the yes-no question transformation moves the form of *be* to the left of the subject NP, as in this example.

$$\underset{\text{NP}}{\underline{\text{The world}}} \quad \underset{V_{be}}{\underline{\text{is}}} \quad \underset{\text{NP}}{\underline{\text{a stage.}}} \quad \rightarrow$$

$$\underset{V_{be}}{\underline{\text{Is}}} \quad \underset{\text{NP}}{\underline{\text{the world}}} \quad \underset{\text{NP}}{\underline{\text{a stage?}}}$$

When the main verb of an input sentence is not *be*, things get more complicated. First, let us consider the case of input sentences that have an Aux verb, such as, "George is coming tomorrow." In this case, the transformation moves the Aux to the left of the subject NP, like this:

$$\underset{\text{NP}}{\underline{\text{George}}} \quad \underset{\text{Aux}}{\underline{\text{is}}} \quad \underset{V}{\underline{\text{coming}}} \quad \underset{\text{Adv}}{\underline{\text{tomorrow}}} \quad \rightarrow$$

$$\underset{\text{Aux}}{\underline{\text{Is}}} \quad \underset{\text{NP}}{\underline{\text{George}}} \quad \underset{V}{\underline{\text{coming}}} \quad \underset{\text{Adv}}{\underline{\text{tomorrow}}}$$

Notice that in both of these cases an Aux verb or a main verb *that can be used as an Aux verb* is moved to the left of the subject NP. Other examples of the transformation applied to input sentences with Aux verbs include:

> Will you take out the garbage?
> Has Marsha been forgetting her meds?
> Could someone please jumpstart my car?

The final possibility for an input sentence to the yes-no question transformation involves a sentence with no Aux verb and a main verb other than *be*, that is, sentences in the simple present or simple past tense, like these:

> Dr. Jekyll becomes a different person after the experiment.
> Dr. Jekyll became a different person after the experiment.

Because such sentences have no Aux verb or main verb *be* that can be inverted with the subject NP, we must add the Aux verb *do*, which produces these structures.

> Dr. Jekyll does become a different person after the experiment.
> Dr. Jekyll did become a different person after the experiment.

Now, the yes-no question transformation can invert the new Aux with the subject NPs as follows:

> Does Dr. Jekyll become a different person after the experiment?
> Did Dr. Jekyll become a different person after the experiment?

Notice that the tense markers on the words *considers* and consider**ed** are now attached to the Aux verbs that begin the sentences in the form of *does* and *did*. The operation of the transformation can be represented as follows:

Dr. Jekyll	became	a different person	after the experiment	→
NP	V	NP	PrepP	

Did	Dr. Jekyll	become	a different person	after the experiment
Aux	NP	V	NP	PrepP

Let us also note that the yes-no question transformation is one of the steps in changing a statement into a wh- question (a question that begins with words like *what where*, *when*, and *why*). For example, here are some statements followed by the corresponding wh- questions. The elements that have been moved or added are in bold.

> My socks **are** somewhere.
>> Where **are** my socks?
> George **should** have left for the airport sometime.
>> When **should** George have left for the airport?
> Marsha made something.
>> What **did** Marsha make?

When a sentence begins with a wh- word, the subject and a verbal form (either an Aux or main verb *be*) are inverted, just as in a yes-no question. In the next section we will see that this inversion can also occur in other kinds of sentences that begin with a constituent other than the sentence subject, such as:

> For Banquo's issue **have** I fil'd my mind,
> For them the gracious Duncan **have** I murther'd...
>> William Shakespeare, *Macbeth*
> In Xanadu **did** Kubla Khan
> A stately pleasure-dome decree...
>> Samuel Taylor Coleridge, "Kubla Khan"

> Anger, fear, aggression; the dark side of the Force **are** they.
>
> Yoda, *The Empire Strikes Back*

As these examples show, subject-verb inversion is a feature of much literary language, or at least language that looks literary or old-fashioned.

To end this section, we will sum up the transformational rules we have encountered so far.

ADVERB FRONTING	NP V AdvP → AdvP NP V	An AdvP can be moved to the front of an S.
PREPOSITIONAL PHRASE FRONTING	NP V PrepP → PrepP NP V	A PrepP can be moved to the front of an S.
NP FRONTING	NP_1 V NP_2 → $NP_2 NP_1$ V	A direct object NP can be moved to the front of an S.
PASSIVE	NP_1 V NP_2 → NP_2 Aux(*be*) V(past part.) *by* NP_1	1. move the direct object of the active sentence to subject position, 2. move the subject of the active sentence into a prepositional phrase with *by*. 3. add a form of the verb *be* in Aux position. 4. mark one of the verbal elements as a past participle.

YES-NO QUESTION

a. **When the main verb is *be*** — Move the verb *be* to the left of the NP that is the subject of the sentence.

$$NP \quad V_{be} \quad → \quad V_{be} \quad NP$$

The world is a stage. →
NP — is(Vbe) — a stage(NP)

Is(Vbe) the world(NP) a stage(NP)?

$$\underline{\text{The}\ \ \text{world}}\ \ \underline{\text{is}}\ \ \underline{\text{a}\ \text{stage.}}\ \ →$$
$$\ \ \ \ NP \ \ \ \ \ \ V_{be} \ \ \ \ \ NP$$
$$\underline{\text{Is}}\ \ \underline{\text{the}\ \ \text{world}}\ \ \underline{\text{a}\ \text{stage}}?$$
$$V_{be} \ \ \ \ \ \ NP \ \ \ \ \ \ \ NP$$

b. **When there is an Aux verb** — Move the Aux to the left of the NP that is the subject of the sentence.

$$NP \quad Aux \quad → \quad Aux \quad NP$$

$$\underline{\text{George}}\ \underline{\text{can}}\ \ \ \ \underline{\text{come}}\ \underline{\text{tomorrow}} →$$
$$NP \ \ \ \ V_{aux} \ \ \ \ \ V \ \ \ \ \ Adv$$
$$\underline{\text{Can}}\ \ \ \ \underline{\text{George}}\ \underline{\text{come}}\ \underline{\text{tomorrow}}$$
$$V_{aux} \ \ \ \ \ NP \ \ \ \ \ V \ \ \ \ \ Adv$$

c. **When there is no Aux verb** — Insert a form of the auxiliary verb *do* to the left of NP that is the subject of the subject of the sentence. This rule applies to sentences in the simple present and simple past tenses.

$$NP \quad V \ → \ V_{do}\ NP \quad V$$

$$\underline{\text{Marsha}}\ \underline{\text{watched}}\ \underline{\text{the}\ \text{game}}\ \underline{\text{today}} →$$
$$NP \ \ \ \ \ V \ \ \ \ \ \ \ NP \ \ \ \ \ \ Adv$$
$$\underline{\text{Did}}\ \underline{\text{Marsha}}\ \underline{\text{watch}}\ \underline{\text{thegame}}\ \underline{\text{today}}?$$
$$V_{do} \ \ \ \ NP \ \ \ \ \ V \ \ \ \ \ \ NP \ \ \ \ Adv$$

Exercises 6–9 cover the material presented in this section.

4.3 Canonical Word Order

We saw in the last section that transformations provide options that authors can use to add variety and nuance to their writing rather than always expressing things in the most basic way. Stylistics assumes that authors always make choices (conscious or unconscious) among the various options that a language allows, and that choosing the best syntactic option for creating a particular literary effect is at the heart of good writing. In this section, we will briefly look at how authors can exploit their syntactic options to achieve literary effects.

The fact that transformations apply after phrase structure rules suggests that the original word order is more basic than the stylistic variants created by transformations. The basic word order generated by our phrase structure rules is as follows: NP (Aux) V (NP) (PrepP) (Adv), as in "Marsha saw John at the game, yesterday." Townsend and Bever (2001) cite a great deal of evidence showing that at least part of this order, NP V NP (that is, subject, verb, direct object), is by far the most common word order in English, and they propose a psycholinguistic model of sentence comprehension in which listeners first assume that incoming sentences have this order. Because the word order generated by our phrase structure rules is common and expected, it is called **canonical word order**. Allowing for a little flexibility in regard to adjectives and conjunctions, our phrase structure rules will generate the following made-up lines, which obey canonical word order.

> I have traveled in the realms of gold much
> And I have seen many goodly states and kingdoms;
> I have been round many western islands...

Fortunately, Keats did not stick to canonical word order in his poem "On First Looking into Chapman's Homer." Instead, he wrote:

> Much have I traveled in the realms of gold,
> And many goodly states and kingdoms seen;
> Round many western islands have I been...

The canonical lines are instantly forgettable, but Keats's lines have survived through the years, and the deviation from canonical word order contributes to their striking quality. Let us take a look at some of the ways Keats has diverged from canonical English word order. In the second line the direct object *many goodly states and kingdoms* has been moved to a position in front of the verb *seen*, as allowed by the NP fronting transformation. The third line moves the PrepP *round many western islands* to the front of the S, as allowed by the prepositional phrase fronting transformation. This line (like the first line) also inverts the subject and the Aux by means of a transformation similar to the yes-no transformation. This kind of deviation from the expected word order results in foregrounding, a feature of literary language that was discussed in Chapter 1 and which we will take a closer look at in the next two sections.

Exercise 10 covers the material in this section.

4.4 **Phrases, Clauses, and Sentences**

Our phrase structure rules define S as an NP followed by a VP, and this is what traditional grammar calls a **clause**. A sentence consisting of a single clause is called a *simple sentence*. Of course, sentences can contain more than one clause, and in this section we will consider four different kinds of clauses, which can be combined to make up three different kinds of sentences. But first let us examine in more detail a structure that we have already encountered many times: the phrase. Phrases differ from clauses because (with the exception of VP) they lack a **finite verb**, which is a verb that expresses tense. For example, in (30) the second verb is finite because the -ed suffix marks the past tense. But, the first verb *blowing* is not finite because it has no tense marker. So, although (30) has two verbal forms, it is still a simple sentence with one finite verb and one present in a participial phrase.

(30)   Her scarf blowing in the wind, Marsha skateboarded down the railing.

The structure of (30) looks like this:

Her scarf blowing in the wind	Marsha skateboarded down the railing
present participial phrase	S (Independent Clause)

S (Independent Clause)

Notice that participial phrases can also be formed with past participles:

Her scarf torn to shreds	Marsha skateboarded down the railing
past participial phrase	S (Independent Clause)

S (Independent Clause)

Notice also that the long clause "Her scarf torn to shreds, Marsha skateboarded down the railing" contains the shorter clause "Marsha skateboarded down the railing" within it. But, because the longer clause still contains just one finite verb, it is a simple sentence.

4.4.1 Independent Clauses

When simple sentences are joined together with a coordinating conjunction the result is a compound sentence like (31). The coordinating conjunctions are: *and, or, but, nor, yet, so,* or *for*.

(31)   John danced   and   Marsha sang.
     IndC   IndC

Notice that each of the clauses in (31) can stand alone as a sentence by itself (yes! sentences can begin with *and*); therefore, these clauses are called **independent clauses** (IndC) (also called *main clauses*).

The constituent structure of (31) looks like this:

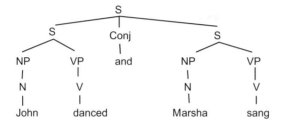

The general form of a compound sentence looks like this:

4.4.2 Dependent Clauses

Clauses that cannot stand alone as sentences are called dependent clauses, and there are three types: adverb clauses, relative (or adjective) clauses, and noun clauses. We will consider each of these in turn.

4.4.2.1 Adverb Clauses

As we saw in Section 3.4, AdvPs provide information about when, where, how, and why the action described by a verb takes place. This information can also be provided by an *Adverb clause* (AdvC), as shown in the following pair of sentences.

Paul Newman could handle a pool cue very well.
                                    AdvP.
Paul Newman could handle a pool cue like Tiger Woods handles a putter.
                                    AdvC

An adverb clause can be joined to an independent clause by means of a *subordinating conjunction* which, like an adverb, shows relationships of

113

time or reason. The subordinating conjunctions include: *before, after, while, as soon as, when, because, unless, if, although, even though,* and *though.* Like all dependent clauses, the adverb clause cannot stand alone as a sentence, as shown in (32) and (33).

(32) <u>Marsha dried the dishes</u>   <u>after John washed them.</u>
            IndC   AdvC

(33) <u>Marsha dried the dishes.</u>   <u>*After John washed them.</u>
            IndC   AdvC

Combining an AdvC (or any dependent clause) with an IndC produces a *complex sentence.* The constituent structure of the complex sentence (32) looks like this:

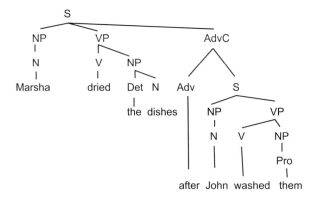

In a complex sentence containing an AdvC, there is a canonical order of clauses: the AdvC is expected to come after the IndC, just as in a simple sentence an AdvP is expected to come after the other elements. And, just as you can move an AdvP to the front of its clause, you can also move an AdvC to the front of its sentence, as shown in these examples.

When the tide was full, the ship set sail.
Because he was the only applicant, Wally got the job.

Complex sentences with fronted AdvCs are more difficult to process mentally than complex sentences that maintain canonical order (the same is true of simple sentences with fronted AdvPs), and authors can exploit this fact to emphasize an idea by slowing the reader down, as we will see in later chapters.

4.4.2.2 Relative Clauses

Like AdvPs, AdjPs have a clausal counterpart called the *relative clause* (RelC). The relationship between AdjPs and a RelCs can be seen in the following examples.

(34)   The early bird catches the worm.
       AdjP

(35)   The bird that is early catches the worm.
          RelC

(36)   I preferred the first comedian.
          AdjP

(37)   I preferred the comedian who was first.
           RelC

The phrase structure of (37) looks like this:

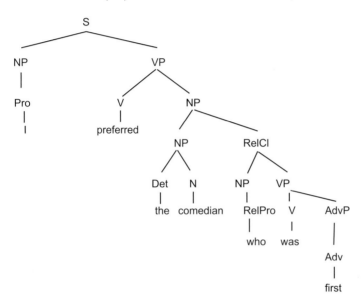

A RelC can be used to express the information contained in two IndCs more concisely, as in the following examples.

James Bond shot the agent. The agent was on the boat.
James Bond shot the agent who was on the boat.
                RelC

That lady is my wife. You saw that lady.
That lady who(m) you saw is my wife.
       RelC

Notice that when a sentence with a RelC is created from two independent clauses, as in the last two examples, a *relative pronoun* (RelPro) (the relative pronouns are *who, whom, which,* and *that*) replaces the second NP and refers to the first NP. Thus, in the first example *who* refers to *the agent* and in the second example *whom* refers to *that lady*. The NP that a relative pronoun refers to is called its *antecedent*.

A RelC can interrupt the independent clause of a sentence as seen in the second example above, but notice that in the James Bond example the RelC comes after the IndC, and research has shown that sentences with an interrupting RelC are more difficult to process mentally than sentences with a non-interrupting RelC because the reader must retain the antecedent in memory during the processing of the interrupting RelC in order to later process the remainder of the independent clause. These observations will be relevant when we discuss the complexity of texts.

All of the RelCs we have looked at so far have contained a relative pronoun, but this is not always the case. In order to understand RelCs without a relative pronoun we must take a closer look at the internal structure of RelCs. Like all clauses, RelCs must have a subject and a finite verb. The subjects of the relative clauses in the following examples are labeled, and in each case the verb immediately follows the subject.

> Structuralists liked to make binary distinctions between contrasting elements
> [which define each other by their difference].
> subject

> In linguistics, cohesion refers to the grammatical elements [that bind a text together].   subject

In both of these examples the relative pronoun is the subject of the RelC, but relative pronouns can also serve as the direct object of their clause, as in this example:

Mrs. McBee gives a pie to a woman [whom she has not met before].
                                   object

Here the subject of the RelC is *she* and the verb is *has met*. Notice that *whom* is logically the receiver of the pie, and also that *whom* is in the objective form. Therefore, *whom* is the direct object within the RelC. When a relative pronoun is the object of its clause, it can be omitted:

> Mrs. McBee gives a pie to a woman Ø she has not met before.

This kind of omission is possible even when the relative pronoun is the object of a preposition in the RelC, as in these examples:

Please return the scissors to the room [that they were borrowed from]. →
                                        object of prep
Please return the scissors to the room [Ø they were borrowed from].

When a relative pronoun is the subject of its RelC, it cannot normally be omitted, though in some vernacular dialects omission does occur. The result sounds gritty and tough, as in these examples from Ed McBain's detective novel *Candyland*.

> Bartender: There was a guy [who] came in around seven-thirty last night. . . .
> RelC
>
> Detective: There's this guy [who]'s a bartender in an after-hours joint on
> RelC
>
>   Second Avenue . . .

To summarize this section, we have seen that the dependent clause in a complex sentence can be a RelC, and that a RelC can interrupt or follow the IndC.

4.4.2.3 Noun Clauses

The third type of dependent clause is the noun clause (NC), which, as you would expect, can replace an NP, as in the following example.

That fact convinced me of the butler's guilt.
  NP

That the body was found in the pantry convinced me of the butler's guilt.
                NC

NCs can appear in any position where NPs can appear. In the example above, the NC serves as the subject of the sentence. NCs often begin with the subordinating conjunction (SubC) *that*, (which should not be confused with the relative pronoun *that*). Here are two more examples of NCs that can begin with *that*. Notice, however, that when the NC follows the IndC, *that* can be omitted.

> The critic insisted (that) there is no such thing as a literary style.
> I can't believe (that) I missed the plane.

The second sentence is diagrammed like this:

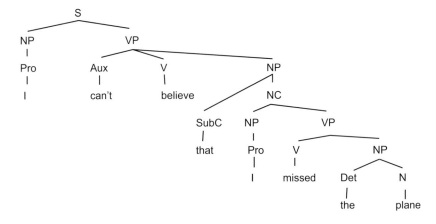

117

A second type of NC begins with a wh- question word, such as *what, where, when, why,* or the honorary wh- word *how,* as in these examples.

I don't know <u>where Sanford went</u>.
                          NC
I don't know <u>what Sanford did</u>.
                          NC
I don't know <u>how Sanford did it</u>.
                          NC

As most of the examples in this section show, an NC usually serves as the direct object of its sentence, but in the first example of an NC in this section, the NC served as the sentence subject.

The different possibilities for joining independent and dependent clauses combine to make up four types of sentences. The first type is the simple sentence, which, as we have seen, has just one independent clause. The second type is the compound sentence, which has at least two independent clauses and no dependent clauses. The third sentence type is the complex sentence, which has at least one independent clause and at least one dependent clause. The last sentence type is a combination of types two and three, that is, a sentence with at least two independent clauses and at least one dependent clause. This is called a compound-complex sentence. Now that we have studied some of the rules of English syntax, we will discuss how authors can have fun obeying them, breaking them, and playing with them.

Exercises 11–14 cover the material in the last three sections.

4.5 Ungrammaticality

Many authors have fun messing with expected syntactic patterns. For example, in the first sentence of the poem "Jabberwocky" Lewis Carroll writes,

> 'Twas brillig, and the slithy toves
> Did gyre and gimble in the wabe:
> All mimsy were the borogoves,
> And the mome raths outgrabe

As mentioned in Chapter 1, although we have never encountered some of these words, we have a good idea of what they mean, in part because of their place in the syntactic structure of the sentence. For example, *slithy* and *mome* look like adjectives because they come after the article *the* and before words that look like nouns because they end in *–s*, thus conforming to the rule NP → Art Adj N.

While Carroll plugs nonsense words into allowed syntactic patterns, E. E. Cummings plugs real words into these patterns, but they are words from the wrong syntactic category. Two examples can be found in the first line of his poem "anyone lived in a pretty how town." Here is the first stanza:

> anyone lived in a pretty how town
> (with up so floating many bells down)
> spring summer autumn winter
> he sang his didn't he danced his did.

One violation of a syntactic rule involves the NP *a pretty how town*, where the interrogative adverb *how* shows up in a syntactic slot normally reserved for adjectives, like *little* or *old-fashioned*. The result of this substitution is to make us question an expected cliché like "pretty, little town." How is the town pretty? In the rest of the poem we learn that it may not be pretty at all. The second violation of syntactic expectations in the first line is using the pronoun *anyone* where we would expect to find a noun or the pronoun "someone." The indefinite *anyone* suggests that this person is not necessarily a character in the poem but that it could be anybody – even you or me.

There is also a negative connotation here because forms with *any* most often occur in questions or negatives, like "Did you see anyone?" or "I didn't see anyone."[2] So, the use of *anyone* instead of *someone* gives the pronoun's referent a questioned or negative slant, suggesting that this person doesn't quite amount to a someone. Later, in the poem we learn that "anyone" has only one good friend, who is called "no one," a person who seems to be of even less consequence than "anyone" to the people of the town. The townspeople, on the other hand, are not referred to by indefinite pronouns but by nouns, as we would expect, namely "women and men."

The second line in the poem violates the expected syntactic pattern Det N V Adv, which would occur in the grammatical phrase:

many	bells	floating	up and down.
Det	N	V	AdvP

Instead we get this word order:

up	so	floating	many	bells	down
Adv	Adv	V	Det	N	Adv

where the verb *floating* may now be interpreted as an adjective modifying *bells*. The result of this playful word-scrambling not only foregrounds the line but iconically suggests the free ringing of bells. However, the impression we are left with is not entirely positive because the phrase ends with the word *down*, which, as discussed in Chapter 3, metaphorically suggests dysfunction and failure.

4.6 **Complexity and Markedness**

In the following passage from *The Adventures of Huckleberry Finn*, Huck, a boy of about 12, and Jim, an escaped slave, are floating down the Mississippi River on a raft at night. Huck narrates the scene.

> Sometimes we'd have that whole river all to ourselves for the longest time. Yonder was the banks and the islands, across the water; and maybe a spark – which was a candle in a cabin window and sometimes on the water you could see a spark or two – on a raft or a scow, you know; and maybe you could hear a fiddle or a song coming over from one of them crafts. It's lovely to live on a raft. We had the sky up there, all speckled with stars, and we used to lay on our backs and look up at them, and discuss about whether they was made or only just happened. . . . We used to watch the stars that fell, too, and see them streak down. Jim allowed they'd got spoiled and was hove out of the nest.

Huck loves to talk (he narrates the whole book), and his sentences are chatty and rambling. Imagine trying to diagram the sentence above beginning with "yonder." (It is a compound-complex sentence with five clauses, most with multiple prepositional phrases.) Yet there is one sentence in the passage that is different. It is a simple sentence with only seven words: "It's lovely to live on a raft." Set in the midst of Huck's rich verbiage, this sentence grabs our attention. Perhaps the reason for this foregrounding is to alert us to the important passage that comes next, where Huck and Jim gaze at the stars. In the final sentence, Jim says he believes that falling stars were cast out of heaven, and this observation reminds us that he and Huck, who is helping Jim to escape, are fugitives, cast out of society. There is also, perhaps, a reference to Milton's *Paradise Lost*, where Satan and his rebellious angels are cast out of heaven and fall into a fiery lake.

In this section we will focus on foregrounding, but instead of using this literary term we will use the similar linguistic term **marked**. A marked form is one that is deviant and unexpected. Conversely, an **unmarked** form is one that is normal and expected. The notion of markedness applies in many areas of linguistics. For example, consider the paradigm of simple present tense verbs in standard English:

	Singular	Plural
1st person	I go	we go
2nd person	you go	you go
3rd person	he/ she/ it goes	they go

Here, the form "go" is used in five of the six possible positions, so it is the unmarked form. The form "goes," however, deviates from the normal pattern, so it is marked.

In literature we can distinguish two kinds of markedness: internal and external. Internal markedness involves a contrast between expected and unexpected patterns within a particular work, as in the example from *Huckleberry Finn*. External markedness involves a contrast across texts, as when a work is compared to other works within the same genre. For example, the poem "Jabberwocky" (which is included in the exercises to Chapter 2) is marked compared to other narrative poems because it is comic and because it contains nonsense words. Another example of external markedness can be found in Text 1 below, which is taken from Cormac McCarthy's novel *All the Pretty Horses*. The book tells the story of two cowboys who ride their horses into Mexico. In Text 1, a boy who has joined them sneaks into a Mexican house – potentially endangering them all.

Text 1
The boy slid from the horse and picked his way gingerly with his bare feet across the road to the house and looked in. Then he climbed through the window.

  What the hell's he doin? asked Rawlins.
  You got me.
  They waited. He didn't come back.
  Yonder comes somebody.

Some dogs started up. John Grady mounted up and turned the horse and went back up the road and sat the horse in the dark. Rawlins followed.

This passage is written in a very simple style, describing only basic actions, with no details or background provided. In grammatical terms it uses mostly nouns, verbs, and conjunctions, without any elaborating adjectives or adverbs. Notice also that the deviation from standard punctuation contributes to the stark simplicity of the text. Normally, we would expect the first lines of the dialogue to be written and punctuated something like this:

"What the hell's he doin'?" asked Rawlins.
"You got me," said John Grady.

The presentation of dialogue in the text, however, is unexpectedly simple, and is thus externally marked.

The same novel also contains examples of internal markedness, as can be seen by comparing Text 1 to Text 2, which was also discussed in Chapter 3.

Text 2
They rode out on the high prairie where they slowed the horses to a walk and the stars swarmed around them out of the blackness. They heard somewhere in that tenantless night a bell that tolled and ceased where no bell was and they rode out on the round dais of the earth which alone was dark and no light to it and which carried their figures

and bore them up into the swarming stars so that they rode not under but among them and they rode at once jaunty and circumspect, like thieves newly loosed in that dark electric, like young thieves in a glowing orchard loosely jacketed against the cold and ten thousand worlds for the choosing.

Text 2 is also sparsely punctuated, so punctuation is not a point of contrast with Text 1; however, Text 2 is far more complex syntactically. Text 1 contains only simple and compound sentences (with the exception of the sentence containing a quote). Because compound sentences are just conjoined simple sentences, this style gives the impression of straightforward, unnuanced description. Text 2, on the other hand, consists of two compound-complex sentences, the second one containing eight clauses and multiple phrases. This syntactic structure gives the impression of elaboration and nuance.

There are other contrasts as well. In Text 2 the scene is described in detail with a rich complement of adjectives and adverbs. Notice that two of the adjectives are not simple descriptive adjectives like "red" or "tall," but are present participles used adjectivally: the "*swarming* stars," and "*glowing* orchard." The use of these verbal forms as adjectives gives the natural setting of the passage a sense of animacy and underlying motion. Another point of contrast between the two texts is that Text 2 does not describe any action except "They rode out;" instead, it focuses on the details of the setting. In addition, as discussed in Chapter 3, Text 2 contains figurative language including "the round dais of the earth," and "like young thieves."

The two passages clearly contrast, but which one should be called internally marked? Kremel (1998) points out that the elaborate style of Text 2 occurs only a few times in the novel, and is, therefore, the marked style. She conducted a quantitative analysis of representative samples of both styles looking at 12 syntactic features, five of which are shown in Table 4.1.

An easy way to measure the complexity of prose is to count the number of words per sentence. As Table 4.1 shows, there are almost twice as many words per sentence in the marked style as in the unmarked style. Counting syntactic features is a more sophisticated way to measure complexity, and Table 4.1 shows that the marked style contains far more AdjPs and AdvPs than the unmarked style. Another measure of complexity is the number of clauses per sentence, and the marked style contains about twice as many as the unmarked style. None of these comparisons alone is an accurate indicator that two styles exist within the novel, but taken together they show clear differences in the styles.

Having supported the claim that the novel contains both a simple style and a complex style, Kremel (1998) goes on to make an interpretive leap. How does the foregrounding of the elaborate style contribute to the meaning of the text? She claims that *All the Pretty Horses* can be read as a modern-day myth, describing heroes facing trials and dangers on a quest for

Table 4.1 *Syntactic features per sentence in two styles of* All the Pretty Horses

Feature	Unmarked style	Marked style
Words	23.44	42.11
AdjP	1.31	3.95
AdvP	0.38	0.68
Clauses	1.90	3.84
PrepP	3.13	5.63

adventure and justice. But where is the heroic dimension of sneaking in windows or riding horses? Kremel (1998) says that the sudden switches from the unmarked to the marked style suggest that the ordinary events in the novel can have a heroic interpretation. If we look carefully at an ordinary event like riding at night, we can see its beauty and mystery. The heroic aspect is always there if we switch our focus and choose to see it.

There are, of course, other measures of syntactic complexity, such as active versus passive voice, simple versus complex verb tenses, and the number of transformations a sentence has undergone, and we will explore some of these measures in our discussion of language varieties and voice in Chapter 6.

Exercises 15–17 cover the material in this section.

4.7 Is There a Literary Style?

We now return to the question raised in Chapter 1 of whether literary language is different from everyday language, as claimed by the Russian Formalists. Many critics have denied this claim. Simpson (2004:100), for example, points out that works of literature can contain many types of language, as in this poem by Dorothy Parker.

One Perfect Rose
A single flow'r he sent me, since we met.
    All tenderly his messenger he chose;
Deep-hearted, pure, with scented dew still wet –
    One perfect rose.
I knew the language of the floweret;
    'My fragile leaves' it said, 'his heart enclose.'
Love long has taken for his amulet
    One perfect rose.
Why is it no one ever sent me yet
    One perfect limousine, do you suppose?
Ah no, it's always just my luck to get
    One perfect rose.

The first eight lines of the poem recall the style of seventeenth-century Meta-physical poetry, but the last four lines sound more like colloquial American English, and that, of course, is the joke. Eagleton (1983) also says that language in literature is sometimes no different from ordinary speech, observing that realist literature aims to imitate ordinary language and authentic dialogue.

One way to frame this question is from the point of view of sociolinguistics, which, as we will see in Chapter 6, provides tools for analyzing different speech styles. We all know that the way you talk in a bar sounds different from the way you talk in a job interview, and sociolinguists have developed precise ways to describe these stylistic differences. One difference is that a speaker in a bar is likely to "drop their g's," using forms like *drinkin'* and *laughin'*. Another feature of informal speech, one that we have encountered, is using the relative pronoun *who* instead of *whom* as a direct object, as in "The lady who you saw is my wife." Sociolinguists emphasize, however, that the correlation of informal speech features with informal settings is far from perfect. The bar patron will almost certainly hang on to some of those final g's, just as the job interviewer will almost certainly drop a few. So, the difference between formal and informal styles is not absolute; it is a question of the frequency of particular features.

The difference between literary style and ordinary style is also a question of the frequency of particular features, and throughout the book, we have mentioned a number of features that are typical of literary language. For example, in Chapter 1 we mentioned that literary texts are often more cohesive than other kinds of texts with more repetitions of sounds and syntactic patterns. In Chapter 2 we looked at musical devices such as alliteration, assonance, and rhyme, and noted that they are often found in literary texts. In Chapter 3 we saw that although all texts contain metaphors, literary texts usually contain more creative metaphors than other kinds of texts. In this chapter we have looked at the device of foregrounding, which is also typical of literary texts. However, all of these devices are by no means absent from other kinds of texts. So, it seems that literary style and ordinary style lie along a continuum with prototypes of the two styles at either end. This relationship between two concepts is not at all unusual. The fact is that few of the categories designated by words in any field have strict boundaries and hard-and-fast definitions, but rather have fuzzy boundaries. Cups blend seamlessly into bowls, blue merges with green, and lately it's hard to tell the difference between a truck and a sports utility vehicle with a truck bed. What makes something a cup or a truck or a literary text depends on many factors. When these factors combine in an optimal way, we have a prototype of the concept: a teacup, or a '55 Chevy pickup, or a Shakespearean sonnet. So, while ordinary language can be used in works of literature, we can still identify a literary style. The interesting question is: what are the features of this style, and in this chapter we have encountered some of those features that involve syntax.

Notes

1 The one exception to this statement is the yes-no question transformation, which is the final transformation we will discuss.
2 However, one now hears, especially in Midwestern American varieties, expressions like, "Anymore you can get really good salsa around here," meaning, "Nowadays, you can get really good salsa around here."

Summary

Knowledge of syntax can be useful for understanding how authors manipulate language to achieve particular effects. Prototypical literary language contains distinctive syntactic devices, such as frequent deviations from canonical word order. Some of the major syntactic structures that we have discussed include NPs, VPs, PrepPs, AdvPs, and AdjPs. We saw how these structures can be generated by phrase structure rules to form grammatical sentences and how they can be rearranged within a sentence by transformational rules. Sentences can be classified according to the combination of independent and dependent clauses that they contain. The four kinds of sentences are: simple, compound, complex, and compound complex. Knowledge of these syntactic patterns can be used to analyze literature by considering such matters as the complexity and markedness of particular texts.

Exercises

Phrase Structure Rules

1. Label the underlined constituents in the following sentences. When more than one grammatical label can apply to a constituent, use the label that is the most specific, that is, the closest to the bottom of the tree structure. For example, in the sentence below *we* is both an NP and a Pro, but Pro is more specific so it is chosen. Notice that some of the structures go beyond the simple grammar presented in this chapter, but the constituents can be identified, nonetheless.

   Example: We can see George from the bottom of the stairs.
   Pro Aux V N   PrepP   Prep

   a. Beagle puppies are loveable.
   b. Bungee jumping is a dangerous sport.
   c. Ethiopia's situation has turned nightmarish after the long drought.
   d. The new rule will allow for infinite recursion.

125

e. Jove <u>in the clouds</u> had <u>his</u> inhuman birth.

f. <u>The ramshackle, white church on the horizon signals</u> a <u>bucolic</u> ideal.

2. Which of the following sentences is compatible with the following phrase structure rule? Notice that there are no parentheses in the rule, so all of the constituents are required.

VP → V PrepP AdvP

a. George slept.
b. George repaired the couch.
c. George slept on the couch recently.
d. George repaired the couch hastily.

3. Draw partial tree diagrams that include only the underlined segments of the following sentences, as in the examples.

EXAMPLES: The house <u>collapsed</u> in the wind.

EXAMPLES: The house <u>collapsed</u> in the wind.

<u>That passenger</u> landed the plane.

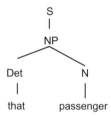

a. A <u>dangerous</u> spy lurks in that alley.
b. The ice was <u>melting</u>.
c. The tired javelina slept <u>peacefully</u>.
d. Those people <u>saw a burglar</u>.
e. <u>The jealous husband</u> has called a good lawyer.
f. Edward turned <u>from</u> the window.
g. We have slept <u>for nine hours</u>.
h. <u>She wore</u> white plastic boots with her brown coat.
i. It <u>has been</u> a pleasure.

4. Write and then draw tree diagrams of sentences that contain: (a) a PrepP; (b) an AdvP; (c) an AdjP in the VP; (d) an Aux verb and an AdjP in an NP.

5. Draw tree diagrams of the following sentences.

   a. Michael Bloomberg is a rich smartie.
   b. His speeches can mimic Ambien.
   c. Donald Trump would build a Great Wall.
   e. The Chair convened the meeting after a long delay.
   f. We will rely on your leadership.
   h. My new management style is exhausting me.
   i. Joe carries many thoughts inside his head.
   j. Both candidates had modified some strong positions.

Transformations

6. Name the transformations, if any, that have applied to the following sentences.

   a. Reluctantly, Marvin surrendered.
   b. Murder, she wrote.
   c. George was ushered into the slumber room by the attendant.
   d. Immediately, Miss Ironwood saw the error.
   e. Has Elvis entered the building?
   f. On my honor, I will do my best.
   g. What men or gods are these?
   h. We got into Milan early.
   i. On a cloud, I saw a child.
   j. Did you eat the plums?

7. Draw derivations for the following sentences. That is, draw the trees generated by phrase structure rules and then show how the relevant transformations change the word order using the shorthand method discussed in the chapter.

   Example: A Jedi he became.

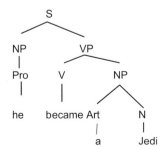

NP fronting:	NP	V	NP →
	NP	NP	V
a	Jedi	he	became

a. After breakfast we left the hotel.
b. Gingerly, Marsha led George down the stairs.
c. Are the tickets expensive?
d. The jello, you can have.
e. Unfortunately, you need a new alternator.

8. Underline any passive verb structures (that is, *be* followed by a past participle) in the following sentences (taken from the book *Slapped Together: The Dilbert Business Anthology* by Scott Adams).

Example: All the complaint forms <u>were taped</u> to the coffee room wall.

a. We were required to account for our time on time cards in SIX MINUTE INTERVALS!
b. The reason for this pickiness is that division potentates were caught messing with the books.
c. The cure for this was not to particularly punish the princes, but rather to flog the peasants by harassing them about every detail of their time.
d. Later on, they caught one of our employees in a sneak audit charging a bathroom break on his time card.
e. He was called on the carpet, and the VP wrote a memo saying heads would roll if this flagrant misbehavior continued.

9. The following two texts are attempts to explain scientific theories to the lay reader. The first text was published in 1859 and the second text was published in 2006. The finite verbs in each text appear in bold.

a. State whether each clause is in the active or passive voice.
b. Compare the two texts in regard to the use of verb tenses and passive voice. If these texts are representative, how has the style of popular science writing (*The Origin of Species* was intended for a general audience) changed over the last century and a half?

Text 1
The original species of our genus **were supposed** to resemble each other in unequal degrees, as **is** so generally the case in nature; species (A) being more nearly related to B, C, and D, than to the other species; and species (I) more to G, H, K, L, than to the others. These two species (A) and (I) **were** also **supposed** to be very common and widely diffused species, so

that they **must** originally **have had** some advantage over most of the other species of the genus. Their modified descendants, fourteen in number at the fourteen-thousandth generation, **will** probably **have inherited** some of the same advantages; they **have** also **been modified** and **improved** in a diversified manner at each stage of descent. . . .

Charles Darwin, The Origin of Species

Text 2
Regional stereotypes **abound** in the US. Most Americans **can** readily **imitate** Southerners (*y'all*), New Yorkers (*fugeddaboudit*), and Californians (yo dude) although these caricatures **are** usually as inaccurate as they **are** unflattering. But if you **ask** someone to imitate the speech of Midwesterners, you **will** probably **be greeted** with silence – even Midwesterners **think** they **speak** without an accent.

Mathew J. Gordon, "Straight Talking from the
Heartland (Midwest)"

Canonical Word Order

10. Charles Dickens is known for his complex style. His novel *Bleak House* begins with this sentence, which obeys canonical word order.

The raw afternoon	is rawest,	and	the dense fog	is densest,	and
NP	VP		NP	VP	

muddy streets	are muddiest,	near that leaden-headed old
NP	V	PrepP

obstruction, appropriate ornament for the threshold of a leaden-headed old corporation: Temple Bar.

But in the next two sentences, Dickens departs from canonical order.

And hard by Temple Bar, in Lincoln's Inn Hall, at the very heart of the fog sits the Lord High Chancellor in his High Court of Chancery. Never can there come fog too thick, never can there come mud and mire too deep, to assort with the groping and floundering condition which this High Court of Chancery, most pestilent of hoary sinners, holds this day in the sight of heaven and earth.

Recast these two sentences in canonical order. How does the emphasis of the original version differ from the recast version?

Phrases, Clauses, and Sentences

11. Identify the sentence types (i.e. simple, compound, complex, or compound-complex) in the examples below, where the clauses and some of the phrases have been labeled.

129

a. The preschoolers rode the carousel, and the nannies sipped their lattes.
   IndC   IndC

b. When I think of my grandmother now, I see her watching wrestling on TV.
   DepC   IndC

c. The cougar curled up beside a tree while the bison grazed on grass.
   IndC   DepC.

d. Although it is not yet fully funded, the College of Medicine campus
   DepC   IndC
   has now accepted 100 students, and it will increase its enrollment next year.
                            IndC

e. A soldier sat outside the door to the garden making crosses and painting on
   them the names, rank, and regiment of the men buried in the garden.
                        IndC

---

12.   Label the following sentences as simple, compound, complex, or compound-complex. Then identify the dependent clauses in the sentences, labeling them as AdvC, RelC, or NC.

      a. Edward G. Robinson is remembered for playing gangsters on the screen.

      b. Julia Child's first show was called *The French Chef*, but she was neither French nor a chef.

      c. With the World Trade Center gone, the lower Manhattan skyline seemed barren.

      d. The administration denied all the requests that the students made.

      e. *Citizen Kane* was highly acclaimed by critics, but it did not make a profit during its first release.

      f. When Lincoln's train passed through towns, thousands turned out to say good-bye.

      g. The US ski team carries a lot of prestige although it doesn't carry American Express.

      h. When the weather turns hot, Maria heads for the mountains and Enrique heads for the pool.

      i. The hurricane weakened rapidly as it moved onshore.

      j. Canyon Ranch is a health spa and not a fat-farm for the rich.

---

13.   Write examples of the following sentence types: (a) simple sentence; (b) complex sentence with a fronted dependent clause; (c) complex sentence with an interrupting RelC; (d) complex sentence with the normal clause order; (e) compound sentence; (f) compound complex sentence with an NC.

---

14.   The following poem describes the feeling of despair.

      There's a certain Slant of light

      There's a certain Slant of light,

Winter Afternoons –
That oppresses, like the Heft
Of Cathedral Tunes –

Heavenly Hurt it gives us –
We can find no scar,
But internal difference,
Where the Meanings, are –
None may teach it – Any –
'Tis the Seal Despair –
An imperial affliction
Sent us of the Air –

When it comes, the Landscape listens –
Shadows – hold their breath –
When it goes, 'tis like the Distance
On the look of Death.

Emily Dickinson

a. In what line has the NP fronting transformation been applied? Recast this line without the transformation. What is the effect of using the transformation?

b. In the last stanza, what two dependent clauses have been moved out of their usual order? Recast these sentences with their clauses in the expected order. How does this re-ordering change the impact of the poem?

Complexity and Markedness

15.   Read the following passage from Donald Bartleme's story "Edward and Pia," which is an example of "absurdist" literature. The style of the passage is externally marked because it is simpler than ordinary English prose.

Edward turned away from the window. Edward received a cable from his wife in Maine. "Many happy birthdays," the cable said. He was thirty-four. His father was in the hospital. His mother was in the hospital. Pia wore white plastic boots with her brown coat.

According to Traugott and Pratt (1980:168), "This experimental literature deliberately draws attention to or foregrounds simple language to support, even establish, a particular point of view – that the world is meaningless, disjointed, and doomed by poverty of experience."

a. Of the seven sentences in the passage, how many are simple sentences?

b. The first two sentences in the passage have canonical word order. The third sentence, however, varies from that order. Recast the third sentence so that it obeys canonical word order.

131

c. Write a single phrase structure rule that will generate sentences 5 and 6. Write a phrase structure rule that will generate sentence 7.

16. In the poem "What the Motorcycle Said" (see Chapter 2), some of the stanzas contain actions and others just express opinions. Compare stanzas 2 and 8. Which one is an action stanza and which one is an opinion stanza? Does one of these stanzas read faster than the other, suggesting speed? What syntactic devices are used to give the impression of rapid motion?

17. One of the measures of syntactic complexity in Table 4.1 is the number of clauses per sentence. Recall that in traditional grammar a clause is the same as an S in generative grammar; that is, a clause must have an NP for each VP, as shown in the example below, which has two independent clauses joined by *and* and is therefore a compound sentence.

Pia was pregnant and she had been sick every day.
NP   VP   NP   VP

But, in sentences like this it is possible to omit the second NP, thus creating a simple sentence with a compound VP, as follows:

Pia was pregnant and had been sick every day.
NP   VP   VP

This new sentence contains only one clause with conjoined VPs. To generate this kind of structure, we need a rule like this:

S → NP VP conjunction VP

Conjoined VP structures are a relatively simple construction because no elements are moved out of canonical order. Kreml (1998) compared the number of conjoined VP structures per sentence in the unmarked and marked styles of *All the Pretty Horses* and, as expected, found them more frequent in the unmarked style. Her findings could be added to Table 4.1 like this:

Feature	Unmarked style	Marked style
VP conj VP	0.72	0.42

Syntactic features per sentences in two styles of *All the Pretty Horses*

a. Which of the following sentences contain a VP conj VP structure (that is, a compound VP)?
   (1) We spotted the overturned van and Pop stopped our car.
   (2) Martin Luther King called for liberty and demanded justice.
   (3) Some Southern states honor Martin Luther King and Robert E. Lee on Martin Luther King's birthday.
   (4) We all had checklists and we checked off what we did.

(5) Many years ago, on a desperately cold evening on the tundra, Genghis Khan's Mongol hordes mounted their horses and did a ride-by "mooning" of the neighboring village.

b. How many VP conj VP structures are there in Text 1 from *All the Pretty Horses* in section 4.6? How many per sentence? Your answer may demonstrate why it is necessary to analyze longer samples of text than Text 1 and to base conclusions about simplicity and complexity on more than just one feature.

18.

In analyzing the complexity of language it can be useful to write out each clause on a separate line. This is done below for a passage from Chester Hymes' detective novel set in Harlem, *The Big, Gold Chain*. First, the passage is presented as written, and then the clauses are separated out. The italics and underlining are explained below.

From the kitchen window he could see the people in the various kitchens across the courtyard sitting down to eat. He figured this would be a good time to call on Mabel. But he was so tired and hungry his wits were blunted. He figured he ought to eat first. He had seen food in the refrigerator but had not paid it any attention.

Now he explored it again. He found three pork chops, two eggs, a saucepan half-filled with cold hominy grits, and a serving dish containing dandelion greens and okra that had been boiled with pig's feet. The pig's feet had already been eaten.

He got out the big iron skillet, poured in some half-rancid drippings from the lard can on the back of the stove and put the chops on to fry. While they were frying, he pried the hominy grits from the saucepan in one piece, and cut it into slices an inch thick.

<u>From the kitchen window</u> he could see the people in the various kitchens
      across the courtyard sitting down to eat.
He figured this would be a good time to call on Mabel.
But he was so tired and hungry
his wits were blunted.
He figured
that he ought to eat first.
He had seen food in the refrigerator but had not paid it any attention.

Now he explored it again.
He found three pork chops, two eggs, a saucepan half-filled with cold
      hominy grits, and a serving dish containing dandelion greens and okra
that had been boiled with pig's feet.
The pig's feet had already been eaten.

133

He got out the big iron skillet, poured in some half-rancid drippings from
      the lard can on the back of the stove and put the chops on to fry.
<u>While they were frying,</u>
he pried the hominy grits from the saucepan in one piece, and cut it into
      slices an inch thick.

It is now easy to see that the passage contains 14 clauses and 10 sentences, for
an average of 1.4 clauses per sentence. It is also easy to spot the passive clauses,
and these have been printed in italics. There are two clauses in the passive voice,
an average of 0.20 passive constructions per clause. It is also possible to spot the
sentence elements that violate canonical word order, and these have been
underlined. Two of the 10 sentences have re-arranged elements. In other words,
20 percent of the sentences have non-canonical word order.

A. Use these techniques to analyze the complexity of the following passage
from William Faulkner's novel *As I Lay Dying*. The voice is that of
Cash, a Southern man about 30 years old. Write out each clause on a
separate line. Then calculate the following figures: (1) the number
of clauses per sentence, (2) the percentage of passive clauses, (3) the
percentage of clauses that violate canonical word order. If the passage
contains any sentence fragments, state how many there are per sentence.

> So we went up the street, toward the square, and he said, "We better take
> Cash to the doctor first. We can leave him there and come back for him."
> That's it. It's because me and him was born close together, and it nigh ten
> years before Jewel and Dewey Dell and Vardaman begun to come along.
> I feel kin to them, all right, but I don't know. And me being the oldest,
> and thinking already the very thing that he done: I don't know.

B. Do the same kind of analysis for this passage from James Joyce's short
story "Araby," which is narrated by an unnamed Irish teenage boy.
Does Hymes's narrator or Joyce's narrator have the more complex
style? What does that suggest about the background of the two narrators? Does any other linguistic information in the passages support your
characterization of the narrators' backgrounds?

> When the short days of winter came dusk fell before we had well
> eaten our dinners. When we met in the street the hours had grown
> somber. The space of sky above us was the colour of ever-changing
> violet and towards it the lamps of the street lifted their feeble lanterns.
> The cold air stung us and we played till our bodies glowed. Our
> shouts echoed in the silent street. The career of our play brought us
> through the dark muddy lanes behind the houses where we ran the
> gauntlet of the rough tribes from the cottages, to the backdoors of the

dark dripping gardens where odours arose from the ashpits, to the dark odorous stables where a coachman smoothed and combed the horse or shook music from the buckled harness. When we returned to the street light from the kitchen windows had filled the areas. If my uncle was seen turning the corner we hid in the shadows until we had seen him safely housed.

---

19. Choose a descriptive passage from your favorite novel and analyze its complexity according to one or more of the following measures.

   a. words per sentence
   b. clauses per sentence
   c. passives per sentence
   d. percentage of clauses that deviate from canonical word order

   How does the complexity of your passage compare to the complexity of the passages from *As I Lay Dying* and "Araby"?

---

20. Steven Pinker is a professor of psychology and cognitive science at Harvard who keeps doing the impossible: he writes books on grammar that become best-sellers. Pinker has recently written a style manual (another *New York Times* best-seller!) that can help others write well. In the introduction Pinker pays proper homage to the most widely read style manual of all time: Strunk and White's *The Elements of Style*. But, Pinker notes that Strunk and White got some things wrong, and the reason is because they didn't know enough about grammar. Some of Strunk and White's bloopers are reproduced below. Comment on the error and suggest how it might be rewritten. You may use a blue pencil if you wish.

   a. Strunk and White urge their readers to avoid the passive voice, providing the following sentence as an example of the passive.

      "There were a great number of dead leaves lying on the ground."

   b. Strunk and White recommend the use of transitive verbs and give the following example of such a sentence.

      "The cock's crow came with dawn."

   c. Comment on the following advice.

      "Many a tame sentence ... can be made lively and emphatic by substituting a transitive in the active voice."

Key Terms

syntax
generate
phrase structure rule
lexicon
parts of speech
parts of a sentence
transformational rule
derivation
canonical word order
clause
finite verb
independent clause
dependent clause
marked
unmarked

Some Abbreviations

Abbreviation	Term	Definition/ example(s)
S	sentence	A string of words with a subject and a finite verb, e.g. *The cat is on the mat* and *George has seen a ghost*; or, two or more such structures joined with conjunctions.
NP	noun phrase	A phrase with a noun as head, e.g., *a beautiful* **mind**.
VP	verb phrase	A phrase with a verb as head, e.g. George **found** *a peanut*.
Aux	auxiliary verb	A verb that can accompany a main verb, e.g., *might, will, can, be, have* – "I *might* mow the lawn today."
Art	article	A type of determiner, namely the words *a, an,* and *the*
Det	determiner	A word that modifies a noun and generally must appear as the first word of an NP, e.g., *a, the, one, this, my*, e.g., "Satan and *his* rebellious angels were cast out of heaven."
Prep	preposition	A function word that usually indicates location, e.g., *on, in, to, at, within*, etc.
PrepP	prepositional phrase	A phrase with a preposition as head, e.g., **to** *the lighthouse*.

(cont.)

Abbreviation	Term	Definition/ example(s)
AdjP	adjective phrase	A phrase with an adjective as head, e.g., "They bought a *large, **purple*** house."
AdvP	adverb phrase	A phrase with an adverb as head, e.g., "He ran *really **fast**.*"
IndC	independent clause	A string of words with a subject and a finite verb that can be a sentence by itself: "While John was resting, *the telephone rang*."
DepC	dependent clause	A string of words with a subject and a finite verb that cannot be a sentence by itself: "*While John was resting*, the telephone rang."
AdvC	adverb clause	A dependent clause that functions as an adverb: "We'll have time for a snack *after we tour the ruins*."
RelC	relative clause	A dependent clause that functions as an adjective: "James Bond saw the man *who was on the boat*."
NC	noun clause	A dependent clause that functions as a noun: "I can't believe *you said that*."

Suggestions for Further Reading

The following three books provide in-depth discussions of English syntax. Greenbaum (1996) is the authoritative reference on English grammar from a traditional perspective. It is appropriate for those who already have some knowledge of grammar, such as readers of the present book. Morenberg (2009) is an introductory text that offers a unique combination of generative and traditional grammar, providing a comprehensive discussion of the field. It is especially useful for students who wish to apply syntax to the analysis of literature. The example sentences are great, and I have shamelessly borrowed some of them for this book. Good chapters on syntax can be found in Fromkin, Rodman & Hyams (2014), Fasold & Conner-Linton (2006), and Yule (2010).

Chapter 5

The Rhythms of Poetry and Speech

"A linguist deaf to the poetic function of language and a literary scholar indifferent to linguistic problems and unconversant with linguistic methods are equally flagrant anachronisms."

Roman Jakobson

In this Chapter ...

The purpose of scanning a poem is to understand how the poet uses the natural rhythm of English, and variations from it, to enhance the poem's meaning. First, we will take a look at some traditional notions of how to measure rhythm and meter in poetry, including the different kinds of poetic feet, such as iambs and dactyls, and the different line lengths, such as tetrameter and pentameter. Then, we will examine some rules for marking stress and rhythm in spoken English within the word, the sentence, and the phrase. Our knowledge of how English is naturally stressed will prove useful in scanning poetry in order to better understand its rhythmic effects and to better appreciate the art of the poet.

5.1 Prosody

The study of the rhythmic and sound effects of poetry and prose is called **prosody**. The term comes from an ancient Greek word that meant the degree of stress given to a particular syllable within a sentence, and prosody has traditionally referred mainly to the study of **rhythm** (where the stresses fall) and **meter** (how many stressed syllables there are within a line in poetry). In this section we will take a look at these two aspects of English prosody.

5.1.1 Rhythm

Rhythm is the repetition of motion or sound. In dance, many different kinds of repeated motions are possible. For example, the rhythm of the waltz is: step, step, close; step, step, close. Speech also has rhythm although it is less regular than the rhythm of the waltz. The rhythm of speech results from the fact that different syllables in a word are stressed differently. A stressed syllable is typically longer, louder, and higher in pitch than an unstressed syllable, as you can see for yourself by pronouncing the word *aware*, where the second syllable is more prominent than the first because it is stressed.

Analyzing a poem's rhythm is called *scansion* and to scan a poem is to go through it line by line marking the stressed and unstressed syllables with a view toward connecting some aspects of the poem's rhythm with its meaning. Books on scansion usually advise readers to decide which syllables are stressed and unstressed by following their intuitions. For example, Vendler (2009:660) says: "Natural intonation makes you stress some words and leave others unstressed, helping you to see how many beats are in the line. ...It is ... natural intonation that tells you where to put the stresses." Fussell (1979:18) argues that scansion is a two-step procedure. Using intuition to mark the natural stresses is the first step. The second step is to let the dominant meter of the poem (iambic pentameter, for example) override the natural stress *where appropriate*. This is excellent advice and will allow us to scan many lines of poetry without encountering problems.

However, sometimes intuitions about stress can vary. Consider, for example, Fussell's (1979:19) scanning of the prose sentence below:

> The only úseful expectátion that a réader can bríng to a póem is that it will bé in cértain wáys uníque, a thíng in itsélf.

Some of this marking is indisputable, such as assigning stress to the first syllable of the two syllable words *úseful*, *réader*, and *cértain*. But, what about *only*? It, too, is a two-syllable word with stress on the first syllable, so why isn't that marked? And what about the stress on *be*? Reading the sentence aloud without stressing *be* sounds as natural as Fussell's reading. Because intuitions can vary, it would be nice to have some guidelines about natural English stress that could serve as a supplement to our intuitions. Fortunately, linguists have developed such guidelines, but before discussing them, let us take a look at some conventions of traditional scansion.

Scanning a poem requires counting the number of stressed syllables per line. Each stressed syllable is usually grouped with one or two unstressed syllables in a unit called a **foot**. English poetry has four basic feet. The most common foot, called an *iamb*, consists of an unstressed syllable followed by a stressed syllable, as in Anne Bradstreet's line:

> If ever two were one, then surely we.

which can be scanned as follows:

> If év | er twó | were óne | than súre | ly wé. |

Notice that the feet are separated by vertical lines. The other three basic poetic feet, and two of the less common types, are shown in Table 5.1.

The last two kinds of feet, spondee and pyrrhic, do not contain both stressed and unstressed syllables, so they must be presented as single

Table 5.1 *Types of poetic feet*

Type of foot	Stress pattern	Example
iamb	˘ /	I cóme to plúck your bérries, hársh and crúde.
anapest	˘ ˘ /	'Twas the níght before Chrístmas and áll through the hóuse
trochee	/ ˘	Gód with hónor háng your héad
dactyl	/ ˘ ˘	Éve with her básket was Déep in the bélls and the gráss.
spondee	/ /	**Áll ná**tions stríving stróng to máke **Réd wár** yet rédder.
pyrrhic	˘ ˘	Wáke, nów my lóve, awáke: **for it** is tíme

˘ = unstressed syllable; / = stressed syllable

examples within a line of poetry containing other kinds of feet because it is impossible to maintain the pattern of successive stressed or unstressed syllables for very long. Spondees and pyrrhics usually represent alternatives, or **substitutions**, for one of the more basic feet in a line of poetry.

5.1.2 Meter

So far, we have used the term **meter** in a broad sense to refer to the type of foot and the length of the line, so that we could say, for example, that the predominant meter of a poem was iambic pentameter. Technically, however, the term *meter* refers only to the length of a line (some authors say the "width"), and in this section we will discuss meter only in this narrower sense.

A line's length is measured by counting the number of stressed syllables and in some cases the total number of syllables, as well. The two principal types of meter in English are *accentual-syllabic* and *accentual*. In accentual-syllabic meter, each line contains the same number of stresses and syllables, as in these lines from Tennyson's poem "The Eagle."

	no. of stresses	no. of syllables
He clásps the crág with cróoked hánds;	4	8
Clóse to the sún in lónely lánds,	4	8
Rínged with the ázure wórld, he stánds	4	8

In accentual meter, each line contains the same number of stresses, but the number of syllables can vary. This is the oldest kind of meter in English poetry, and it can be seen in this translation of *Beowulf*.

	no. stresses	no. syllables
His péople prepáred him	2	6
a fúneral pýre	2	4
húng with hélmets	2	4
shíelds and háuberks	2	5

A third and very popular metrical pattern is called **free verse**. In this pattern neither the number of stresses nor the number of syllables per line is held constant. We saw an example in Chapter 2 in the poem "What the Motorcycle Said," which contains these lines:

Pássed phó | nies in Fórds, | knócked dówn | bíll-boards, | lánd-ed |
On the ó | ther síde | of The Gáp, |and Whée, |
BÝ-passed | hís-tor-y. |

Here the first line contains seven stresses, the second line four stresses, and the third line two stresses. Notice also that the rhythm of the verse is very irregular (like a misfiring motorcycle). There are three anapests, three trochees, two spondees, two iambs, and a dactyl. Despite the lack of rules in free verse (it also doesn't have to rhyme) some free verse poems are more consistent than others. Walt Whitman's poem "Leaves of Grass," for example, is almost regular compared to "What the Motorcycle Said." Whitman's lines below differ in the number of stresses, but the basic rhythm is iambic.

> I lóaf | and in-víte | my sóul |,
> I léan | and lóaf | at my éase | ob-sérv | ing a spéar | of súm | mer grássl.

The freest free verse does away even with lines and stanzas, as in Joy Harjo's poem "Santa Fe."

> The wind blows lilacs out of the east. And it isn't lilac season. And I am walking the street in front of St. Francis Cathedral in Santa Fe. Oh, and it's a few
> years earlier and more. That's how you tell real time. It is here. It is there. . . .

Despite the free form, Harjo's lines are poetic, in part, because of the assonance of *east*, *street*, *Cathedral*, and *real*, as well as some repetition of poetic feet, such as the two anapests in:

> It is hére. | It is thére. |

As Harjo's lines show, poets writing in free verse rely mainly on devices other than meter to distinguish their work from prose. Thus, the verse is not really free; to count as verse it must stand out from ordinary language in some way. One of these ways involves the technique of *internal markedness* (which we encountered in Chapter 4), where a pattern is established and then violated at some important point, as in the first stanza of Donald Justice's poem "Men at Forty."

> Mén at | fór-ty |
> Léarn to | clóse sóft | ly
> The dóors | to róoms | they will | nót be
> Có-ming | báck tó. |

The first three lines of the stanza grow progressively longer: line one contains four syllables, line two contains five syllables, and line three contains eight syllables. But the last line violates this pattern of increasing length by returning to four syllables abruptly, like the closing of a door. The first three lines also cohere because they end in approximate rhyme. The last line again violates the pattern, ending harshly on an unrhymed and stressed preposition.

Returning to metered poetry, there are several possibilities as to how many stressed syllables a line can contain. It can contain one, two, three, four, and so on up to eight stresses. Each of these possible line lengths has a name, as provided below. Notice that the length of a line is not related to the kind of feet that the line contains, but only to the number of stresses. A five-foot line can be iambic, anapestic, trochaic, or dactylic because each of these feet contains only one stressed syllable. Here are the eight most common line lengths in English poetry.

Monometer (one stress per line)
You úsed
to lóve
me wéll.
 Ciara Shuttleworth, "Sestina"

Dimeter (two stresses per line)
Í am Sám.
Sám, I ám
 Dr. Seuss, "Green Eggs and Ham"

Trimeter (three stresses per line)
I choóse upstánding mén
That clímb the streáms untíl
The foúntain leáp, and at dáwn
Dróp their cást at the síde
Of drípping stóne; I decláre
Théy shall inhérit my príde.
 W. B. Yeats, "The Tower"

Tetrameter (four stresses per line)
The créature fróm the Bláck Lagóon
went báck intó the bóg too sóon.
Too sóon!" his dóting móther críed.
"You júst ate lúnch! Come báck insíde!"
That Bláck Lagóon is dárk and dámp.
You're góing to gét a stómach crámp!"
 Adam Rex, "The Creature from the Black Lagoon Doesn't Wait an Hour
 Before Swimming"

Pentameter (five stresses per line)
Lét me nót to the márriage of trúe mínds
Admít impédimént. Lóve is not lóve
Which álters whén it álterátion fínds
 William Shakespeare, "Sonnet 18"

Hexameter (six stresses per line)
Thís is the fórest priméval. The múrmuring pínes and the hémlocks
Béarded in móss, and in gárments gréen, indistínct in the twílight
Henry Wadsworth Longfellow, "Evangeline"

Heptameter (seven stresses per line)
As spríngs in désert fóund seem swéet, all bráckish thóugh they bé,
So mídst the wíthered wáste of lífe, those téars would flów to mé.
Lord Byron, "Youth and Age"

Octameter (eight stresses per line)
Ónce upon a mídnight dréary, whíle I póndered wéak and wéary
Óver mány a quáint and cúrious vólume óf forgótten lóre –
Edgar Allen Poe, "The Raven"

5.1.3 Analyzing Verse

The various kinds of rhythm and meter combine to define the patterns of English poetry: iambic pentameter, anapestic tetrameter, etc. The basic meter of a poem, iambic pentameter for example, can be considered a template to which the poem must generally adhere. However, good poetry often varies from its template. Some of the lines substitute one kind of foot for another, and such variation often enhances the meaning of the poem. For example, consider the first lines of Thomas Gray's "Elegy Written in a Country Churchyard."

> The cúr | few tólls | the knéll | of pár | ting dáy, |
>> The lów | ing hérd | wínd slów | ly o'er | the léa, |
> The plów | man hóme | ward plóds | his wéa | ry wáy, |
>> And léaves | the wórld | to dárk | ness and | to mé. |

The first line is completely regular iambic pentameter, and this establishes the meter of the poem, but three substitutions occur in the remaining lines. A trochee appears in the third position of line 2, and this serves to slow down the poem's rhythm, as we picture a slowly moving herd of cattle. The other substitutions are both pyrrhic feet, which occur in the third positions of lines 2 and 4. Both of these departures from regular meter prevent the verse from straying too far from the rhythms of natural speech and thus make it sound more like a conversation. Perfectly regular meter, on the other hand, can sound like a nursery rhyme:

> Kí tty cat | Kí tty cat | whére have you | béen?

Comic verse often adopts a very regular meter, as in the lines from Seuss and Rex quoted earlier and as in this stanza from Calvin Trillin's poem "The Republican Plan to Stimulate the Economy."

It's vé | ry hárd | to és | ti-máte |
Just whát | it tákes | to stím | u-láte |
A cór | por á | tion, bút | we knów |
These péo | ple néed | a lót |of dóugh. |

More serious poetry establishes a metrical template, and then occasionally or often diverges from it, in the way a jazz musician will play the melody of a piece as a courtesy to the audience and then go on to improvise around it.

Before moving on to the linguistic analysis of stress, let us note three more conventions of scansion, all of which can be observed in Fussell's (1979:33) marking of these lines from Yeats's "Sailing to Byzantium."

An ág | èd° mán | is but | a pál | try thíng, | °The secondary
A tát | tered cóat | u-pon | a stíck, | un-léss | stress on *aged*
Sóul cláp | its hánds | and síng, | and lóud | er síng | was supplied by
For év | ery tá | ter in | its mór | tal dréss | …   Yeats, as explained below.

First, in line 1 we see that **the division of feet does not have to correspond to the division of words**. Here foot boundaries divide the words *aged* and *tattered*. In fact, the division of feet does not even have to correspond to the division of lines. The second convention of scansion is that **we usually mark the stress on words as we pronounce them, not as they are spelled**. This can be seen in line 2. Judged by the spelling alone *tattered* might appear to have three syllables, tat ter ed, but it is pronounced with only two: /tǽ tərd/, and that is the way we scan it. Another example in Yeats's lines is the word *every*, pronounced /évri/, not ev er y. Poets sometimes use typographical conventions to indicate the fact that the intended pronunciation does not accord with the spelling, as in Keats's line:

Thou still **unravish'd** bride of quietness

Whether spelled "unravish'd" or "unravished," the word is pronounced with three syllables, not four: /ən rǽv išt/. A third convention of scansion is that **we can stress a word unconventionally if it fits the meter better**. We see this principle at work in line 1 of "Sailing to Byzantium" in the marking of *agèd*, which is usually pronounced with one syllable, /éyǰd/, but where Yeats has supplied an accent mark to indicate that it should be pronounced with two syllables, /éy ǰid/, a pronunciation that better fits the iambic meter.

Let us note a few more things about Fussell's scansion of Yeats's lines. Notice that there are several substitutions for iambic feet. The most prominent occurs in line 3, where a spondee is substituted for an iamb in first position. As we will discuss, an unexpected stress often serves to capture the reader's attention at a particularly important point, and the spondee here introduces the possibility of a happy alternative to the sad fate of an aged man that is described in the first

145

two lines. This is an example of foregrounding, where a change in the expected pattern tells us to pay attention. We saw the same principle at work in Chapter 4, where we noted that authors can use a marked syntactic structure for the same purpose. Two more substitutions occur in Yeats's lines, where pyrrhics are substituted for iambs. The first of these occurs in the third position of line 2, and the second occurs in the third position of line 4. Fussell (1979:33) suggests that the purpose of these substitutions is "To relieve the metrical monotony of the long-continued, unvaried iambic pentameter . . . ."

Exercises 2 and 3 review this material.

5.2 **Natural Patterns of English Stress**

Having looked at some traditional principles of prosodic analysis, let us examine how words and sentences are stressed in naturally spoken English, keeping in mind that a natural reading is always the first step in scanning a poem. This knowledge will allow us to see to what extent natural English stress is compatible with traditional scanning, and may even prove useful in deciding how to scan lines of poetry.

5.2.1 Word Stress

In some languages there are reliable rules about which syllables in a word are stressed. In Spanish, for example, stress in three-syllable words normally falls on the next-to-last syllable:

alfombra	/alfówmbra/	rug
pintura	/piyntúrə/	picture
vestido	/bestíyðow/	dress

When a three-syllable word is stressed differently, this fact is conveniently marked by the Spanish spelling:

címbalo	cymbal
clásico	classic
hablarán	They will speak.

Unfortunately, there are no reliable rules about how to stress English words. The irregular stress patterns of English partly result from the fact that most of its words are descended from two different languages: German and French. When the Angle and Saxon tribes from what is now roughly Germany began to invade Britain in the fifth century CE, they spoke the Anglo-Saxon language, which was basically a dialect of German, and the most common words in English are descended from Anglo-Saxon.

Germanic words in English tend to be short, and to take primary stress on the first syllable: *fíre, móther, wédding.* When William the Conqueror, who ruled what is now Normandy in France, invaded England in 1066, he and his knights spoke French, and that became the language of the law and the Court in England for the next 150 years. During this period English borrowed many words from French, which in turn had inherited them from Latin. Latinate words in English tend to be long and take primary stress somewhere after the first syllable: *incéndiary, matérnal, matrimónial.* Notice that English often has two words for the same idea, one descended from German and the other from French, as in the examples of Germanic and Latinate words that were just given.

In the discussion of traditional scansion, we distinguished only two degrees of stress within a word: stressed and unstressed. However, dictionaries more accurately distinguish three degrees of stress. For example, Webster's marks the word *capitulate* like this: /kə píč ə lèyt/, where ´ indicates strong or primary stress, and ` indicates weak or secondary stress, and where unstressed syllables are not marked. More examples of the three degrees of stress can be found in these words.

mágazìne	/mǽgəzìyn/
scìentífic	/sàyəntífik/
únivèrse	/yúwnivèrs/
bóokmàrker	/búkmàrkər/
prónòun	/prównàwn/

Notice that all of the unstressed syllables in these words are pronounced /ə/ or /i/. These are the two vowels that are the easiest to produce, and because unstressed syllables go by so quickly, we do not have time to articulate a more difficult sound. In fact, the time that it takes to utter an English sentence is mainly related to the number of stressed syllables, not to the total number of syllables. The following sentences are all spoken in about the same amount of time.

Dógs éat bónes.
The dógs will éat the bónes.
The dógs will have éaten the bónes.

In unstressed syllables, the vowels /ə/ or /i/ often replace the "underlying" vowels that we hear when a word is pronounced carefully, that is, in its *citation form*. This **laxing** of unstressed vowels can be seen in these examples.

word	citation form	form in connected speech
cannot	/kǽnát/	I /kənát/ find my glasses.
together	/tùwgéðər/	We'll go down /təgéðər/.
premature	/prìyməčúr/	The announcement was /priməčúr/.
vocabulary	/vòwkǽbyùwlèriy	Watch your /vəkǽbyələri/ !

Thus, all vowels other than /ə/ and /i/ must receive either primary or secondary stress.

Usually native English speakers can distinguish the stresses on a multisyllable word because they learn the stress pattern when they learn the word, mastering its rhythm along with its phonemes. However, if you find it difficult to determine where the stresses fall, Fromkin, Rodman, and Hyams (2014:319) have this advice, "Try shouting the word as if talking to a person across a busy street. Often, the difference in stress becomes more apparent. (This should not be attempted in a public place such as a library.)" Of course, another possibility, and one that is available to non-native English speakers as well, is to consult a dictionary.

Exercises 4 and 5 review this material.

5.2.2 Sentence Stress

As we have just seen, when words are strung together into sentences, some of the syllables in multisyllable words that take secondary stress in citation form are demoted to become unstressed, and the vowel is laxed to become /ə/ or /i/. Laxing also occurs in many single syllable words when they are used in a sentence. For example, in isolation the word *that* is pronounced in its citation form, /ðǽt/; but, in a sentence the stress and also the vowel change: *Mársha sáid* / ðət/ *she was cóming.* For another example, consider the stress patterns in this sentence:

The car had been brought and was ready to use.

Intuition (accessed in this case without shouting) produces this pronunciation:

/ðə kár həd bin brót ənd wəz rédìy tə yúwz/

Notice that there is no stress of the words *had, been, and, was,* and *to,* and that the vowels in all of these words have been laxed. But, as we have seen, intuitions are not infallible. Fortunately, there are some rules for which words are stressed and unstressed within a sentence, and we will now have a look at these rules.

Linguists divide words into two categories: **function words** and **content words**. Function words include prepositions, determiners, relative pronouns, conjunctions, and other words that serve a grammatical purpose, such as joining two clauses together. The number of function words in English is small, and it cannot be added to easily. For example, in standard American English there are only seven personal pronouns: *I, you, he, she, it, we,* and *they,* and we cannot just make up a new one.[1] The number of content words in English, on the other hand, is large and it is easy to make up new ones, as the politician Sarah Palin did when she unintentionally coined the verb *refudiate* (named as one of the words of the year by the American Dialect Society), which means "to refute and repudiate." Here are the most common kinds of content words and function words.

Function Words
prepositions, determiners, relative pronouns, personal pronouns, possessive adjectives (*my, our, your*, etc.), common conjunctions (*and, but, that, as, if, because* etc.), and auxiliary verbs (*will, would, have had, is, was*, etc.)

Content Words
nouns, verbs, adjectives, adverbs, demonstrative adjectives (*this, that, these, those*) and interrogatives (*who, when, why*, etc.)

We can now state a rule of thumb for applying primary stress to words within a sentence: **only content words receive primary stress.** So, all function words receive either no stress or, in a few cases, secondary stress. For example, if the sentence below were read very slowly with each word in citation form, it would sound as shown.

I want to start around five o'clock.
/áy wánt túw stárt əráwnd fáyv ów klák/

But if the sentence were spoken at normal speed, only the content words would take primary stress, and the sentence would sound like this.

/ày wánt tə stárt əràwnd fáyv ə klák/

Notice that the vowels in *to* and *o'* (which is short for the function word *of*) are laxed and pronounced as schwa. The vowels /ay/ in *I* and /aw/ in *around*, however, are preserved, which means that they are not fully laxed but merely demoted to secondary stress. Nevertheless, *I* and *around* are still function words, and are pronounced rapidly in normal speech, so their secondary stresses are hardly noticed. So, for the purpose of marking sentence stress we will ignore the secondary stresses that some function words, like *I* and *around*, might retain, and mark only the primary stresses within a sentence.

Applying the sentence stress rule to the sentence above, then, produces:

/ay wánt tə stárt ərawnd fáyv ə klák/

Like all rules of thumb the sentence stress rule has exceptions, and here are two of them.

1. The main verbs that can also be used as auxiliaries (*have, be,* and *do*) are normally unstressed. However, they are stressed when they are in a tag question (They shóot hórses, *dón't* they?), or in "exposed position" at the end of a clause (I thóught this was hárder than it *ís*).

2. In two-word verbs,[2] which are made up of a verb and a particle, the particle takes primary stress and the verb takes secondary stress:

George   pìcked   úp   the trash.
             V   Part

Let's try out the sentence stress rule on this sentence from Hemingway's *A Farewell to Arms*:

> The trunks of the trees were dusty and the leaves fell early that year and we saw the troops marching along the road.

If the sentence were read very slowly, all of the words would be pronounced in their citation form and would receive a primary stress, but for normal speech the sentence stress rule removes primary stress from all of the function words, producing this reading (the grammatical class of the content words is also shown):

The trúnks of the trées were dústy and the léaves féll éarly thát yéar and we
     N   N   Adj   N   V Adj dem N

sáw the tróops márching alóng the róad.
 V   N   V   Adv   N

Notice that technically three of the words in this sentence, *dusty, early*, and *marching*, should have secondary stress on the vowel /iy/ of their final syllables and should therefore be marked dústỳ, éarlỳ, and márchìng. However, just as we did not mark the secondary stresses on some function words like *I* and *around*, we will ignore the secondary stresses on multisyllable content words when applying the sentence stress rule, and only mark the primary stresses.

Here is another example of the sentence stress rule, as applied to a sentence from Joan Didion's *Slouching Toward Bethlehem*.

The Mórmons séttled the óminous cóuntry, and thén they abándoned it, but by
     N   V   Adj   N   Adv   V

the tíme they léft the fírst órange trée had been plánted.
   N   V   Adj Adj N   V

All of the words in these two sentences that do not have a primary stress are function words.

The sentence stress rule is not infallible. For example, it is difficult to pronounce many unstressed syllables in a row, so if a sentence contains a string of normally unstressed words, one of them can be stressed, as the following example shows:

The hóuse is being wátched (*being* is unstressed because it is an Aux verb).

The hóuse may have been béing wátched (*being* is stressed because it comes after several unstressed words).

The sentence stress rule is a good first approximation of how to stress a sentence, but we need to add to it because it turns out that not all of the content words within phrases are stressed equally. Therefore, we need a phrasal stress rule, which we will look at next.

Exercises 6 and 7 review this material.

5.2.3 Phrasal Stress

The **phrasal stress rule** marks the stresses within NPs, AdjPs, and AdvPs. First, consider NPs. As we saw in Chapter 4, NPs can look like this:

NP → (Det) (AdjP) N

This rule will generate the phrase *this old house*, which occurs in Gwendlyn Brooks's poem "Sadie and Maud."

> She is living all alone
> In this old house.
>   NP

In order to mark the natural stresses in this NP, we first apply the sentence stress rule.

> She is living   all   alone
> In thís   óld   hóuse.
>   Dem   Adj   N
>   NP

We are now ready for the phrasal stress rule, which says that **only the head constituent in an NP, AdjP, or AdvP can take primary stress.** As discussed in Chapter 4, a phrase can consist of a head and one or more modifiers, and the head is the most important word in the phrase. So, applying the phrasal stress rule to the NP *this old house* demotes the modifiers *this* and *old* to secondary stress, as shown below.

> thís óld hóuse   Phrasal stress rule   →
>   NP
> thìs òld hóuse
>   NP

151

The phrasal stress rule works the same way for adjective phrases and adverb phrases. Here are some examples that show how the sentence stress rule and the phrasal stress rule apply to sentences with an NP, AdjP, and AdvP.

Noun Phrase

The next morning the grandfather was the first one in the car.

Sentence stress rule →

The	**néxt**	mórning	the grándfather was the fírst óne in the cár.
Det (modifier)	Adj (modifier)	N (head)	

NP

Phrasal stress rule →

The	**nèxt**	mórning	the grándfather was the fírst óne in the cár.
Det (modifier)	Adj (modifier)	N (head)	

NP

Here the primary stress on *next* has been reduced to secondary stress.

Adjective Phrase

The chemical that leached into the river was *particularly toxic*.

Sentence stress rule →

The chémical that léached into the ríver was **partícularly** tóxic.
Adv (modifier) Adj (head)
AdjP

Phrasal stress rule →

The chémical that léached into the ríver was **partìcularly** tóxic.
Adv (modifier) Adj (head)
AdjP

Here the primary stress on *particularly* has been reduced to secondary stress.

Adverb Phrase

We've seen a rebound in housing prices *fairly recently*.

Sentence stress rule →

We've séen a rébound in hóusing prices **fáirly** récently.
Adv (modifier) Adv (head)
AdvP

Phrasal stress rule →

We've séen a rébound in hóusing príces **fàirly** récently.
Adv (modifier) Adv (head)
AdvP

Here the primary stress on *fairly* has been reduced to secondary stress.

As these examples show, the head of a phrase is usually the rightmost word in the phrase.

We now have a two-step procedure for marking the important stresses in an English phrase or sentence:

1. Apply the sentence stress rule.
2. Apply the phrasal stress rule.

Let us try out this procedure on this line from George Herbert's poem "Virtue."

Sweet day, so cool, so calm, so bright,

The line is not a sentence because it does not contain a verb but rather is an NP followed by three AdjPs. Nevertheless, our two-step procedure can still be applied, as follows.

1. **Apply the sentence stress rule**

    The sentence stress rule marks all of the words with primary stress because they are all content words.

    <u>Swéet</u>   dáy,   <u>só   cóol,</u>   <u>só   cálm,</u>   <u>só   bríght</u>
    <u>Adj</u>   N   Adv Adj   Adv Adj   Adv Adj
          NP   AdjP   AdjP   AdjP

2. **Apply the phrasal stress rule**

    First we will apply the phrasal stress rule to the three AdjPs. All of them consist of an adjective modified by the adverb *so*: *so cool, so calm,* and *so bright.* The phrasal stress rule demotes the primary stresses on these modifying adverbs to secondary stresses, like this:

    Swéet dáy, sò cóol, sò cálm, sò bríght,

    Next we apply the phrasal stress rule to the NP, where it demotes the adjective *sweet* to secondary stress. So the final version of the line looks like this:

    Swèet dáy, sò cóol, sò cálm, sò bríght,

    Finally, let us consider how our two-step procedure applies to lines that contain an AdvP, like this one from T. S. Eliott's poem "The Love Song of J. Alfred Prufrock."

    And the afternoon, the evening, sleeps so peacefully!

The AdvP here is *so peacefully,* in which the adverb *so* modifies the adverb *peacefully* (adverbs often modify other adverbs in AdvPs, as in *very quickly* and *more slowly*).

153

Step 1 **Apply the sentence stress rule**

> All of the content words receive primary stress, for now.
> And the afternóon, the évening, sléeps só péacefully!

Step 2 **Apply the phrasal stress rule**

> The only phrase that contains two stresses is the AdvP *so peacefully*. Reducing the primary stress on the modifier *so* to secondary stress, the entire line now looks like this:
> And the afternóon, the évening, sléeps sò péacefully!

As you might expect, there is an exception to the phrasal stress rule, but it applies only to NPs. English has a number of nominal expressions, called *compound nouns*, which are made up of two nouns, where the first noun works like an adjective to modify the second noun. Examples include: àpple píe, bràss mónkey, and pènny cándy. As you can see from the stress markings, these compound nouns are *not* an exception to the phrasal stress rule because the main noun receives primary stress and the modifying noun receives secondary stress. However, there is another type of compound noun that *is* an exception to the rule. Examples include físh tànk, píne còne, and háir brùsh. As you can see from the stress markings, in these compound nouns the first noun is stressed more strongly than the second. It can be difficult to tell the two kinds of compound nouns apart, but usually in the físh tànk type (which are called *determinative compounds*) the two nouns work together to define a unique concept, whereas in the àpple píe type (which are called *descriptive compounds*) the first noun just names an attribute of the second noun. Thus, a háir brùsh (determinative compound noun) is a unique concept: a brush for the hair. But a hàir brúsh (descriptive compound noun) could be many things: a brush for polishing cars, grooming cats, or dusting – as long as the brush is made out of hair. In any event, correctly assigning stress to the two kinds of compound nouns should not be a problem because our intuitions tell us which stress patterns correspond to which meanings.

5.3 Application of Natural Stress Rules to Poetry

We now have a two-step procedure for assigning three levels of stress (primary, secondary, and unstressed) to the syllables in a naturally spoken English sentence. But, as we have seen, scanning a line of poetry involves assigning only two levels of stress (stressed and unstressed). In this section we will see how the stresses of natural speech correspond to the stresses of poetry.

5.3.1 A Three-step Procedure for Scanning Verse

We can convert a naturally stressed English phrase or sentence into a scanned line of poetry by adding a third step to our procedure, but before doing so let us pause to consider some of the ways in which traditional scansion matches and diverges from the stress patterns of spoken English. We start by looking at Fussell's scansion of two lines from Yeats's poem "Sailing To Byzantium." Fussell's (1979:34) marking of these lines is shown below with our marking of the natural English stresses shown below it in bold.

Ónce óut of náture I shall néver táke
Ónce óut of náture I shall néver táke

My bódily fórm from ány nátural thíng.
My bòdily fórm from àny nàtural thíng.

The first line of the poem is scanned in exactly the same way. The second lines differ only in that on the stressed syllables we have differentiated between primary stress and secondary stress, while Fussell, using the traditional one-stress system, has not. This difference suggests that the traditional system assigns its one degree of stress to any syllable to which we assign *any* degree of stress, whether secondary or primary. However, this hypothesis isn't exactly right and will have to be amended. To see how, let us examine in some detail Arp and Johnson's (2006) analysis of George Herbert's poem "Virtue." Here is the whole poem.

Virtue
Sweet day, so cool, so calm, so bright,
    The bridal of the earth and sky;
The dew shall weep thy fall to night,
    For thou must die.

Sweet rose, whose hue, angry and brave,
    Bids the rash gazer wipe his eye;
Thy root is ever in its grave
    And thou must die.

Sweet spring, full of sweet days and roses,
    A box where sweets compacted lie;
My music shows ye have your closes,
    And all must die.

Only a sweet and virtuous soul,
    Like seasoned timber, never gives;
But though the whole world turn to coal,
    Then chiefly lives.

Like the other authorities I have mentioned, Arp and Johnson advise the student to begin the scanning process by reading the poem "normally, according to its prose meaning, listening to where the accents fall naturally"(p. 844). Then, the student should determine the basic meter of the poem by looking for the most regularly stressed lines, like this one:

A bóx | where swéets | com-páct | ed líe; |

The rhythm of this line is intuitively obvious: it is iambic, but let us go through our two-step process to see if it gets the same result. First, we apply the sentence stress rule, producing:

A bóx where swéets compácted líe;

There are no NPs, AdjPs, or AdvPs that contain modifiers, so the phrasal stress rule does not apply. We can now divide the line into feet, which produces this result:

A bóx | where swéets | com-páct | ed líe; |

So, it looks like the basic meter of the poem is iambic tetrameter, and that our analysis of this line agrees with that of Arp and Johnson.

We now turn to the first line in the poem, which we analyzed earlier in the chapter with this result:

Swèet dáy, | sò cóol, | sò cálm, | sò bríght, |

Here is how Arp and Johnson scan the line:

Sweet dáy |, so cóol, | so cálm, | so bríght, |

This comparison does not support the hypothesis that the traditional system simply marks as stressed any syllable that we mark with primary or secondary stress. We have marked *sweet* and the three *so*s with secondary stress, but Arp and Johnson leave these words unstressed. So, we will have to look for another way to reconcile the two systems, and it is this: **relative stress is assigned within the foot**. For example, taking the first foot first, we see the following comparison between the poetic marking and the natural pronunciation:

Arp and Johnson: Sweet dáy |
Natural stress: Swèet dáy |

The two analyses agree on the *relative* degree of stress: in both systems, *day* is stressed more strongly than *sweet*: So, to translate the three-stress system of natural speech into the two-stress system of scansion, we first divide the line into feet and then mark the most highly stressed syllable within each foot as stressed and leave the other syllable(s) unstressed (if a foot has two primary stresses, they are both marked as stressed). We will refer to this procedure as the **poetic stress rule**.

The poetic stress rule is the third step for assigning stresses to a line of poetry that was promised at the beginning of this section (in Section 3.3 an optional fourth step will be added). Let us now apply this three-step system to the first two lines of the second stanza of "Virtue," which are repeated here.

> Sweet rose, whose hue, angry and brave,
>   Bids the rash gazer wipe his eye;

Step 1 Apply the sentence stress rules
> Swéet róse, whose húe, ángry and bráve,
>   Bíds the rásh gázer wípe his éye;

Step 2 Apply the phrasal stress rule
> Swèet róse, whose húe, ángry and bráve,
>   Bíds the ràsh gázer wípe his éye;

Step 3 Apply the poetic stress rule
> Sweet róse, | whose húe, | án-gry | and bráve, |
>   Bíds the | rash gá | zer wípe | his éye; |

Like language itself poetry cannot always be neatly pinned down, and there is always room for different interpretations in the reading of a poem. Arp and Johnson (2006) observe that the first foot of the first line of "Virtue" could also be read as a spondee, Swéet dáy, and they discuss which reading would be better. Though both are acceptable, in the end they choose the iambic reading for a rhetorical reason. They note that the first three stanzas all begin with the word *sweet*, and all describe things that must die, whereas the fourth stanza, which begins with *only* (which must be stressed on the first syllable), describes something that does not die. Therefore, stressing *only* but not *sweet* reinforces the different meanings of these stanzas. In the end, however, they say, "Ultimately, ... we are reporting what we hear, ..." (p. 845). We, too, can be guided by what we hear, but knowing that *sweet* receives some degree of stress in natural speech suggests that we might want to stress it in the poem, as well.

A similarly ambiguous situation exists in the second position of the second line of the second stanza.

> Bíds the | rash gáz | er wípe | his éye.

Both our analysis and Arp and Johnson's analysis scan this foot as an iamb; however, our full analysis indicates that in natural speech *rash* receives secondary stress, suggesting that we might want to analyze the foot as a trochee if there is a good reason for doing so. Perhaps there is. The phrase

157

rash gazer stands out in the line because of the partial alliteration of /š/ and /z/, suggesting something out of place – an intruder in the rose's world. So, allowing a trochee to intrude on the iambic pattern would reinforce this point.

Let us now return to the first stanza of the poem and scan its second line,

> The bridal of the earth and sky.

First, we apply the sentence stress rule, which produces:

> The brídal of the éarth and ský.

Next, we look to see if the phrasal stress rule can apply. In this case it cannot because none of the NPs contains two stresses. So, we now apply the poetic stress rule. First, we divide the line into iambic feet, which yields an analysis containing four feet with the substitution of a pyrrhic for an iamb in second position:

> The brí | dal of | the éarth | and ský; |

However, Arp and Johnson disagree, marking the line as follows:

> The brí | dal óf | the éarth | and ský; |

Their analysis preserves the strict iambic meter, but, as we now know, stressing the word *of* risks making the line sound artificial because in natural English speech this function word would be unstressed.

Exercises 8, 9, and 10 review this material.

5.3.2 Interpretation

The question of how much to acknowledge the basic meter of a poem when it differs from natural pronunciation is difficult, and different analysts accord the underlying template different degrees of force. Consider, for example, Abrams's (2009) scansion of these lines from Keats's *Endymion*.

> A thíng | of béau | ty ís | a jóy | for-éver |
> It's lóve | li-néss |in-créas | es, ít | will né-ver |
> Páss in | to nóth | ing-ness, | but stíll | will kéep |
> A bó | wer quí | et for | us, ...

The first four feet are regularly iambic and there are five feet in the line, so the basic meter of the poem appears to be iambic pentameter. Notice that lines 1 and 2 end in a foot containing an extra unstressed syllable. This *anabraic* foot (˘ / ˘) provides a *feminine ending*, which contrasts with the more common *masculine ending*, where a line ends on a stressed syllable. Notice also that in the third position of lines 3 and 4 a pyrrhic has been substituted for an iamb. The main point for the present discussion, however, is to notice is that Abrams has stressed *is* in line 1 and *it* in line 2. This violates the natural stress pattern of English because *it* and *is* are normally unstressed, but stressing them fits the meter. On the matter of choosing between natural stress and the underlying meter, Fussell (1979) comments:

> Our scansions [should] reveal, *where appropriate*, the force of the abstract metrical pattern which presumably lies behind the actual rhythms of the words (p. 27)... [O]nce the metrical contract has been agreed to by both parties, an understanding "silent" metrical continuum proceeds through the poem, and ... this abstract pattern, which the actual words are continuously either reinforcing or departing from, has the power now and then to force a metrical rather than a natural pronunciation of a word or phrase.

But, when is the abstract pattern strong enough to force a metrical pronunciation? In some verses the established meter is so powerful that we are compelled to depart from the natural rhythm of the words, as in these lines from Blake, where the forcefulness of the meter in the first line demands that the two prepositions in the second line be stressed:

Týger, | Týger, | búrn-ing | bríght |
Ín the | fór-ests | óf the | níght, |

Keats's lines, however, are less forceful and more conversational in tone, and Abrams has perhaps inappropriately allowed the iambic template to take over from the natural rhythm of the sentence. So, some critics, and Fussell is among them, give primacy to the natural stresses while other critics, like Abrams, give the metrical template more force.

Let us take a look at how some other critics have scanned some lines and compare their marking to the natural rhythms. Vendler's (2002:660) scan of the following lines by Robert Frost differs from the natural stress pattern, which is shown below.

When Í | see bír | ches bénd | to léft | and ríght |
When I | sée bír | ches bénd | to léft | and ríght |

Vendler stresses the pronoun *I* and de-stresses the verb *see*, in order to fit the iambic template. The effect is to emphasize *I* more than *see*, and this may suggest the personal and subjective nature of the experience of seeing birches, but this effect is perhaps achieved at the expense of making the line sound as though it has been memorized. Another example of natural rhythm conflicting with underlying meter is found in Vendler's scan of William Blake's "Sunflower," where the meter is anapestic (again the difference in the natural stress pattern is shown below).

159

> Where the yóuth | pined a-wáy | with de-síre |
> And the pále | vir-gin shróud | ed in snów |
> And the pále | vír-gin shróud | ed in snów |

The difference in the two markings is that Vendler has allowed the anapestic template to de-stress the first syllable in *virgin*. The resulting difference from natural speech gives the line a sing-song quality.

We have seen that knowing the natural patterns of English stress can sometimes aid the analyst in scanning poetry. The three-step procedure described here[3] allows us to mark the stresses in finer detail, and often more accurately, than simply using our intuition. Having marked the natural stresses, we can then compare the relative stresses within each foot to see which syllable should receive stress under the traditional two-stress system. When decisions must be made about whether to adhere to or deviate from the underlying meter, knowing where the stresses would naturally fall can be helpful. The rule of thumb advocated here is that leaving the natural stress in place is usually the better way to scan a line because whether heard aloud or in the "mind's ear," poetry should be a kind of speech.

5.3.3 Rhetorical Stress

Language is impossible to pin down, a fact that poets love and linguists hate. Unsurprisingly, there are some exceptions to the nice three-step system for scanning poetry presented here, but a major exception can be handled by an optional rule that we seldom need to apply: the **rhetorical stress rule**. As we have noted, the sentence stress rule and the phrasal stress rule will produce the neutral or unmarked reading of a sentence – the way the sentence would be stressed in normal circumstances. But, what if circumstances are not normal and the speaker wants to strongly emphasize a particular word? In this case, the rhetorical stress rule comes into play. This rule says: **any syllable of a sentence can receive extra stress.** Consider Shakespeare's sentence "Let me not to the marriage of true minds/ Admit impediment." Applying the sentence stress rule and the phrasal stress rule produces this neutral stressing of the line:

> Lét me nót to the márriage of trùe mínds/ Admít impédiment.

However, suppose we read this line to a friend who doesn't quite hear us and asks, "Did you just say, 'Let me not to the marriage of true *lies* admit impediment'?" To clarify, we can repeat the sentence, emphasizing the word *minds*. But *minds* already has primary stress, so the rhetorical stress rule allows us to add extra stress. Thus, the rule provides a fourth level of stress, called *rhetorical stress*, which can be added to any word that the speaker wishes to emphasize. Rhetorical stress is marked like this:

Lét me nót to the márriage of trùe mi'nds/ Admít impédiment.

Similarly, giving rhetorical stress to the word *me* in the same sentence produces this marking:

Lét me nót to the márriage of trùe mínds/ Admít impédiment.

Poets do not often use rhetorical stress, but Mathew Arnold does in the first stanza of "To Marguerite."

Yes! In the sea of life enisled,
With echoing straits between us thrown,
Dotting the shoreless watery wild,
We mortal millions live *alone*.

The word *alone* clearly receives rhetorical stress, as Arnold indicates by putting it in italics, and it could be argued that the word *yes* in the first line does as well.

Exercises 11–15 review this material.

5.4 **Metrical Variation**

The purpose of the complicated business of scansion is to see how a poem's meter complements and enhances its meaning, and critics have observed that substituting a particular kind of foot for an expected foot often produces a predictable result. For example, successive unstressed syllables can speed up a line, as in Wordsworth's

I wán | dered lóne | ly as | a clóud |

The pyrrhic foot in the third position adds lightness to a whimsical thought that should not be weighed down by a plodding meter. Conversely, piling up stresses slows down a line. Substituting a dactyl or a trochee for an iamb can have this effect, as in these lines of Yeats:

Túrn ing | and túrn | ing in | the wíd | en-ing gýre |
The fál | con can | not héar | the fáll-con-er; |
Thíngs fáll | a-párt; | the cén | ter can | not hóld; |

After starting with a stressed syllable, the first line picks up speed by adding unstressed syllables, with a pyrrhic substitution in third position and an anapest substitution in fifth position. The second line also moves swiftly with a pyrrhic foot in second position and fifth position, which moves us into the third line where we hit a brick wall with a trochee in first position consisting of two stressed words. Here, the speaker moves from the metaphor of the falcon, which merely suggests that it is hard to get our bearings, to the direct assertion that things are falling apart, and the abrupt change in rhythm foregrounds this point.

Another example of a change in rhythm signaling a change in thought occurs in Rachel Hadas's poem "The Red Hat," which describes a mother's feelings when her son begins going to school (and parents will recognize the theme that once children start school, they are basically gone). Here is the last stanza of the poem, describing the contrast between the time when the boy stayed home in the morning and now, when he goes off to school.

> The mornings we turn back to are no more
> than forty minutes longer than before,
> but they feel vastly different – flimsy, strange,
> wavering in the eddies of this change,
> empty; unanchored, perilously light
> since the red hat vanished from our sight.

The lines can be scanned as follows:

> The mórn | ings we | turn báck | to are | no móre |
> than fór | ty mín | utes lón | ger than| be-fóre, |
> but they | féel vást | ly díff | erent – flím | sy, stránge, |
> wá-vering | in the | éd-dies of | this chánge, |
> ém-pty; | un-án | chored, pél | rilous-ly líght |
> since the | réd hát | ván | ished from | our síght. |

The first two lines say that the new morning schedule is actually not so different from the old, and the rhythm moves quickly with three pyrrhic feet among the seven iambs. In line 3, however, things change. The speaker says that mornings without her son feel different, and the rhythm is different too with a pyrrhic followed by a trochee, with unexpected stress on the important word *feel*. In addition, the line is divided into two parts by a pause, which is indicated by the dash. Thus, the stressed phrase *feel vástly different* is foregrounded between a light foot and a pause. The speaker goes on to describe the feel of the new mornings with a series of adjectives that are stressed on the first syllable, which emphasizes their importance: *flimsy, strange, empty, light*. The word *empty* is especially strong because it begins a line. In line 4 the speaker says that she feels uncertain in this new time, and the rhythm of the line is uncertain as well, with one trochee, one pyrrhic, one anapest, and one iamb.

Another way that meter can reflect meaning is to pause in the middle of a line. This pause is called a **caesura** (/seyžurə/), and we have just seen an example in the line

but they feel vastly different – flimsy, strange.

The pause required by the dash makes us dwell for a moment on the word *different*, and perhaps to sense that this line is different from the previous two in its rhythm. A caesura is often signaled by punctuation, as in the example above and as in these lines by Keats, where I have marked the caesuras with double vertical lines.

A thing of beauty is a joy forever;
Its loveliness increases; ‖ it will never
Pass in to nothingness, ‖ but still will keep
A bower quiet for us, ‖ and a sleep
Full of sweet dreams, and health, and quiet breathing.

A caesura can also be signaled by a grammatical boundary. In Sylvia Plath's poem "Mirror" each of the first three lines contains a caesura, but in the second line the pause is signaled not by punctuation but by the boundary between a fronted dependent clause and its main clause.

I am silver and exact. ‖ I have no preconceptions.
Whatever I see ‖ I swallow immediately
Just as it is, ‖ unmisted by love or dislike.

Reading these lines aloud we can hear that the caesura in line 1, signaled by a period, is slightly longer than the caesura in line 3, signaled by a comma, which in turn is slightly longer than the caesura in line 2, which is signaled only by a grammatical boundary. We have already seen another example of a slight pause that is signaled by a syntactic boundary in "The Eagle."

He clasps the crag with crooked hands;
Close to the sun in lonely lands,
Ringed with the azure world, ‖ he stands

Reading these lines aloud we can hear that the caesura in line three, which is signaled by a comma, has parallel pauses (though these are too short to be called caesurae) in lines 1 and 2. These slight pauses are signaled by the beginning of a new syntactic constituent, namely a prepositional phrase.

To conclude this chapter, we should emphasize that the purpose of scanning a poem is not merely to identify the meter but rather to better understand the poem and to better appreciate the poet's craft. In *Paradise Lost* Milton describes Satan's fall from heaven to hell as follows:

Hurled headlong flaming from th' Ethereal Sky
With hideous ruin and combustion down
To bottomless perdition, there to dwell
In adamantine Chains and penal Fire.

Here are the lines scanned:

Húrl'd héad | long flám | ing from | th' Éth| ereal Ský |
With híd | eous rú | in and | com- bús | tion dówn |
To bót | tom-less | per-dí | tion, ‖ thére | to dwéll |
In Ád | a-mán | tine Cháins | and pé | nal Fíre. |

In the first line the fall begins with great energy, reinforced by the alliteration of /h/ and the initial spondee. The speed of the fall is conveyed by unstressed syllables. Line 1 ends in an anapest rather than the expected iamb, and lines 2 and 3 each contain a pyrrhic foot. Satan's fall ends with a caesura, signaled by the comma in line 3 (and a modern editor would insist on at least a semi-colon). Finally, Satan's eternal plight in hell is suggested by the completely regular iambic rhythm of the remaining lines. Scanning this remarkable verse enables us to see in graphic form what our reading of the lines only suggests.

Exercises 16, 17, 18, and 19 review this material.

Notes

1 Attempts have been made to substitute a gender-neutral pronoun, for example *hir*, for *he* and *she*, but these attempts have not been successful.
2 Genuine two-word verbs can easily be confused with a verb followed by a preposition (which is unstressed):

They   clímbed   up   the ládder.
            V   Prep   NP

One way to tell whether a construction is a verb + particle or a verb + preposition is to apply the particle movement transformation, which moves a particle but not a preposition to the right of the direct object.

                George picked up the trash.
Part trans   →   George picked the trash up.
                They climbed up the ladder.
Part trans   →   * They climbed the ladder up.[5]

3 This procedure is described more concisely (and possibly better) in the web materials for this chapter.

Summary

Scansion is a system for identifying the rhythm and meter of poetry. Rhythm is measured in terms of feet, such as iambs (˘ /), and meter is measured by how many feet occur in a line. The traditional system for scanning a poem is based on how we talk, but its two degrees of stress are inadequate for representing natural speech. A more adequate system contains three degrees of stress: primary, secondary, and zero stress, all of which can be seen in the marking of the word *absolute* (/ǽbsəlùwt/). Accurately marking stress in spoken English involves applying two rules. The *sentence stress rule* says to assign stress only to the content words in a sentence. The *phrasal stress rule* says that modifying words within a phrase should receive only secondary stress. The natural stresses in a line of poetry can usually be converted into the two-stress scansion system by applying the *poetic stress rule*, which says to divide the line into feet and mark as stressed only the most strongly stressed syllable within each foot. Good poetry does not have completely regular meter, and poets often insert feet that do not fit the underlying template of the poem. Using an unexpected foot within a line can have the effect of foregrounding the word containing the marked foot. The purpose of scanning a poem is to allow us better to understand the meaning of the poem and better to appreciate the poet's craft.

Exercises

1. Go to the website www.poetryoutloud.org and listen to some recordings of poetry to get a feel for poetic meter. You can also search YouTube for readings of individual poems.

2. Consider the following lines from Henry Wadsworth Longfellow's "Evangeline."

    My fugitive years are all hasting away,
    And I must ere long lie as lowly as they,
    With a turf on my breast, and a stone at my head,
    Ere another such grove shall arrive in its stead.

    a. Using your intuitions, identify the underlying meter.
    b. Are there any interesting substitutions?
    c. How does this rhythm contribute to the meaning of the verse?

3.   Select a stanza from one of your own favorite poems (older poems are usually easier to deal with).

    a. Using your intuitions, identify the underlying meter.
    b. Are there any interesting substitutions?
    c. Did you have any problems assigning stress within any of the feet?

---

4.   Transcribe the words in the list below in our phonemic alphabet as you would pronounce them in isolation, that is, in citation form. Then, using your intuitions, mark the primary and (if present) secondary stresses. Remember, if a vowel is not /ə/ or /i/ it almost certainly takes primary or secondary stress. **EXAMPLE:**

Word	Citation form transcription	Stresses marked
seventeen	/seventiyn/	/séventìyn/
nitrate		
all-purpose		
telegraph		
telegraphy		
anniversary		
clarinet		
adjacent		
regular		
microscopic		

---

5.   All of the words in the first column below take both primary and secondary stress in citation form. Using your intuitions, mark the primary and secondary stresses. Then, transcribe the same words in the second column indicating if laxing has occurred when the word is spoken in a sentence, as in the example (there may be more than one standard pronunciation of a word).

together	Simon and Garfunkel are together again!
/tùwgéðər/	/təgéðər/
abstain	Marsha will have to abstain from this vote.
remark	Just ignore that last remark.
conversation	Thanks for the drinks and the conversation.
eleven	I'll meet you at the Seven Eleven.
anniversary	My daughter and I have the same anniversary.

Extra credit: All of the vowels in this exercise in which secondary stress was reduced to zero stress have something in common in terms of their placement within the word. What is it? In Chapter 6 we will see that in colloquial speech entire syllables in this position can be dropped completely. Can you think of some examples?

6. Using the sentence stress rule, mark the stresses in the following sentences.

   a. In an hóur it will be réady.
   b. They locked the keys in the car.
   c. I don't suppose you can come tonight.
   d. The owner of the bar thought for a moment about my offer.
   e. Everyone respected the quarterback.
   f. I met the couple on my trip to Europe.

7. Mark the stresses in the following passage from *Winnie The Pooh* using the sentence stress rule.

   . . . he thought that if he stood on the bottom rail of the bridge, and leant over, and watched the river slipping slowly away beneath him, then he would suddenly know everything that there was to be known, and he would be able to tell Pooh, who wasn't quite sure about some of it.

   In line 2 *over* takes primary stress even though it is a preposition. Why?

8. Identify the NPs, AdjPs, and AdvPs that contain more than one word in the following sentences, and label their constituents. Then mark the natural stresses within the phrases.

   a. This chocolate is <u>rèally</u> <u>góod</u>
                       <u>Adv</u>   Adj
                                AdjP

   b. Social pressures can encourage young women to starve themselves.
   c. I think we'll have to move extremely cautiously.
   d. It's good to know that we are in such capable hands.
   e. The Minister spoke very touchingly about the disaster.
   f. Exams are becoming increasingly difficult.
   g. Her gold bracelet looks like a goldfish.
   h. He works in the green house.
   i. He works in the greenhouse.

9.   Mark the natural speech stresses in the following lines, as in the example.

   a. If it ráins, we'll càll óff the whòle párty.
   b. There are two ways of accomplishing it.
   c. I'd like you to play a new game.
   d. He rode to the third floor of the courthouse with a turnkey.
   e. The man in the cell to the left was dressed only in gray undershorts.
   f. His sparse hair was the color of Mercurochrome, pasted in oily stains across his head.

10.   Mark the natural stresses in these prose lines from August Wilson's play *Fences* using the three-stress system. Remember that our procedure allows for plenty of exceptions if you wish to emphasize a particular word or syllable.

   I married your daddy and settled down to cooking his supper and keeping clean sheets on the bed. When your daddy walked through the house he was so big he filled it up. That was my first mistake. Not to make him leave some room for me.

11.   Here are some lines from Calvin Trillin's poem "On the Backlash Against the Perfidious French" that have been marked for stress using the sentence stress rule.

   And súre, they cóme on ráther stróng
   If you pronóunce a dípthong wróng.
   And éven if you're quíte contríte,
   They óften fáil to be políte . . .

   a. Apply the phrasal stress rule to the lines.
   b. Apply the poetic stress rule to translate your result into the traditional scansion system.
   c. Identify the rhythm and meter of the lines.
   d. Are there any substitutions or is the meter perfectly regular?

12.   Mark the natural stresses in each of the following selections using the sentence stress rule and the phrasal stress rule. Then translate the natural stresses into poetic feet using the poetic stress rule. Comment on why you chose to scan the lines as you did. You might mention such considerations as where the natural rhythm of the words varies from the underlying meter, how the natural stress pattern can explain any substitutions that occur, and what effect, if any, the substitution has on the meaning of the poem.

Example:

In Máy, when séa-wìnds píerced òur sólitùdes
I fóund the frésh Rhòdára in the wóods, . . .
   Ralph Waldo Emerson, "The Rhodara: On Being
                Asked, Whence Is the Flower?"

In Máy, | when séa- | winds píerced |our sól | i túdes |
I fóund | the frésh | Rho dá | ra in |the wóods, | . . .

A strict iambic meter would stress *in* in the fourth position of the second line, but natural stress would not. Natural stress is probably better here because it leaves the only stresses on fresh, rhodura, and woods, which are connected conceptually.

a. They say of me, and so they should,
   It's doubtful if I come to good.
      Dorothy Parker, "Neither Bloodied
              Nor Bowed"

b. ""Faith" is a Fine Invention"
   ""Faith" is a fine invention
   When Gentlemen who *see!*
   But *Microscopes* are prudent
   In an Emergency!
      Emily Dickinson, ""Faith" is
            a Fine Invention"

c. Before man came to blow it right
      The wind once blew itself untaught,
  And did its loudest day and night
      In any rough place where it caught.
      Robert Frost, "The Aim Was Song"

d. She walks in beauty, like the night
   Of cloudless climbs and starry skies;
   And all that's best of dark and bright
   Meet in her aspect and her eyes;
      Lord Byron, "She Walks in Beauty,
            Like the Night"

e. Piping down the valleys wild,
   Piping songs of pleasant glee,
   On a cloud I saw a child,

> And he laughing said to me:
> William Blake, "Songs of
> Innocence"

---

13.   Comment on this scan of these lines from Shakespeare. How do they conform to or diverge from the natural English stresses? Would you change these markings? Why or why not?

> So lóng as mén can bréathe, or éyes can sée,
> So lóng lives thís, and thís gives lífe to thée.

---

14.   The first of the three scans below was produced by mechanically applying the iambic pentameter template. The second scan was produced by mechanically applying our procedure. The third scan was produced by altering the second scan in a logical way. Which scan do you prefer? How could you justify the third scan according to the principles of natural English stress (in other words, how could you justify deviating from our procedure)?

> a. Shall Í compáre thee tó a súmmer's dáy?
>   Thou árt more lóvely ánd more témperáte;
>
> b. Shall I compáre thee to a súmmer's dáy?
>   Thou art more lóvely and more témperate;
>
> c. Shall I compáre thee to a súmmer's dáy?
>   Thou art móre lóvely and móre témperate;

---

15.   Consider the following stanza from Houseman's poem "Is My Team Plowing."

> Yes, lad, I lie easy,
> I lie as lads would choose;
> I cheer a dead man's sweetheart,
> Never ask me whose.

a. Line 2 is the most regular. What underlying meter does this suggest for the poem?

b. Scan line 3 using the underlying meter strictly. Then, mark the natural English stresses using our procedure. How are the two markings different? What is gained and lost by using the natural rhythm of the words?

c. Scan line 4. How does it vary from the underlying meter? How does this variation contribute to the meaning of the poem?

---

16. Consider these lines from Edward Fitzgerald's *Rubaiyat*.

> I sometimes think that never blows so red
> The Rose as where some buried Caesar bled;
> That every Hyacinth the Garden wears
> Dropt in her lap from some once lovely head.

a. Fussell (1979:19) scans the first two lines as follows:

> I sómetimes thínk that néver blóws so réd
>   The Róse as whére sóme búried Cáesar bléd;

The marking of the first line conforms both to natural stress and to iambic tetrameter meter. The marking of the second line, however, differs from both. Scan the second line according to strict iambic pentameter and then mark the natural stresses in the line. Which of the three markings (i.e. Fussell's, strict iambic pentameter, or natural speech) do you prefer?

b. In natural speech line 4 might be stressed as follows:

> Drópt in her láp from some ònce lòvely héad.

How would you apply the poetic stress rule to the line? Explain how you handled the secondary stresses.

---

17. What is the basic meter of the following poem? Which lines begin with substitutions? How do the substitutions contribute to the meaning of the poem? Which stanza is the most regular and which is the most irregular, sounding more like the rhythm of natural speech? How does this change in the regularity of the rhythm contribute to the meaning of the poem?

> **That Night When Joy Began**
> That night when joy began
> Our narrowest veins to flush,
> We waited for the flash
> Of morning's leveled gun.
>
> But morning let us pass,
> And day by day relief
> Outgrows his nervous laugh,
> Grown credulous of peace,
>
> As mile by mile is seen
> No trespasser's reproach,

> And love's best glasses reach
> No fields but are his own.
> > *W. H. Auden*

---

18.   Mark the caesurae in the following lines from Shakespeare's *The Winter's Tale.*

> It is for you we speak, not for ourselves:
> You are abused and by some putter-on
> That will be damn'd for't; would I knew the villain,
> I would land-damn him. Be she honour-flaw'd,
> I have three daughters; the eldest is eleven
> The second and the third, nine, and some five;
> If this prove true, they'll pay for't. By mine honour.
> > (Act 2, Sc. 1:142–148)

---

19.   Caesurae come in two varieties: feminine and masculine. The feminine caesura is a pause that occurs after a nonstressed syllable in a line and the masculine caesura is a pause that occurs after a stressed syllable.

    a. Label as feminine or masculine the caesurae that you marked in the last exercise.

    b. Mark and label as masculine or feminine the caesurae in the following extract from Keats's "Ode on a Grecian Urn." What effect is created by the many caesurae in the last three lines? Do any other elements of the lines also contribute to this effect?

> Thou still unravish'd bride of quietness,
> Thou foster-child of Silence and slow Time,
> Sylvan historian, who canst thus express
> A flowery tale more sweetly than our rhyme:
> What leaf-fringed legend haunts about thy shape
> Of deities or mortals, or of both,
> In Tempe or the dales of Arcady?
> What men or gods are these? What maidens loth?
> What mad pursuit? What struggle to escape?
> What pipes and timbrels? What wild ecstasy?

Key Terms

prosody
rhythm
foot (poetic)
substitution

meter
free verse
laxing
function word
content word
sentence stress rule
phrasal stress rule
poetic stress rule
rhetorical stress rule
caesura

Suggestions for Further Reading

The reader has probably figured out that much of my understanding of scansion comes from Fussell (1979). Good discussions of rhythm, meter, and scansion from a traditional perspective can be found in Arp & Johnson (2006) and Vendler (2002). Introductory linguistics books either pay little attention to stress or else discuss it from a very technical viewpoint, but perhaps the most useful (though short) discussion is in Curzan & Adams (2009), which also contains an entire chapter on stylistics! Prator & Robinett (1972) is an ancient but still useful primer on English stress, which is intended for students learning English as a second language.

CHAPTER 6

Varieties of English

In this Chapter ...

English has more accents and varieties than any other language in the world, and this chapter discusses those regional and social dialects. First we look at how sociolinguists study language varieties, then at how authors use regional and vernacular speech to portray their characters. Finally, we consider how speech varies according to social class, age, and gender, and how speakers vary their speech according to the speech situation. Authors can represent the different identities and voices of individual characters by showing how their speech varies according to these demographic characteristics.

6.1 Introduction

The sun never sets on the English language. Although Chinese is spoken natively by more people – almost a billion – English is spoken by well over that number if we add in the nonnative speakers. English has only about 375 million native speakers worldwide, but it is spoken by an additional one billion people as a second language (Melchers and Shaw, 2003:8). The countries of the world can be divided into three types according to the role that English plays in their national life: inner circle, outer circle, and expanding circle (Kachru, 1983). In *Inner Circle* countries English is spoken natively by large numbers of people. These countries include Britain, Ireland, the United States, Australia, Canada, and South Africa. Notice that some of these countries, such as Canada and South Africa, are bilingual with English as just one of the official languages. In *Outer Circle* countries, which include India, Pakistan, Nigeria, Kenya, and the Philippines, English is learned as a second language and is used as a lingua franca so that citizens who do not share a native language can communicate. It is also widely used in the schools, especially at the college level. In *Expanding Circle* countries, which include France, Mexico, China, and Japan, English is taught as a foreign language and is used for international communication, especially for business and scientific purposes. This chapter is devoted to literature written in English in two inner circle countries, the United States and Britain.

The written form of English is basically the same in all of the inner circle countries, and the main difference between American English and British English is in pronunciation. The next section discusses some of the differences between these two varieties in more detail.

6.2 British and American Varieties of English

As G. B. Shaw famously remarked, "Britain and America are two countries divided by a common language." To take an example of a difference in syntax, in Britain it is possible to form a question by inverting main verb *have* with the sentence subject (just as you can invert main verb *be* with the subject, as in, "Are you a student?"). Thus, in Britain, but not in America, you might hear, "Have you an appointment?" In both countries the reply might be, "No, but I will have one next week," but only in Britain would you also be likely to hear, "No, but I shall have one next week." There are also well-known differences in vocabulary. In Britain you put the nappies in the boot, but in America you put the diapers in the trunk.

The main difference between American and British varieties, however, is in pronunciation. In order to discuss these differences, it is useful to distinguish between standard and nonstandard dialects. Standard American English is usually defined as the **language variety** that one reads in books and newspapers, studies in school, and hears on news broadcasts (in fact, this variety is sometimes called "network English"). So, standard American English includes phonology as well as morphology and syntax. Standard American English is also associated with a particular geographical area and social class: it is the way educated Midwesterners talk. According to this definition President Jimmy Carter did not speak standard American English but rather standard Southern English, because he had a strong Georgia accent.

It is more difficult to define standard British English because the most prestigious speech is associated not with a geographical area but only with a social class. For this reason, Milroy (1981) defines "standard British English" only in terms of morphology and syntax, not pronunciation. Under Milroy's definition, a speaker may have a Scottish, or Yorkshire, or any other British regional accent but still speak standard British English. So, when Cockney trash collector Alfred P. Doolittle in *My Fair Lady* sang /oym getin mærid in ðə monin/ (I'm getting married in the morning), he was speaking standard British English with a Cockney accent. However, for our purposes we will include accent in the definition of standard British English as well as standard American English. According to our definition, then, standard British English is the variety that one reads in books and newspapers and usually hears on news broadcasts (BBC English), and the one that is used by the British upper class. It is also the variety that is taught in the public schools (which are, of course, expensive private schools) where the children of the upper class are educated.

The phonology, or accent, associated with standard British English is called Received Pronunciation (RP), which originally meant the accent received by the Queen. The major differences between standard American pronunciation and RP involve the pronunciation of vowels and the phoneme /r/. RP is an r-less dialect, like the dialects of New York City, Boston, Charleston, and other American cities that had a Tory affiliation prior to the Revolutionary War. Some of the differences between the standard American accent and RP are listed below (please note that our phonemic alphabet was designed to represent American English, and so only approximates the sounds of RP).

Standard American	RP	Examples
/æ/	/a/	bath, staff, hand, grant,
/ow/	/əw/	so, joke, home, soap
/ir/	/iə/	near, beer, sincere, fear
/er/	/eə/	square, care, where, pear
/ur/	/eə/	cure, poor, tourist, pure

Moving beyond British and American English, Wells (1982) divides the varieties of English spoken in inner circle countries into four types, mainly according to the way vowels and the phoneme /r/ are pronounced.

Type I   "Irish-based"   Provincial Irish southern (interestingly, also valid for Jamaica and Barbados)
Type II   "English-based"   Most accents of England and Wales and of the countries in the Southern Hemisphere: Australia, New Zealand, and South Africa
Type III   "American-based"   American and Canadian
Type IV   "Scottish-based" Scotland and Northern Ireland

These types can be distinguished by these tests.

	Ireland Type I	England & S. Hemisphere Type II	America Type III	Scotland Type IV
1. Does *lawn* rhyme with *corn*?	No	Yes	No	No
2. Does *mirror* rhyme with *nearer*?	No	No	Yes	No
3. Does *good* rhyme with *mood*?	No	No	No	Yes

These differences can be explained historically. "English-based" accents rhyme *lawn* with *corn* because they have no post-vocalic [r]. [r]-dropping began in London during the seventeenth century, where it was associated with educated speech, and it spread to many of the provinces, including New York City and Boston. "American-based" accents rhyme *mirror* with *nearer* because unstressed [ə] disappeared between a vowel and a following [r]. Thus, *mirror* changed from [miərər] to [mirər], producing a feminine rhyme with [nirər]. In "Scottish-based" accents *good* rhymes with *mood* because in the northern part of the British Isles Middle English /uː/ (long /u/) and /uw/ merged so that *good* changed from /guːd/ to present day /guwd/. Because the "Irish-based" accent has undergone none of these changes, it appears to be the oldest. Of course, Wells's (1982) four-way division of inner circle Englishes is very broad. All of the language varieties he mentions can be divided further into **regional** and **social dialects,** and we will now take a closer look at these varieties in America and England.

6.3 **American English**

Approximately two-thirds of the world's native speakers of English live in the United States, and the different kinds of English spoken across America reflect the history of its people.

6.3.1 Regional Dialects

The study of dialects is the province of the branch of linguistics called *sociolinguistics*. The most comprehensive sociolinguistic study of American dialects so far is the *Atlas of North American English*, which is based on telephone interviews with speakers from all over the United States (Labov, Ash, Boberg, 2006). The *Atlas* divides American regional speech into the areas shown in Map 6.1. Notice that the lines, or *isoglosses*, dividing the dialect areas generally run from east to west rather than from north to south. This pattern reflects the migration routes in the earlier history of the United States. The east-to-west isoglosses end in the Great Plains states, and The West is classified as a single dialect area. This is because the settlement of the West largely occurred after the completion of the transcontinental railroad, which made it easier for easterners from all of the dialect areas to migrate to any area of the West. Notice also that some of the larger dialect areas contain smaller dialect areas. For example, The South, contains the

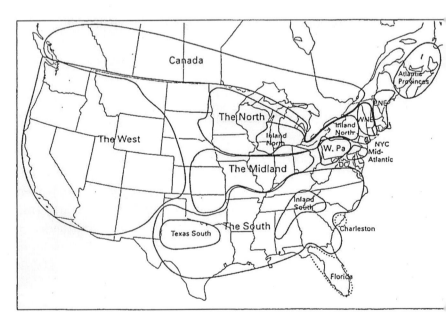

Map 6.1 Dialect areas of the United States
(from Labov, W., Ash, S., Boberg, C. (2006); reprinted in Fasold, R. & Connor-Linton J. (eds.). *An introduction to language and linguistics* (p. 322). Cambridge University Press.)

smaller dialect area, Inland South, which differs from general Southern speech because the so-called "southern vowel shift" is more prevalent. One feature of the southern shift is that low back vowels are fronted and acquire a glide toward the back. Thus, *lost*, *dog*, and *thought* are pronounced, respectively, [læwst], [dæwg], and [ðæwt]. The isoglosses in Map 6.1 are determined mostly on the basis of how speakers in the different regions pronounce vowels. For example, Southern speech can be distinguished from the speech of other regions because the diphthong /ay/, as in *fried* and *Carolina*, contains no glide, or a very short glide, so that these words can sound like [fræd] and [kerəlænə]. There are also, of course, many distinctive features of Southern speech that are not phonological, such as the use of the second person plural pronoun *y'all*, and the use of double model constructions, which allow two modal verbs to be strung together, as in, "I may can mow the lawn today" (which is less likely to happen than "I may mow the lawn today").

Dialect areas can also be distinguished by the way that vowels are shifting their positions of articulation, moving around in the vowel space represented in Table 2.3. English vowels have been doing this for a long time, at least since what is known as the *Great Vowel Shift*. Shakespeare pronounced *east* / eyst/ and *meat* /meyt/, but even as he was writing, some speakers in England were producing the vowel in these words higher in the mouth, so that the pronunciations were changing to present-day /iyst/ and /miyt/. For reasons that are not entirely clear, English vowels are still changing positions in many dialects, as in the example from the southern shift, just mentioned. Another example of vowel shift is in the Western dialect, where young, urban Westerners (especially in California) are fronting their tense, back vowels, so that *so* can be pronounced /səw/, and *dude* can be pronounced /dəwd/.

6.3.2 Social Dialects

People of different social classes within the various regions also speak differently, and so there are social as well as regional dialects. The study of **social dialects** has been the main enterprise of sociolinguistics for the past half century, and it involves the study of **sociolinguistic variables**. A sociolinguistic variable is a feature of language that can be produced in more than one way. For example, words ending in *–ing*, like *darling* and *running*, have a formal and an informal pronunciation, represented in writing as in *running* and *runnin'*, and pronounced /rəniyŋ/ and /rənin/. This alternation is found in all English dialects, and *–in'* is always considered less prestigious than *–ing*. Sociolinguists have found that the *–ing/ –in'* variable shows **class stratification;** that is, working-class speakers use *–in'* more frequently than middle-class speakers, who use it more frequently than upper-class speakers.

Table 6.1 *Percentage of postvocalic [r] in casual speech among New Yorkers (based on Labov 1972a:114)*

Class	Percent postvocalic [r]
Upper middle	18
Working	6
Lower	2

Another example of a sociolinguistic variable that shows class stratification is the pronunciation of /r/ in New York City. New York City English is an "[r]-less" dialect, which allows New Yorkers to delete [r] after a vowel, pronouncing "fourth floor" [foəð floə], but they also sometimes say [forð floər]. The difference between social dialects within the New York City speech community is that middle-class speakers pronounce postvocalic [r] more often than working-class speakers. Labov (1972a) investigated how often the different social classes produced postvocalic [r] in casual conversation and found the results shown in Table 6.1.[1]

Table 6.1 shows that all of the social classes show variation in [r] pronunciation, but that the variation is patterned: each class produces [r] more frequently than the class(es) below it. We will look more closely at New York City [r] deletion later in the chapter.

Syntactic variables can also show class stratification. For example, double negatives, such as, "We've never had no trouble," are more likely to be found in the speech of working-class speakers. Dialects also have lexical differences, and sometimes these are absolute so that people from one region or class cannot understand words from another region or class. If you don't live in the rural American South, you may not understand the difference between Huck Finn's observation, "yonder were the banks and the islands", and the standard American version "over there were the banks and the islands" ("Yonder" is farther away than "over there"). If you travel in the rural South, don't expect dinner at seven o'clock; that meal is "supper." Expect dinner around one o'clock (and expect a lot more food than you would get for "lunch" in the North).

6.3.3 Representing Dialect in Literature

The fact that speech differs according to region and social class allows writers to suggest a character's background by using appropriate vocabulary and syntax and also by altering standard spelling to show how the character sounds, as in this passage from the novel *McBee's Station* by Elise

Sanguinetti. In the passage Mrs. McBee, an upper-class Southerner, is visiting the house of Mrs. Flemming, a working-class Southerner who helps Mrs. McBee in her business. People are gathering at the house because Mrs. Flemming has just been arrested for killing her husband with an axe. Mrs. McBee has brought a pie, which she gives to a woman who is obviously a member of the family but whom she has not met before.

"I'm Mrs. McBee, from across the way," said Mrs. McBee in hushed tones. "Is there anything I can do to help here?"

For the first time she saw that the woman's eyes, similar in color to Mrs. Flemming's but larger, were red with strain. She tried to smile. "Sister's told me a heap about you."

"You're Mrs. Flemming's sister then?"

"Yes'm." She looked about the kitchen. "Just tryin to see what all needs to be done."

"I presume the rest of the family has been called, relatives."

"Yes'm. Lojean done that this morning."

"Lojean. I haven't seen her anywhere."

"No,'m. She and Buster, Junior done took the kid and went to the funeral home to make arrange-mints." The woman's eyes gazed sorrowfully at Mrs. McBee and she shook her head.

Mrs. McBee patted her arm. "I know Mrs. Flemming is relieved to have *you* here."

The woman instantly looked away. "I thank I'm just in a spell, aint able to take none of it in yetta while. I'm not well neither. Just got outta the hospital two weeks ago from a goiter operation."

"Oh dear," sympathized Mrs. McBee. "Well, I think we're all just dazed."

Several features of Mrs. McBee's speech signal her social status. For example, the words "presume," "relieved," and "dazed" suggest that Mrs. McBee is educated. Mrs. Flemming's sister, on the other hand, uses more colloquial words like "heap" and "spell." The most noticeable difference in the two women's speech is the contrast in grammatical forms. Mrs. McBee speaks standard Southern English while Mrs. Flemming's sister speaks working-class Southern English. Nonstandard features in her speech include: "ain't," "what all," and double negatives ("I'm not well, neither"). A particularly interesting feature of this variety is *completive done*, as in "Junior done took the kid and went to the funeral home. . . ." Completive done signifies that an action is final. If she had said, "Junior took the kid and went to the funeral home," we might expect that they would come back soon, but "Junior done took the kid" means they will be at the funeral home

181

for the foreseeable future (but see the further discussion of *done* in the section on African American English).

The women's pronunciation also distinguishes their speech. Mrs. McBee's speech is spelled using standard conventions, but these conventions are broken to convey the sound of the sister's speech, as in "Yetta while," "outta," and "arrange-mints" (a ten-dollar word that may not be familiar to her). Another possible indication of class difference is that the sister addresses Mrs. McBee as "Mam" (shortened in "yes'm" and "no'm"), but Mrs. McBee does not return the favor although this asymmetry may be due to a difference in age. It is also interesting that the author echoes the features of the two women's speech in the quotative verbs and their modifying adverbials as in, " 'Oh dear,' sympathized Mrs. McBee," and "said Mrs. McBee in hushed tones." *Sympathized* and *hushed tones* are words that Mrs. McBee herself might have used rather than the narrator.

6.3.4 Nonstandard Features

Table 6.2 contains a list of nonstandard English features that can be found in literary representations of working-class and rural American speech.

Of course, these features can be found in the speech of real people as well as in the speech of fictional characters, as seen in this narrative recorded by the sociolinguist Crawford Feagin from Flora P., a 74-year-old, rural white woman living in Anniston, Alabama (superscript numbers refer to categories in Table 6.2).

> **An'**[1] another time, honey, **I 'uz**[2] in a – I' uz in a – in a **shore**[3] **'nuff**[4] cyclone, I lived out here at the Alston place out here at Weaver. An uh my sister and my mother an' 'em were down in the field **hoein'**[5] cotton for Mr. Herbert Sims. An' **lemme**[1] see... I don't know – can't remember what year it was.
>
> But anyhow **they'd**[2] been over there in Herbert Sims' cotton patch. **I'ad**[2] seen my mother and them comin' in, an' – I kept **a-watchin'**.[6] It **come**[7] from this direction. An', honey, when it ... was about as far as from here to **that there**[8] house down yonder from our house, and I 'uz settin' there on the back porch a-churnin'. An' I kept a-settin' there, and I said, "well, Lord, if it hits me and kills me, I'll jus" – You intend for it to. (From Feagin, 1979, pp. 113–114)

A feature of nonstandard dialects that was mentioned earlier is that they often contain both standard and nonstandard forms, and that different social classes mark their speech by the percentages at which the different forms are used. This kind of variability can bee seen in Flora's speech. For

Table 6.2 *Nonstandard dialect features found in literary texts. Superscript numbers refer to selected examples in Flora P.'s story (see text)*

Category	Standard	Nonstandard
Phonology		
[5]Pronunciation of *–ing*	"*-ing*"	"in'"
[3]Vowel sounds	No dialect pronunciation marked in spelling	Dialect marked in spelling
[2]Contracted pronunciation of verb form followed by infinitive **or** of aux verb following pronoun	Clear distinction between the two verbs, or slight reduction of juncture as with contractions	Moderate to extreme reduction of juncture, e.g., "gonna", "I'ma", **or** "they'd," "I'ad," "I'uz"
[4]Loss of initial unstressed syllable or vowel sound	Retention of first syllable, e.g., *arithemetic, remember, about, and*	Suppression of first syllable, e.g., *'rithmetic, 'member, 'bout, 'nd*
[1]Deletion of final consonant	*and, next, called*	*an', nex', call'*
Deletion of [r] following a vowel	more, floor, father	mo', flo', fatha
Insertion of [r] following a vowel	Cuba, Washington, among,	Cuber, Warshington, ermong
Verb Forms		
[7]Past tense of irregular verbs	*swim – swam, know – knew, see – saw, take – took*	*swim – swimmed, know – knowed, see – seen, take – taken or taked*
Variation in irregular form of present perfect or past perfect tenses	I've *seen* it; I had *seen* it.	I've *saw* it; I had *saw* it.
[6] A- pre-fixing of verb	He was *running* and *jumping*	He was *a-running* (or *a-runnin'*) and *a-jumping* (or *a-jumpin'*)
The word *ain't*	Infrequent occurrence	Frequent occurence
Nouns and Pronouns		
Plural forms of nouns	*desks, children*	*desses, chirren* or *chirrens*
Relative pronouns	A man *who* doesn't run around is a good catch.	A man *what* don't run around is a good catch.
	This is a word *whose meaning I don't know.*	This is a word *that I don't know what it means.*
	I bought one of Fred's houses, *which everyone knows are built right.*	I bought one of Fred's houses, *which everyone knows he builds them right.*
[8]Demonstrative pronouns	*this thing, those things*	*this here thing, that there thing, them things*
Reflexive pronouns	He washed *himself;* they washed *themselves*	He washed *hisself;* they washed *theirselves*
	He gave the tickets to my friend and *me.*	He gave the ticktets to my friend and *myself.*

Table 6.2 (*cont.*)

Category	Standard	Nonstandard
Possessive pronouns	It's *yours, mine, his.*	It's *yourn, mines, hisn.*
Plural of *you*	*you* as plural form	Yinze, y'uns, yourns, youse, you-all, y'all, you lot
Syntax		
Multiple negatives	He *never* cries; he doesn't *ever* cry.	He don't *never* cry.
Fronting of negative auxiliaries	Nobody has said *anything;* nobody knows *anything.*	Ain't nobody said nothing; *don't* nobody know nothing.
Auxiliary inversion in indirect questions	I wonder if he finished the job.	I wonder *did* he finish the job.
Other Features		
Forms of address	Yes, *madam*; No, *madam*	*Yes'm; No'm*; Yes, *sorr*; No, *sorr*
Rough talk	Infrequent use of derogatory terms	Profanity, obscenity, name calling
Polite terms	thank you, excuse me	thankye', 'scuseme
Direct terms	Softened expressions modal constructions, - e.g., *darn, passed away, Would you shut the door?*	e.g., *damn, upped an' died, Shet the door!*

example, she uses the word *and* nine times, deleting the final [d] six times. So, she deletes final [d] from *and* 66 percent of the time. We would expect that an urban, upper-class woman would also use the deleted form, but that she would use it less frequently than Flora. Another example of variation in Flora's speech involves the forms *verb + ing* and *a-verb+ ing*, as in *I 'uz settin'* and *I 'uz a-settin'*. These forms, unlike the case of *and – an'*, have slightly different meanings. *A-verb + ing* emphasizes the duration of an action more than *verb + ing*. Notice how Flora uses the older *a+verb+ing*, which is no longer available to speakers of standard English, to add drama to her story. As the cyclone approaches, she sits *a-churnin'* and keeps *a-settin'*, thus drawing out the waiting time and the suspense.

Returning to nonstandard speech in literature, Mark Twain tried to accurately represent Missouri dialects in *The Adventures of Huckleberry Finn*. In a note to the reader he claims,

> In this book a number of dialects are used, to wit: the Missouri Negro dialect, the extremist form of the backwoods South-Western dialect,

the ordinary "Pike-County" dialect; and four modified varieties of this last. The shadings have not been done in a haphazard fashion, or by guess-work but pains-takingly, and with the trustworthy guidance and support of personal familiarity with these several forms of speech. I make this explanation for the reason that without it many readers would suppose that all these characters were trying to talk alike and not succeeding.

The subtle differences in Twain's characters' speech can be seen in the following passage from Chapter 19 "The Duke and the Dauphin Come On Board." This episode takes place on Huck and Jim's raft after they have picked up two passengers, who are fleeing from an angry crowd. The passengers are confidence men, who have just run their scams in nearby villages. The older, bald-headed man was running a temperance revival, but was caught drinking. The younger man did a little of everything: selling patent medicines, putting on tent revivals, acting scenes from dramas, mesmerism, and phrenology. Once safely aboard the raft, both men begin another scam, which emerges in the following dialogue. The younger man speaks first.

"Alas!"

"What're you alassin' about?" says the baldhead.

"To think I should have lived to be leading such a life, and be degraded down into such company." And he begun to wipe the corner of his eye with a rag.

"Dern your skin, ain't the company good enough for you?" says the baldhead, pretty pert and uppish.

"Yes, it *is* good enough for me; it's as good as I deserve; for who fetched me so low, when I was so high? *I* did myself. I don't blame *you*, gentlemen – far from it. I don't blame anybody. I deserve it all. Let the cold world do its worst, one thing I know – there's a grave somewhere for me. The world may go on just as it's always done, and take everything from me – loved ones, property, everything – but it can't take that. Some day I'll lie down in it and forget it all, and my poor broken heart will be at rest." He went on a-wiping.

"Drot your pore broken heart," says the baldhead; "what are you heaving your pore broken heart at us f'r? *We* haint done nothing."

"No, I know you haven't. I ain't blaming you, gentlemen. I brought myself down – yes, I did it myself. It's right I should suffer – perfectly right – I don't make any moan."

"Brought you down from whar? Whar was you brought down from?"

"Ah, you would not believe me, the world never believes – let it pass – 'tis no matter. The secret of my birth –"

"The secret of your birth? Do you mean to say –"

"Gentlemen," says the young man, very solemn, "I will reveal it to you, for I feel I may have confidence in you. By rights I am a duke!"

Jim's eyes bugged out when he heard that; and I reckon mine did, too. Then the baldhead says, "No! You can't mean it?"

"Yes, my great-grandfather, eldest son of the Duke of Bridgewater, fled to this country about the end of the last century, to breathe the pure air of freedom, married here, and died, leaving a son, his own father dying about the same time. The second son of the late duke seized the title and estates – the infant real duke was ignored. I am the lineal descendant of that infant – I am the rightful Duke of Bridgewater; and here am I, forlorn, torn from my high estate, hunted of men, despised by the cold world, ragged, worn, heart-broken, and degraded to the companionship of felons on a raft!"

Not to be outdone, the older man then confesses the secret of his own birth.

"Looky here, Bilgewater," he says, "I'm nation sorry for you, but you ain't the only person that's had troubles like that."

"No?"

"No, you ain't. You ain't the only person that's been snaked down wrongfully out'n a high place."

"Alas!"

"No, you ain't the only person that's had a secret of his birth." And by jings, *he* begins to cry.

"Hold! What do you mean?"

"Bilgewater, kin I trust you?" says the old man, still sort of sobbing.

"To the bitter death!" He took the old man by the hand and squeezed it, and says, "The secret of your being: speak!"

"Bildgewater, I am the late Dauphin!"

You bet you Jim and me stared, this time. Then the duke says:

"You are what?"

"Yes, my friend, it is too true – your eyes is lookin' at this very moment on the pore disappeared Dauphin, Looy the Seventeen, son of Looy the Sixteen and Marry Antonette."

"You! At your age! No! You mean you're the late Charlemagne; you must be six or seven hundred years old, at the very least."

"Trouble has done it, Bilgewater, trouble has done it, trouble has brung these gray hairs and this premature baltitude. Yes, gentlemen, you see before you in blue jeans and misery, the wanderin' exiled, trampled on and sufferin' rightful King of France."

In this passage Twain sparingly uses the technique of **eye dialect,** in which a word is misspelled even though it does not change the word's pronunciation. Louis is spelled "Looy" even though both spellings are pronounced /luwiy/. Earlier in the book Huck tells us of unsuccessful attempts to "sivilize" him. "Sivilize", of course, is pronounced the same way as "civilize." Eye dialect can be thought of as a way that a character might spell the word, suggesting a low level of education.

The difference in the Duke's and Dauphin's education is indicated by many features of their speech. In telling the story of his birth the Duke uses learned words and phrases like *alas*, *reveal*, and *by rights*. But when the Dauphin tries to use a similar vocabulary he can't pull it off, coming up with *snaked down*, *disappeared* (meaning lost), and *baltitude*. Twain presents a number of specific contrasts in the men's speech. When the Dauphin asks, "Ain't the company good enough for you?" the Duke replies, "Yes, it *is* good enough for me" (emphasis in the original). When the Duke refers to his "poor (/pur/) broken heart," the Dauphin replies, "Drat your pore (/powr/) broken heart." In his Shakespearian mode, the Duke often uses the formal pronunciation of –ing words, such as "everything" /evəriθiyŋ/, and "dying"/[dayiyŋ]. But the Dauphin cannot manage a single formal form, saying "alassin'," "lookin'", and "wanderin'". The use of nonstandard spelling to represent nonstandard language varieties has been criticized. Kentucky writer Nikole Brown (2003) notes that one book of advice for fiction writers warns against creating "provincial curiosities," and she worries that "... political correctness [has] whitewashed the written word to make it acceptable and understandable to all" (p. 48). Brown denies that accurate representation of vernacular speech is harmful and maintains that Mark Twain would have written the same way even if he knew that some critics would dismiss his portrayal of Huck and Jim as derogatory.

6.3.5 African American English

A particularly interesting variety of English is the one spoken by many (but not all) African Americans throughout the United States. **African American English** (AAE) is remarkably consistent among speakers living in widespread American cities from Philadelphia to Los Angeles. This similarity may be partly due to the relatively recent migration of African Americans from the South to these cities, and it is undoubtedly due to social segregation. AAE shares many features with Southern Vernacular English. In fact, a description of AAE would look very much like the speech of Mrs. Flemming's sister, quoted above. AAE also shares many of the nonstandard features in Table 6.2 though there are some differences in usage, which are listed below.

1. White Southern Vernacular (WSV) uses completive *done* with the auxiliary verb *have*: "She's done gone to bed" (so don't try to get her up).

However, AAE does not require *have*: "She done gone to bed." Notice that in the passage from *McBee's Station* Mrs. Flemming's sister broke this rule when she said, "Junior done took the kid." Sanguinetti appears to have gotten this aspect of WSV wrong.

2. WSV very rarely omits *is* (though it is often contracted). Informants in Feagin's (1989) study of Anniston, Alabama speech omitted *is* only 6.8% of the time, while informants in Labov's (1966) study of Black teenagers in Harlem omitted it 42 percent of the time. Both white and black dialects omit *are* much more often. The Anniston rural working class speakers omitted *are* 56 percent of the time, and higher percentages are found among AAE speakers. Examples of these forms include:

> She fast in everything she do.
> That a bear book.
> They coming over to my home.

3. The best known syntactic feature unique to AAE is **invariant *be***, so called because it is usually not conjugated (although occasionally forms like "It bees that way" are heard). For example, a Detroit teenager said, "My father, he work at Ford. He be tired. So he can't never help us with our homework." "He be tired" means that the father is usually tired. If the speaker had wished to say that her father was tired now, she could have said, "He is tired," "He's tired," or "He tired." Invariant *be* can also be used with a present participle to indicate habitual action.

> **AAE**　　　　　　　　They be playing basket ball everyday.
> **STANDARD ENGLISH**　They play basketball everyday.

This form contrasts with:

> **AAE**　　　　　　　　They playing basketball right now.
> **STANDARD ENGLISH**　They're playing basketball right now.

In questions, invariant *be* can be combined with the auxiliary verb *do*:

> **AAE**　　　　　　　　Do they be playing everyday?
> **STANDARD ENGLISH**　Do they play everyday?

Besides these syntactic and morphological features, AAE also has distinctive phonological features though many of these are shared by other nonstandard dialects. These features include:

1. Initial /ð/ pronounced as [d], as in *them* → [dem] and *the* → [də]

2. Final /θ/ pronounced as [f], as in *bath* → [bæf] and *mouth* → [mawf]

3. Deletion of postvocalic /r/, as in *church* → [čəč] and *more* → [mow]

4. Deletion of middle and final /l/, as in help → [hep] and will → [wi]

6.3.6 African American English in Literature

Some of the features just mentioned, as well as some of those in Table 6.2, can be found in the passage below from the short story "Wife of His Youth" by Charles Chesnutt, which was published in the *Atlantic Monthly* magazine in 1900. Chesnutt was a Black writer who daringly wrote about interracial relationships in the decades before and after the turn of the twentieth century. Born in Cleveland, Ohio in 1858, he became a school teacher and principal. He found some early success as a writer of short stories published by New York City magazines and publishing houses, but, perhaps in part because of the controversial nature of his work, he was unable to support himself as a writer. The true literary value of Chesnutt's work has only been recognized in more recent times.

The protagonist of "The Wife of His Youth" is Mr. Ryder, an educated and well-off African American who belongs to a literary club called the "Blue Veins." The narrator explains the name of the club as follows: "By accident, combined perhaps with some natural affinity, the society consisted of individuals who were, generally speaking, more white than black. Some envious outsider made the suggestion that no one was eligible for membership who was not white enough to show blue veins." In the passage below, Mr. Ryder is approached by Lisa Jane, a small woman "with very bright and restless eyes" who is obviously poor and whose skin color is "very black." The conversation below shows the contrast between Mr. Ryder's standard speech and Lisa Jane's vernacular AAE.

> "Good-afternoon, madam," he said.
>
> "Good-evenin', suh," she answered, ducking suddenly with a quaint curtsy. Her voice was shrill and piping, but softened somewhat by age. "Is dis yere whar Mistuh Ryday lib, suh?" she asked, looking around her doubtfully, and glancing into the open windows, through which some of the preparations for the evening were visible.
>
> "Yes," he replied, with an air of kindly patronage, unconsciously flattered by her manner, "I am Mr. Ryder. Did you want to see me?"
>
> "Yay, suh, ef I ain't 'sturbin' of you too much."
>
> "Not at all. Have a seat over here behind the vine, where it is cool. What can I do for you?"
>
> "Scuse me, suh," she continued, when she had sat down on the edge of a chair. "'scuse me, suh, I's lookin' for my husban'. I heerd you wuz a big man an' had libbed heah a long time, an' I 'lowed you wouldn't

min' ef I'd come roun' an ax you ef you'd ever heerd of a merlatter man by de name er Sam Taylor 'quiririn' de chu'ches ermongs' de people fer his wife Lisa Jane?"

Mr. Ryder seemed to think for a moment.

"There used to be many such cases right after the war," he said, "but it has been so long that I have forgotten them. There are very few now. But tell me your story, and it may refresh my memory."

There are several interesting features in Lisa Jane's speech. Notice first of all that Chesnutt accurately represents the fact that in real speech nonstandard features usually alternate with their standard counterparts. Although -in' and [d] for initial [ð] do not vary, other features do. For example, final [d] is deleted from a consonant cluster in *min'* and *roun'* but not in *heerd*. Also notice that Lisa Jane says "ax" instead of "ask." This pronunciation is still a common feature of AAE. Finally, consider Lisa Jane's use of *I'se* (lookin' for my husban') instead of *I'm*, which is a case of nonstandard subject-verb agreement. Wolfram and Fasold (1974) note that AAE *is* is variable across different African-American communities. "For rural Southern communities, it may be the case that *is* is the only present form of *to be* and the grammar of these dialects calls for its use regardless of person and number" (p. 157). Lisa Jane would, of course, probably come from a rural Southern community.

6.4 British English

Hughes and Trudgill (1996) divide Britain and Ireland into five large linguistic areas, noting that "the drawing of regional linguistic boundaries is a notoriously difficult and somewhat arbitrary task" (p. 64). These areas are: the south of England; the north of England; Wales, the south of Ireland; and Scotland and the north of Ireland, as shown in Map 6.2. Notice that, as in Map 6.1, each of the five divisions contains smaller dialect areas. Although Maps 6.1 and 6.2 do not show this, British dialects are more numerous than American dialects. This is because the settlement of the American continent has been relatively recent, and there has been less time for the speech in different areas to evolve differently. In Britain, as in Europe as a whole, dialect boundaries are more difficult to draw than in the United States because the dialects can merge more seamlessly into one another. For example, as one moves eastward from London to Norfolk, one encounters small differences in the speech of each town rather than sharp boundaries. On the other hand, in the United States as one moves north from Louisville, Kentucky across the Ohio River, there is a rather sharp change from Southern to Midland speech.

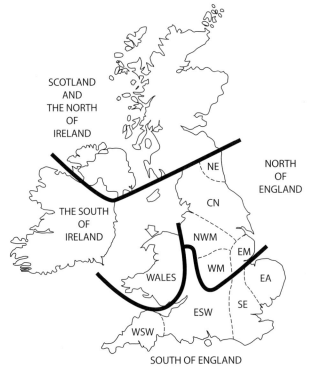

NE = Northeast   CN = Central North
NWM = Northwest Midlands   EM = East Midlands
WM = West Midlands   WSW = Western Southwest
ESW = Eastern Southwest   SE = Southeast
EA = East Anglia

Map 6.2 Dialect areas of Britain

In the remainder of this chapter we will look at one of Britain's regional dialects and at how it has been represented in literature.

6.4.1 East Anglian English

Charles Dickens represented the speech of East Anglia on England's southeastern coast in the novel *David Copperfield*. As in all regional dialects, East Anglian English is marked by a number of features that vary according to a speaker's social class. Two of these features are the deletion of initial [h], so that *Harry* can be pronounced [æriy], and the –*ing/ –in'* alternation discussed earlier. Table 6.3 shows the frequency at which five social classes in Norwich, the capital of East Anglia, "drop" their h's and g's.

Table 6.3 *Percentage of non-prestige forms for two variables in Norwich speech*

	iyŋ → in	h → Ø
Middle middle class	31	6
Lower middle class	42	14
Upper working class	87	40
Middle working class	95	59
Lower working class	100	61

Based on Trudgill (1995, p. 36)

As the table shows, with one exception, all of the classes use both the prestige and the nonprestige forms of both variables and each social class produces more of the prestige forms than the class(es) below it. The table also suggests that dropping an *h* is more stigmatized than *–in'* because speakers in all classes use the former less often than the latter.

In *David Copperfield*, the East Anglian dialect is represented in the speech of members of the Peggotty family. Clara Peggotty (just called "Peggotty" in the novel) was the housekeeper for David's father and mother and, after their deaths, becomes David's life-long friend. An important subplot in the novel involves Clara's brother Daniel Peggotty, a fisherman. Daniel adopts his nephew Ham Peggotty and Ham's cousin Little Emily after they are orphaned. Raised together, the two cousins fall in love and seemed destined for marriage until Emily meets David's wealthy childhood friend Steerforth, who seduces Emily and takes her on a journey through Europe. Grown tired of her, Steerforth leaves Emily in Venice in the company of his abhorrent servant Littimer, suggesting that they marry. Emily disappears and Daniel moves to London in order to search for Emily, hoping that she will turn up there and that they can be re-united. At David's suggestion, David and Daniel try to find Emily's former acquaintance Martha, who may know where Emily is. Like Emily, Martha is a fallen woman. The men locate Martha and follow her to the Thames River, where she is about to drown herself. They save Martha and give her a reason to live: finding Emily. In a passage demonstrating his good character, Daniel expresses regret that he formerly looked down on Martha, remarking, "The time was, Mas'r Davy ... when I thowt this girl, Martha, a'most like the dirt underneath my Em'ly's feet. God forgive me, theere's a difference now!" (Ch. 43, p. 546; all citations refer to The Project Gutenberg EBook of *David Copperfield*; www.gutenberg.org/cache/epub/766/pg766.txt).

The East Anglia dialect is most faithfully represented in the novel in the speech of Daniel and Ham. Here is an example of Daniel's speech in a dialogue with David (with explanations in brackets). They are concerned about Ham because he has been despondent after being deserted by Emily. David speaks first.

> "Do you recollect," said I, "a certain wild way in which he looked out to sea and spoke about 'the end of it'?"
>
> "Sure I do," he said.
>
> "What do you suppose he meant?"
>
> "Mas'r Davy," he replied, "I've put the question to myself a mort [great number] o' times, and never found no answer. And theer's one curious thing – that though he is so pleasant, I wouldn't fare to feel comfortable to try and get his mind upon't. He never said a wured to me as warn't as dootiful as dootiful could be, and it ain't likely as he'd begin to speak any other ways now, but it's far from being fleet water [clear] in his mind where them thowts lay. It's deep, sir, and I can't see down."
>
> "You are right," said I, "and that has made me anxious."
>
> "And me too, Mas'r Davy," he rejoined, "Even more so, I do assure you, than his *venturesome* ways, though both belongs to the alteration in him. I doen't know as he'd do violence under any circumstances, but I hope as them two [i.e., Ham and Steerforth] may be kep assunders (Ch. 46, p. 546).

In examining Daniel's speech we must take into account the fact that *David Copperfield* was published in 1850, and so the book represents archaic varieties of English. Nevertheless, Poussa (2000:31) maintains that the major features of Dickens's East Anglian dialect can still be heard.

Some of the features of American nonstandard speech shown in Table 6.2 can also be seen in Daniel's speech. These include double negatives ("and **never** found **no** answer"), demonstrative pronouns ("I hope as **them two** may be kep asunders"), and the deletion of final consonants from a consonant cluster ("**kep** assunders.) Daniel also uses *ain't*, which could still be heard in cultivated nineteenth-century speech but is not used by David and other middle- and upper-class characters in the novel. One nonstandard British feature of Daniel's speech is not listed in Table 6.2 because it has become standard in American English. This is the so-called "yod dropping" (yod is the character in the Hebrew alphabet that corresponds to /y/), where /y/ is dropped after consonants so that *news* is pronounced /nuwz/ rather than /nyuwz/ as in RP. Thus, *dutiful* (/dyuwtəfəl/ in RP) is spelled "dootiful."

An archaic feature in Daniel's speech is the use of *as* as a relative pronoun and subordinating conjunction – the equivalent of modern English *that*. The relative pronoun use can be seen in: "He never said a wored to me **as** weren't as dootiful as dootiful could be," and the subordinating conjunction use can be seen in: "but I hope **as** them two may be kep asunders." Notice that in Daniel's speech subordinating conjunction *as* alternates with subordinating conjunction *that* ("And theer's one curious thing – **that** ... I wouldn't fare to feel comfortable to try to get his mind upon't"). Such alternation is to be expected in a changing grammatical feature, especially in the speech of a character who has contacts in both the village and the city.

6.4.2 Dialect and Social Evaluation

Unlike the conversation between Huck, the Duke, and the Dauphin, where all the characters use vernacular speech, the conversation between David and Daniel contrasts standard and nonstandard varieties. In fact, chapter 46 of *David Copperfield* presents an extreme contrast between the informal, nonstandard speech of Daniel and Ham (see exercise 4) and the formal, hypercorrect speech of the Steerforth household. Earlier in the chapter, Mrs. Steerforth summons David to her home and informs him that she wishes to locate Emily in order to buy her off so that her son "may be saved from again falling into the snares of a designing enemy" (p. 542) (to this David replies that Emily would rather die than accept a cup of water from Steerforth). David is also addressed by Mrs. Steerforth's snobbish and "fierce" companion Miss Dartle, who despises Emily ("this devil whom you make an angel of", p. 542), and her cruelty is expressed in learned, standard language, which even contains a biblical reference:

> [Emily] may be alive ... if she is, you will desire to have a pearl of such price found and taken care of. We desire that, too, that [Steerforth] may not by any chance be made her prey again. So far, we are united in one interest, and that is why I, who would do her any mischief that so coarse a wretch is capable of feeling, have sent for you to hear what you have heard" (p. 542).

The RP of the Steerforths and Miss Dartle contrasts sharply with the East Anglican dialect of the Peggottys, and the morality of these two households contrasts even more sharply, but perhaps not in the way that nineteenth-century readers would expect. The Steerforths are villainous and selfish while the Peggottys are good-hearted and selfless. David, the young observer, learns a lesson about social stereotypes from these contrasts, and in Dickens's later novel *Great Expectations*, another young observer, the narrator Pip, learns a similar lesson about judging people by the way they speak.

Yet, to make his point Dickens may have stacked the deck. Notice that the excerpt from Daniel's speech (as well as the excerpt from Ham's speech quoted in exercise 4), does not contain the two sociolinguistic variables in Table 6.3, namely *h*- and *g*- dropping. Daniel pronounces [h] in *he*, *his*, and *him*, and says "*thing* and *being*," not "*thin'* and *bein'*." In fact, there is no variation in either Daniel's or Ham's speech in regard to these features throughout the book. Perhaps, then, Dickens' purpose was not so much to present an accurate picture of nonstandard speech (as was the case with Twain) but rather to portray the speakers of the East Anglian dialect in a favorable light. In order to achieve this, he accurately represented the distinctive *regional* features, but did not accurately represent all of the *social* features associated with working-class speech. As we have noted, Daniel's speech does contain many working-class features, such as double negation and final consonant deletion, but *h*- and *g*- dropping are particularly stigmatized, and one of the book's villains, the "'umble servant" Uriah Heep, is characterized by always dropping initial [h] from the word *humble*. Furthermore, another Norwich resident, the lowly cart driver Barkis, drops the *g* in his famous proposal to Clara, "Barkis is willin'." Dickens may have wished to spare his more noble characters the social evaluation that Victorian readers associated particularly with initial *h* and final *g*.

6.5 Identity and Voice

So far, we have mostly considered the differences in the speech of characters who came from different regional, class, and racial backgrounds. But, language varies not only along these dimensions but also along the dimensions of age, gender, and education. In other words, characters from the same region, race, and social class can also show systematic differences in their speech, and authors can exploit these differences to suggest a character's identity.

6.5.1 Age and Social Class

Dorothy Parker portrays characters of a particular age and social class in her short story "The Standard of Living," published in 1952. The situation in the excerpt below is similar to that of the Duke and the Dauphin aboard Huck and Jim's raft, in which characters represent themselves as belonging to a higher social class, and some of the humor in both pieces involves how they give themselves away.

> Together they went over to the shop window and stood pressed against it. It contained but one object – a double row of great, even pearls clasped by a deep emerald around a little pink velvet throat.

"What do you suppose they cost?" Annabel said.

"Gee, I wouldn't even know," Midge said.

The devil nudged Annabel in the ribs. "Dare you to go in and price them," she said.

"Like fun!" Midge said.

"Dare you," Annabel said . . .

. . .

"Is there something – ?" the clerk said.

"Oh we're just looking," Annabel said. It was as if she flung the words down from a dais.

The clerk bowed.

"My friend and myself merely happened to be passing," Midge said, and stopped, seeming to listen to the phrase. "My friend and myself," she went on, "merely happened to be wondering how much are these pearls you've got in your window."

"Ah, yes," the clerk said. "The double rope. That is two hundred and fifty thousand dollars, Madam."

The clerk bowed. "An exceptionally beautiful necklace," he said. "Would you care to look at it?"

"No, thank you," Annabel said.

"My friend and myself merely happened to be passing," Midge said.

In this excerpt the girls' names and voices identify them as young though some of the identifying features of their speech are now archaic. The expression "like fun" has passed from general usage, and "gee" sounds dated. The use of "like," on the other hand, has expanded its semantic range. Annabel and Midge use it to mean "approximately," modifying a certain quantity (of dollars). Now "like" means "approximately" in a looser sense and can modify things that cannot actually be counted, as in:

> Last night Harvey found, like, this giant cockroach in the bathtub, and I'm all like, "Yuck, I don't want to see it."

The first use of *like* is adverbial, and it suggests that the speaker doesn't want to be held accountable for accurately naming the species of bug. The second use of *like* is quotative, that is, it is used like "said," and it suggests that the speaker doesn't remember the exact words she spoke. These uses of *like* imply an ironic distance from the events, suggesting that they weren't important enough to require accuracy. In both Parker's day and our own, the use of "like" is associated with young people.

The girls' informal speech when they are talking outside the shop contrasts with that of the clerk, who bows, calls Midge "madam," uses formal diction, and employs the past modal tense: "Would you care to look at it?" This tense is more polite than the present tense equivalent: "Do you care to look at it?" In an attempt to match the clerk's formality, Midge replies, "My friend and myself merely happened to be passing," a sentence with which she is so pleased that she repeats it at the end of the conversation. However, Midge misses the mark: her sentence is overly formal, with its use of "passing" and "merely." In addition, it is ungrammatical because it uses "myself" instead of the grammatically correct "I." English has recently undergone a change regarding which forms to use in second position when pronouns are conjoined. Nowadays one often hears sentences like, "The seats were reserved for John and I," where the prescriptively correct usage is "for John and me" (*me* is the object of the preposition *for*, so it takes the objective case). The confusion about whether to use "I" or "me" in a phrase of conjoined pronouns has spread to confusion about whether to use the reflexive pronoun "myself" in these phrases, which, though wrong, somehow sounds even more formal. Midge's confusion on this point betrays her real class status.

6.5.2 Class Stratification and Style Shifting

Midge's speech is an example of **hypercorrection**, which occurs when speakers attempt to use the language variety of a higher social class but get it wrong. Labov (1972a) found a fascinating example of hypercorrection in the pronunciation of New Yorkers. As mentioned in Section 6.2.2, New York City English is an "r-less" dialect, in which [r] can be deleted after a vowel, so that *fourth floor* can be pronounced [foəθ floə]. Labov studied this feature by asking New Yorkers from four social classes to speak in five different situations. The results of his study are shown in Figure 6.1.

The horizontal axis in the figure shows the five different speaking situations, which elicited five different speaking styles, and the vertical axis shows the percentage of [r] pronunciation. The style that contains the highest percentage of [r], and thus sounds the most formal, is the minimal pairs style. To elicit this style, Labov asked speakers to read a list of minimal pairs, which, as noted in Chapter 2, are words that are pronounced exactly the same except for one sound. In this case the only difference was that one word contained a post-vocalic [r] and the other did not, such as *guard-god*, both of which can be pronounced [goəd] in New York City English. Notice that all the social classes produced the highest percentage of [r] in the minimal pairs style, with the lower middle class producing [r] about 80 percent. The second most formal-sounding style is word lists style, in which subjects read a list of words containing postvocalic [r]. Continuing along the horizontal axis, the next most formal style is reading style, which involves reading a text. The next most formal style is careful speech, which

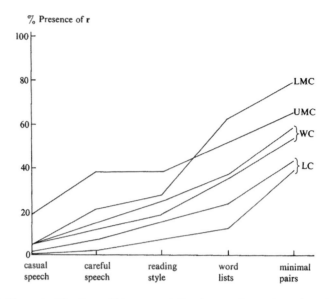

Figure 6.1 Class stratification of [r] pronunciation in *guard, car, beer, beard*, etc. for native New York City adults showing hypercorrection of the lower middle class (based on Labov 1972a:114; reprinted in Fasold, R. & Connor-Linton, J. (eds.). *An introduction to language and linguistics* (p. 317). Cambridge University Press.) key: UMC = upper middle class; LMC = lower middle class; WC = working class; LC = lower class.

involves talking to the interviewer about topics like family and school, but not telling a story. The least formal speaking style is casual speech, which involves telling a story. So, as we move from right to left along the horizontal axis the percentage of [r] for all social classes decreases. Labov explained this pattern by saying that speakers can **monitor** their speech, and are able to pronounce more [r]s when they can devote more attention to how they sound. When telling a story, speakers can't monitor very well because they are focused on the details of the narrative, but when reading a list of words, especially a list of minimal pairs, they can pay more attention to how they sound. The fact that monitoring produces different speaking styles suggests that all New York City English speakers believe that [r] should be pronounced after vowels, and that they try to change their natural (or *vernacular*) speech to include this [r] when they can. This is one piece of evidence that New York City is a cohesive speech community.

A particularly interesting feature of Figure 6.1 is the crossover pattern of postvocalic [r] for the lower middle class in the two most monitored styles. Notice that in almost all of the speaking styles the higher the social class, the higher percentage of [r]. In other words, New York City English shows class stratification. However, there is an important exception. In word list style and minimal pair style the lower middle class speakers use more postvocalic [r] than the upper middle class speakers, thus showing hypercorrection.

Like Midge, these lower middle class speakers are trying to sound like upper middle class speakers but are overdoing it.

Another important point that can be seen in Figure 6.1 is that speakers do not have a single style, but rather can *style shift*, depending on the speaking situation, and this is what Midge attempts to do with the clerk. In Labov's (1972a) study, **style shifting** occurred only when more monitoring was possible, but other researchers (e.g., Bell, 1984, 2001) have found that speakers also style shift depending on whom they are talking to. Bell called this phenomenon *audience design*, but a more widely used term is **accommodation**, of which there are two types: *convergent* and *divergent*. Convergent accommodation occurs when speakers try to sound more like their audience, thus establishing solidarity with them. An example from Bell (1984) is when a travel agent adapted her speech to sound more like that of her customers. Divergent accommodation occurs when speakers try to sound less like their audience, thus putting social distance between them. An example is provided by Bourhis and Giles (1977), who asked a group of ethnically Welsh English speakers to talk to a speaker with a very English English accent. They found that when the conversation focused on Welsh-English differences, thereby potentially threatening the Welsh identity of the informants, these speakers diverged from the speech of the Englishman, emphasizing the Welsh features of their own variety of English. When authors show their characters' style shifting in response to different audiences, they highlight the social relationships that exist in particular conversations. The Duke and the Dauphin attempted divergent accommodation on the raft when they tried to adopt the style of more educated speakers and thus put social distance between themselves and Huck and Jim.

6.5.3 Individual Voices

Adrienne Rich portrays differences in individual personalities as well as age in the voices of her characters in the poem "Letters in the Family."

Letters in the Family
                                        I: Catalonia, 1936

Dear Parents:
            I'm the daughter
    you didn't bless when she left,
    an unmarried woman wearing a khaki knapsack
    with a poor mark in Spanish.
            I'm writing now
    from a plaster-dusted desk in a town

pocked street by street with hand grenades,
some of them, dear ones, thrown by me.
This is a school: the children are at war.
You don't need honors in schoolroom Spanish here
to be of use and my right arm
's as strong as anyone's. I sometimes think
all languages are spoken here,
even mine, which you got zero in.
Don't worry. Don't try to write. I'm happy.
if you could know it.

Rochelle

II: Yugoslavia, 1944

Dear Chana,
         where are you now?
Am sending this pocket-to-pocket
(though we both know pockets we'd hate to lie in).
They showed me that poem you gave Reuven,
about the match:
Chana, you know, I never was
for martyrdom. I thought we'd try our best,
ragtag mission that we were,
then clear out if the signals looked too bad.
Something in you drives things ahead for me
but if I can I mean to stay alive.
We're none of us giants, you know,
just small, frail, inexperienced romantic people.
But there are things we learn.
You know the sudden suck of empty space
between the jump and the ripcord pull?
I hate it. I hate it so,
I've hated you for your dropping
ecstatically in free-fall, in the training,
your look, dragged on the ground, of knowing
precisely why you were there.
               My mother's
still in Palestine. Are yours
still in Hungary? Well, there we are.
When this is over –
             I'm
your earthbound friend to the end, still yours –

Esther

III: Southern Africa, 1986

Dear children:

        We've been walking nights
a long time over rough terrain.
sometimes through marshes. Days we hide
under what bushes we can find.
Our stars steer us. I write
on my knee by a river with a weary hand,
and the weariness will come through
this letter that should tell you
nothing but love. I can't say where we are,
what weeds are in bloom, what birds cry at dawn.
The less you know the safer.
But not to know how you are going on –
Matile's earache, Emma's lessons, those tell-tale
eyes and tongues, so quick – are you remembering
to be brave and wise and strong?
At the end of this hard road
we'll sit all together at one meal
and I'll tell you everything: the names
of our comrades, how the letters were routed to you, why I left.
And I'll stop and say, "Now you,
grown so big, how was it for you, those times?
Look, I know you in detail, every inch of each
sweet body, haven't I washed and dried you
a thousand times?"

        And we'll eat and tell our stories
together. That is my reason.

Ma

A footnote to the poem provided by the author explains that although all of the letter writers are imagined persons, Chana is modeled after Hannah Senesh, who in 1943 joined an expedition of Jews who trained under the British to parachute behind Nazi lines in order to rescue Jews in Hungary, Romania and Czechoslovakia. She was captured by the Nazis and tortured and executed in November 1944. In regard to Rochelle's letter it is helpful to know that the province of Catalonia in northeastern Spain was the site of much fighting during the Spanish Civil War, in which Franco's Fascist forces defeated democratic forces. Rochelle is pictured as a member of the Lincoln Brigade, American volunteers who fought against the Fascists. Ma's letter was written in South Africa before the end of apartheid, the enforced segregation of Blacks, Asians, and Whites. Ma is, no doubt, aiding the anti-apartheid cause. In regard to interpreting the poem, Hunter (1999) notes,

This poem uses different voices, and here they are clearly distinguished as different "historical" characters – Rochelle, Esther, and "Ma," women from three separate places and times who in letter form tell their own stories. In each case, the individual story is part of some larger historical moment, and although all three characters are (as the author's footnote points out) fictional, the three stories together present a kind of history of female heroism in difficult cultural moments. Try reading the poem aloud so you can hear how different in tone the three voices sound. Each woman has distinctive expressions and syntax of her own (p. 68).

Reading poetry aloud is always a good idea, but with the tools you studied in Chapter 4, you can more effectively analyze the distinctive syntax of each voice. Rochelle's and Esther's voices seem to be the most different, with Ma's falling in between these two extremes. The content and style of Rochelle's letter suggest that she is angry, determined, and totally committed to her cause. How is this effect achieved? First, Rochelle's letter is formally punctuated; it contains nine complete sentences, all beginning with capital letters and ending with periods. Second, Rochelle's letter uses only canonical word order, that is, NP V NP PP Adv. There is no inverting of subject and verb in part because the letter contains no questions. Rochelle is telling, not asking. Neither is there any fronting of prepositional or adverbial phrases or clauses. Recall from Chapter 4 that canonical word order is the easiest word order to process mentally, so Rochelle's letter strikes us as straightforward and to the point. Furthermore, Rochelle interrupts a clause only once, with the ironic phrase "dear ones" which, because it is marked, is more forceful. There are no parenthetical expressions or interrupting relative clauses. The result, from a syntactic perspective, is a forceful succession of clauses. However, poets have another device for interrupting phrases and clauses that is not syntactic, called *enjambement*, where a grammatical unit does not end with the line but is carried over to the next line. Rochelle's letter contains only one example, but it is telling. It occurs in lines 10–11, where the new line breaks up not just a grammatical unit, but a word:

> . . .and my right arm
> 's as strong as anyone's. . . .

This sentence is perhaps the strongest expression of Rochelle's bravado, but the enjambement suggests that she hesitates slightly, implying that she is not as sure of herself as she would have her parents believe. As we will see, this interruption of straightforward exposition is repeated in Esther's and Ma's letters.

Another measure of the forcefulness of Rochelle's writing is her use and placement of simple sentences as opposed to the more complicated compound and complex sentences. Rochelle's letter contains nine sentences and four of them (44%) are single clauses, that is, simple sentences, which occur in two pairs. The first pair is in line 10, where Rochelle, hunkered down in a school room, lectures her parents:

> This is a school: the children are at war.

At the end of the letter she repeats a similar syntactic pairing, this time in the form of two commands:

> Don't worry. Don't try to write.

In sum, Rochelle's straightforward syntax suggests focus and determination with only one unconscious but noticeable glitch suggesting vulnerability.

If Rochelle's style is straightforward, Esther's is all over the board. Esther tells us that she is not so committed to her cause, and she often comes across as hesitant and disjointed. The letter begins on a note of uncertainty. The first sentence does not start with a capital letter and rather than making a statement, it asks a question. The second sentence lacks a subject. Esther further violates standard punctuation in line 12, and, more noticeably in line 16, both of which are run-on sentences. Unlike Rochelle, Esther strays from canonical word order. In addition to two questions, positioned at the beginning and the end of the letter, she fronts two dependent clauses ("if I can" and "when this is over"). Processing is also made more difficult by three instances of enjambement (compared to one instance in Rochelle's letter).

There is, nevertheless, a kind of symmetry in the two letters, and it has to do with the breakdown of straightforward exposition. As we have seen, in Rochelle's letter this occurs where enjambement divides a contraction (My right **arm/'s** as strong as anyone's …). Like Rochelle, Esther can write straightforward sentences, and she does it when she is talking about what she doesn't like.

> But there are things we learn.
>> You know the sudden suck of empty space
>> between the jump and the ripcord pull?
>> I hate it. I hate it so,

Here a succession of five canonically ordered clauses, the last four of them simple sentences, forcefully expresses Esther's hatred of what she must do. She then goes further, confessing that her hatred extends to her friend for loving the work, and at this emotional point Ester's syntax breaks down:

> I've hated you for your dropping
>> ecstatically in free-fall, in the training,
>> your look, dragged on the ground, of knowing
>> precisely why you were there.

203

In this sentence "dragged on the ground" modifies "your look," and this construction is hard to process. What Ester means is "your look while being dragged on the ground," but the awkward syntax suggests that the line was written with some emotion. Furthermore, the last two lines of the sentence are not grammatically integrated into the whole sentence. The ideas represented in these lines are semantically but not syntactically well-connected, and, following the previous grammatical sentences, they strike us as deeply felt.

Ma's syntax is more elaborate than Rochelle's and Ester's and thus sounds more mature. Her letter is longer, and it contains more words per sentence: 16.6 words per sentence compared to 12 for Rochelle and 10 for Ester. Her sentences are also more complex, containing an average of two clauses per sentence compared to 1.67 for Rochelle and 1.56 for Ester. Elaboration can also be seen in Ma's variation of canonical word order. Her letter begins with the expected order, but the second sentence shows some variation:

> ... Days we hide
> under what bushes we can find.

Here canonical word order is altered with the fronting of adverbial "Days" and in the Noun Clause "what bushes we can find" ("what bushes" is the direct object of "find" so we don't expect it at the beginning of the clause). Canonical order is also changed with the fronting of the long prepositional phrase "At the end of this hard road" (line 17) and the parallel noun clauses in lines 10 and 11:

> ... I can't say *where we are,*
> *what weeds are in bloom, what birds cry at dawn.*

With these syntactic structures, Ma not only varies her style but also slows us down a bit as we process her words. However, like the younger writers, Ma can also be direct, with short simple sentences like "Our stars steer us" and the fragment "The less you know the better." This marked structure (it is the only fragment in the letter) directly precedes a passage that breaks down a bit syntactically. Like the other writers, Ma's standard exposition changes when she gets personal.

> But not to know how you are going on –
> Matile's earache, Emma's lessons, those tell-tale
> eyes and tongues so quick –

Here we expect the nominal construction "not to know how you are going on" to be the subject of a sentence with a main verb to follow the long parenthetical expression, but there is no following verb; instead a new sentence begins without the signaling capital letter. This irregular syntax is marked in Ma's otherwise standard language, and, as in the previous letters, it underlines the writer's emotional involvement.

In sum, all three writers are risking their lives to further a worthy cause, and all three of their letters share some stylistic features, namely variation between more elaborate sentences that mostly supply background information and simple, canonical sentences that make important points. In addition, the standard syntax of all three writers breaks down at points of emotional involvement. Nevertheless, on the whole, Ma's syntax is more complex, suggesting that she better understands her situation and can better portray it to her audience. We will next consider another device for measuring syntactic complexity and exercise 11 asks you to use that device to measure the relative complexity of the syntax in the three letters.

Norman Mailer's "nonfiction novel" *The Executioner's Song* won the Pulitzer Prize in 1980. It is a journalistic account of the execution of Gary Gilmore in 1977. Gilmore, who had spent most of his life in prison, was paroled into the custody of his cousin Vern, who provided Gilmore with a job in his cobbler shop in Provo, Utah. For a short time Gilmore got along, visiting with his family and courting Nicole Baker, a young, unmarried mother with only a high school education. But, Gilmore couldn't adapt to life outside prison, and after a few months he robbed and murdered two men. When he was sentenced to death, his case became a cause locally and nationally because his execution would be the first to take place in the United States after a four-year moratorium imposed by a U.S. Supreme Court decision. Several organizations, including the American Civil Liberties Union, organized campaigns to challenge the legality of the execution, but these efforts were not helped by the fact that Gilmore himself wanted to die and fired attorneys who attempted to save him.

Mailer divides the book into two sections: Western Voices and Eastern Voices. In the first section he tells the story of the murders from the point of view of the Utah people who knew Gilmore, writing in a style in which they themselves might write. In the second section he tells the story of the legal battle from the point of view of the lawyers and activists, many of them from the East. The first passage below, from Western Voices, tells how Gilmore met Nicole. The voice is that of the narrator, but it is written from Nicole's point of view, in a style that she might use. The second passage, from Eastern Voices, tells how Julie Jacoby, an older, college-educated woman, and a recent transplant from Chicago, worked to challenge the execution. Here the narrator adopts Julie's point of view using a style that suggests Julie's voice.

Nicole's Voice

When he [Gary Gilmore] returned with the beer, she was leaning against the door, and he put the six-pack on her knee. She joked and said, Oh that hurts. He started rubbing her knee. He did it decently not too personal, but it felt pretty good in a nice simple way, and they went on home. When they got to the end of Sterling's driveway, before she got out to the car, he turned around and looked at her and asked if she would kiss him. She didn't say anything for a minute, then said, Yes. He reached across and gave her a kiss and it didn't do any harm at all to what she thought about him. In fact, to her surprise, she felt like crying. A long time later, she would remember that first kiss. Then they went back to the house.

Now Nicole didn't ignore him quite so much, although she still made a point of sitting across the room. Sue obviously couldn't stand the fellow, and was paying even less attention in his direction. In fact Nicole was surprised how indifferent he seemed that Sue disliked him. Sue might be obviously pregnant now, but in Nicole's opinion she was a beautiful-looking blond. Maybe even the more spectacular of the two of them. Yet he didn't care, seemed ready to sit by himself. Sterling was also quiet. After a while, it began to seem as if the evening would all go nowhere.

Julie's Voice

Julie Jacoby had a good opinion of Shirley Pedler and thought her very attractive with that long thin build and her beautiful long hands. The strain of the Gilmore situation, however was really making Shirley lose too much weight. She had been a pretty intense woman to begin with, but after these last weeks, she was beginning to resemble a cigarette.

Although Shirley was twenty-four years younger, Julie Jacoby thought they were a lot alike. They would both rather be reclusive, yet were always in the middle of political activity. So Julie was not surprised when Shirley, during the Christmas week, asked her to aid in the formation of the Utah Coalition Against the Death Penalty.

Of course Julie had not been doing a great deal in the year since she and her husband moved from Chicago to Utah. It was nothing like the Days of Rage in Chicago in the summer of 1968 when people were beaten by the police. That was when, in her own mind, she moved on from being little more than just another society lady from the North Shore who came down to United Charities twice a week to spend an afternoon sympathizing with the mothers of black children who came into the office in various states of coma from eating lead paint that had peeled off the walls. Some of these society ladies used to appear for work wearing diamond rings, and Julie had spent time trying to get the idea across that these ladies ought not to carry more wealth on their finger than the person in need across the desk could make in a year.

Julie's style is clearly more complex than Nicole's, and so far in the book we have discussed several devices for measuring such syntactic complexity, including words per sentence, clauses per sentence, percentage of passives, and canonical word order (see Table 4.1). Another measure of complexity was developed by educational researcher Kellogg W. Hunt (1965), who studied children's writing. Hunt proposed the "minimal terminal unit" or **t-unit** as a measure of sentence complexity. A t-unit consists of a main clause and all of its modifiers, including any embedded or attached clauses or phrases. In his words, "cutting a passage into t-units will be cutting it into the shortest units which it is grammatically allowable to punctuate as sentences" (p. 13). In other words, dividing a passage into t-units means re-punctuating it into the largest number of sentences possible (remembering that coordinating conjunctions can begin sentences). Here are some examples of t-units from "Nicole's voice."

TU1	When he [Gary Gilmore] returned with the beer, she was leaning against the door,	(12 words)
TU2	and he put the six-pack on her knee.	(8 words)
TU3	She joked	(2 words)
TU4	and said, Oh that hurts.	(5 words)
TU5	He started rubbing her knee.	(5 words)
TU6	He did it decently not too personal,	(7 words)
TU7	but it felt pretty good in a nice simple way,	(10 words)
TU8	and they went on home.	(5 words)

This passage has a total of eight t-units and 54 words for an average of 6.65 words per t-unit. Hunt discovered that as children matured, they used more words per t-unit in their writing. He noted:

> Throughout the school years, from kindergarten to graduation, children learn to use a larger and larger number of sentence-combining transformations per main clause in their writing. Skilled adults carry the same tendency still further.... (1970, p. 9).

Because Julie is more educated than Nicole, we might expect that Julie's voice would contain more syntactic elaboration, and thus more words per t-unit, than Nicole's voice. Let us test this hypothesis by calculating the number of words per t-unit in the first paragraph of "Julie's voice".

TU1	Julie Jacoby had a good opinion of Shirley Pedler and thought her very attractive with that long thin build and her beautiful long hands.	(24 words)
TU2	The strain of the Gilmore situation, however, was really making Shirley lose too much weight.	(15 words)

| TU3 | She had been a pretty intense woman to begin with, | (10 words) |
| TU4 | but after these last weeks, she was beginning to resemble a cigarette. | (12 words) |

In this paragraph Julie's voice has a total of 61 words in four t-units for an average of 15.25 words per t-unit, which turns out to be more than twice the number of words per t-unit than in the sample of Nicole's voice. In other words, Julie uses longer clauses and more dependent clauses than Nicole, and this syntactic elaboration is one way in which Mailer signals Julie's greater maturity and education.

Note

1 The use of slash and bracket notation can be confusing. Remember from chapter 2 that the English phoneme /t/ has the allophones [t] and [tʰ]. Similarly, New York City English has the phoneme /r/, which is often pronounced as [r]. However, speakers of this dialect can produce a different allophone of /r/ when it occurs after vowels, namely [Ø] (i.e. nothing). Thus, in New York City English, /r/ has the allophones [r] and [Ø].

Summary

English is the most commonly spoken language in the world. The two varieties with the largest number of speakers are American English and British English, which differ from each other mostly in pronunciation. Both of these varieties contain regional and social dialects, and authors can employ features of these dialects in their characters' speech to suggest the characters' identities. Social dialects differ from each other mainly in the percentage at which particular features are used. For example, working-class speakers pronounce –ing as [in] more frequently than middle-class speakers. Real speakers and fictional characters can *style shift*, changing the formality of their speaking style according to their audience and the speaking situation. The syntactic complexity of prose can be measured in several ways, including words per sentence, clauses per sentence, percentage of passives, canonical word order, and words per t-unit. Authors can shift to more or less complex syntax to foreground a particularly important passage, and complex syntax is often associated with characters who are more mature and more educated.

Exercises

1. a. A number of differences were noted in the speech of the Duke and the Dauphin in the quote from *Huckleberry Finn*, such as the contrast between "poor" and "pore." What other contrasts in the two men's speech can you find? What orthographic conventions does Twain use to convey nonstandard pronunciation?

    b. The Duke has a background in theater. How is that reflected in his speech? What features give away his true identity?

2. Find the following features of AAE in Lisa Jane's speech in the passage from "The Wife of His Youth." The features are listed in the order in which they occur in the passage.

    a. Deletion of final /r/
    b. Deletion of final consonant
    c. Past tense of irregular verbs
    d. Loss of initial unstressed vowel sound
    e. Deletion of medial /r/

3. In the passage from "The Wife of His Youth,"

    a. Does Chesnutt use eye dialect? If so, find one or more examples.
    b. Does Mr. Ryder use any nonstandard forms? How does the representation of Mr. Ryder's and Lisa Jane's speech contribute to the meaning of the passage?

4. In the passage below from *David Copperfield*, Ham Peggotty requests that David write a letter to Emily expressing his feelings toward her after she has run off with Steerforth. Find examples of the following nonstandard features:

    a. loss of unstressed vowel
    b. use of *as* as a subordinating conjunction
    c. use of *as* as a relative pronoun
    d. past tense of irregular verb
    e. deletion of consonant from a cluster
    f. subject-verb agreement
    g. Ignoring the nonstandard features, how would you characterize Ham's ability as a speaker? What point is Dickens making by the contrast of dialect and style?

    I loved her – and I love the mem'ry of her – too deep – to be able to lead her to believe of my own self as I'm a happy man. I could only be happy – by forgetting of her – and I'm afeerd I couldn't hardly bear as she should be told I done that. But if you, being so full of learning, Mas'r Davy, could think of anything to say as might bring her to believe I wasn't greatly hurt, still loving of her, and mourning for her, anything as might bring her to believe as I was not tired of my life, and you was hoping for to see her without blame, where the wicked cease from troubling and the weary are at rest – anything as would ease her sorrowful mind, and yet not make her think as I could every marry, or as she was – I should ask of you to say that – with my prayers for her – that was so dear. (Ch. 51, p. 457)

---

5.   Charles Dickens' novel *Great Expectations* is set in Victorian England and tells the story of Pip, an orphan boy who finally comes into his inheritance. The passage below contains three voices: Miss Havisham, Joe Gargery, and Pip, who narrates the passage. What linguistic features mark the different social classes of the characters? As the passage states, Pip was raised by Joe Gargery. Is Pip's speech more like Joe's or Miss Havisham's? How might this be explained sociolinguistically?

"You are the husband," repeated Miss Havisham, "of the sister of this boy?"

It was very aggravating but, throughout the interview, Joe persisted in addressing me instead of Miss Havisham.

"Which I mentersay, Pip," Joe now observed, in a manner that was at once expressive of forcible argumentation, strict confidence, and great politeness, "as I hup and married your sister, and I were at the time what you might call (if you was any ways inclined) a single man."

"Well!" said Miss Havisham. "And you have reared the boy, with the intention of taking him for your apprentice; is that so, Mr. Gargery?"

"You know, Pip," replied Joe, "as you and me were ever friends, and it were looked for'ard to betwixt us, as being calc'lated to lead to larks. Not but what, Pip, if you had ever made objections to the business – such as its being open to black and sut, or such-like – not but what they would have been attended to, don't you see?"

"Has the boy," said Miss Havisham, "ever made any objection to it? Does he like the trade?"

"Which is well beknown to yourself, Pip," returned Joe, strengthening his former mixture of argumentation, confidence, and politeness, "that it were the wish of your own hart," (I saw the idea suddenly break upon him that he would adapt his epitaph to the occasion, before he went on to say.) "And there weren't no objection on your part, and Pip it were the great wish of your hart!"

---

6.   In *The Black Book* Ian Rankin emphasizes the novel's Scottish setting by using local vocabulary words that the reader must try to understand from the context. The book opens with the passage below, a scene in the north of Scotland where two men are disposing of a body by dropping it off a cliff into the sea.

a. Try to guess the meanings of the local vocabulary words in bold from their context. Translations are provided at the end of the exercises.

b. According to the discussion of varieties of inner circle English, would *bloody* ("A bloody answer to everything") likely be pronounced /blədiy or /bluwdiy/?

There were two of them in the van that early morning, lights on to combat the **haar** which blew in from the North Sea. It was thick and white like smoke. They drove carefully, being under strict instructions.

"Why does it have to be us?" said the driver, stifling a yawn. "What's wrong with the other two?" ...

The passenger was not a conversationalist, but maybe talk would keep the driver awake.

"It's just temporary," he said. "Besides, it's not as if it's a daily chore."

"Thank God for that." The driver shut his eyes again and yawned. The van glided in towards the grass **verge**.

"Do you want me to drive?" asked the passenger. Then he smiled. "You could always **kip**." ...

The body had been placed in two thick plastic fertilizer sacks, one pulled over the feet and one over the head, so that they overlapped in the middle ... They carried the grotesque parcel low, brushing the wet grass. Their shoes were squelching by the time they passed the sign warning about the cliff face ahead. Even more difficult was the climb over the fence though it was rickety enough to start with.

"Wouldn't stop a bloody kid," the driver commented. He was **peching**, the saliva like glue in his mouth.

"**Ca' canny**," said the passenger.

---

7.   Answer these questions about the poem that follows.

a. Who are the two speakers in the poem? What seems to be their relationship?

b. Translate the dialect in the second line of stanza 2. What linguistic features differentiate the speech of the two women? What does their speech suggest about their backgrounds?

c. How does the use of *ain't* in the last line alter our impression of Amelia?

The Ruined Maid

"O 'Melia° my dear, this does everything crown!　　　　°Amelia
　　Who should have supposed I should meet you in town?
And whence such fair garments, such prosperi-ty?" –
"O didn't you know I'd been ruined?" said she.
　– "You left us in tatters, without shoes or socks,
Tired of digging potatoes, and spudding up docks°;　　　°spading up weeds
And now you've gay bracelets and bright feathers three!" –
"Yes: that's how we dress when we're ruined," said she.

　– At home on the barton° you said 'thee' and 'thou,'　　°farmyard
And 'thik oon' and 'theas oon,' and 't'other'; but now
Your talking quite fits 'ee for high company-ny!" –
"Some polish is gained with one's ruin," said she.
　– "Your hands were like paws then, you face blue and bleak
　But now I'm bewitched by your delicate cheek,
　And your little gloves fit as on any la-dy!" –
　"We never do work when we're ruined," said she.

　– "You used to call home-life a hag-ridden dream,
　And you'd sigh, and you'd sock°; but at present you seem　°hit out
　To know not of megrims° or melancho-ly!"　　　　°migraines
　"True. One's pretty lively when ruined," said she.
　– "I wish I had feathers, a fine sweeping gown,
And a delicate face, and could strut about Town!" –
"My dear – a raw country girl, such as you be,
Cannot quite expect that. You ain't ruined," said she.

Thomas Hardy

8.　Compare Nicole's and Julie's voices in the passages from *The Executioner's Song* in terms of some or all of the following features: (a) punctuation; (b) standard English grammar; (c) diction; (d) canonical word order; (e) interrupted clauses; (f) metaphorical language.

9.　Calculate the number of words per t-unit in the passage from *A Man in Full* by Tom Wolfe, which is quoted in exercise 4 following section 7.2.2. Is the narrator's voice in Wolfe's passage more or less complex than Julie's voice according to this measure?

10.　Compare the syntactic complexity of the following two stanzas from poems by Emily Dickinson and Carl Sandburg in terms of t-units. Which stanza has more words per t-unit? According to Kellogg W. Hunt's definition of mature writing, who is the more mature writer, Dickinson or Sandburg? Please remember that Hunt devised his measure to be used for the writing of school children, not great poets. Nevertheless, the comparison is interesting.

It Sifts from Leaden Sieves
It sifts from leaden sieves,
It powders all the wood.
It fills with alabaster wool.
The wrinkles of the road.
It makes an even face
Of mountain and of plain –
Unbroken forehead from the east
Unto the east again.
Emily Dickinson

The Harbor
Passing through huddled and ugly walls
By doorways where women
Looked from their hunger-deep eyes,
Haunted with shades of hunger-hands,
Out from the huddled and ugly walls,
I came sudden at the city's edge
On a blue burst of lake,
Long lake waves breaking under the sun
On a spray-flung curve of shore;
And a fluttering storm of gulls,
Masses of great gray wings
And flying white bellies
Veering and wheeling free in the open
Carl Sandburg

11. Compare the syntactic complexity of Rochelle's, Esther's and Ma's letters in "Letters In The Family" using words per t-unit. Which letter has more words per t- unit? According to this measure, who is the more mature writer?

12. Using the instructions for exercise 7 in Chapter 8 ask someone you know to tell you a story, which you record. Then, transcribe all of the words that would be spelled ending in –*ing*, noting whether they are pronounced [iyŋ] or [in]. What is the percentage of [in] words? How does this percentage compare to Flora's use of –*ing* and the use of other characters discussed in this chapter? If several students do this exercise, how do the various informants' percentages of [in] use compare? Can you explain these differences in terms of the identity of the informants?

Local Terms from *The Black Book*

haar   a cold mist or fog
verge   a narrow border that runs alongside a road (this term is in general use in Britain)
kip   a nap
peching panting
Ca' canny go carefully

Key Terms

language variety
regional dialect
social dialect
sociolinguistic variable
class stratification
eye dialect
African American English
hypercorrection
monitor
style shifting
accommodation
t-unit

Suggestions for Further Reading

The definitive book on North American dialects is Labov, Ash & Boberg (2006). Though it contains a lot of technical discussion, the dialect area maps are accessible to all. Melchers & Shaw (2003) provides very detailed discussions of the Englishes spoken in inner, outer, and expanding circle countries. Trudgill (2000) is concise, interesting, and accessible to readers with no previous knowledge of linguistics. Wardhaugh (2010) is the best textbook in general sociolinguistics, thoroughly covering many more aspects of the field than are mentioned in the present volume. Wolfram & Schilling (2016) is a thorough and authoritative survey of American English dialects, written for undergraduate students.

Chapter 7

Morphology, Semantics, and Pragmatics

In this Chapter ...

We first observe that linguists have described language at different levels of organization, such as the phonetic and phonemic levels, and then note that these levels reflect the way that language is organized in the brain. We next discuss three levels of linguistic organization that have not yet been covered in the book and show how literature can be analyzed at each of these levels. *Morphology* is the study of how words can be broken up into smaller meaningful units called morphemes, such as *–ed*, which signals that the action of a verb took place in the past. The repetition of morphemes, like the repetition of phonemes in alliteration, can add cohesion to a work of literature.

Semantics studies how language represents meanings. Case Grammar is an area of semantics that uses a set of universal notions, like Location, Time, and Agent, to characterize the relationships between NPs within a sentence.

Pragmatics studies the way the relationship between speaker, audience, and speaking context can affect language form and meaning. Context, for example, can dramatically change the meaning of the utterance "There's a gun in Mary Lou's handbag," which in different circumstances could be a warning, an admission, or even a boast.

7.1 Linguistic Levels

In Chapter 2 we saw that linguists have analyzed the sound system of English at two different levels, the phonemic and the phonetic, and that these levels are arranged hierarchically, so that the phonemic level is more abstract than the phonetic. The abstract phoneme /t/, for example, is made up of the actual sounds [t] and [tʰ]. The notion of linguistic levels is not just useful for describing the sound patterns of a language – these levels also correspond to steps in mental processing when language is produced. According to Levelt's (1989) speech production model, the brain stores word meanings together with their phonemic representations, so that, for example, the word *pen* is stored with the information that its pronunciation involves the phonemes /p/, /e/, and /n/. If a speaker wants to say "pen," the phonemes are mentally transformed into the appropriate allophones for their linguistic environment, namely: [pʰ], [ẽ], and [n] (or, in the case of speakers from the American South (for whom /e/ → [i] before nasals) [pʰ], [ĩ], and [n]). Allophones can be thought of as mental plans for activating the appropriate vocal tract muscles for pronouncing the sounds.

Language as a whole is also mentally organized as a hierarchy containing different levels of information. Let us look at a somewhat simplified version of Levelt's model of speech production using the example sentence, "The cat chased the mouse." (The reader may wish to consult Figure 7.1 during this discussion.) The process begins at the **conceptual level**, where the speaker calls up the concepts: CAT [+specific], MOUSE [+specific], CHASE and PAST and also the pragmatic information (to be discussed) that the proposition will be expressed as a sentence in the active voice. At this level, the concepts, which will eventually be realized as words, are not fully specified; for example, the concept CAT might eventually be realized as "cat," "pussy," or "kitty." At the conceptual level a prospective sentence also contains information about how the concepts that will eventually be realized as NPs are logically related to each other. For example, the abstract concept of CHASE includes the information that the notion of chasing involves a thing to act as an Agent (to do the chasing) and another thing to act as a Patient (to be chased). The conceptual level may also include information about whether particular concepts are specific (e.g. if the speaker is thinking about a particular cat) or nonspecific (e.g. if the speaker is thinking about cats in general). This information may eventually be expressed by the morphemes *the* or *a*.

The information assembled at the conceptual level is passed on to the **lexical level**. At the lexical level concepts are matched with the appropriate lexical entries (words) in the mental lexicon; for example, CAT is matched

Conceptual level

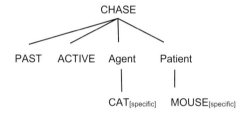

Lexical level

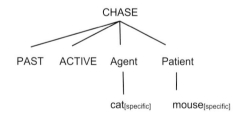

Syntactic level

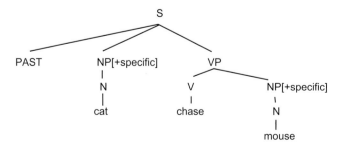

Figure 7.1 Simplified version of Levelt's (1989) model of speech production

217

Morphemic level

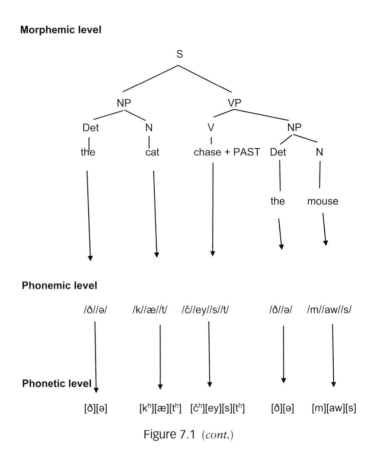

Figure 7.1 (*cont.*)

with *cat* or *kitty*. The mental lexical entries, like the entries in a dictionary, contain both syntactic and semantic information. For example, the entry for *chase* specifies that this lexical item is a verb and that it requires an NP that acts as an Agent and an NP that acts as a Patient. In addition, at this level the lexical item *cat* is assigned the Agent role and *mouse* is assigned the Patient role. The output from the lexical level becomes input for the **syntactic level** where, as we saw in Chapter 4, syntactic rules generate a phrase structure tree with the NP *cat* as the first NP (and thus the sentence subject) and the NP *mouse* as the second NP (and thus the sentence object). In other circumstances, it might be more appropriate to express the same basic information in a passive structure, and this would be specified by pragmatic considerations represented at the conceptual level. If this were the case, *mouse* would be assigned to the first NP position. Notice, that this step in production is different from the generation of passive sentences described in Chapter 4. In that chapter, phrase structure rules generated an active sentence that was turned into its passive version by means of the passive transformation. But, in Levelt's model the passive form is directly generated from the information at the conceptual level by means of a phrase structure rule for passives.

The output of the syntactic level becomes input to the **morphemic level**. As discussed later in the chapter, a morpheme is the smallest unit of meaning in a language. Many words, like *tree, river*, and *sky*, consist of a single morpheme, but other words contain more than one morpheme, such as *treetop, riverbed*, and *skylark*, each of which contains two morphemes. Notice that in these examples, the morphemes can stand alone as words, and are therefore called *free morphemes*. However, some morphemes must be attached to a word stem, and these are called *bound morphemes*. Examples include the plural morpheme, as in *treetops*, and the past tense morpheme, as in *chased*. Returning to our discussion of Levelt's model of how the sentence "The cat chased the mouse" is produced mentally, at the morphemic level any free morphemes that are required by conceptual considerations, such as *the*, or *a*, are inserted. In our example sentence, *the* is required before both *cat* and *mouse* because both of these NPs were marked +specific at the conceptual level. In addition, any necessary bound morphemes, such as PAST or PLURAL, are attached to the appropriate word stems. In our example, the past tense morpheme is attached to the verb *chase*, producing *chase* + PAST.

We are already familiar with Levelt's final two levels of processing. The output from the morphemic level is fed into the **phonemic level**, so that the string

the cat chase + PAST the mouse

becomes

/ð//ə/ /k//æ//t/ /č//ey//s//t/ /ð//ə/ /m//aw//s/

Notice that at this level the PAST morpheme is expressed as /t/, which is appropriate for the word *chased*. Other verbs incorporate the PAST morpheme differently. For example, *see* + PAST is expressed as *saw*.

Finally, at the **phonetic level** the appropriate allophones of the phonemes are produced, namely,

[ð][ə] [kʰ][æ][tʰ] [čʰ][ey][s][tʰ] [ð][ə] [m][aw][s]

We should note that this final step is different in speaking and writing. In speaking the language user utters the appropriate sounds, but in writing the user produces the appropriate graphic symbols, namely:

The cat chased the mouse.

Figure 7.1 illustrates the different levels of processing that we have just discussed.

So far in the book we have examined in detail several of the levels of linguistic organization just described, including the phonemic and phonetic levels in Chapter 2 and the syntactic level in Chapter 4. In this chapter we will take a brief look at some of the other levels at which linguists have studied language and which also appear to correspond to levels of mental processing, namely the morphemic, semantic, and pragmatic levels.

7.2 **Morphology**

We first examine a unit that falls between the phoneme and the word, called the **morpheme**. As already mentioned, morphemes are the smallest units of meaning in a language. For example, the word *moonbeam* contains two morphemes: *moon* and *beam*. A less obvious morpheme can be found in the word *moonbeams*, which is made up of *moon, beam,* and *–s*. The *–s* signifies that the word is plural. Prefixes and suffixes are morphemes that modify the stem of a word. For example, *restarted* contains three morphemes: *re* (which means "do again"), *start* (which means, well, "*start*"), and *ed* (which means that the action occurred in the past). Similarly, *unhappiness* contains three morphemes: *un* (which means "not"), *happy* (which means "happy)" and *ness* (which means that the word is a noun).

Many of the world's languages like to string morphemes together into long words that can translate into English as whole sentences. For example, in Amharic, a Semitic language related to Arabic and Hebrew that is spoken in Ethiopia, the word /yfeligutal/ translates as "He/she likes it." The morphemes in the word can be sorted out as follows:

y	felig	ut	al
he/she	like	it	present tense (for *he* or *she*)

Like phonemes, morphemes can be repeated and contrasted for poetic effect. Of course, because morphemes are made up of phonemes, their repetition can also involve the repetition of sounds, but this is not necessarily so. Consider, for example, this stanza from William Blake's poem "The Clod and the Pebble."

Love seeketh not itself to please,
Nor for itself hath any care;
But for another gives its ease,
And builds a Heaven in Hell's despair.

The stanza contains a number of cohesive elements. At the phonetic level, we notice the end rhymes, with the repetition of *please* and *ease*, *care* and *despair*. A less obvious repetition is the consonance of *seeketh* and *hath* in lines 1 and 2 and of *gives* and *builds* in lines 3 and 4. At the phonetic level, these two sets of repetitions are not related, but at the morphemic level they are. The morpheme *–s* means that the verb is in the present tense and that its subject is third person singular, and the morpheme *–eth* is an older form that means the same thing. The contrast between the forms *–s* and *–eth* stands out to modern readers, and it would have been apparent to Blake's late eighteenth-century readers as well, even though they would be more exposed to the older form. Why did Blake use the older form in the first two lines, and then switch to the more modern form? The poem was published in Blake's 1794 book *Songs of Innocence and Experience*, which contrasted a romantic philosophy of innocence, to which human beings are born (symbolized by the clod), with a more practical and worldly philosophy of experience, which human beings develop after exposure to the corrupting influences of society (symbolized by the stone). The first two lines of the poem state the Clod's innocent vision of love, and using the older English form *–eth* gives these lines dignity, making them sound like a universal truth. Switching to the newer form makes lines 3 and 4 sound more contemporary, like a modern comment on a biblical homily.

7.2.1 Free and Bound Morphemes

As we have noted, some morphemes, like *love*, can stand alone as words, and these are called *free morphemes*. Other examples of free morphemes include: *not, to, please, nor, for, any, care*. However, morphemes like *–eth* and *–s* (as well as the *un–* of *unnecessary* and the *–ible* of *edible*) must be combined with a word stem, and these are called *bound morphemes*. All four of the morphemes in /yfeligutal/ are bound morphemes because the stem *fellig* is not a word by itself. English also contains examples of words whose stem is a bound morpheme that cannot stand alone, such as *grateful*. The suffix *–ful* usually changes a noun into an adjective (as in *graceful* and *wonderful*), but unlike *grace* and *wonder*, the stem *grate* is not also a word, and so it is classified as a bound morpheme. Another example involves the prefix *un–*, which is usually attached to an adjective or noun to reverse its meaning, as in *unhappy* and *unhappiness*. But, consider the word *uncouth*. The Early English word *couth* (meaning "sophisticated") has fallen into disuse, leaving us with only the word *uncouth*. Therefore, today both *un–* and *–couth* are bound morphemes.

7.2.2 Morphemes and Allomorphs

It may seem curious that we have called both *–eth* and *–s* instances of the same morpheme because they don't look anything alike, but these are not the only examples of morphemes that have different graphic and phonetic forms. For example, the plural morpheme is spelled *s* in *books*, but *es* in *kisses*. Furthermore, even when the plural morpheme is spelled *s*, it has two phonetic realizations. As a short experiment, try saying out loud the words *bugs* and *bucks* and then phonetically transcribing these words. Your transcriptions should look like this:

bugs [bəgz]   bucks [bəks]

A simple phonological rule (which applies at Levelt's phonemic level) explains how we unconsciously know when to pronounce which version of the plural morpheme that is spelled *s*. If the word stem ends in a voiceless sound, the plural morpheme is pronounced as the voiceless alveolar fricative [s], but if the word stem ends in a voiced sound, it is pronounced as the voiced alveolar fricative [z]. In other words, the final alveolar fricative agrees in voicing with the last sound of the word stem. Other pairs that show this pattern include:

rips   [rips]   ribs   [ribz]
pats   [pæts]   pads   [pædz]
picks   [piks]   pigs   [pigz]

A similar principle explains how to pronounce plurals spelled with *–es*, like *roses* [rowzəs] and *glasses* [glæsəz]. Adding [z] or [s] to such words wouldn't work because the words already end in one of those sounds. The solution is to add the vowel [ə] before the final alveolar fricative or, in the case of spelling, to add the letter *e* before the final *s*. This rule produces the desired plurals, as in *gin fizzes* [ǰin fizəz] and *angel kisses* [eynǰəl kisəz] (it's a cocktail made with cream and coffee liquor). In fact, this principle for forming the plural morpheme applies not only to word stems that end in [z] and [s] but also to stems that end in the similar sounds [č] and [š], like *watches* [wačəz] and *rashes* [ræšəz].

   Of course, the plural morpheme has even more forms: *–en* is the plural morpheme in *oxen*, and *–i* is the plural morpheme in *cacti* (although having lived among sahuaros and prickly pears for 30 years, I have never heard this Latin plural used in a conversation). So, the same morpheme can be realized phonetically in several different ways. We encountered a similar phenomenon in Chapter 2 when we discussed the difference between phonemes and allophones. Recall that the phoneme is an abstract unit that contrasts with the other abstract units in the phonological system. Nobody has ever pronounced a phoneme because it must be realized as a specific phonetic pronunciation called an allophone, and a single phoneme can have several allophones. To repeat an example from Chapter 2, the phoneme /p/ is usually realized as the allophone [pʰ] (aspirated, bilabial stop), but when /p/ occurs after a fricative, as in *splash*, it is realized as the allophone [p] (unaspirated, bilabial stop). So, /p/ has at least two pronunciations: [pʰ] and [p]. The same thing occurs with morphemes. The plural morpheme is an abstract unit of meaning (PLURAL) that can be realized in several ways. In writing it can be realized by adding the letter *s* to the stems of words of a certain class. For words of another class, however, we add the letters *es* (as in *dishes*), and for words of yet another class we add the letters *en* or *ren* (as in *oxen* and *children*), etc. These different realizations of the plural morpheme are called **allomorphs**. Another example of a morpheme with more than one allomorph is the progressive morpheme, as in "Marsha is play**ing**." The word *playing* contains two morphemes: *play* and *–ing, where play* means "play" and *–ing* means that the action is ongoing, as discussed in Chapter 6. However, the progressive morpheme is commonly pronounced and spelled in two different ways: [iyŋ] and [in], as in *playing* and *playin'*. Thus, [iyŋ] and [in] are allomorphs of the progressive morpheme in regard to pronunciation, and *–ing* and *–in'* are allomorphs of the progressive morpheme in regard to writing.

7.2.3 Lexical and Functional Morphemes

In Chapter 5 we noted that words can be divided into two groups, one of them large and the other small. We called the words in the large group "content words" and the words in the small group "function words." We can now use more technical names for these two word classes. Content words are also called **lexical morphemes**, and, as mentioned in Chapter 5, they include nouns, verbs, adjectives, and adverbs. This word class can easily be added to, as shown by these relatively recent additions to English dictionaries: *blog* (a noun), *text* (a verb), and *meh* (an adjective borrowed from Yiddish meaning neither good nor bad). So, lexical morphemes are said to constitute an *open class*. The words in the small class are called **functional morphemes,** and they include articles, prepositions, and personal pronouns. The class of functional morphemes is a *closed class* because it cannot be added to easily although occasionally people try, as in recent attempts to add gender-neutral pronouns to English to replace the awkward expressions *he or she, him or her,* and *his or hers*. For example, the video game LambdaMOO allows players the option of using the pronouns *e* (for "he or she"), *em* (for "him or her") and *eir* (for "his or hers"). Another difference between lexical and functional morphemes is that lexical morphemes seem to have a clear sense of meaning: we can even form a mental picture of words like *dog* and *car*. But, the meaning of the functional morphemes is more abstract. For example, *at* is used to show a spatial relationship between two objects that is difficult to specify exactly, and whole chapters have been written (but not in this book) about the different meanings of *a* and *the*.

7.2.4 Derivational and Inflectional Morphemes

So far, we have distinguished between lexical and functional morphemes and observed that each type contains both free and bound morphemes. Continuing this categorization, functional, bound morphemes can be divided into two types: inflectional and derivational, as shown in Figure 7.2.

Because both derivational and inflectional morphemes are also functional and bound, we have already encountered some of them in the discussion so far. The **derivational morphemes** in English include both suffixes and prefixes. The derivational suffixes serve to change the grammatical category of words. For example, adding *–able* to a verb changes it into an adjective, as in *affordable*, *remarkable*, and *doable*. Similarly, adding *–ly* to an adjective changes it into an adverb, as in *quickly*, *presently*, and *remarkably*. Derivational suffixes can be strung together to form words with considerable internal structure such as:

noun	flaw
adjective	flaw·less
noun	flaw·less·ness

verb	pay
noun	pay·ment
adverb	pay·ment·wise

noun	danger
adjective	danger·ous
adverb	danger·ous·ly

Derivational prefixes change the meaning of a word but not its grammatical category. There are far fewer derivational prefixes than suffixes, and they include: *un–*, *pre–*, *ex–*, *mis–*, *co–*, and *re–*, as in:.

wise	adjective		pay	verb		wife	noun
un·wise	adjective		pre·pay	verb		ex·wife	noun

Inflectional morphemes add some aspect of meaning to words of particular grammatical categories. For example, the plural morpheme attaches

Table 7.1 *The eight inflectional morphemes in English*

Morpheme Name	Attaches to	Examples of allomorphs for spelling
plural	nouns	cat**s**, ox**en**, stimul**i**
possessive	nouns	Marsha**'s** house, the boy**s'** house
past tense	verbs	want**ed**, wr**o**te, sw**a**m, b**ou**ght
progressive	verbs	runn**ing,** runn**in'**
3rd person singular	verbs	Marsha sing**s**. John danc**es**.
past participle	verbs	I have eat**en**. George has finish**ed**.
superlative	adjectives	the cool**est**
comparative	adjectives	hungri**er**

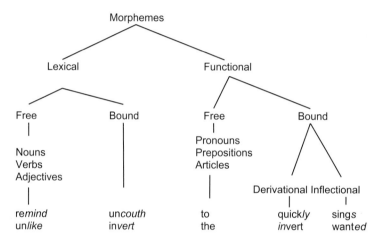

Figure 7.2 Classes of morphemes

only to nouns, and it indicates that there are more than one. Some languages categorize nouns into three numerical groups: singular (just one), dual (just two), and plural (three or more). For example, in Inuktitut (an Eskimo language) the word for *house* can be inflected as follows:

[iglu] one house
[iglu**k]** two houses
[iglu**t**] three or more houses

There are only eight inflectional morphemes in English. All of them are suffixes, and, unlike the derivational morphemes, all of them have names. They selectively attach to different grammatical classes of words, as shown in Table 7.1.

Notice that different morphemes can have allomorphs that look and sound exactly the same. For example, as we have seen, *–s* and *–es* are allomorphs of both the plural morpheme (cat*s*) and the third person

225

singular morpheme (jump*s*), and, of course, these forms are pronounced the same regardless of which morpheme they represent. Another example is –*ing*, pronounced (iyŋ]), which is an allomorph of the inflectional progressive morpheme (jump*ing*). But this form is also an allomorph of two derivational morphemes. In the first case, –*ing* changes verbs into gerunds (verb forms used as nouns) as in "**Skiing** (from the verb *ski*) is fun" and in the movie title *The Shining* (from the verb *shine*). In the second case, –*ing* changes verbs into adjectives, as in "**swimming** pool," "**hitching** post," and "**death-defying** leap."

7.2.5 Morphemes in Literary Analysis

As we have seen, the bound morphemes constitute a set of meaning elements that can be attached to word stems, including word stems that have recently entered the language, as in *snarky*. They can also be attached to made-up word stems, where they serve to give us some idea of the meaning of the made-up word. We saw examples of this in the first stanza of the poem "Jabberwocky," which is repeated here.

> 'Twas brillig, and the slithy toves
> Did gyre and gimble in the wabe:
> All mimsy were the borogoves,

We've never heard the words *toves* and *borogoves*, but the use of the inflectional morpheme –s signals that these words are nouns. Similarly, the use of the derivational morpheme –y on *slithy* and *mimsy* signals that these words are adjectives that modify *toves* and *borogoves*.

New words are entering the English language all the time, and a common point of entry is when names for specific products become generic, as with *levis* (any brand of jeans), *tylenol* (any version of the drug), and *coke* (in the South any soft drink). Another process for coining new words is to extend the meaning of an existing word or phrase. For example, *child-friendly* consists of three morphemes *child* (a noun), *friend* (a noun), and –*ly* (a derivational affix that changes nouns into adjectives). But, the first morpheme, *child*, can be replaced by other nouns, as in *user-friendly*, *customer-friendly*, and *pet-friendly*. I haven't yet heard the word *senior-friendly*, but I know what it would mean and, I will probably be hearing it soon. The ease with which English combines free and derivational morphemes allows writers to play with the language by inventing new words. Gillian Flynn does this in the novel *Gone Girl*, where the girl in question, who has assumed the persona of a *cool girl* (someone she thinks will please men), writes in her diary,

I've gotten so retro... shuffling out the door in my **swingy** tweed coat, my lips painted red, going to the *beauty parlor*.

Here the author has transformed the verb *swing* into the made-up adjective *swingy*, by adding the derivational suffix –y, whose diminutive [iy] sound suggests frivolity and silliness. Elsewhere in the diary the character writes about her boyfriend,

I find myself steering the course of conversations – **bulkily**, unnaturally – just so that I can say his name aloud.

The unnaturalness of the conversations is reflected in the unnatural, but still perfectly understandable, word *bulkily*, where the noun *bulk* has been pressed into service as an adverb by adding the derivational suffix –ly.

In discussing "The Clod and the Stone" we saw that Blake repeated and contrasted morphemes in order to create cohesion in the poem. As another example of these techniques, consider this poem by Lawrence Ferlinghetti.

Constantly risking absurdity

Constantly risking absurdity	1
and death	2
whenever he performs	3
above the heads	4
of his audience	5
the poet like an acrobat	6
climbs on rime	7
to a high wire of his own making	8
and balancing on eyebeams	9
above a sea of faces	10
paces his way	11
to the other side of day	12
performing entrechats°	13
and sleight-of-foot tricks	14
and other high theatrics	15
and all without mistaking	16
any thing	17
for what it may not be	18
For he's the super realist	19
who must perforce perceive	20
taut truth	21
before the taking of each stance or step	22

° A jump in ballet where the dancer crosses the legs a number of times

in his supposed advance	23
toward that still higher perch	24
where Beauty stands and waits	25
with gravity	26
to start her death-defying leap	27
And he	28
a little charleychaplin man	29
who may or may not catch	30
her fair eternal form	31
spreadeagled in the empty air	32
of existence	33

Ferlinghetti's poem is an example of *carmen figuration*, a form of verse where the graphic shape of the poem mimics the poem's subject. The awkward indenting of the lines suggests an acrobat tentatively making his way across a high wire, swaying and teetering with each step. The poem contains three stanzas. The first stanza, which comprises roughly half of the poem, describes what an acrobat does and metaphorically suggests what a poet does. The mood in this stanza is one of movement and danger, an impression that is conveyed not only by the line indentations but also by the use of action verbs. Looking first at the finite verbs we see that the acrobat/poet *performs*, *climbs*, and *paces*. In the last two stanzas, where the poet tells us why he does these things, the mood is more passive, as suggested by the verbs *be*, *perceive*, *stand*, and *wait*.

But finite verbs are not the only verbal forms in the poem. There are also a number of words ending in the morpheme *–ing*, and we might ask whether these words also contribute to the sense of action in the first half of the poem and passivity in the second half. In fact, the –ing words in the first half are more like verbs, suggesting action, and the –ing words in the second half are more like nouns, suggesting lack of action. To justify this claim, we will have to take a short grammar lesson.

When attached to a verbal stem, the –ing morpheme can create a present participle (which functions like a verb), or a gerund (which functions like a noun), or an adjective. Let us consider the adjective case first. One clue that *death-defying* in line 27 is an adjective is that it comes before and modifies the noun *leap*. Another clue is that *death-defying* has the determiner *her* in front of it, so, the structure *her death-defying leap* is an NP consisting of Det + Adj + N, with *death-defying* as the adjective.

Now let us consider the participles and gerunds. Participles are more verb-like than gerunds or adjectives and can, in fact, be considered truncated finite verb phrases from which some form of AUX *be* has been deleted, as shown in (1a,b).

Full verb form	Participle
(1a) While they *are exercising,* they listen to Bach.	While *exercising,* they listen to Bach.
(1b) While he *is balancing,* the acrobat performs entrechats.	While *balancing,* the acrobat performs entrechats.

Gerunds are verbal forms used as nouns, and like nouns, they can be preceded by determiners like *the* and *his*, as is shown in (2a–d).

(2a) **The skiing** was a lot of fun.

(2b) ... before **the taking** of each stance or step (line 22)

(2c) **His gambling** was getting worse.

(2d) ... a high wire of **his** own **making** (line 8)

These observations suggest a test for whether an –*ing* word (that is not an adjective) is a participle or a gerund. If you can parenthetically put a determiner in front of the –*ing* word and the phrase is still grammatical, then the word is a gerund; if the phrase is not grammatical, the word is a participle. Let us apply the gerund test to the –*ing* words in the poem, starting with *risking* in line 1.

Constantly **risking** absurdity and death whenever he performs...

Inserting *the* before *risking* we get

*Constantly, **the risking** absurdity and death whenever he performs...

That sounds bad. "The risking **of** absurdity and death" would be ok, but there is no *of* in the line, so *risking* must be a participle. Notice also that the line sounds fine if you restore the deleted verb *be* and its subject from in front of the participle:

Constantly, **he is risking** absurdity and death whenever he performs...

Now let's try the next –*ing* word.

... a high wire of his own **making** (line 8)

This phrase already contains the determiner *his*, so *making* has to be a gerund.

Now let's try

... and all without **mistaking** anything for what it may not be...

229

Placing a determiner in front of mistaking we get:

... and all without **his mistaking** anything for what it may not be...

This phrase sound fine, so *mistaking* is a gerund.

Counting up the results of the adjective and gerund tests for the whole poem, we find that that the first half contains three participles and two gerunds while the second half contains no participles, one gerund, and one adjective. This contrast in the number of participles supports the claim that the *–ing* forms in the first half of the poem are more verb-like than the *–ing* forms in the second half, and that this distribution contributes to the impression of more movement and action in the first half of the poem.

Exercises

1. Write examples of the following.
    a. A single free morpheme.
    b. A word with two bound morphemes.
    c. A morpheme that has two allomorphs in pronunciation (please list the allomorphs).
    d. A word with at least two morphemes containing a root that is not a free morpheme.
    e. A phonetic form that is an allomorph of two different morphemes.

2. Identify the bound morphemes in the following sentences.
    a. James Cagney thought of himself as a singer and a dancer.
    b. Calling a Texan a liar will usually cause a fight.
    c. Helping drug abusers means walking an emotional tightrope.

3. Identify the bound morphemes in the following sentences. If they are inflectional morphemes, give their names.
    a. The camera-toting tourists swarmed from the monorail, joining Epcot's late afternoon rush.
    b. I stood for hours at Cincinnati's riverfront dock, awaiting a Mississippi steamboat – a paddlewheeler named the *Memphis Queen*.

4. a. Bring up Linda Pastan's poem "To a Daughter Leaving Home" at the website http://www.loc.gov/poetry/180/075.html (or just google it).
    b. Identify the words containing past tense morphemes and the words containing progressive morphemes (the first two examples are done below). Remember that the past tense morpheme indicates that the action of the verb is in the past and the progressive morpheme indicates that the action is ongoing. Which kind of morpheme is more associated with the mother? Which with the daughter? Is there a change in this association as the poem progresses? How does this association contribute to the meaning of the poem?

Example:

To a Daughter Leaving Home

When I **taught** you   **past (associated with mother)**
  at eight to ride
a bicycle, lop**ing** along . . .   **progressive (associated with mother)**

7.3 **Semantics**

Semantics is the study of meaning in language, and in Chapter 3 we discussed an important area of semantics, namely how language maps our mental concepts onto words and sentences by means of metaphor and metonymy. In this chapter we will discuss another area of semantic research that can be applied to literary analysis called Case Grammar.

7.3.1 Semantic Case Roles

In the first part of this chapter we saw that in Levelt's (1989) psycholinguistic model of sentence production, verbs in the mental lexicon specify what NPs must accompany them. The verb *chase*, for example, must be accompanied by an NP that acts as the Agent of the chasing and an NP that acts as the Patient of the chasing. The verb *put* requires not only an Agent and a Patient but also a Location. You can't say,

> *Marsha put the book.
> AGENT   PATIENT

You have to say,

> Marsha put the book on the table.
> AGENT   PATIENT   LOCATION

(or specify some other location, like shelf or floor).

The study of the relationships among the NPs that particular verbs require is called *Case Grammar* and notions like Agent, Patient, and Location are called **semantic case roles**, or *case roles* for short (in some grammars they are called *thematic roles*). The notion of semantic case is similar to the notion of the parts of a sentence, like subject and direct object, that we studied in Chapter 4, but Case Grammar redefines and expands these traditional notions. Here are some more examples of sentences in which the semantic case of the NPs has been specified.

(3) Marsha   elbowed   John.
     <u>AGENT</u>   <u>PATIENT</u>

(4) Milhous   was sleeping.
     <u>PATIENT</u>

(5) Selena   hit   Venus   the ball.
     <u>AGENT</u>   <u>GOAL</u>   <u>PATIENT</u>

In sentence (3) Marsha is the Agent or doer of the action of elbowing, and John is the Patient or receiver of that action (some case grammar systems call this element the Theme). In sentence (4) Milhous doesn't perform any action, so he is not an Agent; rather, Milhous would also be called the Patient even though he does not receive an action but is just described by the verb. In (5) Venus is the Goal or intended destination to which Selena hits the ball.

Case roles can be thought of as the roles that NPs play in the little drama described by the verb. The drama in sentence (5) involves an NP playing the semantic role of Agent hitting an NP playing the semantic role of Patient to an NP playing the semantic role of Goal. Now consider sentence (6).

(6)   Selena   hit   the ball   to Venus
       <u>AGENT</u>   <u>PATIENT</u>   <u>GOAL</u>

Notice that this analysis confirms our intuition that the semantic relationship of the NPs in (5) and (6) is the same regardless of the different word orders. That is, we know that Venus is the intended destination for the ball regardless of whether the word *Venus* comes directly after the verb or after the preposition *to*. Similarly, the verb *put* describes a drama in which an Agent places a Patient in some Location, as in (7),

(7)   George   put <u>the plums</u> on <u>the top shelf</u>.
       <u>AGENT</u>   <u>PATIENT</u>   <u>LOCATION</u>

Case grammars contain several other case roles that characterize the semantic relationships that NPs can have within a sentence. Here are the case roles that we will use. They are customarily abbreviated by using just the first letter, but we will spell out Path to avoid confusion with Patient.

Agent   the NP that performs an action.
Patient   (sometimes called the **theme**) the NP that is affected by the action or described by the verb. Patient serves as a kind of default case role – if it is not clear what role an NP plays in a sentence, it is probably a Patient.
Goal   the NP to which another NP (usually the Patient) moves or is directed.
Source   the NP from which an NP (the Patient) moves or is directed.
Path   the route along which an NP moves.
Location   the place where an NP (the Patient) is located.

Experiencer   the NP (a usually a person) who has a feeling or experiences a sensation.
Instrument   the NP that the agent uses in fulfilling an action.
Time   the NP denoting the time at which an event takes place.

Here are some examples of how these case roles are used.

Melvin sprayed insecticide onto the tree last week.
  A   P   G   T

John grabbed the sandwich from Harvey.
  A   P   S

(Notice that John could also be considered to have a double role: both A and G.)

Attach the roof assembly to the uprights with two 3″ hexagonal bolts.
          P   G   I

The ant slowly traveled across the picnic table.
  A   Path

The bottle rolled off the table, along the deck, and into the pool.
  P   S   Path   G

Harvey was shocked when the White House issued its denial.
  E   A   P

Notice that in the last sentence *the White House* is a metonym for the President of the United States (see Chapter 3). For this reason, the case role Agent, which is almost always assigned to an animate NP, is assigned to what is literally an inanimate object. However, it is not always so obvious that an inanimate NP should be assigned an Agent case role because it is construed figuratively. For example, what case role should be assigned to *the wind* in the following sentence: "The wind blew down the tents"? Here, it seems appropriate to consider *the wind* a Patient because it does not purposefully blow down the tents. But what about this similar sentence: "The angry wind blew down the tents"? In this case, the adjective *angry* personifies the wind and suggests that it intentionally blew down the tents, so the Agent case role would be appropriate. Similarly, in the following lines from Thomas Hardy's poem "Channel Firing" the guns are personified and should be considered Agents.

Again the guns disturbed the hour,
       A   P

Roaring their readiness to avenge,
           P

As far inland as Stourton tower;
                G

And Camelot, and starlit Stonehenge.
      G   G

The examples discussed so far are relatively straightforward, but there are many instances where it is less clear how to assign case roles. Consider, for example, sentence (8).

(8)   The lawn mower sputtered to a stop.

Is the lawnmower an Agent or a Patient? Clearly, we are using *sputtered* figuratively bcause lawnmowers don't have mouths, so they can't literally sputter. So, does that mean that the lawnmower is personified and should be considered an Agent? In this case, probably not because *sputter to a stop* has become a conventional metaphorical expression to describe how gasoline engines quit working, so the role of Patient should be assigned. In general, the decision about whether an NP should be construed literally or figuratively depends on the context in which the NP occurs and on the overall interpretation of the text.

7.3.2 Case Roles in Literature

Now let us see how semantic case analysis can be used to analyze literature. Dennis Lehane's novel *Gone, Baby, Gone* is about the kidnapping of a four-year-old girl. Private detective Angie Gennero insists to her partner Patrick Kenzie that they must find the girl. In the following scenes, Lehane first portrays Angie's intense dedication to the search for the child and then describes her utter emotional and physical exhaustion following their initial failure. Marking the case roles that relate to Angie in the two scenes sheds light on how Lehane vividly contrasts her two moods.

First scene

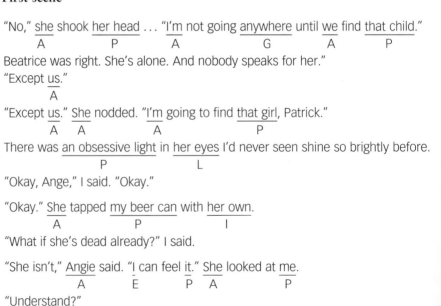

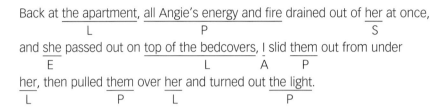

She drained her beer, tossed the can into the bag at my feet.
A   P   P   G   L
"Sure," I said.

Second scene

Back at the apartment, all Angie's energy and fire drained out of her at once,
      L   P   S
and she passed out on top of the bedcovers, I slid them out from under
   E   L   A   P
her, then pulled them over her and turned out the light.
L   P   L   P

In the first scene Angie is the Agent of almost all of the verbs. Such *agentive verbs* tend to be action verbs. Angie shakes her head, vows to find the child, and taps Patrick's beer can for emphasis. In the second scene Patrick is the Agent, and Angie is the inactive Source from which energy drains. Finally, she becomes merely a Location around which events take place. We could make the same point using the vocabulary of traditional grammar by saying that in the first scene Angie is the subject of transitive verbs, and is therefore shown to be acting on some object, while in the second scene she is mainly the subject of intransitive verbs or the object of prepositions, which shows her in a more passive role. However, semantic case analysis provides a more specific vocabulary and thus lets us see more clearly how the two scenes work.

Next, let us consider the semantic case roles in the first two stanzas of William Blake's poem "London." Below, the case roles of the major NPs have been marked. Notice that, as in the passage from *Gone, Baby, Gone*, when an NP contains another NP, only the higher NP is marked. For example, the phrase *where the chartered Thames does flow* is an NP that acts as the object of the preposition *near*. This NP contains the NP *the chartered Thames*, but the lower NP is not labeled here.

London

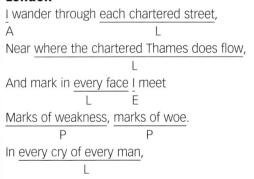

I wander through each chartered street,
A   L
Near where the chartered Thames does flow,
              L
And mark in every face I meet
         L   E
Marks of weakness, marks of woe.
        P   P
In every cry of every man,
          L

235

In <u>every infant's cry of fear,</u>
         L

In <u>every voice,</u> in <u>every ban,</u>°   °curse
      L   L

<u>The mind-forged manacles</u> <u>I</u> hear.
      P   E

The poem describes the experience of walking through the streets of London. The narrator first mentions encountering two of the city's landmarks: the chartered (planned and controlled) streets and the chartered Thames (in fact, the Thames' course was artificially altered). Both of these sights are physical locations, so the NPs that refer to them are marked with L. The narrator then describes encountering some of the human aspects of the city: the faces, the cries, and the curses. Like the physical landmarks, these aspects are presented in prepositional phrases containing an NP functioning as a Location, and this foregrounding serves to equate the faces and voices with the streets and the river. Similarly, the last four Location NPs, *every cry of every man, every Infant's cry of fear, every voice,* and *every ban,* should be interpreted metaphorically as Locations because all of them are preceded by the preposition *in,* which suggests an object situated in a place. But, here the NPs are not physical places (like a face) but sounds, namely cries, voices, and bans, in which mind-forged manacles are contained. Sounds, of course, cannot literally contain anything, so a metaphor is at work, namely the conceptual metaphor SOUNDS ARE CONTAINERS, which underlies expressions like: "I heard regret in her voice," and "There was a hesitation in his reply." This conceptual metaphor, then, construes the voices of the London streets as Locations, where mind-forged manacles are figuratively to be found. Thus, both the case role semantics and the conceptual metaphors in these lines equate the cries, curses, and bans with the river and the streets of London, suggesting that they are part of the permanent landscape of the city.

Exercises

1. Identify the semantic case of the NPs in the following sentences by writing the correct abbreviation below the NP.

    Example: <u>Popeye Doyle</u> shot <u>the man</u> on <u>the boat.</u>
                    A   P   L

    a. John washed the shirt in the bathtub.

    b. The rain washed the blood from the pavement.

    c. This material washes nicely.

   d. Marsha loaded the hay onto the wagon.
   e. Marsha loaded the hay with a pitchfork.
   f. The hay was loaded onto the wagon.
   g. A yellow-bellied sapsucker was spotted by Mr. Wolfe in the garden.
   h. George walked along the ridge from the saddle to the summit.
   i. Alice felt like a new woman.
   j. The kickoff took place at exactly seven o'clock.

2.   a. Identify the case roles of the underlined NPs in the following passage
          from *Pudd'nhead Wilson* by Mark Twain.

          Tom set his candle on the stairs, and began to make his way toward
          the pile of notes, stooping low as he went. When he was passing his
          uncle, the old man stirred in his sleep and Tom stopped instantly –
          stopped, and softly drew the knife from its sheath, with his heart
          thumping and his eyes fastened upon his benefactor's face. After a
          moment or two he ventured forward again – one step – reached for his
          prize, and seized it, dropping the knife-sheath. Then he felt the old
          man's strong grip upon him, and a wild cry of "Help! help!" rang in
          his ear.

       b. Twain's description of this incident is concrete and precise. How does his
          use of case roles contribute to this impression?

3.   Examine the case roles assigned to Gary Gilmore and Nicole Baker in
       the first paragraph of the passage from *The Executioner's Song* in
       section 6.5.3. Compare the number of Agent, Patient, and Experiencer
       roles assigned to Gary versus the number of these roles assigned to Nicole.
       How does this difference in case usage reflect your impressions of Gary
       and Nicole?

4.   In the following passage from Tom Wolfe's novel *A Man in Full*, the most
       important NPs have been underlined.
       a. Identify the case roles of the underlined NPs.
       b. If the passage were to be divided into two parts, where would the
          division come?
       c. What is the difference in the mood of part 1 versus the mood in part 2?
          How do the different case roles in the two parts help to create these
          different moods?

          On those magical evenings in San Francisco when the fog rolls in from
          the Pacific Ocean and people emerge from the hotels of Nob Hill and go
          for brave walks down the staggeringly steep slopes of Powell Street and
          [they] shiver deliciously in the chilly air and [they] listen to the happy

237

clapper clangor of the cable cars and the mournful foghorns of the freighters heading out to sea and all at once life is a lovely little operetta from the year 1910 – at that moment, likely as not, barely five miles to the east, a brutal sun has been roasting Contra Costa County for thirteen or fourteen hours, and the roof of the Croker warehouse is still swimming in caloric waves, even though the stars are out and the mercury remains swollen up to 90 degrees, down from 104 at 3 p.m., and the employees' parking lot, which is dirt, has been cooked to cinders until it's as parched, pocked, dusty, and godforsaken as the surface of Mars.

7.4 Pragmatics

Pragmatics is concerned with how the physical and social context of speaking influences the use of language. To see the importance of physical context consider the adverbs *here*, *there* and (in some dialects) *yonder*. In isolation, these words have no fixed meaning the way the word *cat* does. *Here* means the place where the speaker is located; *there* means a place some distance from the speaker, and *yonder* means a place at an even greater distance. So, when these words are used in speaking, their meanings can only be understood if we know the physical situation in which they are uttered. Social context is also important in the study of pragmatics. As we saw, in Levelt's (1989) model of speech production, pragmatic notions, such as whether the sentence should be framed in the active or passive voice, are represented at the conceptual level, the deepest level of meaning. The choice between active and passive depends on the context of speaking, and this context involves social considerations. Thus, as we saw in Chapter 4, the passive voice is often chosen if the Patient is more important than the Agent. For example, the active sentence

A streetcar ran over Antonio Gaudí.

seems less respectful of the great architect than the passive version

Antonio Gaudí was run over by a streetcar.

Similarly, forms of address, such as whether a suitor should address his girlfriend's father formally as "Mr. Jones" or informally as "George" are determined at the most basic level of sentence construction. Although Levelt (1989) does not discuss the details of how social context influences the production of sentences, it is apparent that pragmatic notions are involved at the conceptual level.

7.4.1 Speech Acts

A main tool of pragmatic investigation is the *illocutionary act* or **speech act**, and, like phonemic and syntactic analysis, speech act analysis can be used to break samples of language into their component parts. A speech act is what an utterance (or group of utterances) does, rather than how it is structured. For example, consider this famous dialogue.

WIFE: There's the phone.
HUSBAND: I'm in the tub.
WIFE: OK.

A Martian linguist trying to make sense of this exchange would be baffled. What does being in the bathtub have to do with the telephone, and what, exactly, is OK? Labeling the speech acts in the conversation makes the meanings clear.

WIFE: There's the phone. [This utterance acts as a *request* for the
            husband to answer the phone.]
HUSBAND: I'm in the tub. [This utterance acts as a *denial* of the request and
            also as an *excuse* for the denial (notice that an utterance can
            sometimes work as more than one speech act).]
WIFE: OK. [This utterance acts as an *acknowledgement* of the denial
            and the excuse.]

As the example shows, speech acts are used to do things with words, such as: request, deny, acknowledge, accept, apologize, command, invite, compliment, state, ask. The speech act that an utterance accomplishes is called its **illocutionary force**. The illocutionary force of the utterance "There's the phone" in the dialogue is to request the husband to answer the phone, but in a different context, say a motel owner showing a room to guests, the same utterance could have the illocutionary force of a statement pointing out the location of the phone.

There seems to be a large number of words that describe possible speech acts. Besides those mentioned above there are *deny, forbid, ask, vow, thank, resign*, and many more. The British philosopher J. L. Austin, who pioneered the study of speech acts, noticed that some speech acts are more closely related than others so that it is possible to group speech acts into broad categories. There have been many attempts to sort out the different kinds of speech acts, but we will use the system proposed by Parker and Riley (2005, p. 13), which includes the following six categories of speech acts.

Representatives describe some state of affairs. They include stating, informing, quoting, predicting, denying, notifying, admitting.
Questions ask for information. They include asking, questioning, querying, inquiring.

Directives try to get the listener to do something. They include requesting, ordering, suggesting, advising, warning, recommending.

Commissives commit the speaker to some course of action. They include promising, vowing, agreeing, pledging, betting, offering.

Expressives express an emotional state. They include exclaiming, apologizing, rejoicing, thanking, congratulating, complimenting, welcoming, deploring.

Declaratives change the state of the social world. They include marrying, hiring, firing, resigning, awarding, christening, arresting, sentencing.

7.4.1.1 Direct Speech Acts

Another way of classifying speech acts is according to whether they are **direct** or **indirect**. The illocutionary force of a direct speech act is usually clear as the examples to follow will show, but the exact illocutionary force of an indirect speech act can sometimes be difficult to determine. Direct speech acts can be further broken down into four types according to how we recognize their illocutionary force. The first type is the e*xplicit performative*, where the verb in the utterance names the speech act that the utterance performs:

> "I apologize for calling you an elitist." [**apology**]
> "I hereby request to be transferred." [**request**]
> "I command you to disperse." [**command**]
> "I christen this ship Titanic." [**christen**]
> "You can't fire me – I resign!" [**resignation**]

The second type of direct speech act conveys its illocutionary force without actually naming it. Instead, the illocutionary force is conveyed by a special syntactic form associated with the speech act, as in these examples.

> "Have you eaten yet?"

This utterance has the illocutionary force of a **yes-no question**, that is, a question that requires the answer yes or no. In yes-no questions an auxiliary verb (in this case *have*) must come before the sentence subject (in this case *you*) as we saw in Chapter 4.

> "Where are my socks?"

This utterance has the illocutionary force of a **wh- question**.

In wh- questions a wh- word like *where, when,* or *who* must come at the beginning of the sentence. As in yes-no questions, the subject and auxiliary verb are inverted.

> "Open the window."

This utterance has the illocutionary force of a **command**. In commands the subject of the sentence need not appear because it is understood to be *you*.

The third type of direct speech act uses certain expressions that are conventionally associated with a particular illocutionary force. For example, the expression "I'm sorry" is a direct apology because it is conventionally associated with apologies. Similarly, the word "please" is associated with requests so that "Will you please pass the salt?" is a direct request even though its syntactic form is used for yes-no questions.

The fourth type of direct speech act uses the most common syntactic form in English: the declarative, where the subject of the sentence precedes the verb. Several categories of speech acts share this form, including representatives, commissives, and declaratives. Examples include:

> "Columbus discovered America." [**statement, a type of representative**]
> "I'll give you a ride." [**promise, a type of commissive**]
> "You did a great job!" [**compliment, a type of expressive**]

Because these classes of direct speech acts do not have a unique syntactic form, their illocutionary force is conveyed by the meanings of the words in the utterance along with the context in which the utterance is expressed.

The question of whether a direct speech act is performed by means of a conventional expression (type 3) or by the overall meaning of the utterance (type 4) is controversial. Everyone agrees that an utterance that begins with the expression "I'm sorry" is, under normal circumstances, an apology. But what about the expression "I can't stand…" as in "I can't stand white limousines." Do we know that this utterance is a complaint because the first three words are conventionally associated with complaints or because of the meaning of the entire utterance?

7.4.1.2 Indirect Speech Acts

Speech acts can also be performed indirectly. To understand the illocutionary force of an indirect speech act the listener needs to know the context in which the utterance takes place. For example, the utterance "There's a gun in Mary Lou's handbag!" is, on its surface, a statement. But, it could also, under the right circumstances, serve as a warning, an admission, or even a boast. Notice that if this utterance were intended as, for example, a warning, there are actually two speech acts involved: the *literal speech act* (what the utterance appears to be on its surface, in this case a statement) and the *primary speech act* (the warning). Thus, the primary speech act is what conveys the illocutionary force. As another example, consider the utterance, "Can you open a window?" If a doctor were to say this to a patient with an arm injury, the patient would understand the utterance as a direct speech act with the illocutionary force of a yes-no question (are you able to open a window with your injured arm?). But, if a speaker addressed the sentence to someone who was sitting next to a window in a hot room, the hearer would understand the utterance as an indirect speech act of requesting. In this case the literal speech act would be a yes-no question and the primary (indirect) speech act would be a request. The reason the hearer knows that the literal speech act is not intended to convey any illocutionary force is because asking this question in these circumstances makes no sense, so the listener looks for some other way to interpret the sentence. Because the room is hot, it makes sense to interpret the literal question as an indirect request to cool things off by opening a window.

It is sometimes difficult to decide whether a particular speech act is intended to be direct or indirect, especially when family members are involved, as in this actual conversation.

YOUNGEST SISTER: Look, there's a new Johnson's Ice Cream.
OLDEST SISTER: We're not stopping.
MIDDLE SISTER: She's not asking to; she's just saying there it is.

Here only the middle sister correctly interpreted the youngest sister's utterance as a direct statement, not as an indirect request. In the case of asking "Can you open a window?" in a hot room, the illocutionary force is entirely that of a request. But, sometimes the literal act as well as the primary act can have some illocutionary force. For example, one friend might say to another "Would you like to go to a movie tonight?" intending the utterance to be both a real question (the literal act) and a suggestion that they go to a movie (the primary act). As we will see in the next section, it can be difficult to tease out all of the illocutionary intent in a particular utterance.

Often, specific speech acts are used in a predictable order in a **speech event**. A speech event has a recognized social purpose and is often conducted by people with particular social roles or positions. For example, a classroom lecture is a speech event involving a teacher and students, and it normally consists of a series of statements made by the teacher, followed by questions or comments made by the students, which are followed, in turn, by answers and comments from the teacher. Of course, sometimes teachers conduct classes by just asking questions, but such a class would not be characterized as a lecture. An interview on a late-night talk show is a speech event that includes the guest walking onto the stage to be greeted by the host, questions from the host that elicit jokes and stories from the guest, a signal from the host to end the conversation, such as a thank you or a handshake, and mutual good-byes, followed by applause (and a commercial). Other speech events include telling stories, asking a stranger for directions, making a sales transaction, and, as we will discuss, praying.

All of these speech events have a particular pattern or *script* (see Chapter 3) that includes an expected succession of speech acts.

7.4.2 Speech Acts in Literature

Practically everything we say or write is some kind of speech act and to understand ordinary conversation, we must closely follow which actions are being performed, as seen in the dialogue between the husband and the wife that was discussed earlier. Literature can also be analyzed in terms of speech acts. For example, consider the pragmatic structure of the following passage from Amy Tan's novel *The Joy Luck Club*, which is set in the Chinese immigrant community of San Francisco. The two main characters are a mother and a daughter, and the book is widely regarded as autobiographical with the author as the daughter. Examining the mother's and daughter's speech acts helps to illuminate the relationship between these characters. In the passage below the mother's utterances are numbered, and the corresponding numbers that appear below the passage identify the speech acts. Remember that an utterance can have more than one illocutionary force.

> My mother believed you could be anything you wanted to be in America. You could open a restaurant. You could work for the government and get a good retirement. You could buy a house with almost no money down. You could become rich. You could become instantly famous.
>
> **"Of course you can be prodigy, too,"**[1] my mother told me when I was nine. **"You can be best anything.**[2] **What does Auntie Lindo know?**[3] **Her daughter, is only best tricky."**[4]
>
> . . .
>
> We didn't immediately pick the right kind of prodigy. At first my mother thought I could be a Chinese Shirley Temple. We'd watch Shirley's old movies on TV as though they were training films. My mother would poke my arm and say, *"Ni kan"* – **You watch.**[5] And I would see Shirley tapping her feet, or singing a sailor song, or pursing her lips into a very round O while saying, "Oh my goodness."
>
> **"Ni kan,"**[6] said my mother as Shirley's eyes flooded with tears. **"You already know how. Don't need talent for crying!"**[7]
>
> Soon after my mother got this idea about Shirley Temple, she took me to a beauty training school in the Mission district and put me in the hands of a student who could barely hold the scissors without shaking. Instead of getting big fat curls, I emerged with an uneven mass of crinkly black fuzz. My mother dragged me off to the bathroom and tried to wet down my hair.
>
> **"You look like Negro Chinese,"**[8] she lamented, as if I had done this on purpose.

The instructor of the beauty training school had to lop off these soggy clumps to make my hair even again. "Peter Pan is very popular these days," the instructor assured my mother. I now had hair the length of a boy's, with straight-across bangs that hung at a slant two inches above my eyebrows. I liked the haircut and it made me actually look forward to my future fame.

In fact, in the beginning, I was just as excited as my mother, maybe even more so. I pictured this prodigy part of me as many different images, trying each one on for size. I was a dainty ballerina girl standing by the curtains, waiting to hear the right music that would send me floating on my tiptoes. I was like the Christ child lifted out of the straw manger, crying with holy indignity. I was Cinderella stepping from her pumpkin carriage with sparkly cartoon music filling the air.

In all of my imaginings, I was filled with a sense that I would soon become *perfect*. My mother and father would adore me. I would be beyond reproach. I would never feel the need to sulk for anything.

But sometimes the prodigy in me became impatient. "If you don't hurry up and get me out of here, I'm disappearing for good," it warned. "And then you'll always be nothing."

1. Literally this utterance is a statement, but it may indirectly convey the illocutionary force of a compliment and also some kind of directive suggesting that the daughter should become a prodigy.
2. This utterance seems to work just like the previous one.
3. Literally this utterance is a wh- question but it works indirectly as a statement that Auntie Lindo knows nothing; in other words, it is a criticism in the form of a rhetorical question.
4. Literally this utterance is a statement, but it works indirectly as a criticism of the daughter.
5. This is a direct command.
6. This is also a direct command.
7. Literally these two utterances are statements, but they work indirectly as a criticism of the daughter for crying too much.
8. Literally this utterance is a statement, but it works indirectly as a lament and as a criticism of the daughter for somehow being responsible for how her hair looks.

The mother's tone throughout the passage is mostly one of criticism. As the verb after quote 8 tells us, "You look like Negro Chinese" is a lament, but the narrator then says that the mother's words also convey the illocutionary force of a criticism – as if the daughter were responsible for her ruined hair. The mother also criticizes Auntie Lindo's daughter in quote 4. Quotes 1 and 2 constitute praise for the daughter by saying that she can be successful; however, given the overall tone of the passage, we might look to see if there is also some indirect illocutionary force. The phrase "of course" seems to vitiate the praise implied in "you can be prodigy, too," suggesting that it shouldn't really be that hard, and although I have not seen the speech act "nag" mentioned in the literature, these statements seem to have the illocutionary force of nagging.

The daughter's voice contrasts with the mother's. She does not speak directly, but her imaginings convey a tone of hope, as in the sentence, "I was filled with a sense that I would soon become *perfect*." Against the background of these two sharply contrasting voices, a third voice appears, the voice of the daughter's "inner prodigy":

> "If you don't hurry up and get me out of here, I'm disappearing for good," it warned. "And then you'll always be nothing."

The quotative verb tells us the illocutionary force of these utterances: they are warnings. This voice, then, is not the hopeful voice of the girl, but rather the internalized and critical voice of the mother.

Let us now consider the speech act structure of two poems. When analyzing a poem, it can be useful to get an overview of what's going on by mapping out who says what to whom and identifying the speech acts that each voice in the poem performs. We will first apply this technique to Shelley's "Ozymandias."

Ozymandias

I met a traveler from an antique land
Who said: Two vast and trunkless legs of stone
Stand in the desert ... Near them, on the sand,
Half sunk, a shattered visage lies, whose frown,
And wrinkled lip, and sneer of cold command,
Tell that its sculptor well those passions read
Which yet survive, stamped on these lifeless things,
The hand that mocked° them, and the heart that fed:
And on the pedestal these words appear:
"My name is Ozymandias, king of kings:
Look on my works, ye Mighty, and despair!"
Nothing beside remains. Round the decay
Of that colossal wreck, boundless and bare
The lone and level sands stretch far away.

Percy Bysshe Shelley

° mocked them up, i.e., sculpted them

The speech act structure of the poem is complex. It consists of an account provided by the main speaker, which contains within it an account provided by a traveler, which in turn contains a quote from an ancient emperor. These voices are shown below in different type faces, where regular type is the voice of the main speaker, italic type is the voice of the traveler, and boldface is the voice of the Emperor.

I met a traveler from an antique land
Who said: *Two vast and trunkless legs of stone*
Stand in the desert … Near them, on the sand,
Half sunk, a shattered visage lies, whose frown,
And wrinkled lip, and sneer of cold command,
Tell that its sculptor well those passions read
Which yet survive, stamped on these lifeless things,
The hand that mocked them, and the heart that fed:
And on the pedestal these words appear:
"My name is Ozymandias, king of kings:
Look on my works, ye Mighty, and despair!"
Nothing beside remains. Round the decay
Of that colossal wreck, boundless and bare
The lone and level sands stretch far away.

This speech act structure is shown in Figure 7.3, where each speaker's speech acts are noted.

Two observations emerge from Figure 7.3. The first is that the poem consists almost entirely of statements, as we might expect from a short narrative. The exception is Ozymandias's two commands, "Look on my works, ye Mighty" and "despair." The second observation is that these commands are buried deep within the poem. In fact, the commands are conveyed to us third-hand, through the sculptor,

1st Voice:	narrator
Speech acts:	statements
2nd Voice:	traveler
Speech acts:	statements
3rd Voice:	Emperor (reported by sculptor)
Speech acts:	statements, commands
4th Voice	narrator
	statements

Figure 7.3 Voices and associated speech acts in "Ozymandias"

the traveler, and then the narrator. Taking the interpretive leap, we can say that this distancing underlines the point made in the last lines of the poem: that power and glory are fleeting and will be destroyed by time. The Emperor's commands are buried as deeply in the pragmatic structure of the poem as the ruins of the Emperor's statue are buried in the sand.

Finally, we will consider John Donne's poem "Holy Sonnet 14," which constitutes the speech event of a prayer.

Holy Sonnet 14

Batter my heart, three-personed God; for You
As yet knock, breath, shine and seek to mend;
That I may rise and stand, o'erthrow me, and bend
Your force to break, blow, burn, and make me new.
I, like an usurped town, to another due,   5
Labor to admit You, but O, to no end;
Reason, Your viceroy in me, me should defend,
But is captived, and proves weak or untrue
Yet dearly I love You, and would be loved fain,
But am betrothed unto Your enemy,   10
Divorce me, untie or break that knot again;
Take me to You, imprison me, for I,
Except You enthrall me, never shall be free.
Nor ever chaste, except You ravish me.

John Donne

Reading the poem, especially reading it aloud, we are struck by its power. Some of this impression is achieved by means of meter and alliteration. In general, the meter is iambic, as in the regularly stressed last line.

Nor éver cháste excépt you rávish mé.

But some of the lines depart from the iambic pattern and pile up several stressed syllables in a row, as in this line:

and bend
Your fórce to bréak, blów, búrn, and máke me néw.

The strong effect of the three consecutive stresses is enhanced by their alliteration.

But, perhaps the most powerful aspect of the poem involves the speech acts that the speaker performs. This is not how one usually addresses God. Nine times the speaker commands God, ordering Him to batter, o'erthrow, make new, divorce, etc. This forceful language contrasts sharply with the polite language of direct requests usually found in prayers, such as, "I ask," and "I pray," and is thus externally foregrounded.

Let us again map out the speech act structure of the poem. This time there is only one speaker, but the speaker performs a variety of speech acts. These are shown below, where the poem is laid out with one clause (or reduced clause) per line with the quatrains separated. The indirect speech acts in the poem are labeled with the literal act first and the primary act second.

Batter my heart, three-personed God; [**command**]
for you As yet knock, breath, shine and seek to mend;
[**statement/complaint**]
That I may rise and stand, o'erthrow me, [**command**]
and bend Your force to break, blow, burn, and make me new.
[**command**]

I, like an usurped town, to another due, labor to admit You, [**statement**]
but O to no end; [**statement/complaint**]
reason, Your viceroy in me, me should defend, [**statement**]
but is captived, and proves weak or untrue. [**statement/complaint**]

Yet dearly I love You, [**declaration**]
and would be loved fain, [**statement/request**]
but am betrothed unto Your enemy. [**statement/confession**]
Divorce me, [**command**]
untie or break that knot again; [**command**]
Take me to You, [**command**]
imprison me, [**command**]

For I, except You enthrall me, never shall be free. [**statement**]
Nor ever chaste, [**statement**]
Except You ravish me. [**statement/request**]

As the title says, the poem is a sonnet, a verse form that contains three quatrains followed by a rhyming couplet, and often the quatrains address somewhat different themes. Examining the illocutionary forces in the poem, we can see that this is the case here. The poem contains three complaints (which like commands are not expected in a prayer), all of which occur in the first and second quatrains. Beginning in the third quatrain, the tone of the poem changes, in part because of the different illocutionary forces that the quatrain conveys. The first line of this quatrain contains a direct declaration of love followed by an indirect request to be loved in turn, which is followed by an indirect confession. These are the kinds of speech acts we expect to find in a prayer, making the voice in these three lines softer than that of the preceding quatrains. Notice also that these lines violate strict iambic pentameter by substituting unstressed syllables, which also helps to soften the tone. The twelfth line (Divorce me) resumes the forceful tone of the poem with four commands. The poem ends on a milder note with two rhyming statements, the second of which is an indirect request, couched in fairly regular meter. Thus, the poem not only contains the expected voice of the supplicant, which states, declares, and requests, but also the unexpected voice of the claimant, which complains and commands. The result is a poem of unusual power.

Exercises

1. Read the dialogue below and answer the questions that follow.

   JOHN: Can you pass the salt?
   MARSHA: Here it is.

   a. Identify the illocutionary force (i.e. the speech act) in each line of the dialogue.
   b. The first sentence has the syntactic form of a yes-no question, but Marsha doesn't answer yes or no. Why did she answer as she did? How did she know that the sentence was not really a yes-no question?

2. Someone stands between you and the TV you are watching, so you decide to say one of the following utterances. Identify the illocutionary force of each utterance and state whether the speech act is direct or indirect, mentioning the literal act and the primary act if the speech act is indirect.

   a. Move!
   b. You're in the way.
   c. Could you sit down?
   d. Please get out of the way.
   e. You make a better door than a window.

3. Name the illocutionary force in each of the following utterances. Then state whether the speech act is direct or indirect. If the speech act is direct, state whether or not it is an explicit performative.

   a. The English language originated in England.
   b. I promise to do the work.
   c. Don't take too long.

d. I'm sorry I broke the glass.

e. I declare this meeting adjourned.

f. You might give me a hand with this.

g. And you are ... ?

h. Could you keep quiet?

i. Do you have the time?

j. How right you are.

k. [A boss to an employee] "I suggest you rewrite this memo."

l. [A sign at the side of the road reads] *Construction Ahead.*

m. [In the corner of an envelope, there is a printed message stating] "Post Office will not deliver mail without proper postage."

---

4.   Name the illocutionary force in the following messages found in Chinese fortune cookies. Remember that an utterance can contain more than one illocutionary force. You need not say whether the speech act is direct or indirect, only what illocutionary force(s) is conveyed. Possibilities include: prediction (that is, an actual fortune), advice, compliment, insult, warning, and nag.

a. You will find happiness in mind and heart.

b. In order to have great friends, you must first learn to be a great friend.

c. Remember yesterday, but live for today.

d. If you are given an open book exam, you will forget your book.

e. Start a new project at work – or start a new job altogether.

f. Pray for what you want, but steal what you need.

g. The star of success is shining on you.

h. Your heart is pure and your mind is clear.

i. Do not be overly judgmental of your loved one's intentions or actions.

j. Your winsome smile will be your sure protection.

k. Be careful in whom you place your confidence.

---

5.   Read the following poem and map out its speech act structure by answering the questions that follow.

Grass

1 Pile the bodies high at Austerlitz and Waterloo.

2 Shovel them under and let me work –

3   I am the grass; I cover all.

4 And pile them high at Gettysburg

5 And pile them high at Ypres and Verdun.

6 Shovel them under and let me work.

7 Two years, ten years, and passengers ask the conductor:

8 What place is this?

9 Where are we now?

10   I am the grass.

11   Let me work.

Carl Sandburg

a. What is the main voice in the poem (that is, who is the main speaker)?

b. What is the main illocutionary force in the poem (that is, the most common speech act)?

c. Write three examples of this speech act from the poem.

d. What other voice is heard in the poem?

e. What speech acts does this voice perform?

f. The theme of this poem is something like: "Past battles are soon forgotten." In which lines is this theme most clearly revealed? What voice is speaking in these lines?

g. (Extra credit) Your answers to questions 3 and 4 were mainly observations about the structure of the poem. Now take the "interpretive leap" and explain the significance of your answers. That is, what is the significance of the fact that the main voice in the poem mostly utters the speech act that you identified in question b.?

6. The following passage (from Labov, 1972b, p. 356) is the beginning of a story told by Larry, a pre-adolescent living in Harlem. Identify the illocutionary force(s) of the speech acts in the underlined lines. If the speech act is indirect, state the literal act and the primary act. Extra credit: which lines have regular meter? What modern musical genre does this narrative remind you of?

a. An' then, three weeks ago I had a fight with this other dude outside.

b. He got mad 'cause I wouldn't give him a cigarette.

c. Ain't that a bitch?

d. Yeah, you know I was sittin' on the corner an' shit, smokin' my cigarette, you know

e. I was high, an' shit.

f. He walked over to me,

g. "Can I have a cigarette?"

h. He was a little taller than me, but not that much.

i. I said, "I ain't got no more, man,"

j. 'cause, you know, all I had was one left.

k. An' I ain't gon' give up my last cigarette unless I got some more.

[**Example:**   line a. statement]

Summary

Linguists have studied language at a number of different levels, and these levels appear to correspond to how linguistic knowledge is organized in the brain. In this chapter we have examined three of the levels. **Morphology** focuses on units smaller than the word, such as prefixes, suffixes, markers of tense, and markers of plurality. The repetition of morphemes, like the repetition of phonemes (as in alliteration) can add cohesion to a work of literature. Case grammar, a topic within the field of **semantics**, uses a system of universal semantic notions to analyze the relationships of NPs within a sentence. Semantic cases include Agent, Patient, Instrument, Source, Goal, Location, Time. Particular verbs require particular case roles. For example, *put* requires an Agent, a Patient, and a Location. Looking at the semantic cases within a text can provide insight into how an author creates scenes of action (with many Agentive cases), scenes of physical sensation (with many Experiencer cases), and so on. **Pragmatics** looks at how language is used rather than at how grammatical sentences are formed. One unit of pragmatic analysis is the speech act, such as an apology, a warning, or a question. Practically every utterance performs a speech act of some kind. Speech acts can be direct, as in "Pass me the salt," which is a command, or indirect, as in "Can you pass me the salt?" which is literally a question but has the illocutionary force of a request. Identifying the speech acts in a poem or dialogue is a good way of mapping out what is going on and also allows us to understand the pragmatic motivations of the speakers.

Key Terms

speech production model
morpheme
allomorph
lexical morpheme
functional morpheme
derivational morpheme
inflectional morpheme
semantics
semantic case roles
pragmatics
speech act
illocutionary force
speech event

Suggestions for Further Reading

Fromkin, Rodman & Hyams (2014), Fasold & Conner-Linton (2006), and Yule (2010) all contain good introductions to pragmatics and morphology, but their discussions of case grammar are brief. As usual, Fromkin, Rodman & Hyams (2014) is best for readers of the present book who wish to look further into these matters. Students who want to look more deeply into case grammar should read Cook (1989), which presents a comprehensive and clearly written introduction to case grammar. Fillmore (1968) provides a more advanced discussion. Students who would like to delve into speech act theory should read Austin (1962). This seminal work is written in a clear and elegant style and will reward anyone interested in language. Jeffries & McIntyre (2010) presents insightful analyses of some of the literary devices that authors have used at the different levels of language organization mentioned in this chapter.

CHAPTER 8

Discourse Analysis

"A reader only reads what he brings to the book. A writer constantly learns he was wrong."

Oscar Wilde

"Everybody has a story to tell."

William Labov

In this Chapter ...

So far in the book we have mainly looked at small chunks of language, starting with individual sounds and working up to individual sentences. In this chapter we will look at how sentences can be put together to form coherent texts, and how authors can create entire fictional worlds, called *text worlds*. We will observe that just as there are rules for building sentences, there are rules for building different kinds of text worlds, such as true stories and first-person fictional narratives. To understand how authors construct text worlds we will build upon concepts from cognitive science that were introduced in Chapter 3, in particular the cognitive model, which is a type of schema. We will see that authors use various linguistic tools, such as the pragmatic notion of deixis, to build text worlds in the minds of their readers. Characters also have ways of understanding the text worlds they inhabit and sometimes, as in the case of children, these ways are very different from the ways in which the reader understands the text world. Such ways of understanding are called the character's *mind style*. Finally, we will look at how computers can be used to study literary discourse.

8.1 Introduction: Schema Theory

A schema is any mental representation, as we learned in Chapter 3, where we paid particular attention to three types of schemas: concepts, cognitive models, and scripts. Recall that a concept is a mental representation of an object, such as a bird, or an event, or a bird landing on a branch. A cognitive model is a network of concepts that shows how the concepts are related to each other. For example, the cognitive model for a dog show contains the concepts of *dog*, *judge*, and *prize*, and relates these concepts to each other, indicating, for example, that if a dog bites a judge, it won't win a prize. A simplified cognitive model for publishing was shown in Figure 3.3. A script also shows how concepts are related to each other, but it includes instructions for how to act in particular situations. Figure 3.1 shows a script for what to do if you are approached by a strange dog. In short, concepts, cognitive models, scripts, and other kinds of schemas underlie and make possible our understanding of the world.

Schemas are not just deposits of knowledge stored in a mental vault, but rather are continually constructed as we attempt to understand what is going on around us. When we walk down the street, for example, we construct a schema of our surroundings that is based on what we see and hear. This kind of construction is called *bottom-up* or *stimulus-driven* processing, and it is guided by any schemas for the street that are already stored in memory, thus allowing us to anticipate rough spots in the

255

sidewalk, angry dogs, etc., and check to see whether any of these remembered elements might apply to the present moment. Checking our perceptions against existing schemas in memory is called *top-down* or *conceptually driven* processing. Bottom-up processing is guided by external stimuli and top-down processing is guided by prior knowledge, but the two processes work together. This procedure of schema activation followed by prediction followed by confirmation or disconfirmation by the senses applies to understanding all of our experience in the world. For example, in a restaurant we don't have to ask the server whether we should leave a tip because our restaurant script tells us that we should. However, for a restaurant in another country we might find that our restaurant script is wrong and must be modified.

Visitors to a foreign country often lack the appropriate scripts for dealing with everyday situations, and the result can be "culture shock," which after a few months can result in serious depression. I experienced some culture shock when I moved to Barcelona for a two-year stay, and one frustrating experience occurred in a bakery. I walked in and, seeing that there was no line at the counter, ordered some croissants, whereupon everybody in the bakery turned to me and said, "No! No! No!" I started for the exit, but then a nice lady explained to me that when you enter a bakery in Barcelona you are supposed to ask, "Who is the last one?" and the last person to enter will say, "It's me." Then you know that you will be served after that person. I proceeded to modify my bakery script to include the actions appropriate in a Spanish bakery.

Schemas allow us to understand texts as well as real-world experiences, and Goodman's (1967) widely accepted theory of reading comprehension involves a combination of bottom-up and top-down processing. In Goodman's theory people mentally assemble letters into words (or first translate them into sounds, which are then assembled into words) and assemble words into sentences. This is bottom-up processing. The sentences then activate a relevant schema in memory that allows the reader to predict what will come next. This is top-down processing. The prediction is then either confirmed or disconfirmed by more bottom-up processing. As Goodman says, "Reading is a psycholinguistic guessing game. It involves an interaction between thought [i.e. schemas] and language [i.e. texts]" (1967:108).

The psychology literature is full of experiments in which undergraduate students are asked to comprehend a text that does not contain enough clues for them to call up an appropriate schema for predicting and confirming what the text is about. Here is the text from an experiment by Bransford Johnson (1972). See if you can activate the schema that will allow you to understand it.

The procedure is actually quite simple. First you arrange things into different groups. Of course, one pile may be sufficient depending on how much there is to do. If you have to go somewhere else due to lack of facilities that is the next step, otherwise you are pretty well set. It is important not to overdo things. That is, it is better to do too few things at once than too many. In the short run this may not seem important but complications can easily arise. A mistake can be expensive as well. At first the whole procedure will seem complicated. Soon, however, it will become just another facet of life. It is difficult to foresee any end to the necessity for this task in the immediate future, but then one never can tell. After the procedure is completed one arranges the materials into different groups again. Then they can be put into their appropriate places. Eventually they will be used once more and the whole cycle will then have to be repeated. However, that is part of life (p. 722).

In Bransford and Johnson's experiment one group of participants listened to just the quoted paragraph above, and, probably like you, they didn't think it made much sense and later could hardly remember any of it. A second group of participants listened to the same paragraph but this time they were given its title, "Doing Laundry." These participants thought that the text made perfect sense, and later they remembered most of it.

A lot of bad writing can be blamed on an author's inability to activate the appropriate schemas in the reader. In his how-to-write book *The Sense of Style*, Pinker (2014) devotes an entire chapter to explaining "the curse of knowledge," which is the difficulty that experts face in explaining their fields to a lay audience. The problem, of course, is that the experts cannot easily put themselves in their readers' shoes and anticipate what schemas the readers already possesses regarding the experts' specialized field. As Pinker (2014:61) says, "It simply doesn't occur to the writer that her readers don't know what she knows," and the result of this failure, Pinker believes, is no less than "a pervasive drag on the strivings of humanity, on par with corruption, disease, and entropy" (p. 62).

Literary authors must also to some extent anticipate what schemas their readers possess, and all literary passages assume considerable background knowledge about their settings. For example, consider the opening paragraph of Katherine Mansfield's short story "Her First Ball," published in 1921.

Exactly when the ball began Leila would have found it hard to say. Perhaps her first real partner was the cab. It did not matter that she shared the cab with the Sheridan girls and their brother. She sat back in her own little corner of it, and the bolster on which her hand rested felt like the sleeve of an unknown young man's dress suit and away they bowled, past waltzing lampposts and houses and fences and trees.

The first schema that the passage activates is the schema for *ball*, and Mansfield assumes that her readers will know that a ball is an occasion where men and women dance with partners of the opposite sex, where the men wear dress suits, and where the women touch the sleeves of those suits. This background knowledge allows her to explore the metaphor that the cab taking Leila to the ball, and not a young man, is Leila's first dancing partner. The second schema that the text activates is the schema for *cab*, and here modern readers may experience some confusion. The cab apparently held six people including the driver (there are four Sheridan siblings), and it is hard to imagine how this would work in a modern taxi cab. Were three people sitting up front? And what is the bolster where Leila rested her hand? Because the story is set in Wellington, New Zealand in the early twentieth century, Mansfield is probably evoking the schema for a horse-drawn carriage, which had room for six people inside with the driver sitting outside. The bolster refers to the upholstery of the seat. So, the cab schema that Mansfield aimed to activate is not present in modern readers' minds, and must be constructed by a modern editor in a footnote to the story. Such footnotes often provide schema construction for period literature.

The way schemas allow us to understand oral and written texts is addressed by text world theory, a branch of stylistics that emerged in the 1990s. We will take a look at this theory in some detail after considering some actual texts in the form of stories.

8.2 The Structure of Narratives

A narrative is the representation of past experience in language, and narratives can be found in many genres, including biography, news reports, jokes, and stories, which can be true or fictional. Stories have been extensively studied by psychologists and sociolinguists, and in this section we will look at them from both of these perspectives.

8.2.1 Folktales

Probably the most famous story in cognitive psychology is "The War of the Ghosts," a Native American tale that was used by Bartlett (1932) in pioneering studies of how schemas enable us to understand texts. This story is difficult for Europeans and European-Americans to understand because it does not conform to their schemas of life and death. It tells of a young man who encountered a war party made up of ghosts. He joined the party, and they traveled up a river in canoes and engaged in a battle with an enemy tribe, where the young man was wounded. He then returned to his village, where he told his story and then died. The Native American audience for whom the story was intended believed that death is a spiritual as well as a physical process, so they understood that the young man's death began when he joined the ghosts. This process continued in the ghostly battle where the young man was wounded and ended in his village when he physically fell after telling his story. However, when Bartlett's European-American participants were asked to retell the story, they changed it to fit their schema for death so that the cause of the young man's death was thought to be his physical wounds and not his encounter with the ghosts. Bartlett concluded that his participants' understanding and memory of the story were mediated through their pre-existing schemas.

Mandler (1984) studied the structure of folktales, mostly from European sources, and found that they share a structure so common that it can be described by a phrase structure grammar, whose rules (such as rule 1 below) can be considered psychologically real schemas for a prototype story. A simplified version of this grammar looks like this:

1.   story → setting, episode

2.   episode → beginning, development, outcome

3.   development → action, (action), (action), etc.

Mandler's story grammar can be used to analyze the Mother Goose nursery rhyme "The Old Woman Who Lived in a Shoe," as shown in Figure 8.1.

There was an old woman who lived in a shoe.
She had so many children, she didn't know what to do.
She gave them some broth without any bread;
And whipped them all soundly and put them to bed.

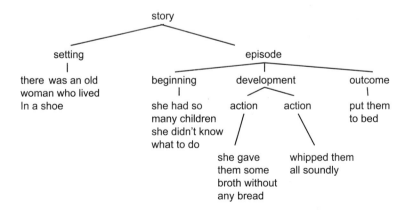

Figure 8.1 "There Was an Old Woman Who Lived in a Shoe" analyzed using a simplified version of Mandler's story grammar

Of course, stories don't have to conform to the pattern generated by Mandler's story grammar ("The War of the Ghosts" is one example), and to test the psychological reality of the grammar, Mandler (1984) wrote some stories that fit the grammar and some that did not. She then asked students at different grade levels to read the stories and rate how good they were. She found that her participants liked the stories that conformed to the story grammar better than those that did not, and also that they remembered the "grammatical" stories better. In sum, Mandler's research suggests that readers have a schema specifying the prototypical form of a story, and that they appreciate and remember stories more when they conform to this schema.

8.2.2 Personal Narratives

The sociolinguist William Labov, whom we met in Chapter 6, has studied personal narratives, which are stories that people tell informally about their own experiences, like the time they almost drowned, or when they got into trouble with the law. Labov found that personal narratives typically have a structure that is very similar to Mandler's story schema, and in this section we will examine this structure in some detail.

The structure of personal narratives can be seen in a story collected by the anthropologist Shirley Brice Heath (1983) in a small community in the North Carolina Piedmont. The storyteller is Sue, the leader of a group of women who have gathered at her home for religious instruction. Following the lesson, the conversation turns to domestic topics.

MRS. MACKEN:	Sue, you oughta tell about those rolls you made the other day, make folks glad you didn't try to serve fancy rolls today.
MRS. DEE:	Sue, what'd you do, do you have a new recipe?
MRS. MACKEN:	You might call it that. . . .
MARTHA:	Now Millie [Mrs. Macken], you hush and let Sue give us *her* story.
SUE:	Well, as a matter of fact, I did have this new recipe, one I got out of *Better Homes and Gardens*, and I thought I'd try it, you see, it called for scalded milk, and I had just started the milk when the telephone rang, and I went to get it. It was Leona... I thought I turned the stove off, and when I came back, the burner was off, uh, so I didn't think anything about it, poured the milk in on the yeast, and went to kneading. Felt a little hot. Well, anyway, put the stuff out to rise, and came back, and it looked almost like Stone Mountain, thought that's a strange recipe, um so I kneaded it again, and set it out in rolls. This time I had rocks, uh, sorta like 'em, the kind that roll up all smooth at the beach. Well, I wasn't gonna throw that stuff all out, so I cooked it. Turned out even harder than those rocks, if

260

that's possible, and nobody would eat 'em, couldn't even soften 'em in buttermilk. I was trying to explain how the recipe was so funny, you know, see, how I didn't know what I did wrong, and Sally piped up and said, "Like yea, when you was on the phone, I came in, saw this white stuff a-boiling, and turned it off." (Pause) Then I knew, you know, that milk was too hot, killed the yeast. Guess I'll learn to keep my mind on my own business and off other folks'.

Labov (1972b) has identified five parts that most oral narratives contain, namely the *abstract, orientation, complicating action, resolution, evaluation*, and *coda*.

1. The *abstract* is a short summary at the beginning of the story to give listeners an idea of what the story is about. In Sue's story the abstract is provided by Mrs. Macken. In her invitation to Sue to tell the story, she lets the audience know that the story is about making rolls that didn't turn out so well. A more typical abstract can be seen in Flora P.'s story in Chapter 4 (which is not complete, only the first part is quoted). The abstract in that story is the following clause: "An' another time, honey, I 'uz in a – I 'uz in a – in a shore 'nuff cyclone. . . ."

2. The *orientation* sets the stage for the action of the story. It tells who, where, what, and when. The orientation in Sue's story is everything that comes before the clause "I had just started the milk," where we learn that Sue was trying out a new recipe that called for scalded milk. Because we know that the story involves cooking, we also understand that the setting is in Sue's kitchen.

3. The *complicating action* is the only non-optional part of a narrative. The action is related in *narrative clauses,* which drive the plot of the story forward. The first action in Sue's story is when she puts the milk on the stove, so the first narrative clause is "I had just started the milk." The next narrative clause is "when the telephone rang." The next clause, "it was Leona," is not a narrative clause because no action takes place. The temporal order of the actions described in narrative clauses cannot be changed without changing the nature of the story. If Sue had talked on the telephone before she started the milk, the story would be very different. Therefore, a test to see whether a clause is a narrative clause or not is to move it to a different location and see if this changes the story. For example, the clause "Felt a little hot" is not a narrative clause because it can appear after the next clause without changing the story, as follows: "Well, anyway, put the stuff out to rise although it felt a little hot. . . ."(also, of course, this clause does not describe an action). All of the narrative clauses taken together comprise the *foreground* of the story. Everything else is part of the *background*.

4. The *resolution* describes how the story turned out. In Sue's story the resolution begins with the clause, "… and then Sally piped up…" and ends with the phrase, "killed the yeast."

5. The *evaluation* expresses the narrator's opinion about or stance toward the narrative. For example, when Sue says, "I was trying to explain how the recipe was so funny, you know, see, how I didn't know what I did wrong, …" she is emphasizing how puzzled and frustrated she was. Another function of evaluative statements is to let the listener know why the story is important. Labov (1972b) says that the worst thing a storyteller can hear from a listener is, "So what?" indicating that the story wasn't unusual or interesting enough to be told. To avoid this reaction, storytellers often point out the unusual and important features of the narrative, sometimes exaggerating them, as when Sue says, "This time I had rocks, …" The most important evaluative statement in Sue's story is the last line, which acts as a moral (don't gossip): "Guess I'll learn to keep my mind on my own business and off other folks'." This statement frames the story as a parable that is instructive and worthwhile for the audience, not just the story of a silly mistake.

6. The *coda* is a short statement following the narrative proper that connects the story to the present time, thus signaling that the story is over. The coda in Sue's story is the last line, which, as mentioned, also serves as an evaluative statement. A more typical coda would be something like: "Nowadays, I always turn off my phone when I'm cooking."

Let us now examine a shorter oral narrative, looking for the six parts identified by Labov. The following story was told by Benny, an eighth-grade student in Tucson, who was talking to me about a time when he got in trouble.

That wasn't the worst time.	1
The worst time was	2
when I hit some little boy through a window.	3
It was because	4
he was on the other side of the window	5
'n' he kept makin' faces at me,	6
'n' I just go with my fist,	7
'n' hit him,	8
'n' broke the window.	9
He had all kinds of cuts.	10
They took me to Juvi [Juvenile Court].	11

The first thing to do when analyzing an oral narrative is to find the first narrative clause, where the action begins. In Benny's story it is line 6, "he kept makin' faces at me." This is a continuing action and so might seem to be part of the orientation, but it must occur before Benny hits the little boy. If this action had occurred after the hitting, the story would not be the same. Notice that the verb in the next sentence, "go," is in the present tense although it describes a past event. This is the *historical present* tense, which good storytellers can use to heighten the immediacy of their narrative. The abstract of Benny's story is lines 1–3, where he provides a brief preview of what the story is about. The orientation is lines 3–6. Notice that line 3 has two functions. It is part of the abstract because it previews the story and also part of the orientation because it tells us who was involved. Line 5 tells us where Benny and the little boy were, and line 6 tells us why Benny did what he did. Several clauses in the story provide evaluation, letting us know why this story is worth listening to. Line 1 tells us that this was the worst trouble that Benny has gotten into; line 10 tells us that the little boy was badly hurt, and line 11 tells us that this event was serious enough to land Benny in court. These last two lines also provide the resolution to the conflict – the antagonist is defeated, but Benny pays a price. Benny's narrative contains no coda.

As the analysis of Sue's and Benny's stories suggests, personel narratives are usually easier to analyze than literary narratives, which can begin at the end of a story (detective novels often begin with the murder and work backwards), or jump back and forth in time. Indeed, the Russian Formalists distinguished between the *story* and the *plot* of a narrative. The story is the chronological order of events as they must have transpired whereas the plot is the order of events in which they are presented to the audience, along with the motivation for those events. For example, the movie *Citizen Kane* begins with the death of the protagonist, after which his life story is told in a series of flashbacks and flashforwards. Narratives in novels can also intertwine with other narratives and can be spread out over many chapters. Nevertheless, literary works often contain small narratives embedded within the larger plot structure, as in the haircut story in *The Joy Luck Club* (see Chapter 7, Section 7.4.2), and these stories-within-a-story often stick to the traditional narrative format.

8.3 Text World Theory

We now return to the question of how schemas allow us to understand texts. In life, when we walk into a bakery or encounter a strange dog, what we see and hear interacts with the schemas in our memory to allow us to understand the situation directly. But, when we communicate with other people, understanding becomes less direct. Werth (1999) proposed that the act of communicating by means of language, whether spoken or written, can be analyzed on two levels. The first level is the discourse world, which is "the situational context surrounding the speech event itself" (Werth 1999: 83). The situational context – the discourse world – for Sue's story of the ruined rolls was a gathering of friends in her living room, where Sue was the speaker and her friends were the audience. If we wanted to describe this discourse world in more detail, we could mention that Sue's house was located in "Roadville," which is in the North Carolina Piedmont, where the group had met to study the Bible, and that the Bible study portion of the meeting was over, so the women were just socializing. The discourse world of a communicative event also includes cultural information, so we could add that in Sue's subculture personal narratives are expected to be without exaggeration or embellishment ("don't lie"), and that a story which reflects badly on someone can only be told by that person or in that person's presence or the presence of their representative ("don't gossip"). In short, the term *discourse world* refers to that part of the real world that is relevant to a particular speech event, whether spoken or written.

In a face-to-face conversation, the speaker and the audience are in the same physical location, but in other communicative events they are not. For example, two people talking on the phone or skyping are usually separated in space; nevertheless, they are both participants in the same discourse world. In the case of reading a text, the author and the reader are separated not only in space but also in time. In fact, the creation of a written text may have taken place centuries before and continents away from the actual act of communication, which occurs when the reader reads the text. Nevertheless, the discourse world of reading still contains a real-life author and a real-life reader. These situations are called split discourse worlds.

The second level of analysis in text world theory is the text world, which consists of the schemas that are created in the minds of listeners or readers when they understand spoken or written words. In the discourse world of Sue's living room two main text worlds were created. The first text world was created by the conversation among Sue's friends before Sue began her story. It consisted of the following discussion:

MRS. MACKEN: Sue, you oughta tell about those rolls you made the other day, make folks glad you didn't try to serve fancy rolls today.
MRS. DEE: Sue, what'd you do, do you have a new recipe?
MRS. MACKEN: You might call it that. . . .
MARTHA: Now Millie [Mrs. Macken], you hush and let Sue give us *her* story.

Here, Mrs. Macken, Mrs. Dee and Martha jointly constructed a schema – a text world – in their minds and in the minds of the others in the room that included the information that Sue had made rolls that didn't turn out so well. The second main text world was created by Sue when she told her story.[1] Thus, two text worlds emerged from the same discourse world. However, these text worlds differ in several ways, including their purpose, time, and location. The conversation text world was created in order for the discourse world participants to comprehend what was being said in real time, but the story text world was created by Sue so that her audience could understand a past event. The location and the time of the two text worlds differed as well. The physical location of the conversation text world was Sue's living room and the time was the here-and-now, whereas the location of the story text world was Sue's kitchen and the time was several days in the past. The participants in the two text worlds overlapped a bit but not completely. The text world created by the conversation included all of the discourse world participants – Sue, Mrs. Macken, Mrs. Dee, Martha, and others – whereas the text world created by the story included Sue and Mrs. Macken but also Katie, who was not a participant in the discourse world. In literary fiction there is often no overlap between the participants in the discourse world (the author and the reader) and the characters[2] in the text world, as we will discuss. In sum, a text world emerges from a discourse world, but may or may not share its place, time, purpose, or participants.

The participants in the discourse world where Sue tells her story share more than a physical context: they also share a lot of background knowledge. For example, they all know Katie, and they also know the script for making rolls, so they understand that rolls will not rise without the presence of living yeast cells, which will be killed if you douse them with scalding milk. In addition, these participants know about Stone Mountain and about rocks that have rolled up on the beach, as well as many other pieces of background information that Sue assumes in her story. In a split discourse world, the language producer and the audience also share some amount of background information, though as we saw in the discussion of "Her First Ball," when the background schemas of author and reader are different, misunderstandings can result.

8.3.1 Cognitive Concepts

Text world theory is based on the discipline of cognitive linguistics, which attempts to understand how the mind works. So, before turning to the analysis of written texts, we will take a brief look at a cognitive linguistics explanation of how human beings communicate with each other. As we have seen, people understand what goes on around them in the real world by means of the interplay between external stimuli and internal schemas. We know what to do when we walk into a McDonalds because we can see the "McDonalds" sign and because we have walked into a McDonalds at least a few times before. This interplay of bottom-up and top-down cognitive processing creates an on-line schema for understanding our surroundings. When people communicate by speaking, they create a text world, and to understand this world a similar procedure of bottom-up and top-down processing occurs. In this case, however, the stimuli for the bottom-up processing are not sights like a McDonalds sign, or natural sounds like lake water lapping. Rather, the stimuli are the sights of the discourse world setting (as when a speaker points to a cat) and the sounds of the phonemes that the speaker utters. Let's say that speaker A wishes to share with listener B the proposition "The cat chased the mouse," which we can represent conceptually using the notation introduced in Chapter 7, Section 7.1 as in (1).

(1)

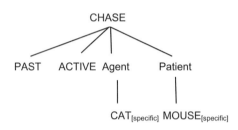

To communicate this idea, A must create a very simple text world (it contains only two characters) in B's mind that corresponds to his own schema. He can do this by uttering the phonetic sequence [ðə kʰætʰ čʰeystʰ ðə maws], which B's language comprehension system will convert through the various levels described in Chapter 7 (this time working backwards from the phonetic level to the conceptual level) into schema (1). This process can be represented pictorially as in Figure 8.2.

In this example, A's original idea and the text world that he creates in B's mind are identical, but in communicating more complex schemas, there can be discrepancies between what A has in mind and what B understands, as we saw in the discussion of "Her First Ball."

The differences in readers' interpretations is widened when one moves beyond the literal understanding of a text. Recall from Chapter 1 that the reader-response critic Rosenblatt (1978) distinguished between the efferent and aesthetic modes of reading. In the efferent mode the reader focuses only on the literal meaning of a text while in the aesthetic mode the reader focuses on the feelings and memories that a text evokes. In the aesthetic mode readers' interpretations can vary widely. To take a small example, consider the text in Figure 8.2 "The cat chased the mouse." The figure represents only the literal meaning of the text, which is represented by

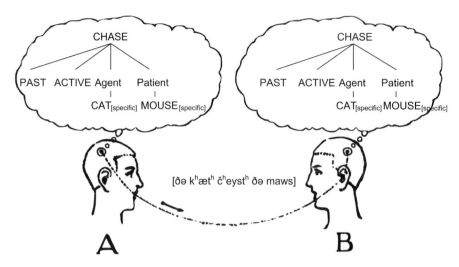

Figure 8.2 Diagram showing how a speaker creates a schema, or text world, in the mind of a listener

identical schemas in the minds of A and B. But A and B might have very different associations and memories associated with cats and mice. If A is a farmer, he might have positive associations with the statement, whereas if B is an animal rights activist, the statement might evoke horror.

Most of the schools of culture-oriented literary criticism mentioned in Chapter 1, including Marxism, feminism, and African-American criticism, aim to expand the reader's aesthetic understanding of a text, thus changing the reader's schemas regarding the areas relevant to the particular interests of their school. For example, a Marxist critic of *Pride and Prejudice* might draw attention to the rigid class structure that the novel portrays, while a feminist critic might emphasize the subservient position of women in eighteenth-century English society, and an African-American critic might point out that the wealth and prosperity of the upper class that is depicted in the novel depended to some extent upon the African slave trade. Nevertheless, all of these critics would agree on the literal meaning of the novel. In Section 8.3.6 we will further consider how literature can change readers' schemas regarding an area of knowledge and thus change the way that they view the world.

In the next section, we will look in more detail at how speakers and authors build text worlds.

8.3.2 Deixis

Einstein taught us that measuring time and space is always relative to an observer. For example, if a passenger on a spaceship traveling very fast looks at the clock on the wall and can somehow simultaneously see a clock on a wall on earth, the earth clock will appear to be moving slower than the

267

spaceship clock. However, someone on earth looking at both clocks will observe that the space clock is moving slower. So, the relative speed of the two clocks depends on who is looking at them. In some ways it is the same with how language refers to things in time and space. Many expressions can only be understood relative to a particular speaker (not an observer). For example, as we saw in Chapter 7 *here* means the place where the speaker is located and *there* means a place some distance from the speaker. Similarly, the meaning of the phrase "See you tomorrow" depends on the time that the speaker utters it. "Tomorrow" can mean "Monday" only if the phrase is spoken on a Sunday. The study of such relational expressions is called deixis (from the Greek meaning to point the finger), and this is the main tool that speakers and authors use to build text worlds.

Any communicative context (that is, any discourse world) involves a number of dimensions, and over the years linguists have tried to specify exactly what these are and how they are related to each other. A basic list of the dimensions that define a discourse world includes the time, the place, the speaker/writer, and the audience. For example, the dimensions of the discourse world in which Benny told his story were as follows:

Time: the past
Place: an empty classroom
Speaker: Benny
Audience: me

The prototype situation for the use of deixis is a real-life conversation where everybody can see each other, and where a speaker might actually point their finger at a person or a location to emphasize the meaning of a deictic expression, such as *that girl* or *over there*. In conversation, the speaker is indicated by the deictic pronoun *I* or one of its inflected forms *me* and *my* (*we*, *us* and *our* in the case of politicians and authors). The audience is indicated by *you* or one of its vernacular alternates such as, *y'all*, *youse*, *yinze* or *you lot*. The people or things being talked about are indicated by a form of *he*, *she*, *it* or *they*. Notice that none of the deictic pronouns have a fixed meaning. Their meanings depend completely on who is speaking and who is being spoken to or about.

Like pronouns, verb tenses are deictic and are based on the speaker's perspective. For example, the past tense in "They took me to Juvi" is only appropriate if that action occurred prior to the moment of speaking. In a similar way, place can be indicated by deictic adverbs like *here*, *there*, and (in some dialects) *yonder*, which identify particular locations in relation to the speaker. The demonstrative pronouns *this*, *these*, *that* and *those* are also deictic. The first pair modify objects that are close to the speaker and the second pair modify objects that are farther away. Earlier varieties of English also used *yonder* as a demonstrative pronoun allowing for a three-way division of the distance from speaker to the object being referred to, as in "What light from *yonder* window breaks?" To summarize, because deictic words locate people, time, objects, and places in relation to a speaker, they serve to establish the speaker as the center of the communicative setting.

The articles *a* and *the* are also deictic. The rules for using them are complicated and depend on several characteristics of the noun phrases that they are part of, but articles always indicate some relationship between a noun phrase and the speaker and the audience. For example, consider the following text:

A princess lived in *a* castle. *The* castle was drafty.

The reason that *a* is used with the first instance of *castle* is that the speaker knows about the castle but the audience does not, so *castle* is new information in the discourse. *The* is used with the second *castle* because now both the speaker and the audience know about the castle, so it is old information. As we saw in Chapter 1, this way of signaling new and old information serves to create cohesion in the text. Speakers can often assume that their audience already knows about a noun phrase that has not so far been mentioned in a discourse. For example noun phrases that are unique to a particular context are assumed to be publicly known within that context. If I say, "Please open *the* door," you know that I mean the door to the room that we are in because that is the only relevant door. Similarly, we usually refer to the nearest star as "*the* sun" because that is the only sun that is relevant to our communicative context, making it unique and thus a kind of assumed or old information.

Everybody knows about the sun, but in many speech situations only a particular speaker and audience share certain information. For example, a mother might say to a father, "Did you get presents for *the* kids?" meaning *their* kids, which both of them know about, but which many other people in the world do not. Similarly, one co-author might say to another, "Have you received the check yet?" where only they know which check they are expecting. Thus, the context in which unique reference (and use of *the*) is determined is not just the physical context of the communication, but the entire world knowledge of the discourse world participants.

Let us now take a look at how Benny used deixis to create a text world when he told his story. As already mentioned the participants in this discourse world were just Benny and me, and the setting was an otherwise empty classroom, where I had been helping Benny with his homework. But, this speech event was not like the conversation among Sue's friends, where the time and location of the discourse world and the text world were the same. Rather, in telling his story Benny, like Sue, created a text world set in

269

a different time and place. For convenience, we will consider just the first part of Benny's story, which is repeated here.

That wasn't the worst time.	1
The worst time was	2
when I hit some little boy through a window.	3
It was because	4
he was on the other side of the window	5
'n' he kept makin' faces at me,	6
'n' I just go with my fist,	7
'n' hit him,	8
'n' broke the window.	9

In text world theory the text world that Benny created can be represented by a diagram like Figure 8.3, where the elements and propositions of the text world are displayed. Notice that the propositions are displayed in the form:

elements   →   actions or states
   (NPs)   (VPs)

Benny builds his text world first of all by using noun phrases to establish (or *nominate*) entities, such as *window*, and characters, such as *little boy*, and he uses verb phrases to nominate actions, such as *go with my fist*, and *broke the window*. He also uses deixis. The deictic pronoun *I* in line 3 establishes Benny as the center of the text world, and the simple past tense, as in *was* and *broke*, establishes that the story took place before the speaking event. Notice that the phrase *the worst* is also deictic because it ranks this incident in relation to the other times Benny got in trouble. In line 3 Benny uses the article *a* to introduce the object *window* into the text world, but after this he says "*the* window" because now this information is

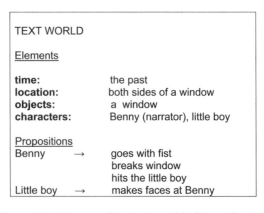

Figure 8.3 Diagram of the text world of Benny's story

known to both of the discourse world participants. Similarly, Benny nominates the second text world character with the indefinite phrase "some little boy," but after that he uses the pronouns *he* and *him* because now this information is shared between speaker and audience. These uses of deixis serve to create a cohesive text world centered on the narrator of the story.

Deixis is used for world-building in the split discourse world of written texts just as it is in face-to-face storytelling. However, authors often use a deictic device that is rare in storytelling: they pretend that the reader is already familiar with the text world. For example, consider the first sentence of Hemingway's novel *A Farewell to Arms*.

> In the late summer of *that* year we lived in *a* house in *a* village that looked across *the* river and *the* plain to *the* mountains.

Whereas Benny used the indefinite articles *a* and *some* to nominate entities and participants into his text world, the narrator of *A Farewell to Arms* uses the definite article *the* and the demonstrative pronoun *that*. In this context both of these words assume that the reader already knows about the noun phrases that they are part of. But, of course, we don't know what year the narrator is talking about, and we don't even know who *we* refers to. Nevertheless, it's nice of the narrator to pretend that we do because it invites us into a text world that we are assumed to be familiar with and implies a personal relationship between the narrator and the reader. We do not know everything about this text world, however. For example, the narrator mentions *a* house in *a* village, implying that we are not already familiar with these places, but he also mentions *the* river, *the* plain and *the* mountains, implying that we already know about these general landmarks. So, the deictic expressions in the first sentence of the novel creates a text would in which the reader seems to know the context in which the novel is set and to be a friend of the narrator.

Before leaving *A Farewell to Arms*, observe that, as in Sue's story, many elements of this world are not specifically mentioned in the text but are supplied by the reader's knowledge of the real world. For example, no dates are provided in the novel, but the reader can infer that it is set in World War I (1916–1918) because of the mention of gas masks, machine guns, horses, and other instruments of war that are appropriate for that era. We will return to this topic in Section 8.3.5.1.

We should also note that while deictic words can help to create a text world by establishing its time, place, and participants, language also has non-deictic ways of indicating these things. For example, instead of saying, "See you tomorrow," I could say, "See you on January 1, 2018 of the Common Era," and instead of saying, "Please come over here" I could say, "Please come over to the table in the kitchen of the house at 51 Elm St. in

Tucson, Arizona, USA." The meanings of these awkward expressions are said to be "public," that is, they do not depend on the time, place, and speaker in the context where they were uttered. But you can see why languages need a system of deixis.

In this section we have examined four text worlds: the conversation in Sue's living room prior to Sue's story, Sue's story, Benny's story, and the beginning of *A Farewell to Arms*. In the first case, the text world was jointly created by the discourse world participants in order to understand an ongoing conversation. At first glance the last three cases might appear to be different from that conversation because the stories were told or written by a single person, suggesting that they were created just by the speaker or author. But, we have seen that this is not the case because all of the text world creators asumed some background knowledge on the part of their audiences. If you didn't understand that hot milk kills yeast, then you didn't understand the resolution of Sue's story, and if you didn't know that Juvi means Juvenile Court, you didn't understand the coda of Benny's story. Hemingway went even further, assuming that his readers knew about *the* river, *the* plain, and *the* mountains. So, creating a text world requires the active involvement of the participants in whose minds the text world is being built. In a conversation this involvement is both vocal and mental, but when listening to a story or reading a book the involvement is only mental. Therefore, although I have used and will continue to use expressions like "the text world that Benny created" it should be understood that all text worlds are a joint creation of a speaker/author or a listener/reader. Semino (1977) uses the terms *project* and *construct* to describe this process, so that speakers/writers *project* a text world and listeners/readers *construct* one. In Figure 8.2 the projected world and the constructed world are identical, but of course this is not always the case, as we saw in the discussion of "Her First Ball," where modern readers may construct a different concept of "taxi" than Mansfield projected. Furthermore, audiences from different backgrounds and with different life experiences can construct very different text worlds from the same text.

8.3.3 Pragmatics

We are already familiar with some of the discourse tools that people use in conversations to get their meanings across, or as we might now say, the tools that they use to build text worlds in the minds of their listeners. In Chapter 7, for example, we saw how the physical context of a discourse world helps to determine the illocutionary force of an utterance. If a doctor asks a patient with an arm injury, "Can you open the window?," the doctor is probably asking a real question, but if someone in a hot room says the same thing to a person sitting next to a window, they are probably making an indirect request. Similarly, in the discourse world of Sue's living room, the text world that the participants construct by their on-going conversation helps them to determine the illocutionary forces of utterances. When Mrs. Macken says, "Sue, you oughta tell about those rolls you made the other day," the literal speech act is a statement, but the primary speech act (which carries the illocutionary force) is a request.

As mentioned in Chapter 7, the way a listener can figure out what illocutionary force a speaker intends an utterance to have is to consider whether a speech act makes sense if it is taken at its literal or face value. If it does not, the listener looks for some other possible illocutionary force. This method of inferring meaning is possible because of what Grice (1975) called the *cooperative principle*, and speakers often take advantage of this principle when building text worlds. The cooperative principle states that in a conversation people usually try to make their intentions clear by conforming to four basic rules or *maxims*. Grice's conversational maxims boil down to these four guidelines: (1) be informative, (2) be truthful, (3) be relevant, and (4) be clear. Mrs. Macken's remark "Sue, you oughta tell about those rolls you made the other day," breaks maxim (1) *be informative* because if it is taken as a statement, people will naturally wonder why she ought to tell about the rolls, and Mrs. Macken does not explain this. So, it makes sense to construe the utterance as a request for that information. We saw many other examples of breaking (or "flouting") a conversational maxim in Chapter 7. For example, if someone is standing between you and the TV, you might directly request them to move by saying, "Please move." Or, if you wanted to be indirect (and snarky), you could say, "You make a better door than a window." Taken literally, this utterance is a statement, but understood that way it breaks both the truthfulness and the relevance maxims, so your audience will look for some other interpretation and will understand that you are indirectly requesting them to move.

Verbal irony is a literary device that often depends on violating the truthfulness maxim. For example, in *Harry Potter and the Order of the Phoenix* Harry describes Professor Quirrell as follows: "Yeah, Quirrell was a great teacher. There was just that minor drawback of him having Lord Voldemort sticking out of the back of his head." The first sentence is literally a compliment, but because we know that Harry despises Quirrell we know that he has broken the truthfulness maxim, so we look for another illocutionary force and understand that the primary speech act is, in fact, an insult. Similarly, in *Julius Caesar*, after Brutus has helped to murder Caesar, Mark Anthony says, "But Brutus says he [Caesar] was ambitious;/ And Brutus is an honorable man." Because we know that Brutus and Mark Anthony are enemies, we know that the second sentence breaks the truthfulness maxim, and so also carries the illocutionary force of an insult.

273

8.3.4 Point of View

The term point of view refers to the question of who tells the story and how much of the text world they have access to. The most common points of view are *first person, third person limited*, and *third person omniscient*, but there are many other possibilities such as *second person*. We will take a look at all of these in turn. In the discussion we will see how our pre-existing knowledge of the real world affects our understanding of the text world.

8.3.4.1 First-Person Narrators

The narratives we have looked at in this chapter, including those of Sue, Benny, and Frederick Henry (the narrator of *A Farewell to Arms*) are first-person narratives, using the pronoun *I*, where the narrator is a character in the text world, on whom the story is centered. In first-person narration, the reader sees, hears, and knows only what the narrator experiences, and has access only to what the narrator is thinking, as when Sue says, "I thought I turned the stove off," and "Well, I wasn't gonna throw that stuff all out...."

In first-person narration there is an important difference between fiction and non-fiction. In non-fiction, including autobiographies and personal narratives, the author and the narrator are the same person. Thus, in Benny's and Sue's stories the discourse world speaker is the same individual as the text world narrator. For Benny's story, this situation can be illustrated by expanding Figure 8.4 as follows.

Fiction is different. In first-person fictional narratives the discourse world author and the text world narrator are not the same. For example, in *Moby*

Figure 8.4 Expanded diagram of the discourse world and text world of Benny's story

Dick the narrator Ishmaei is not the same person as the author, Herman Melville. The separate identities of author and narrator are made clear in the opening passage of *The Adventures of Huckleberry Finn*.

> You don't know about me without you have read a book by the name of The Adventures of Tom Sawyer, but that ain't no matter. That book was made by Mr. Mark Twain and he told the truth mainly. There was things which he stretched but mainly he told the, truth. That is nothing. I never seen anybody but lied one time or another... (p. 1).

Here, Huck the narrator, who exists only in the text world, refers to Mark Twain, the author, who exists only in the discourse world (except for this passage). The relationship between the author and the narrator in *A Farewell to Arms*, which is typical of split world narration, can be seen in Figure 8.5.

In first-person fiction, readers often identify the text world narrator with the real world author despite their different identities. This is natural because of the familiar relationship deictically established between the narrator and the reader, as already mentioned. But, this identification can be reinforced by facts about the author's life. For example, it is well known that Ernest Hemingway, like Frederick Henry, was an ambulance driver for Italy during World War I, that he was wounded, and that he fell in love with the nurse who cared for him. Of course, there are also many examples of novels and short stories where the author cannot be identified with the narrator, such as *Gone Girl* by Gillian Flynn, which is partly narrated by a male character, and the chapters in *As I Lay Dying* by William Faulkner that are narrated by Benjy, a mentally challenged adolescent. However, when it is plausible to identify the narrator with the author, readers are likely to do so because it counteracts the split in the discourse world with its

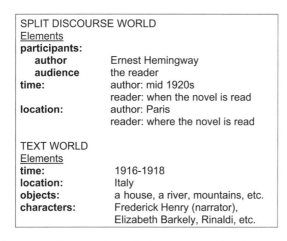

Figure 8.5 Diagram of a split discourse world and text world

lack of a conversational partner. As Gavins (2007) says, "A text-world entity, the narrator, becomes a substitute co-participant in the discourse. Readers accept and process the world building information … as though the text world narrators responsible for [it] were discourse-world human beings" (p. 129). Perhaps it is also for these reasons that in lyric poetry the speaker is usually identified with the author. For example, the voice that asks "How do I love thee?/ Let me count the ways" is assumed to be that of the poem's author Elizabeth Barrett Browning. Notice also that throughout this book I have followed the common practice of referring to the speaker of a poem with either *he* or *she* according to the gender of the author.

8.3.4.2 Other Points of View

There are two main kinds of third-person narration: limited point of view and omniscient point of view. In limited-point-of-view narration the narrator is not a character in the text world but does tell the story from the point of view of one of the characters, so that the reader only has access to that character's thoughts and sensations. For example, the main character of "Her First Ball" is referred to as *she* or *Leila*, and the reader sees and hears only what Leila sees and hears and can look only into her mind, as when the narrator says, "Exactly when the ball began Leila would have found it hard to say." A limited-point-of-view narrator need not be a main character, however, as in *Moby Dick*, where the tale is told by Ishmael, a lowly harpoon thrower.

In omniscient-point-of-view narration the narrator is again not a character in the story, but in this case the reader has access to much more of the text world than in limited-point-of-view narration, including some or all of the characters' thoughts and perceptions. An omniscient narrator may, however, focus on the thoughts and perceptions of a particular character; who is called a focal character. This technique can be seen in the following passage from the novel *War And Remembrance* by Herman Wouk.

> [Commander Victor] Henry had won his wife five years [after applying to the Naval Academy], though she was a couple of inches taller than he, and though her prosperous parents had looked for a better match than a squat Navy fullback from California, of no means or family. Courting Rhoda, he had come out of his single-minded shell of ambition to show much tenderness, humor, considerateness, and dash. After a month or two Rhoda had lost any inclination to say no. Mundane details like height differences had faded from sight (p. 5).

Here, the omniscient narrator is positioned somewhere outside the story, but he can look into of the minds of the characters, seeing that Victor was encased in a shell of ambition before courting Rhoda, and that Rhoda was initially inclined to say no to Victor because of their height difference, but that after a month or two she lost that inclination.

Although the narrator and the author are obviously different in omniscient third-person narration, readers are still likely to identify the narrator with the author, as they do in first-person narration. This is because the world created by omniscient narrators is conceptualized as though it is true within the discourse world, like a personal narrative, rather than just true within the text world. In other words, a well-told story seems real to us. This effect enhances the familiar relationship between the narrator and the reader that is established by deixis, extending it to a relationship between the author and the reader.

Second-person narration uses the pronoun *you* (always referring to the second person singular and not the plural, as far as I can tell). Novels and stories told from this point of view are rare, but one example is *Bright Lights, Big City* by Jay McInerney. Here is an excerpt:

> At the subway station you wait fifteen minutes on the platform for a train. Finally, a local, enervated by graffiti, shuffles into the station. You get a seat and hoist a copy of the *New York Post*. ... The train shudders and pitches toward Fourteenth Street, stopping twice for breathers in the tunnel. You are reading about Liz Taylor's new boyfriend when a sooty hand taps your shoulder. You do not have to look up to know you are facing a casualty, one of the city's MIAs. You are more than willing to lay some silver on the physically handicapped, but folk with the long-distance eyes give you the heebie-jeebies.

Second-person narration puts readers in the role of the protagonist, allowing them to enter the text world more completely than in first- or third-person narration. Nevertheless, there is an artificial quality to experiencing a text world from this point of view, perhaps because the reader has no actual control over what the protagonist does.

8.3.4.3 Unreliable Narrators

In non-fiction the discourse world author and the text world narrator (who are the same person) are expected to abide by Grice's Second Maxim (Be Truthful). Perhaps this is because real people can check out the truth of a storyteller's claims. If Sue had lied about Katie's turning off the stove, Katie herself could set the record straight. Because the information in true narratives is accessible to people in the discourse world, this genre is said to be participant-accessible. The authors of realistic fiction, however, are never held to the truthfulness maxim; after all, they are making the whole thing up. But, what about the text world *narrators* in realistic fiction? Should we trust Ishmael or the third-person narrator of "Her First Ball" not to mislead us about the true nature of the text world?" Of course, statements about the nature of the text world are not reader-accessible, but they are character-accessible, which is to say that lies about what is really going on in the text world can only in principle be detected by the characters of that world. Perhaps for this reason, fictional narratives are more likely than personal narratives to contain a narrator who intentionally or unintentionally breaks the truthfulness maxim and misleads the reader. When this happens we have an unreliable narrator.

Unintentionally unreliable narrators include Huck Finn, who naively reports that the bald-headed con man who joins him on the raft is the rightful King of France, and Nick Carraway, the narrator of *The Great Gatsby*, whose sympathetic portrayal of the title character glosses over the fact that Gatsby was a gangster. The omniscient narrator of Ambrose Bierce's story "An Occurrence at Owl Creek Bridge," on the other hand, intentionally misleads the reader. The story describes the hanging of a Confederate saboteur by Union troops during the American Civil War. At the story's climax, the narrator recounts:

> As Peyton Faquhar fell straight downward through the bridge he lost consciousness and was as one already dead. From this state he was awakened – ages later, it seemed to him – by the pain of a sharp pressure upon his throat, followed by a sense of suffocation. … Then all at once, with terrible suddenness, the light about him shot upward with the noise of a loud splash; a frightful roaring was in his ears, and all was cold and dark. The power of thought was restored; he knew that the rope had broken and he had fallen into the stream. … He opened his eyes and saw above him a gleam of light, … and he knew that he was rising to the surface (p. 65).

The narrator proceeds to describe how Faquhar swims to shore, escapes through the woods, and manages to return to his house, where he runs to embrace his wife. At that point, switching to the historical present tense, the narrator continues:

> As he is about to clasp her he feels a stunning blow upon the back of the neck; a blinding white light blazes all about him with a sound like the shock of a cannon – then all is darkness and silence!

> Peyton Farquahar was dead; his body, with a broken neck, swung gently from side to side beneath the timbers of the Owl Creek bridge (p. 69).

So, Farquhar has only imagined his escape during the few seconds in which he fell to the end of the rope, and for most of the story the reader has been led to believe in a miraculous escape by an unreliable narrator.

The historical novel *War and Remembrance* mixes narration that is accessible to both participants and characters. The story is mostly told by an omniscient and reliable narrator, but it also contains a brief "history" of World War II written by the fictitious German General Armin von Roon, who presents a Nazi point of view. In the passage below, von Roon describes his disillusionment with Adolph Hitler after the Allies' successful landing in Normandy, France.

> Stamped on my memory is a briefing conference about the time Cherbourg was falling. Hitler was standing at the map, wearing his thick glasses, and with a compass and ruler he was gleefully showing us what a small part of France the invaders held, compared to the area we still occupied. This he was telling to senior generals who know, and who had been warning him for weeks, that with the defensive crust at the coast smashed and a major port gone, the rest of France was open country for enemy operations, with no tenable German position short of the West Wall at the border and the Rhine. What a sorry moment; scales fell from my eyes, and I knew once and for all that the triumphant Führer had degenerated to a pathological monster, trembling for his life behind a mask of bravado (p. 1162).

Because *War and Remembrance* mixes fact and fiction, Wouk could have relied only on the reader's general knowledge (participant-accessibility) to detect the false and self-serving notes in von Roon's tardy reassessment of Hitler's character. But, just in case the reader misses this point, the character Victor Henry adds this comment to von Roon's "history," thus demonstrating the possibility for character-accessibility:

> As for Hitler "degenerating" into a pathological monster, he never was anything else, though he had a good run in his first flush of brigandage. Why his demagogic bunkum ever spurred the Germans to their wars and their crimes remains a vastly puzzling question. The scales did not fall from Roon's eyes. They had to be shot off.

So, in a text that mixes non-fiction and fiction, the reliability of a narrator can be judged both by the reader in the discourse world and by a character in the text world.

In this section we have looked at both true and fictional narratives. In the next section we will take a closer look at the difference between these genres and at the nature of fictionality.

8.3.5 Possible Worlds

Possible worlds theory is a branch of philosophy that has proved helpful for understanding fiction. The theory involves the question "What is truth?"

Kant distinguished between necessary truths and contingent truths. Necessary truths include mathematical statements that are true by definition, like: "2+2 = 4," and linguistic statements that are logically true, like: "Either George ate the plums or he didn't." Contingent truths depend upon the state of the world. For example, the statement "Debre Marcos is the capital of Ethiopia" can only be judged true or false by checking to see what the actual capital of Ethiopia is (the statement is false; the real capital is Addis Ababa). A classic problem in philosophy is what to make of counterfactual statements like: "The present King of France is bald," which presupposes something that is false, namely that there is a present king of France. Traditionally, philosophers considered such statements to be neither true nor false; however, possible worlds theory provides another way to look at things. We can imagine a world where there is a present king of France, and in that world it would be possible to find out whether or not the man is bald. A similar kind of reasoning can apply to fictional text worlds. As we have seen, the truth value of statements about such worlds is character-accessible and so can often be determined by the reader by using evidence from the text. For example, the statement, "Leyla hated the ball" is obviously false, based on our knowledge of Leila's excitement as described in the passage that we read.

8.3.5.1 Impossible Worlds

Because truth in a possible world is not the same as truth in the real world, possible worlds do not have to follow the laws of nature. Stories and poems can contain hobbits, fairies, and waist-coated rabbits; they can describe other galaxies and future times, and they can construct societies where war is peace, freedom is slavery, and ignorance is strength, and so require the suspension of our disbelief. So far, we have looked only at text worlds that do not differ in their physical aspects from the real world, and have seen how narrators furnish these worlds with believable objects and characters. Now let us look at how a narrator constructs a possible world that differs from the real world. J. K. Rowling's novel *Harry Potter and the Chamber of Secrets* describes Harry's first dueling lesson as follows:

> "Face your partners!" called Lockhart, back on the platform, "and bow!"
>
> Harry and Malfoy barely inclined their heads, not taking their eyes off each other.
>
> "Wands at the ready!" shouted Lockhart. "When I count to three cast your charms to disarm your opponent – only to disarm them – we don't want any accidents. One ... two ... three ..."

Harry swung his wand over his shoulder, but Malfoy had already started on "two": his spell hit Harry so hard he felt as though he'd been hit over the head with a saucepan. He stumbled, but everything still seemed to be working, and wasting no more time, Harry pointed his wand straight at Malfoy and shouted "*Rictusempra.*"

A jet of Silverlight hit Malfoy in the stomach and he doubled up, wheezing. . . .

Harry had hit him with a Tickling Charm, and he could barely move for laughing.

The first two sentences of the passage describe duelists facing each other and bowing, and this description could apply to a duel in the real world. In the third sentence, however, the narrative begins to depart from reality, as we learn that the duelists are using wands instead of swords. The fourth sentence moves us entirely into the world of magic by referring to the casting of charms, and the rest of the passage furnishes this world with particular charms, which are cast by uttering words in Latin. Notice, however, that the text world of Harry Potter is actually not so different from the real world. Although uttering the word "Rictusempra" will not really make someone laugh, the effects of laughing on Malfoy are the same as if he had heard a really good joke: he doubles over and gasps for breath. These observations show that fictional worlds work exactly like the real world unless the reader is informed otherwise. To take another example, in *The Lord of the Rings* we learn the extraordinary text-world fact that trolls turn to stone if they are touched by sunlight. But, we don't have to be told that the sun will come up in the morning. We assume that, in general, the natural laws of Middle Earth are just like the laws of the real earth. This assumption is called the principle of minimal divergence, and it explains why even though we know that Harry and Malfoy are unusual boys in some respects, we still assume that they each have two legs and one head. The possible worlds of fiction are therefore said to be *parasitic* on the real world.

A corollary of the principle of minimal departure is that possible worlds do not have to be fully furnished. We do not know what color Malfoy's eyes are or whether he has any siblings, nor can we find out unless Rowling tells us in another book. In fact, all text worlds are inherently incomplete, and this is why we employ top-down processing to access the schemas that are stored in our memory in order to fill in the details. Of course, it could also be argued that our understanding of the real world is similarly incomplete. For example, we do not know whether President Kennedy would have continued the Vietnam War if he had lived, but as Semino (1997:84) has

pointed out there is a difference in principle between our incomplete understanding of the real world and a text world. In theory it would be possible to
find out Kennedy's intention regarding the war, and his intention might, in
fact, have been known to some of his friends and advisors. However, it is
inherently impossible to find out the color of Malfoy's eyes or the number of
Lady Macbeth's children.

8.3.5.2 Accessibility

The degree to which a possible world differs from the real world is called its
degree of accessibility. The text world of a true story contains real characters and settings, so it completely corresponds to,[3] or is "accessible to," the
real world. However, the text world of a fantasy like *Harry Potter* differs
considerably from the real world and so is said to be less accessible. Ryan
(1991) has suggested several ways in which a text world can differ from the
real world, and has devised rules that a story must uphold in order to be
considered non-fiction. It turns out that the extent to which a story upholds,
bends, or breaks these rules can be used, in part, to define different genres of
narrative. True stories uphold all of the rules, and fantasies break them all,
to some extent. An author can consistently break rules throughout a text or
just break them occasionally, as explained below. If a rule is only occasionally broken, I will say that it has been "relaxed." In the discussion that
follows, I have greatly simplified Ryan's seven accessibility rules, reducing
them to the three that are listed below:

1. The **characters rule** requires that the characters in the text world correspond to real people, as they do in Sue's true story. If Sue had claimed that
   her imaginary evil twin had scalded the milk, her story would not
   completely uphold this rule, and would not be entirely true. However,
   the appearance of one imaginary relative would not completely break the
   rule but merely relax it, because most of the characters would still
   correspond to real people.
2. The **places rule** requires that all of the places in the text world correspond to real places. If Sue had said that Millie had telephoned her from
   Oz, her story would relax this rule.
3. The **features rule** requires that the people, places, and things in the text
   world have the same characteristics as they do in the real world; that is,
   that they appear and behave as we would expect them to. This rule
   follows from the principle of minimal departure. It means that we can
   assume, for example, that Victor Henry wears shoes (probably wing-
   tips), that Sherlock Holmes's London is the capital of England, and that
   cars cannot fly. If Sue had claimed that the hot milk turned her rolls into
   Moon Pies, her story would relax this rule.

Table 8.1 *Relative accessibility of four narrative genres*

Accessibility rules

Genre	Characters	Places	Features	Index score
True story	1	1	1	3.0
Historical novel	0.5	0.5	1	2.0
Realistic fiction	0	0.5	1	1.5
Fantasy/Science fiction	0	0.5	0.5	1.0

The rows display the genres and the columns display the accessibility rules (see text). 1 = rule is always upheld; 0.5 = rule is relaxed; 0 = rule is never upheld.

Now let us see how the accessibility rules are associated with some different genres of narrative. We will consider non-fiction (e.g. Sue's and Benny's personal narratives); historical fiction (e.g. *War and Remembrance*); realistic fiction (e.g. "Her First Ball," and *A Farewell to Arms*); and science fiction/fantasy (e.g. *Harry Potter and the Chamber of Secrets*). Of course, these five categories are not air-tight, and there are many narratives that are difficult to place within them; however, the texts we will discuss represent prototypes within each category. Here is how these narrative genres uphold, relax, or break the accessibility rules. The discussion is summarized in Table 8.1.

(1) **Non-fiction** (true stories) always upholds all of the rules.
(2) **Historical fiction** includes real people and places but adds fictional people and places. By adding these elements, this genre relaxes the characters rule and the places rule, but because all of the characters and places are just as we expect them to be, this genre upholds the features rule. If, on the other hand, the Washington, DC of *War and Remembrance* were located on the West Coast, the novel would relax the features rule.
(3) **Realistic fiction** contains only fictional characters, so it always breaks the characters rule. It relaxes the places rule to a great extent, but not entirely, because realistic fiction is usually set in a real place, as *A Farewell to Arms* is set in Italy and "Her First Ball" is set in Wellington, New Zealand. However, there are exceptions to this observation: some realistic narratives are set in an unspecified location. For example, Poe's poem "The Raven" is set in a library in an unknown city. Ryan (1991:36) describes such geographically unanchored text worlds as "eerie" and "foreign," which certainly describes the scene of "The Raven."Nevertheless, following the principle of identifying the narrator with the author we can suppose that this fictitious library is located in a

city on the American East Coast where Edgar Allen Poe lived, probably Baltimore (which has an ample supply of ravens). Like historical fiction, realistic fiction follows the principle of minimal divergence, so the people, places, and things of the text world look and work the way they do in the real world, thus upholding the features rule.

(4) Like realistic fiction, the genres of **fantasy and science fiction** break the characters rule (everybody is fictitious), but they only relax the places rule because these stories often include real places. For example, Harry Potter's fictitious school, Hogwarts, is set in a real place, Scotland. The features rule, of course, is relaxed because in this genre rabbits can talk and trees can walk. Nevertheless, the minimal divergence principle is obeyed unless we are told otherwise. Relaxing the features rule has an important consequence regarding how much this genre can relax the characters rule because it entails that the characters need not have all, or even most, of the features of real people. So Malfoy can cast spells and Mandrake the Magician can read minds. Relaxing the rule even further, we encounter characters who are partly or not at all human, thus allowing for Mr. Spock, Superman, and Chewbacca, and many fantasy worlds are populated with a menagerie of fictitious species including hobbits, wizards, elves, orcs, trolls, and balrogs. Similarly, relaxing the features rule means that the real places in fantasies need not have their expected properties. For example, in the TV series *Star Trek* San Francisco is the capital of the United Federation of Planets. Another effect of relaxing the features rule is that real objects can have fabulous properties, like Harry Potter's wand, and that fictitious objects like starship cruisers can exist.

I have lumped fantasy and science fiction into the same category of narrative genre because the three criteria of characters, places, and properties cannot distinguish them. In order to do that we need to add a fourth criterion: natural law. In true science fiction all natural laws are obeyed. Of course, we may not yet know about some of these natural laws, such as the possibility of time travel. But, although science fiction can thus relax the features rule, it never invokes magic or the supernatural to explain deviations from reality. Rather, this genre extends present scientific knowledge, and sci/fi stories often go into considerable detail about exactly how science will be extended in the future. Fantasy, on the other hand, does not usually bother with explanations. We don't need to know how Harry's magic wand works, just that it does.

The relationship between the accessibility rules and the narrative genres just discussed can be displayed in an implicational table like Table 8.1. In this table the flexibility of the rules within each genre is indicated numerically, so that 1 means that the rule is always upheld, 0.5 means that the rule is relaxed, and 0 means that the rule is never upheld. So, reading across the row for realistic fiction, we see that the characters rule is never upheld; the places rule is relaxed; and the features rule is always upheld. Notice that as we read down the rows of the table, the possible worlds within each genre become more removed from the real world, so that true stories uphold all of the rules and fantasy/science fiction relaxes or breaks all of them. Adding up the numbers across each row of the table produces an index of accessibility, so that the lower the index number the further the genre is from the real world. Table 8.1 also allows us to see specifically how a given genre differs from the other genres. For example, historical fiction differs from realistic fiction because historical fiction includes at least some real characters, and realistic fiction differs from fantasy/science fiction because only in the latter genre can the fictional characters and places have different properties than people and places in the real world. Of course, quantifying the differences in narrative genres as in Table 8.1 is not necessary for understanding the differences between the genres; however, Table 8.1 does provide a handy way of displaying what the major differences are.

8.3.5.3 Worlds We Often Make

Finally, it should be emphasized that possible worlds that depart from the laws of nature are not just found in novels and stories – they are also common in everyday talk. Ordinary language allows us to create text worlds describing a present that does not exist or a past that never was. A common device for such world creation is the conditional clause with the conjunction *if*, as in "If that contact lens were a snake, it would bite you," or "If I were you, I'd put down that axe!" Of course, I'm not you, but I can imagine that I am in order to increase the strength of this indirect threat. Counterfactual *if* clauses are also common in songs and poems, as in Pete Seeger's line, "If I had a hammer, I'd hammer in the morning," and Lorenz Hart's verse,

> If they asked me, I could write a book
> About the way you walk and whisper, and look.

In earlier varieties of English it was also possible to construct conditional clauses (and thus alternate realities) without using *if* by inverting the subject and tensed verb in a clause, as in Andrew Marvell's lines:

> Had we but world enough and time
> This coyness lady were no crime.

The conditional clauses in the examples so far are *present conditionals*, which create a possible world in the present. Past conditional clauses create a possible world in the past. The structure of past conditionals is similar to the structure of present conditionals, except that the verb tenses are moved further into the past. So, Hart's line can be changed from the present conditional to the past conditional as follows:

> If they had asked me, I could have written a book
> (Of course, they didn't ask, so I didn't write one).

Past conditionals seem to be less popular than present conditionals in songs and poetry, but they do crop up in country music (which is often about regret for past mistakes), as in the following examples. Notice that in the second example a nonstandard tense is used in the two *if* clauses, as we would expect in a country song.

> And Jane if I had known –
> I might have stopped kissing right then.
> It's just as well we don't know
> When things will never be that good again.
>   *Greg Brown*, lyrics from "If I had Known"

> If you'd have been there, if you'd have seen it
> I becha you would have done the same.
>   *John Kander*, lyrics from "Cell Block Tango"

Of course, imagining unrealized possibilities and considering how things might have been are common human activities, the stuff of daydreams and children's play as well as of practical planning and strategizing, and possible-worlds theory merely provides a way of talking about this uniquely human ability.

8.3.6 Text Worlds Change Schemas

In Chapter 1 we saw that the Russian Formalists believed that describing an experience in an unaccustomed way, for example in verse, or from the point of view of a dead person, "defamiliarized" the experience, allowing us to see it with fresh eyes, and throughout the book we have observed how particular linguistic constructions can, in a similar way, foreground a concept and make it more vivid. To take a trivial example, applying the NP fronting transformation to the sentence "I love pizza" draws our attention to the pizza: "Pizza, I love." More substantive examples include extending conceptual metaphors, as when Robert Frost extends the LIFE IS A JOURNEY metaphor to include the problem of choosing between two paths in "The Road Not Taken" (see Chapter 3, Section 3.2.7.1). Cook (1994) elaborates on this idea, claiming that disrupting accustomed ways of processing information prompts readers to reconsider their prejudices and stereotypes, and he calls such changed understanding schema refreshment, which, he believes, is the most important function of literature.

Of course, building and altering schemas is the main purpose of educational texts, whose authors hope that their readers will come away with new, refreshed, interesting, and useful schemas for the subjects covered in their textbooks. However, Cook says that stories and poems can alter schemas more effectively than expository texts because they have the ability to simulate real-life experience.[4] As we have seen, Twain increases our understanding of nineteenth-century rural Missouri, in part, by accurately representing the sounds of the local dialect and by presenting Huck's strict moral world view in the language of the uneducated. By doing so, he likely decreased the linguistic prejudices of his readers. Similarly, Yeats allows us to experience the light and sounds of an unspoiled island by means of visual and sound imagery in "The Lake Isle of Innisfree," a vicarious experience that may increase our appreciation of natural beauty and our desire to preserve it.

Sometimes authors of fiction explicitly try to alter our understanding of things. For example, in the following passage from C. S. Lewis's *Out of the Silent Planet* the narrator explains why the region of space beyond the moon's orbit should not be considered cold and lifeless but warm and full of life. There is a religious subtext here, namely that the realm of the planets should be thought of as part of heaven, the dwelling place of angels, as it was in medieval Europe. In the following passage the focal character of the novel, who is traveling from earth to Mars in a small spacecraft, experiences the spiritual effects of traveling in the heavens.

> But Ransom, as time wore on, became aware of a ... progressive lightening and exultation of heart. A nightmare, long engendered in the modern mind by the mythology that follows in the wake of science, was falling off him. He had read of "Space": at the back of his thinking for years had lurked the dismal fancy of the black, cold, vacuity, the utter deadness, which was supposed to separate the worlds. He had not known how much it affected him till now – so that the very name "Space" seemed a blasphemous libel for the empyrean ocean of radiance in which they swam. He could not call it "dead"; he felt life pouring into him from it every moment. How indeed should it be otherwise, since out of this ocean the worlds and all their life had come? (p. 34).

In this passage the narrator does not just describe Ransom's experience of bathing in heavenly light but also editorializes, implying that science fosters an outlook that is cold and dead but that religion embraces warmth and life. The more usual way of refreshing schemas, however, is to do it implicitly.

We saw an example in the semantic case structure analysis of Blake's poem "London" (Chapter 6, Section 6.2.2), in which the narrator describes wandering through London's streets. The narrator first reports on the places he sees, namely the streets and the River Thames, using NPs that take the semantic case Location. He then reports on the human elements of London, including the weary faces that he sees and the cries of fear that he hears, also using NPs of Location. This parallelism equates the permanent landmarks of the city with the unchanging human misery that the narrator witnesses, and may thus refresh readers' schemas regarding the condition of London's poor.

Certain books have changed history by immersing readers in a text world that altered their schemas for important areas of life. For example, Harriet Beecher Stowe's sentimental novel *Uncle Tom's Cabin* depicted the reality of slavery, which was not widely understood in 1852 when the book was published, and converted many people to the abolitionist cause. A more recent example involves the text worlds in Ayn Rand's novels, including *Atlas Shrugged*, which idealize rugged capitalist individualism. Alan Greenspan, who served as Chairman of the Federal Reserve Bank of the United States for five terms, was a devotee of Rand, and as Chairman he enacted the free-market, anti-consumer protection philosophy of her novels in the form of federal regulations governing banks and Wall Street. When these policies led to the Great Recession of 2008, Greenspan admitted that he had been wrong, testifying to a Senate committee that he had "found a flaw" in his schema for how capitalist economies work and stating: "Those of us who have looked to the self-interest of lending institutions to protect shareholders' equity, myself included, are in a state of shocked disbelief." So, too, of course, were the many investors who lost their homes and life savings ("Greenspan Concedes Error in Regulation" by Edmund L. Andrews, *New York Times*, October 23, 2008, downloaded on April 27, 2016 from NYT.com2008/10/24/businesseconomy).

Text worlds can also strengthen schemas, and Cook (1994) mentions Jane Austen's works as examples of novels that for modern readers "evoke, maintain, and indeed reinforce quite rigid schemata about acceptable and desirable behavior" (p. 194). However, Cook notes that at the time some of Austen's writing may have been schema refreshing. For example, the character Jane Fairfax in *Emma* is described as an independent woman "of excellent education ... [whose] heart and understanding had received every advantage.... ." Yet, Jane is a revolutionary, who breaks society's strongest taboos by having a secret affair with a man who is below her class. This portrait of a well-educated and non-conformist woman was "schema-breaking" in 1816 when the novel was published, and Cook notes that "Literary discourse that were once schema-refreshing can become schema-reinforcing" (p. 194).

8.4 Mind Style

Fiction allows readers to enter a narrator's or character's mind, and these fictional minds may view the textual world in many different ways. Fowler (1977) coined the term "mind style" to refer to the ways that narrators and characters understand things. According to Leech and Short (1981) individual mind styles can be placed along a continuum from conventional to unconventional. At the unconventional end we might find the world views of children or the mentally impaired. According to Fowler different mind styles can be conveyed by different linguistic patterns, and the best way to see how linguistic choices can reflect the workings of a fictional mind is to look at mind styles that differ from the ordinary. In this section we will take a look at several examples of individual mind styles, starting with one that is definitely unorthodox.

Semino (2002) discusses Louis de Bernières' novel *Captain Corelli's Mandolin* (also a major motion picture), which is set on a small Greek island during Italy's invasion of Greece during World War II. One of the focal characters is the shepherd Alekos, who lives on the side of a mountain and has little human contact. The following passage describes how the war enters Alekos's life.

> But this time he looked up, perhaps from instinct, and beheld a particularly pretty sight. A sort of white mushroom was drifting down with a tiny man suspended underneath, and what was marvelous about it was that the rising sun was glinting from the silk before it had had time to become more than a suspicion of a glow upon the horizon. Alekos stood up and watched it with fascination. Perhaps it was an angel. It was certainly garbed in white. He crossed himself and struggled to remember a prayer. He had never heard of an angel that floated about below a mushroom, but you never knew. And it seemed that the angel had a big rock, perhaps a package, hanging from his feet on a rope (p. 333).
>
> ...
>
> The most intriguing thing about the angel was that when it wanted to speak to God or one of the saints, it fiddled about with the metal box and made lots of interesting whines and hisses and crackles. And then God would speak back in angel speech, sounding so far away and stilted that Alekos realized for the first time how difficult it was for God to get himself heard by anyone. ... Another odd thing about the creature was that it carried a pistol, a light automatic, and a number of very heavy khaki-coloured iron pine cones with metal levers that he was not allowed to touch. All the angels he had ever seen in pictures

289

carried swords or spears, and it seemed odd that God had seen fit to modernize (p. 334).

In these passages the third-person omnipotent narrator takes us inside Alekos's head, so that we can see how he is experiencing the world. An obvious feature of Alekos's thought is that he lacks the background knowledge for understanding the new things he is observing, so he thinks of them in terms of his existing schemas. For example, he thinks of the paratrooper as an angel. In portraying the workings of an unsophisticated mind authors can use the technique of underlexicalization, which means referring to something unknown with a descriptive phrase instead of a word ("metal box" for "radio") or with an inaccurate word ("mushroom" for "parachute"). Another example of underlexicalization is the phrase "heavy khaki-coloured pine cones with metal levers" for hand grenades.

Leech and Short (1981) provide an example of the mind style of a narrator, rather than a character, in their analysis of the following passage from William Faulkner's short story "The Bear." Notice that although the mind style is distinctive, it is a lot closer to conventional than that of Alekos.

> There was a man and a dog too this time. Two beasts, counting Old Ben, the bear, and two men, counting Boon Hogganbeck, in whom some of the same blood ran which ran in Sam Fathers, even though Boon's was a plebeian strain of it and only Sam and Old Ben and the mongrel Lion were taintless and incorruptible.

Leech and Short (1981:200) observe that in this passage the narrator blurs some traditional mental categories. As we saw in Chapter 4, few mental categories have strict boundaries and hard-and-fast definitions, but rather have fuzzy boundaries so that cups blend into bowls, and it is impossible to find a clear border between blue and green on the color spectrum. Furthermore, particular concepts are sometimes arbitrarily assigned to a category. Is a minivan an example of a car or a truck? It seems a lot more like a car, but the United States Department of Transportation classifies minivans as trucks because trucks do not have to comply with as many environmental regulations as cars. In Faulkner's passage, the narrator, like the DOT, engages in some category-bending. He divides the characters in the scene he is describing into two categories, beasts and men, but each of these categories is modified by a participial phrase: "beasts, *counting old Ben the bear*" and "men, *counting Boon Hoggenbeck*." These parallel phrases hedge the category assignments, and suggest that the bear is not exactly a beast, and that Boon Hoggenbeck is not exactly a man. The narrator also suggests that Boon's plebian blood is one reason why he is a bit closer to the beasts. The traditional category boundaries between men and beasts are further blurred when the narrator considers whether the characters are "taintless and incorruptible." We would suppose that these features might only apply to human beings, but in the narrator's mind they also apply to Old Ben and Lion, the dog. In fact, while the two beasts qualify for membership in the incorruptible category, Boon, the man, does not. Leech and Short (1981) describe the effect of this category manipulation as follows:

> In Faulkner's world animals and men are thus portrayed not as being distinct.... . This way of dividing up the cosmos is at odds with the stereotyped categories of our language.... . Indeed, when we read Faulkner casually we may not even notice the way in which he has rearranged our view of the world for us" (p. 201).

While Faulkner uses semantic manipulation to suggest a particular way of viewing the world, syntactic manipulation can do this as well, and (without using the term "mind style") we have already noted how particular linguistic patterns can convey a character's way of thinking. For example, in Chapter 6 we noted the syntactic differences between Rochelle's and Esther's letters in the poem "Letters in the Family." There, we characterized Rochelle's style as "straightforward" because it contained only canonical word order and a high percentage of simple sentences, and we characterized Esther's style as "hesitant" because it often violated canonical word order and contained sentence fragments. We can now claim that these differences in syntactic style not only convey a difference in the tone of the letters but also reveal differences in the mind styles of the two fictional writers. Rochelle views the world, and her place in it, in a simple and straightforward way, as revealed in these forceful lines:

> I'm writing now
> from a plaster-dusted desk in a town
> pocked street by street with hand grenades,
> some of them, dear ones, thrown by me.

Esther's view of the world, however, is confused, as suggested by these halting and ungrammatical lines:

> I've hated you for your dropping
> ecstatically in free-fall, in the training,
> your look, dragged on the ground, of knowing
> precisely why you were there.

Rochelle knows precisely why she is in Spain fighting the Fascists, but Rochelle is not entirely sure why she is in Yugoslavia fighting the Nazis, and these world views are in part created by the respective writing styles.

Another example of how syntactic differences can suggest different mind styles can be seen in Nicole's and Julie's voices in *The Executioner's Song*, which were also discussed in Chapter 6. There, we noted that Julie's voice was considerably more complex than Nicole's, containing more than twice as many words per t-unit. This difference was interpreted to reflect a difference in the characters' maturity and education, but we might now suggest that it also reflects a difference in mind style, with Julie's view of the world being more complicated than Nicole's.

8.5 Corpus Stylistics

In recent years stylisticians have employed computers to analyze literary discourse. These studies involve analyzing a database, or corpus, of written or spoken language for particular linguistic features and patterns. A number of online corpora are now available, such as the British National Corpus of 100 million words of written and spoken British English. A computer can easily search a large corpus for particular words or constructions. For example, asking the computer to look for some form of the verb *be* closely followed by a past participle form will identify the passive constructions in a corpus.

Biber (1995, Biber et al., 1998) conducted pioneering studies of the distinguishing features of various linguistic registers. A register is a variety of language used for a particular purpose or in a particular social setting, such as the language of computer technicians or lawyers. Biber sought to identify the distinguishing features of the registers that are used in articles in certain academic disciplines, in general fiction, and in face-to-face conversations. Recall that in our discussion of regional and social dialects in Chapter 6 we noted that dialects usually do not differ because they use different features but rather because they use the same features at different frequencies. Biber found this to be true of register variation, as well. Among the linguistic features that he examined were passive constructions, conjunctions, and dependent clauses. Biber found that in all registers writing contains higher frequencies of these features than speaking, and he suggested that this difference contributes to the less personal tone of written texts. Having determined the frequencies at which particular linguistic features are used in very formal texts (like academic articles) and in very informal texts (like personal letters), Biber was able to place any individual text, spoken or written, on a scale ranging from formal to personal, according to the percentage of relevant features that the text contained. He found, for example, that general fiction is more formal than face-to-face conversation, and that ecology articles are more formal than history articles. It makes sense that ecology articles would contain a large number of passive constructions because in scientific articles human agents are usually not important to the natural phenomenon being discussed, as we saw in Chapter 4, Section 4.2.6, whereas in history articles it usually does matter which human agents or political entities perform which actions, so passives are less common.

Corpus scholars have also examined texts to identify words that always or often occur together, which are called collocations. One kind of collocation is a fixed expression that cannot be altered, such as "no *ifs, ands*, or *buts*, or "you can't get there from here." A more flexible kind of collocation is the *grammatical construction*, where a phrase requires a specific word or words from a particular grammatical category. For example, the *way* construction, as in "Marsha painted her way across the room," must adhere to the following formula: NP, V, possessive pronoun, *way*, PrepP, as these examples show.

NP	V	possessive pronoun	*way*	PrepP
Marsha	painted	her	way	across the room
Harry	bluffed	his	way	past the guard
Rocky	couldn't punch	his	way	out of a paper bag

A more elusive kind of collocation involves words that do not adhere to a formula but nevertheless often occur together. The value of identifying such associations is that a word can take on the semantic coloring of words that it often occurs with. For example, Jeffries McIntire (2010:184) report that in the British National Corpus the word *priest* most frequently occurs with the word *lecherous*, adding a dark connotation to a word that until recently had mainly positive associations.

Louw (1993) used a collocational analysis to interpret Philip Larkin's poem "Days," which is presented below.

Days
What are days for?
Days are where we live.
They come, they wake us
Time and time over.
They are to be happy in:
Where can we live but days?

Ah, solving that question
Brings the priest and the doctor
In their long coats
Running over the fields.

The first stanza of the poem asks an unexpected question and tries to provide an upbeat answer: days are to be happy in. Yet, there is an undeniably melancholy tone to the stanza, and that tone foreshadows the unsettling second stanza, where the poet points out that the end of our days will involve the doctor and the priest, in other words, sickness and death. The melancholy mood of the first stanza is enhanced by the fact that it consists of two questions, suggesting that the speaker is not altogether sure of just how happy our days will be, but Louw suggests that the mood is also enhanced by the collocation *days are*. Searching for this phrase in several corpora, he found that it is frequently followed by the words *gone*, *over*, and *past*, all of which are associated with the end of life.

SUVs = Sport Utility Vehicles

Notes

1 Remember that schemas are created in the minds of individual listeners/ readers, so each of Sue's listeners created her own slightly different schema of the rolls story. Nevertheless, we usually speak of *the* story schema or *the* restaurant schema (as though there were only one) because within a culture individual schemas for such uncomplicated things are a great deal alike. Similarly, we talk about *the* text world that a speaker or author creates, even though there are really as many individual text worlds as there are listeners or readers.

2 In text world theory, text world characters are called "enactors" but in the interest of simplicity I will stick to the traditional term "characters."

3 Strictly speaking, these text worlds correspond to our *schemas* of the real world. The philosophical question of how we understand reality is addressed in the web materials for this chapter.

4 In fact, Cook (1994:189) claims that literary discourse can change schemas more effectively than real-life experience itself because experience is "too important" to be altered, but when reading we can "withdraw from interaction," and thus more easily alter our ideas.

Summary

This chapter has taken a cognitive linguistics approach to discourse analysis, emphasizing the function of mental schemas in understanding and producing literary texts. We noted, for example, that our schema for personal narratives leads us to expect particular narrative elements in a particular order. Text world theory claims that communication by speaking or writing involves a speaker/author projecting a schema, called a "text world," which is interpreted by a listener/hearer. The linguistic tools that speakers/authors use to create text worlds include deixis and pragmatics. In building a text world an author always adopts a particular perspective, or point of view. The most common points of view are first-person, third-person limited, and third-person omniscient. Possible worlds theory holds that a text world can correspond closely to the real world, as in a true story, or can differ considerably, as in a fairy tale. A text world that differs from a reader's existing schemas has the potential to change those schemas, thus broadening the reader's understanding. In addition, stories that are told from a particular character's point of view can reveal the character's "mind style," which is how he or she views the world. Finally, computers can be used to analyze a corpus of spoken and/or written language to find collocations or words that often occur together. This knowledge can aid the literary critic because our understanding of a word is affected by the contexts in which the word appears.

Exercises

1. We have seen that appropriate schemas are necessary for understanding written texts because they usually assume a considerable amount of background knowledge. Consider this text from the discussion of speech acts in Chapter 7.

    WIFE: There's the phone.
    HUSBAND: I'm in the tub.
    WIFE: OK.

    As mentioned in Chapter 7, a Martian reading this dialogue would have no idea what was going on, and we can now see that this is because he lacks the relevant schemas. What are some of the schemas that the Martian would have to have in order to understand the dialogue?

2. A nemesis of first-year writing students is the dangling participle, as in these examples:

    The robber ran from the policeman, still *holding* the money in his hands.
    Walking back from the bar, my wallet got lost.
    Flitting from flower to flower, the athlete chased the butterfly.

    First-year writing instructors sometimes warn their students that dangling participles will confuse their readers, but in fact this is seldom the case. How does schema theory explain that in the examples above (and others that you may come up with) the dangling participles may raise some stylistic hackles and even some smiles but will present no danger of semantic confusion?

3. Sometimes narrative clauses do not indicate what actions have occurred but rather what speech acts have occurred. For example, the second clauses of these two sentences are narrative clauses, with the narrative verbs in italics:

    "Drop those plums," he *warned*.
    "Says who?" she *replied*.

    With this in mind read Larry's fight narrative in exercise 6 of chapter 7 and identify the lines that comprise: (a) the abstract, (b) the orientation, (c) the first narrative clause, (d) other narrative clauses, and (e) evaluative clauses.

4. Analyze the narrative structure of the poem "Jabberwocky," in exercise 13 of chapter 2, mentioning which narrative parts appear in the poem. Stanza 2 consists of a warning from the parent to the son. Is this part of the background or the foreground?

5. Analyze the haircut narrative from Tan's novel *The Joy Luck Club*, which appears in section 7.4.2. First, you must decide where the story proper begins and ends. Then, analyze the haircut narrative itself, noting the presence or absence of the abstract, orientation, first narrative clause, resolution, coda, and evaluative clauses. Please quote the lines in which these features occur.

6. a. Record, transcribe and analyze a personal narrative. Try to find an informant who will have an interesting story to tell, perhaps an older person or a person who has traveled a lot. A roommate or spouse is usually not a good informant because they are likely to view the speech event as a classroom exercise rather than as an opportunity to tell a good story. Begin the interview by asking about the person's family, a topic that usually puts people at ease:

     "Do you come from a big family?
     Tell me about it."

     Your goal is to get your informant to talk casually, so you need to be relaxed and refrain from talking yourself. After the family question, ask a question that you think will elicit a narrative. Here are some suggestions that are usually successful.

"Were you ever in a situation where you were in serious danger of being killed and where you said to yourself, 'This is it'?

Tell me about it."

"Were you ever in a fight?

Tell me about it."

"What was the most frightening experience you ever had?

What happened?"

"What was the best day of your life?

Tell me what you did."

b. Transcribe just the narrative part of the interview, writing out one sentence per line. If you like, you can use orthographic conventions, like 'em for *them,* or phonetic script to represent your informant's pronunciation.

c. Analyze the narrative, noting the presence or absence of the following parts: abstract, orientation, first narrative clause, evaluative clauses, resolution, and coda. Write the numbers of the lines in which each of these parts occurs.

d. Explain how your informant used deictic devices and pragmatics to project the text world of the story.

e. Provide the following demographic information about your informant (a pseudonym should be used): age, gender, racial/ethnic group, occupation, where born and raised.

A feature of many narratives that was not mentioned in the chapter is the *climax,* where the action and suspense reach a peak. In Benny's narrative, the climax comes in these lines:

'n' I just go with my fist,
'n' hit him,
'n' broke the window.

Analyze the following narrative, submitted by a student for the assignment in exercise 6, locating the major parts of the narrative including the climax and the resolution. The narrative was told by Henrietta, a 56-year-old retired nurse who was born and raised in Boston.

I was a new graduate nurse, working at my first job at Cardinal Cushing Hospital. After about two weeks at work, there was too much help on our surgical floor. So, they floated me to take care of a critically ill patient in a private room, who was on a monitor and unconscious. And, all of a sudden the alarm went off. So, I thought the patient had gone into cardiac arrest. So, I pushed a button above the patient's bed that connected to the nurse station, and I said: "Code Blue." Code Blue means the patient has gone into arrest, and the team that is in the hospital is supposed to come to that room. There's a Code Blue team that comes with a crash cart and all the drugs you need to revive a patient, with a defibrillator – doctors, nurses, anesthesiologists – you know, various doctors that come in. And they all came running. And a nurse went over, and said "The leads had come undone from his chest." She pushed on it, replaced the adhesive, and the monitor went back to a normal rhythm. And I was mortified. Before I call a Code Blue, I will make sure all the leads are still attached to the patient's chest.

8. Who do you think constitute the discourse world participants for the text of the book you are presently reading? What aspects of the discourse world do they probably share? What aspects of the discourse world vary from individual to individual?

9. Text worlds can contain subtext worlds, that is, different scenes within the same general setting. How many subtext worlds (different scenes) would you say are in the following passage from Hemingway's short story "Big Two-Hearted River"? What are the objects and who are the participants within each subtext world?

> The train went up the track out of sight, around one of the hills of burnt timber. Nick sat down on the bundle of canvas and bedding the baggage man had pitched out of the door of the baggage car. There was no town, nothing but the rails and the burned-over country. The stone was chipped and split by the fire. It was all that was left of the town of Seney. Even the surface had been burned off the ground. Nick looked at the burned-over stretch of hillside, where he had expected to find the scattered houses of the town and then walked down the railroad track to the bridge over the river.
>
> The river was there. It swirled against the log spiles of the bridge. Nick looked down into the clear, brown water, colored from the pebbly bottom, and watched the trout keeping themselves steady in the current with wavering fins. As he watched them they changed their positions by quick angles, only to hold steady in the fast water again. Nick watched them a long time.

10. Identify the points of view and the focal characters represented in the following excerpts.

> a. From the opening sentences of Charlotte Perkins Gilman's "The Yellow Wallpaper."

John is practical in the extreme. He has no patience with faith, an intense horror of superstition, and he scoffs openly at any talk of things not to be felt and seen and put down in figures. John is a physician and *perhaps* – (I would not say it to a living soul of course, but this is dead paper and a great relief to my mind) – *perhaps* that is one reason I do not get well faster. You see, he does not believe I am sick! And what can one do?

b. From the opening sentences of Stephen Crane's "The Blue Hotel."

The Palace Hotel at Fort Romper was painted a light blue, a shade that is seen on the legs of a kind of heron, causing the bird to declare its position against any background. . . . Pat Scully, the proprietor, had proved himself a master of strategy when he chose his paints. It is true that on clear days, when the great transcontinental expresses, long lines of swaying Pullmans swept through Fort Romper, passengers were overcome at the sight, and the cult that knows the brown-reds and the subdivisions of the dark greens of the East expressed shame, pity, horror, in a laugh. But to the citizens of this prairie town and to the people who would naturally stop there, Pat Scully had performed a feat. With this opulence and splendor, these creeds, classes, egotisms that streamed through Romper on the rails day after day, they had no color in common.

c. From the opening sentences of Tom Wolfe's *A Man in Full*.

Charlie Croker, astride his favorite Tennessee walking horse, pulled his shoulders back to make sure he was erect in the saddle and took a deep breath ... Ahhhh, that was the ticket ... He loved the way his mighty chest rose and fell beneath his khaki shirt and imagined that everyone in the hunting party noticed how powerfully built he was. Everybody; not just the seven guests but also his six black retainers and his young wife, who was on a horse behind him on a team of La Mancha mules that pulled the buckboard and the kennel wagon (p. 4).

1. What deictic devices does Edwidge Danticat use to build a text world and establish a familiar connection to the reader in these opening lines of "Night Talkers"?

He thought that the mountain would kill him, that he would never see the other side. He had been walking for two hours when suddenly he felt a sharp pain in his side. He tried some breathing exercise he remembered from medical shows on television, but it was hard to concentrate. All he could think of, besides the pain, was his roommate Michel, who'd had an emergency appendectomy a few weeks before in New York. What if he was suddenly stricken with appendicitis, here on top of a mountain, deep in the Haitian countryside, where the closest village seemed like a grain of sand in the valley below?

12.   The discussion of how accessibility rules are related to narrative genres in
        this chapter is somewhat simplified, as noted in the text. For example, i
        could be argued that there is a genre of "true fiction," which would include
        Norman Mailer's *The Executioner's Song* (discussed in Chapter 6, Section
        6.5.3) and Truman Capote's *In Cold Blood*, which Capote called a "non
        fiction novel." In this genre all of the places in the text world correspond to
        real places. How would you expand Table 8.1 to reflect this fact? How does
        true fiction differ from a true story? Does this difference suggest that we need
        to create a new accessibility rule?

13.   Urban legends are stories that, like many fairy tales, contain a moral. Here is
        an urban legend that I heard when I was a teenager, and that has appeared in
        many versions over the years.

> A boy and a girl drove up into the foothills to park, listen to the radio
> and make out. The music was interrupted by an announcer who said that
> an inmate that had been convicted of rape and robbery, and whose right
> hand had been replaced by a hook, had escaped from the state mental
> institution. The girl asked the boy to drive her home immediately. He
> didn't like the idea, and they argued, but eventually he gave in. When they
> stopped in the girl's driveway, the boy walked around the car to let her
> out, and he saw a metal hook hanging from the door handle.

Recount or write your own urban legend and then analyze it, explaining
how you used deictic devices and pragmatics to project a text world.

Key Terms

text world theory
discourse world
split discourse worlds
text world
deixis
conversational maxim
point of view
limited point of view
omniscient point of view
focal character
participant-accessible
character-accessible
unreliable narrator
possible worlds theory
principle of minimal divergence
degree of accessibility
schema refreshment

mind style
underlexicalization
corpus
register
collocation

Suggestions for Further Reading

Labov's research on personal narratives is presented in Chapter 9 of Labov (1972b). Anderson (2015) provides a good introduction to schema theory, which is related to literature in Cook (1994). Semino (1997) engagingly discusses most of the topics covered in this chapter. Leech & Short (1981) is a classic text in stylistics with a good discussion of mind style, and Semino (2002) provides an update on their discussion. The best introduction to text world theory is Gavins (2007).

CHAPTER 9

Alternative Texts

"Though we travel the world over to find the beautiful, we must carry it
with us or we find it not."

Ralph Waldo Emerson, "Art"

In this Chapter ...

So far, in the book we have used insights from linguistics to analyze literature. In this chapter
we consider how these insights might apply to analyzing visual images, including cartoons,
advertisements, and religious art. We first note that, like language, art can diverge from
literally representing reality, and that this mismatch can be interpreted metaphorically. The
expression "I could just wring his neck" is not literally true, but metaphorically suggests that
the speaker is pretty angry. Similarly, a cartoon of a man with daggers coming out of his eyes
is not realistic, but metaphorically suggests the same emotion. The method of analysis that
has been most fruitful in analyzing art is called Systemic Functional Grammar, and in this
chapter we consider how this method compares to Fillmore's case grammar and Chomsky's
generative grammar. We then look at some conventional rules of artistic composition and
point out how they are similar to rules for composing sentences, according to the
functionalist approach. Finally, we return to the notion of conceptual metaphor that was
introduced in Chapter 3, noting that realistic images can convey meaning by referencing
these metaphors. For example, the familiar Christmas card scene with angels looking down
on the manger references the conceptual metaphor DIVINE IS UP, which underlies
expressions like "Elijah ascended to heaven."

9.1 Introduction

Throughout the book, we have seen how writers employ the basic elements of language, such as phonemes, clauses, speech acts, and metaphors, to create stories, poems, plays, and other works of literature. We might ask whether visual images, such as photographs, drawings, and paintings, are also built up out of more basic components according to particular rules. Is there a grammar of visual art? The answer is yes, and in this chapter we will take a look at how visual media can be analyzed using insights from the approaches to language study we have already used, as well as from a new approach that is introduced in this chapter. First, we will look at visual metaphors (the graphic equivalent of metaphorical expressions) in comics, and then show how images, like clauses, can be analyzed in terms of basic, recurring elements.

9.2 Literal and Metaphorical Art

We saw in Chapter 3 that language can be used both literally and metaphorically. Surprisingly, visual images can be literal or metaphorical, as well. Recall these examples of literal and metaphorical language from Chapter 3, where the writer starts out using only literal language:

> I told [the VP of Engineering] that there was a problem, and I showed him the graph. He took the graph, looked at it, and said "Wow!... How did you make this graph?" (Adams, 2000:304).

But, metaphors soon begin to pop up:

> Over the next two weeks I *spent* most of my time creating graphs for our VP of Engineering to use in his Corporate Management Committee meetings, where he was finally able to *upstage* all the marketing *bozos* (other VPs) with their Mac graphics that their secretaries had *spent* a week working on (p. 304).

Kennedy (2008) argues that pictures, too, can be literal or metaphorical. The claim that pictures can be literal representations of reality is based on our understanding of the human optical system which is, of course, genetically determined and the same in all human beings. Kennedy (2008) explains:

> To see the world, vision uses optic input from surfaces, edges, shadows, shapes of objects, and perspectives dictated by the observer's vantage points. Pictures use contours, lines, and patches on surfaces to re-create the key features of this highly informative optic input. Vision is largely the servant of rich, physical optic laws. Pictures piggyback on these laws (p. 450).

The human optical system has evolved in such a way that it is able to detect lines, contours (a contour is the edge of an object), and surfaces (a surface is the region inside a contour). Our ability to perceive surfaces allows us to see the basic spacial relationships between objects. For example, one object is in front of another if the surface of the first object hides part of the surface of the second object. Kennedy (2008:453) notes that the Songe tribe of Papua New Guinea do not have pictures in their culture, but they recognize outline drawings of trees, houses, birds, and people on first exposure to them. So, photographs, paintings, and even line drawings can realistically represent nature, and when they do, they are the equivalent of literal language. If realistic images correspond to our perceptions of objects and scenes in nature, deviations from realism invite a metaphorical interpretation, just as deviations from literal language invite a metaphorical interpretation.

9.2.1 Visual Metaphors Can Break Line and Contour Rules

One way that images can deviate from realistic representations involves distortions of surfaces and edges. A famous example is Duchamp's painting "Nude Descending a Staircase", where the basic lines of the body including the torso and legs are multiplied as they would appear in successive postures as the woman descends the stairs (See Figure 9.1. The reader should also google this painting in order to see the color version). In addition, the image is blurred, as moving objects sometimes appear in photographs. As Kennedy (2008:453) observes, "Motion is not … multiplication, leaning, blur, or trailing lines, but these suggest motion, that is, they are metaphors for it." It is important to emphasize that even simple drawings can be perceived as realistic. McCloud (1993:29) illustrates this fact in Figure 9.2.

Kennedy (2008:450) answers the question that McCloud poses in the second word balloon of Figure 9.2 as follows:

> In literal pictures lines, contours, and patches depict in surprisingly few ways … Lines and contours give us vivid impressions of the scene

Figure 9.1 *Nude Descending a Staircase* by Marcel Duchamp

Figure 9.2 Detailed images can be simplified to lines, contours, and surfaces yet remain realistic.
(from McCloud, S. (1993). *Understanding comics: The invisible art* (p. 29). New York: HarperCollins

surfaces – so realistic at times even a line drawing can deceive the observer into thinking the real thing is present ... The strong affinity between contours and surface edges allows any other use of line and contour to be distinct, and plausibly nonliteral.

Figure 9.3 Motion lines. The lines trailing behind the Gorg's arm suggest that it is in motion (from Rex, A. (2007). *The true meaning of Smekday* (p. 184). New York: Hyperion)

If the laws of visual perception allow artists to depict reality by representing the basic contours and surfaces of objects, then artists can break these laws in order to create a visual metaphor. Comic strip artists take full advantage of this possibility, with the extension and elaboration of lines, contours, and surfaces. One example is the motion line, a single line or several lines trailing behind an object in motion, as shown in Figure 9.3. Another realistic way to represent motion in a medium that, unlike movies or television, does not allow motion is to use sequential pictures, a method that dates from 1300 BCE, when it was used by Egyptian artists to depict the harvesting of grain in the tomb of Meuna (McCloud, 1993:14). A cartoonist following Duchamp might use this method to depict a nude descending a staircase by drawing the nude at the top of the stairs in the first panel, on the first step down in the second panel, and so on. However, this more realistic way of portraying action was replaced by metaphorical suggestion in the comics of the early 1900s with the introduction of the motion line, and this technique has been streamlined and conventionalized so that now it is instantly recognizable. Over the years, comics have introduced many other distortions of reality that metaphorically suggest various meanings, and these devices have also become conventionalized, as McCloud explains in Figure 9.4. To name just a few of these conventional visual metaphors, a two-headed figure suggests rapid back-and-forth motion of the head, as in a double take; jagged lines around a red, enlarged thumb suggest pain; hearts surrounding a head suggest love; stars and motion lines circling a head suggest dizziness; and daggers emerging from a man's eyes depict the metaphorical expression "He was staring daggers." We will explore some more comic conventions shortly.

Finally, we should note a difference between metaphorical expressions in language and visual metaphors in comics. Writers often invent original

Figure 9.4 One kind of visual metaphor in comics.
(from McCloud, S. (1993). *Understanding comics: The invisible art* (p. 128). New York: HarperCollins

linguistic metaphors, but it is more difficult for artists to invent original visual metaphors in comics because the great majority of these metaphors are conventionalized.

9.2.2 Visual Metaphors Can Violate What We Know to Be True

Another way that images can deviate from a literal representation of reality is to show something that is different from what we know to be true, such as Salvador Dali's paintings of rubbery clocks draped over branches (which suggest that time is flexible and subjective) or the image of the White Rabbit in Walt Disney's movie *Alice in Wonderland*. This latter image asks us to think of a rabbit as a person by depicting a rabbit that walks on his hind legs, wears a frock coat, and carries a gold watch. Like metaphorical expressions, visual metaphors can be analyzed by asking three questions:

1. What are the two conceptual domains?
2. Which is the source domain and which is the target domain?
3. What features are mapped from source to target?

Let us ask these questions of the White Rabbit image. The source domain is a man, and the target domain is the rabbit. The features that are mapped include the human posture onto the rabbit posture, human arms onto the rabbit's front legs, and, of course, the ability to speak. Another example of a

307

visual metaphor is the kind of nativity scene that can be found on Christmas cards, where angels hover above the manger (an example can be found in the web materials for Chapter 9). Here we are asked to view an earthly scene as part-heavenly, so heaven (the home of angels) is the source domain and the earthly manger is the target domain. The features mapped from heaven to earth commonly include the angels, their harps, and some heavenly light around the holy family.

Notice that an expression or an image can differ from reality but not be a metaphor. It can just be wrong. For example, compare these two statements:

The capital of the United States is Tucson.
The capital of the United States is New York City.

The first statement is wrong but not metaphorical because there is no obvious way to interpret Tucson as the US capital. The second statement, however, could be metaphorically interpreted because New York City is the home of many powerful corporations that influence the American economy and elections, and so in some ways it could be thought of as the seat of government. Similarly, a map of the United States with Arizona drawn disproportionately large is inaccurate but does not have any obvious metaphorical interpretation, but a map with New Hampshire drawn disproportionately large has a metaphorical interpretation because New Hampshire is the state with the first presidential primary election, so it is disproportionately important in electing the American President. To take another example, a picture of a banker swimming in a pool filled with money has an obvious metaphorical interpretation, but a picture of children swimming in the same pool does not.

9.2.3 Comic Conventions

Visual metaphors, whether created by distorting reality or falsely depicting it, range along a continuum from conventional to unconventional, just like metaphorical expressions. The manger scene with angels above the crèche is so conventional as to be a cliché, but we can still tease out the underlying metaphorical sense, just as we can with conventional metaphorical expressions like: "I *spent* most of my time creating graphs for our VP. . . ."

Shifting to the other end of the conventionality continuum for visual metaphors (and to another art form), we find Claes Oldenburg's giant sculptures of everyday objects, such as the 60-foot-high clothespin that stands next to Philadelphia's City Hall. This giant household implement is a visual metaphor that links the conceptual domains of the old-fashioned laundry room to the conceptual domain of the modern urban landscape.

nd the metaphor can be interpreted in several ways. One way is to consider the clothespin to be the source domain and City Hall to be the target domain. In this interpretation the ordinariness and utility of the clothespin are mapped onto the giant building, thus making it seem less imposing and bringing it down to size. As Oldenburg explained, "The clothespin is intended to relate to the skyscrapers around it, and especially to the soaring freestanding tower of City Hall" (Philadelphia Museum of Art website downloaded, November 23, 2013). And, of course, as with ironic metaphorical expressions like: "He's two cans short of a six-pack," the artist gives his audience a wink and a smile.

During the Renaissance an art movement, called *emblematica*, arose that made extensive use of conventional visual metaphors (Vicari, 1993). According to these conventions a lion in a painting represented a king. A dolphin twined around an anchor appearing on a piece of jewelry or on a commercial emblem represented both speed and stability, in other words, "make haste carefully." In these two metaphorical mappings the features that are transferred were fairly obvious, but other metaphors were more obscure. For example, a vulture represented a mother because it was believed that all vultures were female, and a goose represented a son because it was believed that the Egyptian words for "goose" and "son" were similar.

Comics also contain many conventional features that are not distortions of realistic images like those discussed in Section 9.2.1 but that can work metaphorically. A good example is the word balloon, which comes in two basic types: the speech balloon and the thought balloon, both of which are shown in Figure 9.5. The arrow connecting Donald to his speech is sharper and clearer than the bubbles connecting Scrooge to his thoughts, metaphorically suggesting that words are more substantial and perhaps more important than thoughts. Because these two kinds of word balloons are well-established conventions, English readers will have no trouble understanding their different meanings, but what are they to make of the apparent burst of light in Japanese comics, or *manga*, as shown in Figure 9.6?

The message is obviously emphatic, but is it a shout or a thought? In fact, these words are the character's thoughts. In manga, thoughts can also be expressed in a Western-style bubble balloon, but important thoughts, like realizations or epiphanies, are presented in a flash balloon, perhaps metaphorically suggesting that they are more important than ordinary thoughts or even speech.

Notice that comics employ these graphic conventions to convey notions that writing conveys with quotative verbs and punctuation marks. The prose equivalents of the word-balloon quotes in Figure 9.5 are something like: Donald **said**, *"This gun has hypnotized you! You're in my power!"*;

309

Figure 9.5 The word balloon and the thought balloon.
(from "Hypno-gun" from *Walt Disney's comics and stories* no. 1 (October, 1952), copyright 1952 Walt Disney Enterprises. Reprinted in Speigelman, A. & Mouly, F. *The Toon Treasury of classic children's comics* (2009)) (p. 133). New York, Abrams

Figure 9.6 The flash balloon in manga comics.
(from Seino, S. (2004). *Girl got game*, Vol.1. Los Angeles: Tokyopop)

and *Scrooge **thought**, "He really believes it! . . . Should I play along with the gag?"* Figure 9.7 shows how the quotative verbs *shouted* and *whispered* can be metaphorically represented by word balloons, as in examples (1) and (2) below, and the figure also contains the graphic equivalent of an adverb and an adverbial phrase that modify quotative verbs, as in (3) and (4), respectively.

(1) "Timber!" shouted John.
(2) "It's so quiet!" whispered Doris.
(3) "Oh, it's you," Marsha remarked, icily.
(4) "Hee, hee, hee, hee, hee," laughed William in a silly voice.

The graphic devices used to indicate tone of voice in Figure 9.7 consist of different balloon shapes and different lettering. Different kinds of lettering

Figure 9.7 Word balloons drawn metaphorically.
(from McCloud, S. (1993). *Understanding comics: The invisible art* (p.134). New York: HarperCollins

can also, of course, be used in prose. For example, in the detective novel *Doll* Ed McBain writes,

> The message went out on the teletype at a little before ten Thursday morning:

> MISSING PERSON WANTED FOR QUESTIONING CONNECTION HOMICIDE XXX EARNEST MESSNER ALIAS CYCLOPS MESSNER XXX WHITE MALE AGE 66 XXX ... (p. 74).

This text is not literally a teletype message, but its style of lettering and punctuation metaphorically suggests one. Also, recall Ferlinghetti's acrobat/ poet metaphorically teetering across the unconventional lineation of "Constantly Risking Absurdity" that was discussed in Chapter 7. But, these kinds of visual metaphors are forbidden in fully conventional prose and poetry.

In this section, we have discussed two media, print texts and comics, and have found that each has different ways, or affordances, of conveying information metaphorically. In the following sections we will examine two other visual media, magazine ads and religious art, and explore the affordances that these media provide.

9.3 Functional Analysis

Before considering another approach to analyzing both language and visual images, let us pause to consider what we have done in the book so far from a theoretical point of view. Most of our linguistic analysis could be called *structuralist* because, like chemists, we have looked for basic elements that can be combined to make up larger structures. For example, we have seen that clauses are made up of different kinds of phrases, and that phrases are made up of words from different grammatical categories, often in a particular order. Structuralism has been the main school of linguistic thought since the beginning of the twentieth century, and it has been most fully developed by the school of generative linguistics, which was founded by Noam Chomsky. The phrase structure and transformational rules in Chapter 4 are based on those developed by Chomsky in the 1960s. However, notice that our method of analysis in that chapter looked only at the *form* of sentences, with no attention to their meaning. This approach to language study contrasts sharply with the approach of cognitive linguistics, which we adopted in Chapter 3 to analyze metaphor and metonymy. In that chapter we looked at concepts and cognitive models, observing how the semantic aspects of a source domain can be mapped onto a target domain. This more recent approach to language study is obviously rooted in how language conveys *meaning*. We now turn to an approach to language study that embraces both structure and meaning, called functionalism. We have already done a bit of functional analysis in our discussion of case grammar in Chapter 7, where we saw that an NP can function as an Agent, Experiencer, Patient, etc. in a sentence. Speech act analysis is also a functionalist approach to language study, and in Chapter 7 we saw that utterances can serve different functions depending on their context. For example, the sentence "Can you open the window?" can function as a request, a suggestion, a question, and so on.

9.3.1 Systemic Functional Grammar

The linguist most associated with functional analysis is M. A. K. Halliday, and his method of analyzing language, called Systemic Functional Grammar (SFG), has been adapted for analyzing images, as well. In this section, we will take a look at Halliday's approach to language study, and in the next section we will consider its application to art. Halliday asks what people *do* with language and finds that language has three primary purposes, or metafunctions: ideational, interpersonal, and textual. The ideational metafunction is to represent aspects of the world as experienced by human beings, as in the sentence, "It's a lovely day." The interpersonal metafunction is mainly to represent the social relationship between a speaker and hearer, as when using someone's first name instead of their title and last name. The textual metafunction is to create messages and texts that are cohesive internally and coherent to the intended audience, as discussed in Chapter 7. We will now consider each of these metafunctions in more detail.

The ideational function of language is to "model reality," so that we can talk about the world with others on the basis of such models. Halliday invites us to:

> imagine that we are out in the open air and that there is move-
> ment overhead. Perceptually the phenomenon is all of a piece; but
> when we talk about it we analyze it as a semantic configuration –
> something which we express as, say, *birds are flying in the sky...*
> (1996:106).

Before looking at Halliday's method of analysis, let us review how we would analyze a sentence like "Birds are flying in the sky" using the Chomskian framework presented in Chapter 4. The similar sentence "Birds are eating seeds on the ground" would look like this:

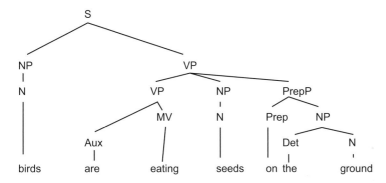

This analysis displays what are traditionally called the *parts of speech*, like Noun, Verb, and Preposition, as well as their organization into more abstract units, like NP, VP, and PrepP. But, our tree diagram does not explicitly label the *parts of a sentence*, namely the subject, verb, direct object, and object of a preposition. These latter terms name how the elements of a sentence function within the sentence. For example, the subject is roughly what the sentence is about; the verb describes the action of the sentence or the relationships described by the sentence, and so on. As we saw in Chapter 4, however, the parts of a sentence can be identified using purely formal techniques, rather than the semantic technique of asking how the parts function within the sentence. Thus, the subject of a sentence is the NP node directly below an S node; the object of a preposition is the NP node directly below a PrepP node, etc.

Unlike the generative grammar, SFG explicitly labels the parts of a sentence. So, an SFG analysis of our sentence would look like this.

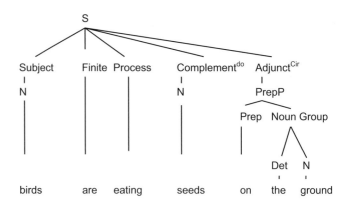

The two tree diagrams look similar, but there are some differences. The constituent that we have been calling the AUX is called Finite in the Hallidayan analysis, and at this level of representation our Verb translates to what Halliday calls Process. Also, notice that in the generative tree diagram all of the nodes are included even if they are redundant. Thus, the N *birds* is attached under an NP even though there are no other elements in the NP. But, in the SFG tree the equivalent of NP, namely *Noun Group*, is included only if it branches into two or more elements. The most important difference, of course, is that the SFG tree names not only the parts of speech, like N and PrepP, but also the parts of a sentence, like Subject, right on the tree, although, as mentioned, in a generative grammar tree it is possible to figure out the parts of a sentence from the configuration of the constituents. We should also note that the labels for the different parts of a sentence in SFG are mostly different from the labels in generative grammar. The term "subject" is used in both systems, but in SFG the direct object is labeled Complement[do] because this N functions as a verbal complement (that is, it completes the verb). In our example sentence, PrepP is attached under the node Adjunct[Cir]. An adjunct is a part of a sentence that is optional and not required by the verb. The label [Cir] stands for "circumstances"; in other words this Adjunct describes the circumstances (in this case the place) of the eating. Thus, SFG explicitly spells out the functional relationships within a sentence that our grammar (as well as the latest version of generative grammar) specifies only indirectly.

Another level of analysis provided by SFG is very similar to one we have already studied, namely case grammar. Remarkably, two linguists, Halliday and Charles Fillmore (whose modified system of semantic cases we have been using), developed different versions of case grammar independently in the mid-1960s. Halliday's case roles are, of course, different from Fillmore's, and Halliday developed his system more fully than Fillmore. In Chapter 7 we saw that verbs like *hear*, *see*, and *know* require a noun in the

Experiencer case, so that the sentence "George heard the shots" would be analyzed like this:

George   heard   the shots.
Experiencer   Patient

Fillmore (1968) called verbs like *hear*, *see*, and *know* "experiencer verbs," and he spoke of a verb's "valence." This metaphor is taken from chemistry, where atomic nuclei require a certain number of accompanying electrons. In a similar way, experiencer verbs require an NP in the Experiencer case. Thus, Fillmore looked at the meaning of a particular verb and asked what accompanying NPs that meaning required. Halliday, on the other hand, looked not at language but directly at human experience and asked how it is represented in language, as the flying birds quote suggests. He found that language characterizes reality in terms of participants (that is, things, which are usually realized linguistically as nouns) and processes (the relationships between participants, which are usually realized linguistically as verbs). For example, our experiences of hearing, seeing and knowing are mental processes, and so the verbs that represent these experiences, like *hear*, *see*, and *know*, require a human or animal participant, the equivalent of Fillmore's Experiencer. Halliday calls this kind of participant a *Sensor,* and he calls the participant that the Sensor experiences (that is, the sound, sight, or thought) a *Phenomenon.* So, he would analyze the sentence "George heard the shots" like this:

George heard   the shots.
Sensor   Process Phenomenon

As you can see, the two approaches wind up with fairly similar analyses.

Let us consider one more parallel between the system of semantic case roles that we have been using and the system of processes and participants used by SFG. What Halliday calls *material processes* involve "doing verbs" like *take*, *hit*, and *sneeze*. In Fillmore's system these would be called "action verbs," and they require an Agent NP. So, "Marsha took the money" would be analyzed by Fillmore as:

Marsha took the money.
Agent   Patient

In the SFG system, the sentence would be analyzed as:

Marsha took the money.
Actor   Process Goal

Notice that Halliday's Actor corresponds to Fillmore's Agent, and that Halliday's Goal (a term Fillmore uses to mean something entirely different) corresponds to Fillmore's Patient.

315

A nice feature of Halliday's system is that is it possible to display more than one level of analysis at the same time and to do so without drawing trees. Thus, we can display both the "parts of a sentence" analysis and the "processes and participants" analysis in a table, such as the one below, which analyzes the sentence "Marsha took the money."

Sentence:	Marsha	took	the money
Part of a sentence	Subject	Process	Complement[do]
Process and participants	Actor	Process (material)	Goal

Having looked at some of the basics of SFG, let us see how Halliday's approach to language analysis has influenced the analysis of visual images.

9.3.2 Image Analysis

We have already noted that according to Halliday language has three primary purposes or metafunctions: ideational, interpersonal, and textual. These functions can also be found in visual images, as we will discuss in this section.

9.3.2.1 Ideational Function

The book *Reading Images: the Grammar of Visual Design* by Gunther Kress & Theo Van Leeuwen, first published in 1996, is a seminal work in understanding visual images, and much of it is based on SFG. For one thing, Kress and Van Leeuwen find analogues in pictures to Halliday's Processes and Participants. Consider, for example, Figures 9.5 and 9.6. We might ask which of these scenes primarily represents a material process (requiring an Actor) and which primarily represents a mental process (requiring a Sensor). Although several processes can be found in both images, clearly the primary process in Figure 9.6 is a mental process, namely perceiving and recognizing Chiharu Eniwa. The primary process in Figure 9.5, on the other hand, is the material process of Donald aiming the hypnogun at Scrooge. Let us now identify the participants in the two pictures. In Figure 9.6 the girl (yes! it is a girl in disguise) who has the startling recognition participates in a mental process, so her image corresponds to the participant role of Sensor. In the material process shown in Figure 9.5 Donald is the Actor, and Scrooge is the Goal. To identify the participants and process in an image it is helpful to ask how the scene might be represented in language. One representation of Figure 9.5 would be "Donald aimed the hypnogun at Scrooge." Halliday's analysis of this sentence would look like this:

Donald	**aimed**	**the hypnogun**	**at**	**Scrooge.**
Actor	Process (material)	Goal		Beneficiary

Notice that the basic relationship described by the functional analysis does not change if a different syntactic structure is chosen. For example, in the passive version of the sentence the relationship of the participants remains the same:

The hypnogun	**was**	**aimed**	**by Donald**	**at**	**Scrooge.**
Goal	Finite	Process (material)	Actor		Beneficiary

In our discussion of comic conventions, we saw how action can be represented by motion lines. There are no such lines in Figure 9.5, yet we have claimed that the scene primarily depicts a material process in which Donald is the Actor. How does the drawing suggest the action of aiming a gun even though the gun does not move? Kress and Van Leeuwen maintain that action can be suggested by compositional elements in an image that indicate directionality, called vectors, which are created by the position of a participant's finger, arm, line of sight, or other device. So, the hypnogun and Donald's arm form a vector pointing at Scrooge, as shown in Figure 9.8, where the action of pointing is the primary process in the drawing. There are also some secondary processes. The direction of Donald's gaze also forms a vector, as also shown in Figure 9.8, suggesting a secondary process that might be rendered verbally as "Donald glared at Scrooge." Other secondary processes include Donald's telling Scrooge that he is under his power, and Scrooge's hands enclosing his money. Indeed, pictures often

Figure 9.8 Vectors are created by visual elements that point in a particular direction. (adapted from "Hypno-gun" from *Walt Disney's comics and stories* no. 1 (October, 1952), copyright 1952 Walt Disney Enterprises. Reprinted in Speigelman, A. & Mouly, F. *The Toon Treasury of classic children's comics* (2009)) (p. 33). New York: Abrams

depict many processes, as suggested by the saying "A picture is worth a thousand words."

Finally, we should note that our ability to find linguistic analogues in visual images does not imply that images work in the same way as language, but only, as Kress and Van Leeuwen (2006:50) note, "that they can 'say' (some of) the same things as language – *in very different ways* " [emphasis in the original].

9.3.2.2 *Interpersonal Function*

The second metafunction of language, according to Halliday, is the inter-personal function, which creates some kind of relationship between the speaker and the audience or suggests the speaker's stance toward a topic. We encountered this use of language in Chapter 6, where we discussed the phenomenon of style shifting. We saw, for example, that New Yorkers use less postvocalic [r] when they are telling a story than when they are reading a list of words. In his studies of New York City speech Labov (1972a) found that people also style shift according to what they are talking about, supplying more post-vocalic [r]s when they are discussing formal topics like school and language than when they are discussing more everyday topics like children, or when they are going off on a tangent. Labov (2001) suggests that children acquire style shifting because the first speech they are exposed to is that of their caretakers, most often their mothers and other women, who address the children in an informal style. Of course, all speaking styles include both formal and informal variants, but in the home informal variants are more frequent. Later, when children venture outside of the family environment, and especially when they go to school, they encounter the formal style, with a higher percentage of formal variants. Thus, informal style is associated with warmth and intimacy and formal style is associated with discipline and social distance.

Kress and Van Leeuwen find similarities between speaking styles and the interaction between an image and its viewer. They distinguish between pictures where the participants are looking at the viewer and pictures where they are not, noting that

> there is a fundamental difference between pictures from which ... participants look directly at the viewer's eyes, and pictures in which this is not the case.... . Vectors formed by the participant's eyelines connect the participant with the viewer (p. 117).

So, when the participants make "eye contact" with the viewer an imaginary personal relationship is created, and this relationship can be either formal or informal. Formality is established when the viewer is at a distance from the participant, or when the participant looks down at the viewer, as well as by the participant's facial expression. Intimacy is established when the viewer is closer to the participant (perhaps just seeing the face and neck as in a portrait), when participant and viewer are at the same level, or when the participant smiles or uses body language to signal an informal and welcoming attitude. When the participants in a picture do not look at the viewer, Kress and van Leeuwen describe the viewer as an *onlooker*, not personally engaged with the participants. The online materials for this chapter contain illustrations of these various possibilities.

9.3.2.3 Textual Function

In Chapter 7 we saw that personal narratives usually present information in a particular order: abstract, orientation, complicating action, resolution, and coda. There are principles for organizing the information in images, as well, and we will consider them in this section.

The first principle of composition is that **old information usually appears on the left of an image and new information usually appears on the right**. This principle also applies to sentence production. In Chapter 4 we noted that one reason a writer might choose to use a passive instead of an active sentence involves old versus new information. Good sentences, like good lectures, begin with what is known and move on to what is new. So, the passive sentence "Marsha is loved by John" is appropriate if we have been talking about Marsha, whereas the active version "John loves Marsha" is appropriate if we have been talking about John, or if the context is neutral. It is the same with many images, where old or given information is presented on the left side of the page and new information is presented on the right. This is true at least for images intended for an audience whose language is written from left to right, but as Kress and van Leeuwen (2006:182) show, images intended for an audience whose language is written from right to left, such as Arabic, often present old information on the right and new information on the left.

The old-before-new scheme is evident in some of the cartoons we have looked at. For example, Figure 9.2 shows that line drawings can seem almost as realistic as photographs. A photograph is obviously realistic, so that notion is the given information, and thus the photo appears on the left in Figure 9.2. The notion that a line drawing can seem realistic is the new information, so the line drawing appears on the right. Another example of this organization can be seen in Figure 9.5, which contains both text and images (and is thus "multi-modal"). Of course, the text reads from left to right, with Donald speaking before Scrooge mentally responds to Donald's statement. But, the figures in the frame are also ordered according to given

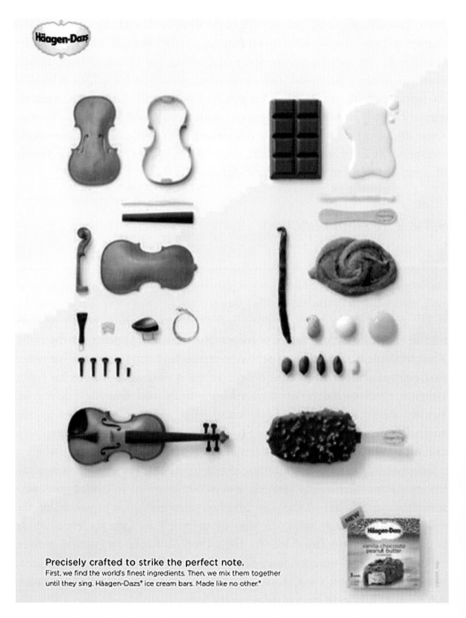

Figure 9.9 Visual metaphor and information in an advertisement

information before new information. In the story Donald has already used the hypnogun on several people, and in Figure 9.5 he once again points it at someone, so that is old information and it appears on the left of the frame. But, this time there is a new goal for the hypnogun, namely Scrooge, so that information appears on the right.

Advertisements have been a favorite subject of image analysis, and the principle of old information on the left, and new information on the right, can be found in many ads, such as the one in Figure 9.9. Before discussing the composition of this ad, we should note that it is structured around a metaphor, namely that making a Häagen-Dazs ice cream bar is like making a violin. So, let us first discuss the metaphorical aspect of the ad and then turn to its composition. As we saw in Chapter 3 metaphorical expressions map features of a source domain onto features of a target domain, and we expressed this graphically using the left-to-right organization in the chart reproduced below, which analyzes the metaphorical mapping in the poem "Life the Hound Equivocal".

Features of the hound (source)		Features of life (target)
comes at a bound	→	events occur suddenly
can rend a person by biting	→	can damage a person in many ways
can befriend a person by licking, nuzzling, etc.	→	can bring desirable things in many ways

The ad does the same thing using images instead of words. The left side of the ad contains features of a violin (the source domain), which are pictorially mapped onto features of an ice cream bar (the target domain). The similarity of the features in the two domains is their shapes: the ebony fingerboard of the violin neck is mapped onto the stick of the ice cream bar; the curled violin strings are mapped onto the round egg yolk, etc. Even the arrows of the chart above have counterparts in the image by the vectors that are formed by the horizontal elements of the picture, such as the completed violin at the bottom, which points from left to right.

Turning to the composition of the Häagen-Dazs ad, we can observe another principle of composition (one that does not have a linguistic counterpart), namely that **abstract or ideal information is presented at the top and real or practical information is presented at the bottom**. This vertical organization of the information in the ad is signaled by the vectors formed by the brown violin neck and black tailpiece on the left side, and the seed pod and seeds on the right side, all of which direct our attention downward. Notice that as the eye moves down the page, it encounters three stages of making both a violin and an ice cream bar. The first stage is shown in the top third of the page, which contains the most basic ingredients of both products, wood in the basic shape of a violin on the left and pure chocolate and cream on the right. These raw ingredients constitute a promise or abstract of the products. The next section downward, marked off by the vectors formed by the black fingerboard and the ice cream stick, shows the second stage of the construction, where the ingredients are partially assembled, with the violin body fit together and the chocolate and cream mixed. The third vertical section of the ad contains the finished products: instrument and ice cream bar. The bottom section of the page contains a print text

Figure 9.10 *Christ Healing the Sick* by Rembrandt. (Downloaded on February 2, 2017 from https://en.wikipedia.org/wiki/Hundred_Guilder_Print#/media/File: Rembrandt_The_Hundred_Guilder_Print.jpg)

that summarizes the fabrication processes we have just observed, along with an image of the Häagen-Dazs box that we should look for at the grocery counter. The composition of the ad, then, exemplifies a very old scheme of vertical organization in which the ideal is presented at the top of an image and the real or practical is presented at the bottom. We have already encountered another example of this organization in the image of the traditional crèche scene, where angels, who are ideal beings, appear at the top and their earthly equivalents, the Holy Family, appear just below them. The animals, who are further down in the hierarchy of creation, often appear at the bottom of the scene.

The crèche scene also exemplifies a second and complementary principle for organizing the elements of an image, namely that **the most important elements appear at the center**. In the Christmas card nativity scene found in the web materials, Jesus is at the center with Mary and Joseph to either side and the animals and angels (who are less involved in the birth) at the margins. This principle can also be seen in Figure 9.10, Rembrandt's etching *Christ Healing the Sick*, which we will discuss in detail in Section 9.4. But, for now, let us note that the most important participant in the image is, again, Christ, who is located near the center. The other participants, including the disciples on the left and people in the darkened room on the right, are at the margins of the image.

Often, there are elements in an image that stand out and capture our attention. We have observed that there are similar elements in language that are salient because they deviate from an expected pattern. Thus, in Chapter 5 we noted that English sentences usually conform to a particular pattern of stress, but that this pattern can be violated when the speaker wishes to emphasize a particular word, as in this dialogue, where speaker B uses emphatic stress on the word *me*:

> A: Lét me hóld the báby!
> B: Nó, lét me hóld the báby!

Salience in speech and art is, of course, a form of foregrounding, which we have discussed at length, observing that foregrounding works by deviating from what we would expect find.

In pictorial art, elements can be made salient in a number of ways. One way is to use maximally contrasting colors. Because of the construction of the human optical system, certain pairs of colors are perceived as maximally different and other pairs of colors as not so different. For example, green and blue are not perceived as very different, and many languages refer to these hues by the same word, which anthropologists have called "grue." Different languages have different systems for naming colors, but the simplest system has only two basic color terms, which denote maximum contrasts in our color perception: light-warm and dark-cool (Berlin and Kay 1969). When societies with this two-word system expand their color vocabulary, perhaps as a result of contact with a language with more color terms, a common sequence in the emergence of new terms is observed. The range of hues designated by the term for light-warm is divided along lines of maximum perceptual contrast resulting in terms for white, yellow, and red, and the dark cool range is divided into terms designating dark-cool (grue) and black. Thus, many languages have four basic color terms (English has eleven), which are: white, yellow, red, dark-cool and black, and these terms designate regions of the color spectrum that appear maximally distinct to human beings.[1]

The Häagen-Dazs ad makes use of these maximal color contrasts to highlight its product, as can be seen by viewing the ad at https:www .pinterest.com/pin/384283780684473058. The basic color contrasts in the image are the light-warm colors of the violin on the left versus the dark-cool colors of the chocolate on the right. Within each of these vertical fields salient hues appear. On the left, the black of the violin's fingerboard, tailpiece, and pegs contrast with the light-warm of the violin's body, emphasizing the vector function of these darker elements. The right side of the image presents even starker contrasts. Against the predominant dark-cool hues of the chocolate, the bright yellow egg yolk and the red-topped box of Häagen-Dazs ice cream bars stand out. Thus, the bottom right of the image, which contains the new and useful information about the product that we are supposed to buy, is especially salient in the image.

Another technique for foregrounding is repetition, or parallelism, and in Chapter 1 we noted that repetition in poetry involves many techniques, including rhyme, assonance, alliteration, refrain, and so on. Foregrounding in visual art can be accomplished by the repetition of shapes. In *Nude Descending a Staircase* the figure is foregrounded in part by its light-warm colors against the cool-dark background but also by the repeated geometric shapes of the torso, buttocks, and legs. In the Häagen-Dazs ad the repetition of basic shapes on the left and right sides of the image suggests the transferred features of the visual metaphor, as noted above, but the most exact repetition of shapes is the image of the violin and the ice cream bar at the bottom of the page, making this aspect of the image especially salient.

In sum, repetition is a powerful tool of composition in both written and visual texts, as Kress and van Leeuwen (2006) emphasize in this statement: "It is from the sense of rhythm and the sense of compositional balance that our aesthetic pleasure in texts [is] derived" (p. 202).

9.4 Halliday Meets Lakoff

In Figure 9.10 we see Rembrandt's etching *Christ Healing the Sick*, which he completed around 1649. Kress and van Leeuwen (2006) call this kind of picture a "narrative image," meaning an image that tells a story. In fact, the picture tells three stories, all of which are found in Matthew, Chapter 19. The main story, related in verses 13 and 14, reads as follows in the King James version:

> Then there were brought unto him [Jesus] little children that he should put his hands on them, and pray: and the disciples rebuked them. But Jesus said, Suffer [allow] little children, and forbid them not, to come unto me: for of such is the kingdom of heaven.

The second story in the etching, as the title states, is about Jesus healing the sick. Although healing is not directly portrayed, many of the figures in Jesus' presence are clearly sick or lame. The third story involves the figure dressed in fine clothing who is leaving Jesus' presence at the bottom right of the picture. This is the rich young man who told Jesus that he had always obeyed the commandments and asked what else he should do to lead a righteous life. Jesus said that he should give all of his possessions to the poor and follow him, which the young man refused to do.

The Halliday-based principles of composition that we have just discussed can be employed to analyze this image. The most important participants in the image are Jesus, the mother approaching him with her child, and the disciples, who stand to Jesus' right. The closest disciple, Peter, tries to bar the woman and the child with his hand, thus forming a vector that excludes them. This material process, however, is secondary in the image. The primary material process involves Jesus raising his right hand and arm, thus creating a vector that excludes the disciples from his attention and includes the mother and child, as well as the other children and the sick on Jesus' left. This situation can be represented in a Hallidayan framework as follows:

Jesus	**excludes**	**the disciples**
Actor	Process (material)	Goal

and

Jesus	**includes**	**the children and the sick**
Actor	Process (material)	Goal

Other vectors can also be found in the image. For example, vectors are formed by the eye lines of the participants who are looking at Jesus and thus direct our attention toward him. The vectors formed by eye lines do not represent material processes, but rather *reactional processes*. For example, the process represented by the mother looking at her child can be represented like this:

The mother	**looks at**	**her child**
Reactor	Process (reaction)	Phenomenon

When two participants reciprocate their gaze, a mutually reactive process occurs, and the only such process in the etching is between Jesus and the child. Notice that the vectors of three eye lines, those of Jesus, the child, and the mother, create two sides of a small triangle, and that this central area of the painting contains the three participants who are central to the main story, with Jesus and the mother focusing their attention, and ours, on the child.

Turning to a metaphorical interpretation of the etching, recall that Kennedy (2008) argues that visual metaphors can be created by breaking the conventions of realistic art, as when dollar signs appear in the eyes of Scrooge McDuck. However, Lakoff (2006) argues that metaphorical meaning can also be conveyed by unaltered, realistic art when it alludes to a conceptual metaphor. Figure 9.10 contains evidence for this claim. The most obvious compositional feature of the image is the contrast between the light and dark areas (one of Rembrandt's specialties). Jesus and the figures in front of him and to his left and immediate right are bathed in light, but the mysterious background and some of the foreground, including the rich young man, are in shadow. Thus, the lighting divides the participants in the image into two groups. This compositional structure suggests the conceptual metaphor PEOPLE IN THE SAME GROUP ARE INSIDE A CONTAINER, which underlies metaphorical expressions like, "Mel's coming *in* with us on the deal," and "Martha was kicked *out* of the club." The metaphorical interpretation of the figures in and out of the light is, of course, that those in the light are Jesus' followers, while those outside the light, including the rich young man, are not. Notice also that Jesus is at the center of the area of light, and his head is its highest point. This configuration suggests the conceptual metaphors CENTRAL IS THE MOST IMPORTANT and DIVINE IS UP, as seen in expressions like: "That concept is *central* to our plan" and "Elijah *ascended* to heaven."

The main source of light in the etching is Jesus' face, and this reflects the Christian understanding of God as the source of good (where light symbolizes good) and invokes the conceptual metaphors GOODNESS IS LIGHT ("You are the light of my life," "Let in the light of reason"). However, there is another light source in the image, namely the window above Jesus' head, to which he points with his left hand, forming a vector. This light appears to be coming directly from heaven, thus symbolizing God and invoking the two conceptual metaphors just mentioned. So, images can be analyzed not only in terms of conventional elements of composition, such as vectors and the placement of participants, but also in terms of the conceptual metaphors that they suggest.

Note

1 See the discussion in Adamson (2009):183–185.

Summary

Like language, visual images can convey meaning literally and metaphorically. Visual metaphors can arise when an image diverges from a realistic representation of an object. For example, dollar signs in a cartoon character's eyes suggest avarice. Many such visual metaphors have become conventionalized in comics, including motion lines and the shapes of word balloons. Visual metaphors can also occur when a picture violates what we know to be true, as when the painter Dali draws rubbery clocks hanging from branches.

Visual images are also like language because they are composed of basic elements that can be arranged according to particular rules, some of which are similar to the linguistic rules of Halliday's Systemic Functional Grammar. This school of linguistics looks not just at the form of elements, such as what a Noun Group consists of, but also at how the various forms function within a clause. For example, a Noun Group can function as an Actor, Sensor, Goal, etc. Halliday claims that language has three metafunctions. The ideational metafunction is used to communicate facts about the world, and realistic images can do this, as well. For example, the figures and objects within an image can be construed as participants that perform the functions of Actor, Sensor, Goal, etc. The interpersonal metafunction establishes formal or informal relationships between participants in a conversation, and images can also establish such relationships with viewers, as when the subject of a portrait looks directly at the viewer, implying an informal relationship. The textual metafunction concerns how a text is organized, and two principles for analyzing how an image is organized are: **old information appears on the left**, and **the most important elements appear at the center.**

Finally, Lakoff has observed that realistic images can convey metaphorical meaning by referencing conceptual metaphors. For example, the light surrounding a holy figure in a painting references the conceptual metaphor GOODNESS IS LIGHT.

Exercises

1. Analyze the image in Figure 9.11 by identifying the primary process it depicts and the functional (case) roles that the process requires. Identify any comic conventions that the cartoonist has employed.

2. Go to the website Comic Strip Library (http://www.comicstriplibrary.org/display/414), and find another cartoon to analyze using the same tools that you used for exercise 1 OR, analyze one of the pictures on the website http://www.comicstriplibrary.org/display/68.

3. Go to the website of the National Portrait Gallery, London (http//www.npg.org.uk) and find portraits that exemplify the following relationships between the participants in the portraits and the viewer: (1) the viewer is an onlooker;

Figure 9.11 Panel from a Krazy Kat cartoon strip.
(from Herriman. Krazy Kat, January 1, 1922. Downloaded from The Comic Strip Library http://
www.comicstriplibrary.org/display/68, January 19, 2014)

(2) the participant establishes a formal relationship with the viewer; (3) the participant establishes an informal relationship with the viewer.

4.   Rembrandt's etching *Christ at Emmaus* is a narrative image, and the story it tells can be read in the Bible, Luke 24, 13–35. After reading this story, access the etching, which can be found at http://www.wikiart.org/en/rembrandt/, and then identify the main elements in the composition (including processes, participants, and vectors) as well as any conceptual metaphors that are visually referenced.

5.   Google the phrase *Starbucks Advertisements* and find an ad with human beings in it (there are surprisingly few). Analyze the ad identifying the main elements in the composition (including processes, participants, and vectors) as well as any conceptual metaphors that are visually referenced.

Key Terms

visual metaphor
affordances
functionalism
Systemic Functional Grammar
metafunctions (of language)
participants
processes
vector
salient

Suggestions for Further Reading

The classic work on comic conventions is McCloud (1993). It is also a lot of fun to read because it is all in cartoons. Kress & van Leeuwen (2006) is the groundbreaking work on image analysis, but an earlier book on this subject, which Lakoff acknowledges greatly influenced his thinking, is Arnheim (1969). Bloor & Bloor (2004) is an accessible introduction to Halliday's Systemic Functional Grammar. Halliday (1994) is the less accessible but authoritative work. Lakoff's take on image metaphors is presented in Lakoff (2006).

References

Abrams, M. H. (1953). *The mirror and the lamp: Romantic theory and the critical tradition*. New York: Oxford University Press.

Abrams, M. H. & Harpham, G. (2009). *A glossary of literary terms* (9th edn). Boston: Wadsworth.

Adams, S. (2000). *Slapped together: The Dilbert business anthology*. New York: HarperCollins.

Adamson, H. D. (2009). *Interlanguage variation in theoretical and pedagogical perspective*. New York: Routledge.

Anderson, J. R. (2015). *Cognitive psychology and its implications*. London: Macmillan.

Arnheim, R. (1969). *Visual thinking*. Berkeley: University of California Press

Arp, R. (1997). *Perrine's sound and sense: An introduction to poetry*. Fort Worth: Harcourt.

Arp, T. R. & Johnson, G. (2006). *Perrine's literature: Structure, sound, and sense* (9th edn). Boston: Thompson.

Austin, J. L. *How to do things with words*. Oxford: Clarendon Press.

Barker, S. (2008). A bench mark for volunteerism. *Tucson Lifestyle* (March), pp. 120–134.

Barry, P. (1995). *Beginning theory*. Manchester: Manchester University Press.

Bartlett, F. C. (1932). *Remembering: A study in experimental and social psychology*. Cambridge: Cambridge University Press.

Bell, A. (1984). Language style as audience design. *Language in Society* 13(2), 145–204.
    (2001). Back in style: Reworking audience design. In Eckert, P. & Rickford, J. R. (eds.), *Style and sociolinguistic variation* (pp. 139–169). New York: Cambridge.

Berlin, B. & Kay, P. (1969). *Basic color terms: Their universality and evolution*. Berkeley: University of California Press.

Biber, D. (1995). *Dimensions of register variation: A cross-linguistic comparison*. Cambridge: Cambridge University Press.

Biber, D., Conrad, S. & Reppen, R. (1998). *Corpus linguistics: Investigating language structure and use*. Cambridge: Cambridge University Press.

Bierce, A. (1991/1891). "An occurrence at Owl Creek Bridge." In Bain, C. E., Beaty, J. & Hunter, J. P. (eds.), *The Norton introduction to literature* (shorter 5th edn) (pp. 63–69). New York: Norton.

Bleich, D. (1978). *Subjective criticism*. Baltimore: The Johns Hopkins University Press.

Bloor, T. & Bloor, M. (2004). *The functional analysis of English* (2nd edn). Arnold.

Bourhis, R. Y. & Giles, H. (1977). The language of intergroup distinctiveness. In Giles, H. (ed.), *Language, ethnicity and intergroup relations* (pp. 19–135). London: Academic Press.

Bransford, J. D. & Johnson, M. K. (1972). Contextual prerequisites for understanding: Some investigations of comprehension and recall. *Journal of Verbal Learning and Verbal Behavior*, 11(2), pp. 717–726.

Bressler, C. E. (2007). *Literary criticism: An introduction to theory and practice* (4th edn). Upper Saddle River, NJ: Pearson/Prentice Hall.

Brown, N. (2003). Writing in the mother tongue: Approaches to dialect and colloquial speech. *The Writer's Chronicle* 35, 48–57.

Cook, G. (1994). *Discourse and literature*. Oxford: Oxford University Press.

Cook, W. A. (1989*). Case grammar theory*. Washington, D.C.: Georgetown University Press.

Crews, F. C. (2003). *Postmodern Pooh: Rethinking theory*. Evanston, IL: Northwestern University Press.

Curzon, A. & Adams, M. (2008). *How English Works* (2nd edn). Boston: Pearson.

Cudden, J. A. (1991). *A dictionary of literary terms and literary theory* (3rd edn). Oxford: Blackwell.

Dickens, C. (1850). *David Copperfield*. Charles Dickens Online. www.dickens-online/david-copperfieldohtml.

Drew, P. (1992). Contested evidence in cross examination. In Drew, P. & Heritage, J. (eds.), *Talk at work: Interaction in institutional settings*. New York: Cambridge University Press.

Eagleton, T. (1983). *Literary theory: An introduction*. Minneapolis: University of Minnesota Press.

Fasold, R. & Conner-Linton, J. (eds.) (2006). *An introduction to language and linguistics*. Cambridge: Cambridge University Press.

Fillmore, C. (1968). The case for case. In Bach, E. & Harms, R. T. (eds.), *Universals in linguistic theory* (pp. 1–88). New York: Holt, Rinehart, & Winston.

Fish, S. (1980) What is stylistics and why are they saying such terrible things about it? In S. Fish (ed.). *Is there a text in this class? The authority of interpretative communities* (pp. 68–96). Cambridge, MA: Harvard University Press.

Fowler, R. (1986). *Linguistic criticism*. Oxford: Oxford University Press.

Fromkin, V., Rodman, R., & Hyams, N. (2014). *An introduction to language* (10th edn). Boston: Thompson.

Fry, P. (2009). *Introduction to theory of literature*. Yale Open University Courses. https://oyc.yale.edu/English/engl-300.

Fussell, P. (1979). *Poetic meter and poetic form* (rev. edn). New York: McGraw-Hill.

Gavins, J. (2007). *Text world theory: An introduction*. Edinburgh: Edinburgh University Press.

Goodman, K. (1967). Reading: A psycholinguistic guess game. *Journal of the Reading Specialist*, May, pp. 126–135.

Greenbaum, S. (1996). *The Oxford English grammar*. Oxford: Oxford University Press.

Grice, H. P. (1975). Logic and conversation. In Cole, P. & Morgan, J. L. (eds.), *Syntax and Semantics, Vol. 3, Speech Acts* (pp. 41–58). New York: Academic Press.

Guerin, F. C. (2005). *A handbook of critical approaches to literature* (5th edn). New York: Oxford University Press.

Halliday, M. A. K. (1994). *An introduction to functional grammar* (2nd edn). London: Arnold.

(1971). Linguistic function and literary style: An inquiry into the language of William Golding's *The Inheritors*. In Chatman, S. (ed.), *Literary style: A symposium* (pp. 330–365). Oxford: Oxford University Press.

Harmon, W. & Holman, C. H. (2000). *A handbook to literature* (8th edn). Upper Saddle River, NJ: Pearson.

Heath, S. B. (1983). *Ways with words: Language, life, and work in communities and classrooms*. Cambridge: Cambridge University Press.

Horace, *Carmen Saeculare, Book 2*. In Thomas, R. F. (ed.) *Horace: Odes and Carmen Saeculare*. Cambridge: Cambridge University Press.

Hughes, A. & Trudgill, P. (1996). *English accents and dialects* (3rd edn). London: Arnold.

Hughes, R. (1992). *Barcelona*. New York: Knopf.

Hunt, K. W. (1965). *Grammatical structures written at three grade levels*. Champaign, IL: National Council of Teachers of English.

(1970). Syntactic maturity in schoolchildren and adults. *Monographs of the society for research in child development*, 35(1).

Hunter, P. J. (1999). *The Norton introduction to poetry* (7th edn). New York: Norton.

Iser, W. (1978). *The act of reading: A theory of aesthetic response*. Baltimore: The Johns Hopkins University Press.

Jeffries, L. & McIntyre, D. (2010). *Stylistics*. Cambridge: Cambridge University Press.

Kachru, B. (1983). Models of non-native Englishes. In Smith, L. E. (ed.), *Readings in English as an international language* (pp. 69–86). London: Pergamon.

Kennedy, J. M. (2008). Metaphor and art. In Gibbs, R. W. Jr. (ed.). *The Cambridge handbook of metaphor and thought* (pp. 447–461). Cambridge: Cambridge University Press.

Kövecses, Z. (2010). *Metaphor: A practical introduction* (2nd edn). Oxford: Oxford University Press.

Kreml, N. (1998). Implicatures of style switching in the narrative voice of Cormac McCarthy's *All the Pretty Horses*. In Myers-Scotton, C. (ed.). *Codes and consequences: Choosing linguistic varieties* (pp. 41–61). New York: Oxford University Press.

Kress, G. & van Leeuwen, T. (2006). Reading images: The grammar of visual design (2nd edn). London: Routledge.

Kuhn, T. (1970). *The structure of scientific revolutions*. Chicago: The University of Chicago Press.

Labov, W. (1972a). *Sociolinguistic patterns*. Philadelphia: University of Pennsylvania Press.

(1972b). *Language in the Inner City*. Philadelphia: University of Pennsylvania Press.

(2001). The anatomy of style-shifting. In Eckert, P. & Rickford, J. R. (eds.), *Style and sociolinguistic variation* (pp. 85–108). Cambridge: Cambridge University Press.

Labov, W., Ash, S., & Boberg, C. (2006). *Atlas of North American English: Phonetics, phonology, and sound change*. New York: Mouton de Gruyter.

Ladefoged, P. (2006). *A course in Phonetics* (5th edn). Boston: Thompson.

Lakoff, G. (1989). *Women, fire, and dangerous things*. Chicago: University of Chicago Press.

(1993). The contemporary theory of metaphor. In Ortony, A. (ed.), *Metaphor and thought* (pp. 202–252). Cambridge: Cambridge University Press.

(2006). The neuroscience of form in art. In Turner, M. (ed.), *The artful mind* (pp. 153–169). Oxford: Oxford University Press.

Lakoff, G. & Johnson, M. (1980). *Metaphors we live by*. Chicago: University of Chicago Press.

Lakoff, G. & Turner, M. (1989). *More than cool reason: A field guide to poetic metaphor*. Chicago: University of Chicago Press.

Leech, G. N. & Short, M. H. (1981). *Style in fiction: A linguistic introduction to English fictional prose*. London: Longman.

Levelt, W. J. M. (1989). *Speaking: From intention to articulation*. Cambridge: M I T Press.

Lewis, C. S. (1997/1938). *Out of the silent planet*. New York: Quality Paperback Book Club.

Louw, B. (1993). Irony in the text or insincerity in the writer? The diagnostic potential of semantic prosodies. In Baker, M., Francis, G. & Tognini-Bonelli, G. (eds.). *Text and technology: In honor of John Sinclair* (pp. 157–76). Amsterdam: John Benjamins.

Mandler, J. M. (1984). Representation and recall. In *Infant Memory*. Moscovitch, M. (ed.) (pp. 75–101). New York: Plenum.

McBain, E. (1965). *Doll*. New York: Avon.

McCloud, S. (1993). *Understanding comics: The invisible art*. New York: HarperCollins.

Melchers, G. & Shaw, P. (2003). *World Englishes: An Introduction*. London: Arnold.

Milroy, L. (1981). *Regional accents of English: Belfast*. Belfast: Blackstaff Press.

Morenberg, M. (2009). *Doing grammar* (4th edn). Oxford: Oxford University Press.

Parker, F. & Riley, K. (2005). *Linguistics for non-linguists: A primer with exercises* (4th edn). Boston: Pearson.

Pinker, S. (2008). *The stuff of thought*. New York: Viking.

(2014). *The sense of style: The thinking person's guide to writing in the 21st century*. New York: Viking.

Poussa, P. (2000). Dickens as a sociolinguist: Dialect in David Copperfield. In Taavitsainen, I., Melchers, G., & Pahta, P. (eds.), *Writing in nonstandard English* (pp. 27–44). Philadelphia: Benjamins.

Prator, C. & Robinett, B. W. (1972*). Manual of American English pronunciation* (3rd edn.). New York: Holt, Rinehart and Winston.

Rex, A. (2007). *The true meaning of Smekday*. New York: Hyperion.

Rosch. E. (1978). Principles of categorization. In Rosch, E. & Lloyd, B. B. (eds.), *Cognition and categorization* (pp. 27–48). Hillsdale, NJ: Erlbaum.

Rosenblatt, L. (1978). *The poem, the text, the reader: The transactional theory of literary work*. Carbondale: Southern Illinois University Press.

Roberts, E. V. & Jacobs, H. E. (2007). *Literature: An introduction to reading and writing* (8th edn). Upper Saddle River, NJ: Pearson.

Ryan, M. (1991). *Possible worlds, artificial intelligence and narrative theory.* Bloomington: University of Indiana.

Saussure, F. (1974/1916). *Course in general linguistics.* Bally, C. & Sechehaye, A. (eds.). London: Collins.

Semino, E. (1997). *Language and world creation in poems and other texts.* London: Longman.

  (2002). Cognitive stylistics and mind style. In Semino, E. & Culpeper, J. (eds.). *Cognitive stylistics: Language and cognition in text analysis* (pp. 95–122). Amsterdam: Benjamins.

Shklovsky, V. (1972). *Mayakovsky and his circle* (ed. and translated by Feiler, L.). New York: Dodd, Mead.

  (2004). Art as Technique. In: Rivkin, J. & Ryan, M. (eds.) *Literary Theory: An Anthology* (2nd ed.) Malden, MA: Blackwell.

Short, M. (1996). *Exploring the language of poems, plays and prose.* London: Longman.

Showalter, E. (2003). *Teaching literature.* Hoboken, NJ: Blackwell.

Shteyngart, G. (2013). From the Diaries of Pussy-Cake, *My double life with Pamela. The New Yorker* (pp. 52–54). June 10, 2013.

Simpson, P. (2004). *Stylistics: A resource book for students.* London: Routledge.

Townsend, D. J. & Bever, T. G. (2001). *Sentence comprehension: The integrations of habits and rules.* Cambridge, MA: MIT Press.

Traugott, E. C. & Pratt, M. L. (1980). *Linguistics for students of literature.* New York: Harcourt.

Trillin, C. (2004). *Obliviously on he sails: The Bush administration in rhyme.* New York: Random House

Trudgill, P. (1994). *The social differentiation of English in Norwich.* Cambridge: Cambridge University Press.

  (2000). *Sociolinguistics: An introduction to language and society* (4th edn). London: Penguin.

Turow, S. (1996). *The Laws of Our Fathers.* New York: Farrar, Straus, Giroux.

Tyson, L. (2006). *Critical theory today: A user-friendly guide.* New York: Routledge.

Ungerer, F. & Schmid, H.-J. (2006). An introduction to cognitive linguistics (2nd edn). Harlow: Pearson.

Vendler, H. (2009). *Poems, poets, poetry: An introduction and anthology* (3rd edn). Boston: Bedford.

Vicari, P. (1993) Renaissance Emblematica, *Metaphor and Symbolic Activity,* 8(3), 153–168.

Wardhaugh, R. (2010). *An introduction to sociolinguistics* (6th edn). Hoboken, NJ: Wiley.

Wittgenstein, L. (1953). Philosophical investigations. New York: Macmillan.

Wells, J. C. (1982). *Accents of English,* Vol. 2. Cambridge: Cambridge University Press.

Werth, P. (1999). *Text worlds: Representing conceptual space in discourse.* London: Longman.

Wolfram, W. & Schilling, N. (2016). *American English: Dialects and variation* (3rd edn). Oxford: Oxford University Press.

Yule, G. (2010). *The study of language* (4th edn). Cambridge: Cambridge University Press.

Glossary

accessibility   The degree to which a possible world differs from the real world. For example, historical fiction has a high degree of accessibility because many of its characters and locations are also found in the real world.

accommodation   Changing speech style to match or diverge from the style of a conversational partner. Changing to match the style of a conversational partner in order to create solidarity is called "convergent accommodation" and changing to diverge from the style of a conversational partner is called "divergent accommodation."

affordances   In discourse analysis an affordance is a resource or capability that a type of media possesses. For example, a comic strip offers the affordance of providing visual metaphors.

African American English   The variety of English spoken by many African Americans in the United States.

alliteration   The use of repeated consonant sounds, as in "I hear lake water lapping with low sounds by the shore."

allophone   A variety of a phoneme. For example, in the word *cat* the phoneme /t/ can be pronounced as [t] (unaspirated) or as [tʰ] (aspirated). So, [t] and [tʰ] are allophones of the phoneme /t/.

allomorph   A particular form of a morpheme. For example, the regular plural morpheme (spelled –s) is pronounced [s] in the word "cats," [z] in the word "dogs," and [iz] in the word "approaches." Therefore, [s], [z], and [iz] are allomorphs of the plural morpheme.

assonance   The repetition of vowel sounds (as in "light a fire") or near vowel sounds (as in "the snow fell sadly").

caesura   A pause in a line of poetry that is made for reasons of natural speech rather than to adhere to the meter of the poem, as in Romeo's line,

But soft! ‖ What light through yonder window breaks?

canonical word order   The most common or expected order of grammatical categories in an English sentence, namely NP V NP.

character-accessible   The situation in fictional narratives where information about the text world cannot be verified by people in the discourse world, but is only available to characters in the text world.

class stratification   When a linguistic variable, such as the –ing/–in' alternation, is pronounced at different frequencies by different social classes. For example, working-class New York City English speakers pronounce –in' more frequently than upper-class New York City English speakers.

clause   A string of words that contains a subject and a finite verb (see *independent clause* and *dependent clause*).

cognitive model   The background knowledge that forms the necessary context for understanding many concepts. For example, the concept of *bachelor* is understood in terms of a cognitive model of a monogamous society where a man is expected to marry at a certain age and where there are women eligible for marriage.

cohesion   "Sticking together." The grammatical and lexical linking within a sentence or text that holds the text together. For example, the agreement of pronouns with their antecedents lends cohesion to a text.

conceptual domain   A concept (including its features) or a cognitive model (including its components) for a particular area of knowledge, for example, knowledge about marriage, or fishing, or irrigation systems.

conceptual metaphor   When one conceptual domain is understood in terms of another. In the conceptual metaphor underlying the expression "Life's like a box of chocolates" the conceptual domain of life is understood in terms of the conceptual domain of a box of chocolates.

collocation   Words that often or always occur together, such as "mother" and "father," or "the die is cast."

conceptual metonym   When a conceptual domain is referenced by mentioning one aspect of that domain, as in THE PLACE STANDS FOR THE INSTITUTION, which underlies the metonymical expression "Signs of a booming economy give *Wall Street* jitters," where *Wall Street* stands for the American stock market.

consonance   When the final consonants of two words are the same, as in *kick* and *flick* and *chuckle* and *fickle*.

content word   A word that has lexical content. Content words include nouns, verbs, adjectives, and adverbs (see *function word*).

conventional metaphorical expression   See *metaphorical expression*.

conversational maxim   One of Grice's four rules to ensure that a conversation is cooperative and effective. For example, the maxim of quality states that the speakers believe what they are saying to be true.

corpus   A database of written and/or spoken language, such as the British National Corpus, which contains 100,000,000 words of written and spoken British English.

creative (or poetic) metaphorical expression   See *metaphorical expression*.

deixis   A word or phrase that cannot be understood without context. For example, the word *here* in the phrase "Come here" can only be understood if we know where the speaker is standing.

dependent clause   A string of words that contains a subject and a finite verb but cannot be punctuated as a sentence by itself but rather must be accompanied by an independent clause (see *independent clause*).

derivation   In generative grammar a tree diagram together with a list of transformations that show how the deep (or logical) structure of a sentence is changed into a surface structure.

derivational morpheme   A morpheme that changes the grammatical category of a word. For example, adding the derivational morpheme *–able* to a verb changes it into an adjective, as in *afford → afford**able***.

discourse world   The situational context surrounding a speech event including the physical setting, the participants, and the background knowledge that the participants bring to the event.

elaboration (of a conceptual metaphor)   Expanding on and supplying details about an aspect of the source domain of a conceptual metaphor. For example, DIFFICULT TO HANDLE THINGS ARE DOGS maps features like unmanageability from dogs to difficult situations, but the poem "Life The Hound Equivocal" elaborates that the hound can lick or bite one's hand.

extension (of a conceptual metaphor)   Mapping an aspect of the source domain of a conceptual metaphor that is not commonly mapped, onto the target domain thus taking the conceptual metaphor in a new direction. For example, DEATH IS SLEEP usually maps only features like inactivity, inability to perceive, and horizontal position from sleep to death. However, in his soliloquy Hamlet extends this conceptual metaphor by noting that in sleep, and therefore perhaps in death, one can dream.

eye dialect   The literary technique of misspelling a word even though it does not change the word's pronunciation. For example, "civilize" might be spelled "sivilize." Eye dialect suggests that the character who is speaking might spell the word that way.

feminine rhyme   When two words share the same last syllables; that is, when the last two or more vowels, plus the consonants that follow them, are the same, as in *fertile/turtle* and *neither/either*.

finite verb   A verb that is marked for tense, as in "Marsha love**s** the beach," where the –s indicates simple present tense. Nonfinite verbs are not marked for tense, as in "Marsha loves **to swim.**"

focal character   The character on whom an omniscient narrator focuses, allowing the reader access mainly to the thoughts and perceptions of this character.

foot (poetic)   A grouping of a stressed syllable and one or more unstressed syllables. For example, the line *'Twas the níght | before Chríst | mas and áll | through the hóuse |* contains four anapestic feet.

foregrounding   When a linguistic structure is different from the structures around it or from the kinds of structures that are expected in a text, thus drawing attention to itself. There are two kinds. *Deviation* occurs when the structure in question deviates from the expected pattern, as when a foreign language word is used in a sentence. *Parallelism* occurs when a structure is repeated, as in a refrain.

functionalism   In regard to grammar, functionalism is the study of how a grammatical structure works rather than how it is formed. For example, in the sentence *The dog bit the man, the dog* functions as the subject of the sentence, and *the man* functions as the direct object.

functional morpheme   A morpheme that serves a grammatical purpose but contains no inherent semantic content. For example, in the phrase "to run" *to* has no inherent meaning but rather serves to indicate that the phrase is an infinitive. By contrast, *run* is a lexical morpheme that means to travel quickly by foot.

function word   A word that mainly serves a grammatical purpose such as joining two clauses together. Function words include conjunctions, prepositions, determiners, relative pronouns.

free verse   Poetry that is free from limitations of regular meter, rhythm, or rhyme.

generate   A technical term meaning "define" or "specify." The phrase structure rule NP → Det Adj N defines an NP as consisting of a determiner followed by an adjective and then a noun.

hypercorrection   When a speaker uses an inappropriate form because it sounds more formal; for example, pronouncing "often" as [aftən] is usually an instance of hypercorrection.

illocutionary force   The speech act that an utterance accomplishes. For example, the sentence "Please come over here" has the illocutionary force of a request, while the reply "No" has the illocutionary force of a refusal.

image metaphor   Image metaphors map aspects of one mental image onto aspects of another mental image. For example, "He clasps the crag with crooked hands" maps parts of the image of a hand onto an eagle's claw.

independent clause   A string of words that contains a subject and a finite verb and that can be punctuated as a sentence by itself (see *dependent clause*).

inflectional morpheme   A morpheme that adds some aspect of meaning to words of a particular grammatical category. For example, the plural morpheme attaches only to nouns, and it indicates that there are more than one.

language variety   A broad term that can refer to any version of language, including a regional dialect, a social dialect, a style, or a register.

laxing   When a tense vowel is changed to the corresponding lax vowel, as when [iy] → [i] or [ey] → [e].

lexical morpheme   A morpheme that contains semantic (as opposed to grammatical) meaning. For example, in the phrase "to run" *run* is a lexical morpheme that means to travel quickly by foot. However, *to* is a morpheme that has no inherent meaning but serves to indicate that the phrase is an infinitive.

lexicon   The part of a formal grammar that contains the words of a language along with their meanings and parts of speech.

limited point of view   A kind of storytelling in which the narrator is not a character in the text world but does tell the story from the point of view of one of the characters, so that the reader only has access to that character's thoughts and sensations.

manner of articulation   One of the three dimensions for identifying consonant speech sounds. The manner of articulation usually has to do with how the sound is produced, and is usually associated with how open the mouth is. For example, the mouth is completely closed for [p], so it is a stop; the mouth is narrowly open for [s], so it is a fricative.

marked   An unusual or unexpected way of expressing a meaning. For example, English does not use different forms for verbs in the simple present tense except for the third person singular form (I go, you go, she **goes**, we go, you all go, they go). So, the form *goes* is marked, or unusual, while the form *go* is unmarked, or usual.

masculine rhyme   When two words have the same final stressed vowel and following sounds, as in *said/red* and *love/of*. This rhyme involves only the final syllable.

metafunctions (of language)   The primary purposes of language according to Systemic Functional Grammar. The three metafunctions are: the ideational function (to represent the world), the interpersonal function (to represent the social relationship between a speaker and a hearer), and the textual function (to create messages and texts that are cohesive internally and coherent to the intended audience).

metaphorical expression   A word, phrase or sentence that expresses a metaphor; for example, the phrase "boys of summer" refers to baseball players.

> *Creative (or poetic) metaphorical expressions* convey a sense of the figurative association. For example, in "Out, out, brief candle" we get the sense of a candle being extinguished.
>
> *Conventional metaphorical expressions* (or dead metaphors) convey no sense of figurative association; they are just the way we say things. For example, in "He passed away" we have no sense of something passing by – it is just how we say, "He died."

meter   The length of (i.e., number of feet in) a line of poetry, for example, tetrameter and pentameter.

metonymical expression   A word, phrase, or sentence that expresses a metonym. For example, in "*the White House* denied the report," *White House* stands for the US President's spokesperson.

metonymy   The substitution of an attribute of a thing for the thing itself. In the expression "There's a *suit* waiting for you in the lobby," *suit* stands for *man dressed in a suit.*

mind style   The ways that narrators and characters understand things within a text world. For example, a child and an adult might have very different understandings of a parent's divorce and thus different mind styles.

monitor   When speakers pay attention to the way they speak. For example, when monitoring, New York City speakers pronounce more post-vocalic [r]s in their speech than when they are not monitoring.

morpheme   The smallest unit of meaning. For example, the word *moonbeams* contains three morphemes: *moon, beam,* and *–s,* which signifies that the word is plural.

New Criticism   A school of literary criticism that focuses on the text itself and not on the historical context of its creation or interpretation. It emphasizes the practice of close reading, where a passage is looked at in great detail and features such as images, sounds, and symbols are analyzed and related to each other.

new historicism   A school of literary criticism that examines literary works along with historical documents to shed light on past cultures.

noun phrase   A string of words that includes a noun and the words that modify it.

omniscient point of view   A kind of storytelling in which the narrator is not a character in the text world and has access to all of the characters' thoughts and sensations.

onomatopoeia   Where the pronunciation of a word imitates the sound the word denotes, as in *whisper, clang,* and *sizzle.*

ontological metaphor   A kind of conceptual metaphor that construes abstract notions, like emotions and processes, as objects or things. For example, LEARNING IS A THING allows us to say that someone *has* (i.e., *possesses*) an education even though an education is not an object that can literally be possessed.

participant accessible   The situation in true narratives where information about the text world can be verified by people in the discourse world (see *character-accessible*).

participants   The constituants of a sentence that are usually realized linguistically as nouns according to Systemic Functional Grammar. For example, in the sentence "The dog bit the man" *the dog* and *the man* are participants.

parts of a sentence   The major divisions of a sentence, such as subject, verb, and direct object.

parts of speech   The categories that words are assigned to according to their syntactic functions, such as noun, verb, and adjective.

personification   The attribution of human characteristics to something nonhuman, as in "The pine trees marched along the ridge line."

phoneme   A distinctive unit of sound in a particular language. Many words differ in only one phoneme. For example, substituting /b/ for /p/ changes the word *pan* to *ban*, so /b/ and /p/ are both phonemes in English (see *allophone*).

phonetic intensive   A word containing sounds that are associated with (but do not imitate) its meaning. For example the *gl* sounds in *glimmer, glisten* and *glow* seem to suggest flickering light.

phrasal stress rule   A rule for assigning stress to English sentences that marks the stresses within NPs, AdjPs, and AdvPs (see text, Chapter 5).

phrase structure rule   A syntactic rule that specifies some grammatical structure. For example, the phrase structure rule NP → Det Adj N defines an NP as consisting of a determiner followed by an adjective and then a noun.

place of articulation   One of the three dimensions for identifying consonant speech sounds. The place of articulation is where the mouth is most narrowly constricted during sound production. For example, in the articulation of [s] and [z] the mouth is most narrowly constricted at the alveolar ridge, so these sounds are alveolars.

poetic stress rule   A rule for scanning a line of poetry after the regular rules for assigning stress have been applied. The poetic stress rule says to assign stress only to the most highly stressed syllable within each foot and to leave the other syllable(s) unstressed.

point of view   The perspective from which a story is told. The most common points of view are *first-person, third-person limited,* and *third-person omniscient.*

possible worlds theory   A branch of philosophy that considers how to deal with the truth value of statements in fictional worlds whose features differ from the features of the real world. For example, within the text world of Superman comics the statement "Clark Kent has x-ray vision" is true.

pragmatics   The study of how physical and social context influence the use of language. For example, the meaning of the sentence "Come over here" depends on where the speaker is standing, and the decision of whether to call someone by his or her first name depends on the nature of the social relationship of the people involved.

principle of minimal divergence   The principle that fictional worlds work exactly like the real world unless the reader is informed otherwise. Following this principle, we can assume that Sherlock Holmes's London is the capital of the United Kingdom.

processes   In Systemic Functional Grammar processes express the relationships between participants (NPs). For example, in the sentence "The dog bit the man" *bit* is the process. The equivalent of *process* in generative grammar is *verb*.

properties   The concepts and relationships that make up a cognitive model. For example, the cognitive model for *restaurant* contains the concept of a waiter who serves the food to the diners.

prosody   The study of the rhythmic and sound effects of poetry.

regional dialect   The variety of a language that is spoken in a particular geographical area, for example Parisian French or Utah English.

register   The variety of a language used for a particular purpose or in a particular social setting, such as the language of computer technicians or the language of sermons.

rhetorical stress rule   This rule says that for emphasis or contrast: **any syllable of a sentence can receive extra stress.**

rhythm   The repetition of motion or sound. In poetry rhythm refers to the type of poetic foot and the number of feet per line, for example, iambic pentameter.

Russian Formalism   A school of literary criticism that focused on the linguistic features of literature, aiming to distinguish literary language from ordinary language.

salient   Language elements that stand out because they deviate from an expected pattern. For example, the adjective *grey* is salient in this line because it comes after instead of before the verb: "While I stand on the roadway, or on the pavements grey...."

schema   Any type of mental representation including concepts, cognitive models, scripts, and text worlds.

schema refreshment   When reading a text disrupts accustomed ways of processing information and prompts readers to change their schemas for understanding the world.

script   A type of cognitive model that specifies what one should do in a particular situation, such as a restaurant or a classroom.

semantic case roles   The roles that noun phrases play in a sentence. For example, in the sentence "The dog bit the man" *The dog* has the case role of Agent/Actor and *the man* has the case role of Patient.

sentence stress rule   A rule for assigning stress to English sentences which says that **only content words receive primary stress.**

slant rhyme (also called *partial rhyme*)   A rhyme in which the stressed vowels, and sometimes the consonants, are slightly different, as in *black/slick* and *full/far* (see masculine rhyme and feminine rhyme).

social dialect   The variety of language that is spoken by a particular social class. The speech of working-class residents of New York City, for example, is a social dialect of English.

sociolinguistic variable   A linguistic feature that can alternate between different forms. For example, the phrase *going to* can be pronounced [gowiyŋ tuw], [goin tuw], or [gənə], and for younger speakers of American English the vowel in the word "plant" can be pronounced [plænt] or [pliənt].

source concept (in metaphor)   The conceptual domain from which features are mapped. In "all the world's a stage" *stage* is the source concept (see *target concept*).

speech act   A speech act is what an utterance (or group of utterances) does, rather than how it is structured. For example, the sentence "Please come over here" functions as a request, while the reply "No" functions as a refusal.

speech event   A series of speech acts that accomplishes some social purpose and is often conducted by people with particular social roles or positions. For example, a classroom lecture is a speech event that involves the speech acts of stating, questioning and answering, and that involves a teacher and students.

speech production model   A psycholinguistic model of how concepts are converted into spoken language.

split discourse world   A discourse world in which the speaker/listener or author/reader are separated in time or space, as when talking on the telephone or when a reader reads a text that was written years ago.

structuralism   In linguistics the theory that elements of a language must be understood in terms of their relationships within an overarching system or structure. For example, the phoneme /a/ can only be understood by examining how it contrasts with other phonemes within a phonological system.

style shifting   Changing speech styles according to the speech topic or situation. For example, when telling a story English speakers normally use an informal style, but they shift to a more formal style when discussing education.

stylistics   A school of literary criticism that uses tools from the discipline of linguistics to analyze literature.

substitution   When one kind of poetic foot is substituted for another. For example, in the line

We thóught | it was | the Júdge | ment-dáy. |

a pyrrhic foot is substituted for an iambic foot in the second position.

synecdoche   A figure of speech in which a part represents the whole or vice versa, as in "*Cleveland* won by six runs," where *Cleveland* stands for the baseball team located in that city.

syntax   The arrangement of words and phrases to create well-formed sentences in a language.

Systemic Functional Grammar   The school of grammar pioneered by the linguist M. A. K. Halliday. His method of analyzing language emphasizes the function rather than the form of grammatical structures.

t-unit   A unit for measuring the complexity of prose. A t-unit is the smallest stretch of discourse that can be punctuated as a sentence; in other words, a main clause and all of its dependent clauses. Prose that contains many words per t-unit is more complex than prose that contains fewer words per t-unit.

target concept (in metaphor)   The conceptual domain onto which features are mapped. In "all the world's a stage" *world* is the target concept (see source concept).

text world   The schema that is created in listeners' or readers' minds when they understand spoken or written texts.

text world theory   A cognitive theory of discourse processing that proposes that when people speak or write they create a semantic schema, or text world, in the minds of their listeners or readers.

transformational rule   A formal rule that changes the order of grammatical categories in a sentence. For example, the statement "George is here" can be changed into the question "Is George here?" by the yes-no question transformation.

tree diagram   A graphic device that looks like an upside-down tree for displaying the syntactic structure of a sentence.

underlexicalization   Using a descriptive phrase or an inaccurate word to refer to something unknown, for example, using "metal box" for "radio," or "mushroom" for "parachute."

unmarked   The normal, usual, expected way of expressing a meaning. For example, English does not use different forms for verbs in the simple present tense except for the third person singular form (I go, you go, she **goes**, we go, you all go, they go). So, the form *go* is unmarked, or usual, while the form *goes* is marked, or unusual.

unreliable narrator   A narrator whom we cannot trust to tell us what really happened within the text world.

vector   The compositional elements in an image that indicate directionality, such as a line or the direction of a gaze.

vehicle   In a conceptual metonym the concept that brings the target concept to mind. In the conceptual metonym AUTHOR FOR BOOK ("Have you read the latest Pinker?") the vehicle is AUTHOR and the target is BOOK. The vehicle corresponds to the source domain of a conceptual metaphor.

visual metaphor   The graphic equivalent of a metaphorical expression. For example, a picture of a man with steam coming out of his ears is a visual metaphor for being angry.

voicing   One of the three dimensions for identifying consonant speech sounds. Voiced sounds are produced with vibrating vocal chords. Examples include [b], [v], [l], and [r]. All vowels are voiced.

Index